SERGEANT MAJOR JOE R. GARNER, U.S. ARMY (RET.)

WITH

AVRUM M. FINE

Simon & Schuster

New York   London   Toronto   Sydney   Tokyo   Singapore

Code Name:

Copperhead

My True-Life Exploits

as a Special Forces Soldier

SIMON & SCHUSTER
Rockefeller Center
1230 Avenue of the Americas
New York, New York 10020

Designed by Hyun Joo Kim
Manufactured in the United States of America

ISBN: 0-671-86435-1

Photos 5, 8, 12, 17, 18, and 19: U.S. Army. All other photos: Collection
of Joe R. Garner

Acknowledgments

I would like to thank all those who contributed to this book. There are many. In particular, I wish to thank the following whose efforts and encouragement were most valuable and appreciated:

Daughter Valerie, son Joey, and my sister Sally Garner Peters, for their love and support; Lee Beitchman, whose devotion to the book went beyond his duties as attorney; Capt. James M. Perry, U.S. Army (Ret.); Col. Stanley Olchovik, U.S. Army (Ret.); Capt. Charles Heaukulani, U.S. Army (Ret.); Maj. Richard D. Bishop, U.S. Army (Ret.); Command Sgt. Maj. Tadeusz Gaweda, U.S. Army (Ret.); Sgt. Maj. Donnie C. Vickers, U.S. Army (Ret.); Sgt. Maj. Gary R. Gilmer, U.S. Army (Ret.); Lt. Col. Jimmy Jones, U.S. Army (Ret.); Lt. Col. Michael L. Lewis, USAR; Sgt. Maj. Gerard T. Infanger, U.S. Army (Ret.); Maj. Richard J. Meadows, U.S. Army (Ret.); Sgt. Maj. John W. Irwin, U.S. Army (Ret.); M. Sgt. Richard W. Altman, U.S. Army (Ret.); Sgt. Maj. Floyd Payne, U.S. Army (Ret.); Col. E. E. Monger, U. S. Army (Ret.); Sgt. Maj. Bobby L. Overfield, U.S. Army (Ret.); Command Sgt. Maj. Harmon D. Hodge, U.S.Army (Ret.); Sgt. Maj. Paul Adair, U.S. Army (Ret.); M. Sgt. Tom Dickerman, U.S. Army (Ret.); M. Sgt. William Langston, U.S. Army (Ret.); Mr. Jimmy Dean, Special Forces Association; Mr. Donald Shealey; Ms. Roxanne Merritt, Curator, JFK Special Warfare Museum; Ms. Hannah Zeidlik, U.S. Army Center for Military History; Mr. Rich Boylan, Military Reference Branch Chief, National Archives; Ms. Joyce Conyers and Mr. Charles R. Smith, USMC Historical Section; Ms. Susanne Forbes, Archivist, John F. Kennedy Presidential Library.

To my brother, Alan, who came up with the idea and provided encouragement every step of the way. Without his tireless efforts, this book would not exist.

To my wife, Kathy, whose patience was remarkable, and her assistance, constant. She is as much responsible for completing the book as anybody.

As reality sets in and I finally realize that I have completed this book, I start to think about things Alan told me; therefore, I must tell Bob Asahina, my editor, how much I appreciate his tremendous efforts, his initial encouragement to Alan for me to do this book, and the end results of his expertise. I also thank Sarah Pinckney, Bob's assistant editor. Her patience, kindness, and availability were extraordinary. She kept the spirit of the book alive.

And it is with the deepest of respect that I dedicate this book to my Special Forces comrades, many of whom never made it back to write their own stories.

Joe Garner
Waynesville, Missouri

Paksane, Laos—White Star *(chapter 5)*

Nakhon Phanom, Thailand—SOG/STRATA Mission Launch Site *(chapters 14, 15, 16)*

Da Nang, South Vietnam—SOG/STRATA Headquarters *(chapters 14, 15, 16, 17, 18)*

Ban Me Thout, South Vietnam—Team B-23 Headquarters *(chapter 12)*

Da Lat, South Vietnam—SOG POW Compound—Team B-23 Headquarters *(chapter 13)*

CHINA

CHINA

Red River
Black River

Dien Bien Phu

HANOI ★ ● Haiphong

Gulf of Tonkin

LAOS

NORTH
VIETNAM

HAINAN

VIENTIANE

▶ 1 ● Muang Huong
● Muang Pak xan (Paksane)

Nakhon Phanom

Mekong River

THAILAND

PLATEAU DES BOLOVENS

HO CHI MINH TRAIL

3 ● Ashau Valley ● Hué
● Da Nang

SOUTH
VIETNAM

South China Sea

Kontum
CENTRAL
● Pleiku
HIGHLANDS

● Ban Me Thuot

BANGKOK

CAMBODIA

Mekong River

▶ 2 ● Da Lat Cam Ranh
DI LINH PLATEAU

PHNOM PENH

● Long Thanh

Gulf of Thailand

SAIGON ●

N

South
China
Sea

1. White Star AO (chapter 5)
2. STRATA AO: Team Practice Mission
         to North (chapter 15)
3. STRATA AO (chapters 17, 18)

0   50   100   150   200
          miles

Contents

Introduction

by Avrum M. Fine

Many pursuits and endeavors have their golden ages to look back upon. U.S. Army Special Forces is no different. I would consider the years from the late 1950s through the late 1970s to be the "golden age of SF."

It was a time of unquestioned commitment and extraordinary valor, when these men were writing the book that others would follow. It was the time of example.

If one were to pick a reason why these men accomplished what they did in the jungles of Southeast Asia and Latin America, it would be that they were bound by a single common thread. They thrived on being out on their own. They reveled in working without fences or fetters. They enjoyed the freedom of answering to no one but themselves.

It was a situation they had been forced into since childhood.

The men I interviewed came from hopeless rural backgrounds and poor blue-collar households. The outdoors was a haven. It was a place to live. It was a place to be safe.

Few had finished high school before joining the Army, some weren't even of legal age, but they saw a chance to get out of desperate situations and grow as men.

When they joined the U.S. Army, the demands came as naturally as life, and when they volunteered to serve in Special Forces, they loved the taste of it. Somehow, they had known they would.

They trained at a fever pitch, stretching the limits of endurance. They also acquired the technical expertise and skills of a college education, twice over. The men emerged physically tough and mentally sharp.

They were SF.

Moreover, each man had earned the rank of NCO, becoming the hardened and dedicated noncommissioned officer that was the military's heart and soul. The men who wore the brass came and went, rotating in and out of the unit. But the NCO was still there to teach and lead.

Joe Garner is from that mold, but he is much more. When you shake his hand, he is rooted to the ground like a tree—solid and sure. His looks are dark and tribal, like an Indian brave's. But his is the blood of the pioneers. His is the strength of the settlers who carved a life out of the wilderness. That's the stock he comes from.

I experienced an incredible rush as I was finishing the first two weeks of interviews with Joe. A chill ran up my back as I realized that I was probably talking to the ghost of Davy Crockett!

Prologue

In August 1982, twenty-two-year-old Joe Garner, Jr., and a friend left their Oklahoma City oil-drilling job for a short vacation in Canada. Their destination was the historic Calgary Stampede.

Returning through a border crossing in South Dakota, their IDs are checked in routine fashion. Joe's friend is Canadian and his driver's license is given back right away. The U.S. Border Patrol agent takes Joe's license into a little stall, also in routine fashion.

After a few minutes he returns with a second Border Patrol agent. They ask Joe to pull his pickup over and get out. The two agents search the truck thoroughly—under the seats, under the hood, under the car—everywhere. All the truck's contents are laid out on the ground.

They are made to wait forty-five minutes more. A U.S. Air Force major appears and asks Joe's Canadian companion to wait in the pickup. Joe is ushered into the Border Patrol station. The Air Force officer begins to interrogate him about his business in Canada and why he left the country. A half hour goes by before the Border Patrol agent confirms through Joe's social security number that he is who he says he is—Joe Garner, Jr.

The problem is that he bears his father's name.

Young Joe, Jr., thinks that will be the end of it. But the Air Force major begins an even more intense line of questioning about the whereabouts of his dad, asking if he is in the country, what he is doing, if he intends to leave the country, and if his father is a mercenary.

Finally, after about three hours, Joe, Jr., and his pal are allowed to go.

But the alarm bells were ringing.

A lot of cages had been rattled by the name Joe Garner.

chapter 1

The Bag

I heard stories when I arrived at Fort Bragg in early 1958. Whenever I got to a new assignment I always tried to find out as much as I could as fast as I could about what was going on.

There were rumors about a top-secret program.

The secure area was a small one-story building at the end of Smoke Bomb Hill, near the barracks where Special Forces lived and trained. Other men would point it out to me as the Greenlight Training Building. It was two buildings down from our barracks, ringed with a chain-link fence topped with barbed wire. An armed guard stood at the entrance.

About every six months Special Forces troops would go in for a couple of weeks and then it would be shut down. All I knew of Greenlight was that it was a hush-hush project about a new type of demolition. If all the scuttle-butt could be believed, it was the kind of thing everyone would be scared to try. I was curious as hell, but I didn't know if I really wanted to get involved or not.

I was just a young E-5 buck sergeant at the time, and 1960 was already a busy year for me. A bunch of us had picked up the banner of the U.S. Army Special Warfare Center's Sport Parachute Club and were logging in a lot of free-fall time on weekends. The club had made a name for itself with the 7th Special Forces Group command, and we were always being called on to represent the center with a show for visiting dignitaries, dropping into the main post parade field. The center liked to have it be a part of events because it was an eye-catching display, and we were good at it.

We were good because we practiced on our own time on the weekends, jumping as many as three times a day, scrounging whatever military aircraft we could—sometimes paying for the fuel out of our own pockets. We were also doing something radical and succeeding—cutting holes in the parachutes to make them steerable.

The Sicily Drop Zone took its toll on our parachutes, and we would spend our evenings at the club cleaning out the North Carolina sand of Fort Bragg. I was in the middle of packing my chute one night when M. Sgt. Harmon Hodge came into the rigging shed. We called him "Preacher" after he got religion and finally got a handle on his violent temper. Hodge was a top jumper and a charter member of the Sport Parachute Club.

Preacher asked for four volunteers for a free-fall jump the next day. VIPs were crawling all over the place again, and the center wanted us for another of our skydiving demonstrations.

This time there was a difference.

"You're going to jump some test equipment . . . the Greenlight device," he said. "Which one wants to jump with the thing?" Hodge was looking right at me. Everyone knew how much Joe Garner loved to jump. I had taken to it like a duck to water. Preacher Hodge knew it, too.

"What the heck," I said. "I'll do it." I had always wanted to find out what Greenlight was all about.

If I hadn't volunteered, Preacher would have picked me anyway. Besides, when the center commanding general made a request, you responded like it was a no-questions-asked order.

At 1300 hours we assembled at the Smoke Bomb Hill parade field. Standing by for us was a familiar H-21 helicopter—two big props, one in front and one in the rear. We called it the "Banana Boat."

A Jeep came out of the Greenlight training area two blocks away. When it drove up, we could see that the four men inside were armed with .45 pistols. They pulled out some parachute harnesses and one rucksack, and approached us.

"Which one is Garner?" one man asked.

They already knew who was going to jump the rucksack. I felt ten feet tall. It was the same kind of feeling I had when everyone trusted and respected me as captain of the junior high school football team.

"Right here," I answered.

The man placed the rucksack at my feet. Whatever was inside filled it out full. It also appeared to be very heavy.

They used one of our men to demonstrate how they wanted us to rig with the special harness. All of us had done tethered static-line jumps with full field gear like the Airborne, but we had never done any high-altitude free-falls with loaded rucksacks. My first thought was that they were going to make us skydive the same way, with our rucksacks in front, and I just knew that the clumsy things would hit us in the face.

"No," one of the men said, "it goes in back. We've got longer straps that will come around and attach to your reserve D-ring."

I was so excited and curious I got ahold of the bag and lifted it. I wasn't prepared for the weight.

"It weighs forty-five pounds in its present condition," the guy said.

"Will the sucker go off if I drop it?"

"It doesn't have a detonator. It won't go off. Don't mess with it. Just jump it. Our boys at the drop zone will take it from you on the ground."

That was fine with me. I was imagining in my head that I might have to run through the woods with it.

The rucksack hung against the small of my back under the main chute. Its straps came around my abdomen and attached to the D-rings of my main chute. "What about my drop line?" I asked. Every jumper loaded with gear had a fifteen-foot line attached to his field pack so he could release the weight to dangle below him and hit the ground before he did. Without it, his legs would break.

"Use it for sure," he said. "You won't have a bone left if you don't."

That was comforting. They rigged up a couple of quick releases that hooked the rucksack to my D-ring from behind, with adjustable straps so I could pull it up tight. With the weight of the bag, I made sure everything was tight—real tight. I didn't want it to slip as I fell.

"Can I have a readout on previous jumps?" I asked.

"We don't have any. We don't know of anybody that has ever jumped it."

Hell, it wasn't only going to be a totally new experience for me, it was going to be a new experience for the whole damned Army.

Our DZ was going to be an old rifle range in the northwest corner of the Macridge weapons training area, an area full of live-fire ranges about five miles west of the main post. We would be jumping in front of a lot of VIPs to demonstrate that my secret device could be carried in on target by a single man in free-fall from a high altitude.

The way everybody was acting, I got the strong feeling that a lot was riding on this jump. The helicopter would be able to slow down enough to provide some accuracy. After that, it was up to me. The Greenlight people were probably concerned about the jumper being able to ride it out to at least eighteen hundred feet before opening. I never doubted I could do it.

As the H-21 headed west toward the DZ, I had a good view of the ground below. I was right next to the open door and could see we were flying over familiar territory. The rifle range showed up ahead. There was a lot of activity and security down there. We could see what appeared to be viewing stands set up at the old firing line and already filling up.

Our jumpmaster was also from the Sport Parachute Club. His job was "spotting the jump"—picking the exact point for us to exit the aircraft. He identified our DZ at the far end of the hundred-yard range. The VIPs in the stands had a good look right down the alley.

We didn't have a pilot briefing like we usually did. The jumpmaster just said that our drop would be from eight thousand feet. That was low enough so that I could make eyeball contact with the DZ. Since it was such a small DZ, we obviously had satisfied the Greenlight people that we wouldn't make any errors. They had made a big point about being accurate in our landing.

At two thousand feet we dropped a twenty-five foot streamer made up of multicolored pieces of crepe paper knotted end to end in checkerboard fashion and attached at one end to three pieces of coat-hanger wire for weight. That was our wind-drift indicator. We all watched as it landed one hundred yards beyond the DZ. The jumpmaster would correct for it and send us out to the opposite side of the DZ. The weather was good—wind below twelve knots, blowing out of the northwest. We picked a road intersection upwind from the DZ as a landmark to open over.

The chopper began to shake as the twin rotors spun up. The back of the

H-21 tilted forward, and we climbed toward eight thousand feet. The controllers down below radioed that we were to go in thirty minutes. The pilot put us into a holding pattern.

The time gave me a chance to think about what all that weight might do to me on the way down and how long it might take me to get flared out and stabilize. Greenlight was one heavy monster.

That's when it hit me. My parachute was deeply cut with control windows set to my weight—180 pounds. That's all it was designed for. And, with fifty jumps already logged, it was about near the end of its life. I thought that it might blow up under the added weight.

I wasn't scared about my butt if the canopy shredded—I had a good reserve. And the Army would give me a new one. The thing was, I would have to shell out $15 for someone to cut and sew all the modifications I needed, and an extra $15 was hard to come by. I couldn't show my feelings to the men in the helicopter. They might have thought I was worried for the wrong reasons.

Five minutes from release, we made a pass over our impact point. Down below we could see smoke marking the spot. The jumpmaster called the pilot in on our jump azimuth, and the H-21 headed into the wind toward the release point.

Over the release point the jumpmaster gave the signal, "Let's do it!" He stepped away from the door and out I went.

All of a sudden all that weight slammed the rucksack against the back of my knees, so I couldn't bend my legs and control my airfoil in flight. It wanted to pull me feet down, making it difficult to stay horizontal to the ground. Under any other circumstance my legs would be free to bend, curled back, and moving to balance. But with that extra-heavy rucksack I couldn't maneuver. I was slipping away from the rest of the men, who were working hard to stay with me.

Within ten seconds I was falling at 125 miles an hour—terminal velocity—and the wind was really whipping at me. In a free-fall every bit of the body is a control surface. You are pushing down as you ride a column of air. When you change body configuration you move the column, and your speed and position to the ground shifts right away.

At first I went into a modified "frog"—pulling in my hands and legs and looking just like a frog in flight. It was a basic position that allowed some stabilization. If I could see my thumbs out of the corner of my eyes, I would be on my way to controlling my free-fall. But what with fighting the heavy rucksack, there was no way.

The hookup wasn't doing its job, and the rucksack was slipping even farther down the back of my legs. I was also dropping more slowly than the other men since I had more wind resistance and thus more lift from the heavy rucksack behind me. The other men were going the other way.

I could see our opening point on the ground and I started to slip away from it. I could not keep from drifting backward, so I went into a partial "Delta" configuration, sweeping my arms back in a V. That gave me acceleration.

My rate of descent increased rapidly until I was falling against a wind of about 180 miles an hour. The weight in the rucksack wanted to shift on me and spin me, but I managed to stabilize through a mile of free-fall.

I popped at eighteen hundred feet, and the chute held. My men were just above me as we started steering toward the DZ. On the way down we crossed over the VIP bleachers at five hundred feet. I thought about letting the thing loose and dropping the bag on them like pigeon crap. It's funny what goes through your mind, even during something serious.

After I passed over the stands I was in the wind line going directly to the target. I was concentrating so hard on where I was going to land I forgot about releasing the rucksack. When I did, it was somewhere between forty and fifty feet. I had released too close to my own impact. About the time the line was fully extended, I was almost on the ground, still carrying all the weight.

When I hit, it felt as if my whole body exploded. It sounded like a fifty-pound sandbag falling one hundred feet onto concrete.

Through the pain, I just smiled at everybody.

I had landed right where I wanted to land. The other men followed in close formation. We came in dead center to the VIP viewing stands—about one hundred yards right down on the range firing line.

On the ground there was a small party waiting. There was also another armed guard. I disconnected the rucksack and turned the device over to the Greenlight officials. We were excused at that point. We rolled up our parachutes and were escorted through a very heavy cordon of security to a waiting truck.

For some reason, my boots were loose as I walked. I looked down and saw that all the shoelaces were broken—snapped clean open. "Damn," I said to myself. "It really *was* a hard landing."

A few years later I found out what Greenlight was all about. It was a man-carried nuclear device. That's when the realization hit me. I was probably the first soldier to free-fall strapped to an atomic bomb.

chapter 2

Wild Card

I almost didn't make it into Special Forces. In fact, making a career out of the military was the farthest thing from my mind that hot Chattanooga summer of 1951. The Korean War was on, and I was a seventeen-year-old Air Force recruit. I knew Mama didn't realize the danger in such a thing. But I wasn't scared. My father had deserted her five years before so I was in to help Mama and the rest of the family with my paycheck, and I took it at that.

I don't remember saying anything to her or the rest of the family in the way of a goodbye. I searched the house for a clean shirt and something decent enough to wear. There wasn't much of a choice. At my induction Mama got the allotment she wanted. It just meant I wouldn't have much money left. Hell, I never had any money anyway.

Lackland Air Force Base was at one corner of San Antonio. It was a dusty place for basic training. Looking around at the other recruits, I knew there would be no problem getting accustomed to military life. I was probably the youngest one there, but I was as big as some of those boys nineteen and older.

After eight weeks in the desert, they shipped me to Tyndall AFB in Panama

City, Florida. I didn't have any skills yet, no military occupational specialty—no MOS. But they found me a job anyway—as a guinea pig. I was given an experimental motion-sickness pill and placed in a cage that spun up, down, and sideways. This went on a couple of weeks. I guess they were satisfied the pill was a success. I kept everything down. But I knew better. The pill didn't have a doggone thing to do with it.

Air Crew School lasted another eight weeks, and all that amounted to was inspecting and repairing vehicles that serviced the jet aircraft. When you're not having much fun you get into trouble. Four of us shared a dormitory-type room in the barracks. One kid would come in at one and two in the morning and crank up his radio. He did it one time too many and I hit him with my footlocker. I could have received Article 15 discipline, but I got only a week restriction. The nights were a lot quieter, though.

For the first time I was homesick. All the time I spent in the woods as a kid had never prepared me for being so far away. I missed Mama and the family, and I missed all the little girls that used to come around when I was a football star. When I wrote Mama, I asked her to send a letter to my commanding officer telling him that my grandmother had died. That got me home on leave. Grandmother died twice.

After a year and a half, my orders for Korea came. I had gotten over being homesick and was relieved to get out of Tyndall and go overseas.

I wound up at an F-86 Sabrejet base in Osan, about thirty miles south of Seoul. The pilots of the 51st Fighter Wing went up against MIG-15s, mostly flown by Red Chinese. Captain Joe McConnell, the top ace of the war with sixteen kills, flew out of Osan.

I still didn't have a real military skill, so about all I ever did was unload wingtip tanks from railroad cars and pull guard duty. The war was already winding down and the only real excitement at the base came when Ted Williams crashed. He was flying with the Marines and came in hard. The jet rolled over, but the rescue crew got him out in a hurry, unhurt.

The base always maintained an alert for possible air attacks. The North Koreans knew how to harass us and occasionally sent over "bed-check Charlie" to make us run for cover. The little turd flew just above the treetops in a small wooden airplane that looked like a big model. He was safe from the Sabrejets, who couldn't operate that slowly. The siren would pull us out of our bunks in the middle of the night, and we grabbed our steel helmets and ran for the sandbag bunkers that were beside the Quonset huts.

Some of us decided to have fun one night during Charlie's visit. The officers had a Quonset next door, with their bunker on the opposite side. We picked up handfuls of the pea gravel that the Air Force used for walkways, and at the right moment tossed the stones over our Quonset onto the metal roof of their Quonset. They started yelling that they were under attack. It scared the hell out of them and we got restricted.

There were the usual dangers outside the base. But there were other things, too. If we saw a mama-san on the road with a young one, we were cautioned to make sure that she didn't throw the child in front of the vehicle. There had been incidents where they would push the kid in your path, and then Uncle Sam would settle with a lot of money, no questions asked.

Shortly after the war ended, men serving in Korea who had completed at least three of their four-year obligation had the option of getting out. I didn't care much for the Air Force. I was just supporting the jet jockeys. I thought if I wanted the Air Force at all, I was going to be a pilot. But I didn't have the education to be one.

I came home to no job—not much of anything. My younger brothers, Larry and Alan, were still at home and hard to handle. I didn't have much luck finding work until older brother Lewis called. He was living in St. Louis and found a job for me there. I was happy for a few months—just running around, going to parties and chasing women. But even that got tiring, so I returned to the family house on Buckley Street.

A new titanium-processing plant was going in and I got a job manning the company's water-pumping station at nearby Chickamauga Creek. It was my responsibility to maintain a constant flow to the construction site. The pay was good for the work, and I thought I had finally landed a decent job.

On the afternoon of my third day, I heard a shotgun blast down the river a short way. That didn't disturb me since a lot of people hunted in the area. Then I heard two young boys screaming and hollering for help. One yelling for help had come up on the edge of the riverbank on the other side.

"My buddy shot off his leg!" he yelled to me.

There was another company worker with me and I told him to call an ambulance. I jumped in the river and swam over. It was only fifty yards, and to me swimming a river didn't mean a thing. The poor kid was losing a lot of blood. His lower leg bone was shot in two. I tore a piece from his pants and tied a tourniquet just above the knee. It didn't take long for the ambulance, and I swam back to the pumping station to find the foreman waiting for me. He wasn't too happy.

The next day was Friday—payday. When I went to collect they gave me my "slip." Hell, to me, helping that boy was more important than the job.

With a pocketful of money, I didn't try to find work again. Four of us were sort of a neighborhood gang just looking for fun—bumming around, really. We were at a drive-in one day and suddenly realized we weren't amounting to anything. Then it hit us all at once. "Let's all go in the service . . . in the Army." We all enlisted, and the old gang was broken up for good.

It was basic training all over again, Army style. At the end of eight weeks at Camp Gordon, Georgia, I was still looking for a skill and didn't know what to get into, so I went wherever they told me.

I reported to the Army Engineers school at Fort Leonard Wood, Missouri, in January 1955. There I found something I excelled at—mines and demolition. The officer in charge of that department saw my progress and asked, "Would you like to stay to instruct?" Since I had no idea where I'd be sent after the school, good or bad, I said, "That'd be fine with me."

I was drinking a lot then, boozing it up with the boys. We'd chase girls at night and guzzle beer. I was letting myself run down and making it worse by taking long weekend drives to Chattanooga and back with no rest. It got so bad that, one morning, I couldn't pull myself out of bed to answer an alert.

When I finally rolled out, I was called on the carpet. "That ain't like me to do that," I told the first sergeant. "There must be something wrong."

He told me to take sick call, and I was escorted to the hospital. There sure was something wrong—a bad case of hepatitis. The doctor looked over my medical records and blamed it on something I might have eaten or drunk in Korea. Whatever it was, it took a long time to incubate.

My drinking didn't help things either, and I thought about that the whole three months I was in that boring hospital bed. They sent me home for thirty days and I made a vow to get back in shape and stay away from alcohol. That kind of infection usually leaves a scar on the liver, but within six months the medics couldn't find one. They gave me a clean bill of health.

By July 1957, I was faced with the same decision all over again, "Do I stay in or get out?" Teaching mines and demolitions was okay, but it wasn't anything to brag about. With discharge coming up in ninety days, I determined that I would go back home, even at twenty-three with no plans for the future. That's when the old recruiting sergeant paid a visit.

I put it to him. "Come up with something good—something that's the best and toughest the Army has, or I'm getting out." He had this book on Army careers and we went through every page. At first he wanted me to go into Ranger training, but that wasn't an organization, just a school.

"That's not what I want," I said.

I said no to everything he had to offer. Then, almost on the very last page, he came to the Special Forces. He went through all the stuff they did: trained like the Rangers in mountain and jungle survival, even scuba; all men airborne qualified.

"They're strictly guerrilla-type unconventional operations," the recruiter said. "None of these ordinary Army maneuvers. They are team-oriented into small groups and perform clandestine behind-the-lines missions."

I had learned about OSS operations in World War II, and moving secretly behind enemy lines appealed to me. I knew I had the qualifications. I was very physically fit and had already completed six years of service, plus an MOS that was used in SF operations. Demolition was one of their requirements and I filled that for sure.

"You've got to take a PT test," the recruiter said, ". . . and this test and that test. We've got to send all this paperwork in to Department of Army, and I don't think there's enough time for all that and a final approval before your tour ends."

I filled out all the applications and flew through the Army Physical Training Test with a 460 score out of a possible 500. SF required 350, so there was no doubt in my mind that I could meet any challenge SF would throw at me. But time began to run out. I had proposed to a beautiful little country girl I met at the PX, and my October 18 discharge date was around the corner. I called Mama and told her to expect me and to get a room ready.

I hadn't heard a thing about the application, and I just knew I was on my way home. But, when I went to pick up my discharge papers on the 18th, the recruiter was waiting in the orderly room. "Garner, I just received your approval."

No one really knows why people do things sometimes. Certainly not me. So, true to my word, I signed up. Corporal Joe Garner was headed for the altar and jump school at Fort Benning, Georgia.

It was a big class—thirty-eight enlisted men from Special Forces and six hundred young officers. It was a physically demanding three-week course. Most of the enlisted men were in top-notch shape, while many of the officers had come directly from their units and hadn't prepared physically. This was their time in hell.

To me, jump school was easy. Everything we did just seemed to come naturally. The enlisted men had a lot of fun, laughing all the time. We had a good reason: having so many officers to worry about kept the instructors off our tails. They were all new officers—Ranger-school graduates, OCS graduates, and West Point ringknockers. The officers were always harassing the instructors, which would backfire, causing the instructors to get on them more, taking all the pressure off us. We did everything they had to do, only without the growling.

Our platoon had a very unusual makeup. We had men who had had prior service in a foreign army, including eight Hungarians from the uprising against the Russians. They had gotten out through the underground and were part of an Army program to use their language skills and knowledge of Eastern Europe in future SF clandestine operations. They were good men.

The last day of the second week was the "parachute drag" phase of the training. You lay on the ground hooked to your parachute harness, and they turned on large fans that inflated the parachute, blowing you through a field. The trick was to recover, get to your feet, and run down the parachute.

I went head over heels rolling all over the field and finally managed to get control of the parachute. My left wrist was hurting as I walked back to the instructor. I mentioned it to him and he looked it over.

"Yeah . . . it looks like it's hurt pretty good," he said. "But if you go to the doc and he X-rays it and finds that it's broken . . . you'll be dropped from the course."

That was terrible news. When I flipped I had no idea it was that bad. Hell, I never had broken bones before.

"Piss on it," I said. "I'm not going to the doctor, then."

The instructor gave me a smile and pulled me to the side. He opened a pouch on his webbed belt and took out an Ace bandage. He was doing whatever he could to see that all our platoon graduated. I could still jump with a hurt wrist. Pulling on the risers to steer your canopy was no strain on it—like doing regular pull-ups. But the wrist still had to stand up to the rest of the exercises in the Army Physical Training Test.

Push-ups would be the hardest to do. You have to open your hand and bend your wrist. You're pushing those bones together with a lot of pain, but the instructor showed me how to use the knuckles and fingers to keep my wrist straight without bending.

So on the day of the test I did it on my knuckles, and when they got sore, I switched to my fingers. I was strong enough to do most with one arm, so I eased off the left arm and put more pressure on the right. I qualified at twenty.

There were a number of washouts before the course ended. Two hundred of the officers never made it. Thirty-four of our thirty-eight got the silver jump wings.

And we headed for Fort Bragg, North Carolina.

chapter 3

Jungle Rot

The world is full of tropical jungles. Unfortunately, after World War II there was more going on in them than what you saw in the pages of *National Geographic*. Some of the most fertile territory for the Red Chinese existed in the thick jungles of Southeast Asia and Malaysia. All you had to do was ask the French and British about that.

Korea was a wake-up call for us, and it was going to be up to outfits like Special Forces to pick up where the OSS of World War II left off. Instead of waging guerrilla warfare against the Japanese from Luzon on across occupied Pacific islands, new U.S. unconventional warfare would concentrate on keeping Communism from gobbling up village after village in the mountains and rice paddies of all those countries that were unlucky enough to be in China's neighborhood.

So far, I had spent the early part of 1958 training in the mountains of North Carolina. Training was constant—day after day and week after week almost without letup. Under the guidance of older SF like M. Sgt. Albert Green, who had been in the OSS, we were given classes in guerrilla warfare and the skills to carry it out—mountain climbing, rappelling off sheer cliffs, hand-to-hand combat, escape and evasion, survival. I was thrilled over doing stuff like that.

You had to respect the men of the OSS. NCO casualties were very high in that elite group. They had the pride. Dying didn't mean anything to them as long as they got the job done. And we were being prepared to fill those shoes.

All us young SF were on "provisional" A-teams. We were working to be fully qualified SF, to reach that "Digit 3" level that meant you could wear the "Full Flash" crest of Special Forces, the insignia that told everybody you were ready anytime to go anywhere the President ordered.

The 77th Group didn't always have the manpower to field a twelve-man A-team. That was my cue to volunteer for as many training exercises as I could—to be a filler on the teams going out. I didn't know how much I needed to earn my Full Flash, but I sure as hell was determined to learn anything and everything.

That's one reason I went along with having my primary MOS switched on my first A-team assignment. "Garner . . . you're a heavy-weapons man." And they handed me a damned Browning automatic rifle. Even though I was fresh from Fort Leonard Wood as an expert in mines and demolition, I took it in stride.

By 1958, SF had already branched out from guerrilla warfare into more direct action—going right after enemy targets. The operations were still covert—sneaking in under their noses and creating all sorts of havoc. And it was looking more and more like we would be doing it in the jungle.

I hadn't been in the jungle yet, but in June I was on a C-123 over the Okefenokee swamps of Georgia. We weren't just dropping into a jungle, we were also jumping at night—the first time outside of Fort Bragg. Standing in the door I couldn't see a thing, even from 1,250 feet. But it didn't make a lick of difference once the green light came on.

It was so dark I didn't realize I was landing in trees until I was about fifty feet over them. I went for a limb and grabbed hold. I was between two giant southern pines. I released my parachute and slid down one tree, using the other for support. As the trunk widened I jumped to the ground. Hitting the ground still didn't mean I was safe. The advance party that cleared the DZ had reported killing thirteen rattlesnakes. The Okefenokee was full of them.

The whole unit had missed the DZ, which was tiny as a dot, and landed in a forest of pines at the edge of the swamp. As I was gathering up my parachute, one man started screaming. He was caught in a tree. The funny thing was, he thought he was stuck at the very top. When I approached him, he took one look at me and didn't know what to say. He was actually only three feet off the ground.

"I dropped my helmet and never heard it hit the ground," he said.

If you're snagged in a tree and it's too dark to see the ground, you drop your steel helmet and wait for it to land. That's how to determine how high up you are. But as soon as he let his loose, it hit the mushy soft, mossy ground, and whatever squish it made was covered up by noise from the rest of us.

It took an hour to get everyone together. Then we were met by the "guerrilla chief," who identified himself with a prearranged code. That was the first phase of the exercise—to link up with the guerrillas of the country we came to help, be escorted through their network, and train them in weapons and tactics as insurgents.

The "insurgents" were men out of nearby Camp Stewart. The "aggressors," who would be on our butts the whole time, were also from Camp Stewart. The guerrilla chief ran the whole show. He was always a top-notch SF, usually a sergeant first class (E-7) or master sergeant (E-8) who had been in the program a long time and knew what to do. In his role, he was very convincing.

It was close to midnight by the time we moved away from the DZ. I always loved being in the woods, and this was right where I wanted to be. Then I heard the alligators all around us. You couldn't see them through the dense underbrush, but you could hear them hit the water. I knew the men running the exercise wanted to see how that would affect us. I never got out of line and stayed right on the trail. It did kind of make your hair stand up having alligators right along the road growling at you when you couldn't see where you were going.

As in our exercises in the mountains, these guerrillas started leading us all over the world. The name of the game was disorientation—keep us guessing where we were. It was easy to see we were being led in circles around the DZ. I could see the moon from our front, sides, and rear. We didn't get to our safe area until just before daylight.

What followed was two weeks of guerrilla "training"—running missions all through the swamps against lines of communication, ammo dumps, tank and truck parks, and everything else that would disrupt the aggressors. That was the easy part.

Once we had used up our last rations, we were set loose in the Okefenokee on the second phase of our training—two weeks of survival. They just put us out and said, "There you are . . . and there's your food. Go get it!"

We were allowed to bring a few modern things along with our hunting knives—like aluminum foil and hot sauce. Earlier field trips had taught us to include also plenty of five-hundred-pound-test parachute cord, fishing hooks with lead sinkers, and long-stem matches in a waterproof container. Two items left from the guerrilla exercises rounded out my survival gear— C-4 plastic explosive and three rounds of blank ammo from my BAR.

We went way back into the swamps before we stopped for the night. The swamp was full of game ripe for the taking. And right where we stopped was this big ol' deer trail going away from us.

"Hot damn," one of the men said. "Let's rig a snare to see if we can catch one of them." It was a noose snare made from our nylon parachute cord. We attached it to a stout tree with some give to it so, when the animal lunged, it wouldn't snap the tree. I tied the noose with what we called a survival knot. You can tighten it but you can't unloosen it. The more the deer pulled, the tighter it would get, and just cut off his wind.

Like most animals, a deer walks with its head low to the ground. When it stops, the deer may raise its head to look around, but when it walks its head is close down, especially in thick underbrush. So the snare was placed over the trail, lying on a little branch just low enough so that the deer's shoulder wouldn't knock the noose off and he couldn't step over it. And, sure as the world, the next morning he took it and we had a big deer in the snare.

At the end of our fourth day we heard a lot of wild hogs near the camp. I pulled out the three blank rounds, dug out the packing wads, and filled one cartridge with powder. Then, I took one of the lead fishing sinkers, shaped it with my knife to fit the shell, and shoved it in. It was soft lead, and it wouldn't mess up the grooves in the gun. Then, rather than keep it round like a pumpkin ball, I gave it a little point so it wouldn't go end over end.

I took a rifle from one of the men and slowly moved to where we had heard the hogs earlier. There was a watering hole where they played in the mud. I climbed a tree and waited. It wasn't thirty minutes before they came in a bunch. With only one round, I shot at the biggest one. He was coming right toward me. The only thing I heard was a large grunt. Then he went wild and timber started falling all over.

I knew I got him real good and we tracked him for about an hour. But our dinner got away. They're pretty tough. I should have shot the littlest. Once the gun went off, that was the end of the hogs. We had to move the next day and didn't have time to do it again.

But all was not lost. We still had C-4. There were a lot of deep "potholes," about eight feet in diameter, that we knew had fish. We put some of the stuff into an empty C-ration can and attached a short fuse. We threw it down a pothole and stood back. BLAM! We got a sackful of fish.

When we went to pick up the fish this four-foot alligator suddenly came to the surface. We stopped fishing then and there. After cooking over an open fire, the alligator tail tasted great. The fish were cooked rolled up in green leaves. All of us gained weight on that survival test.

Camp Stewart looked real good to us. We were given three days to rest before returning to Fort Bragg. The first day there, a C-47 came in and was just sitting there. The crew came up to us and asked, "You boys want to jump while you're down here?"

The next day we assembled to jump. There were so many of us my team was pushed to the third lift to go up. As I waited on the ground the first flight came over and I saw this funny thing come out. It wasn't a person. Even though the parachute opened all right, the landing was very hard. After the SF got back to the ground, they dragged whatever it was over to us. They were so sad.

"Oh, we killed him . . . we killed him."

It was a huge alligator. They had found this long ten-footer, put him in a parachute harness and thrown him out the door. As the parachute popped open he slipped in the harness and landed head down on his nose, breaking his poor neck. The big problem was the team had earlier notified Fort Bragg to prepare an alligator pit in the survival area because they were bringing back a real big one.

By the time all of us had completed one jump they said, "Boys . . . y'all are gonna have to get your rucksacks and go back in the swamp to find us another alligator because Fort Bragg is expecting one." So, for two days, we hunted for another alligator. We found one, but it was only about a three-footer. Fort Bragg sent helicopters for us, and we flew back with our catch.

Colonel Blackburn, the 77th Group commander, was waiting for us, expecting the big one. Then he saw what we brought. "What the hell are you doing with that pitiful little thing? You told us you had a big ol' alligator. We dug a great big pit!"

We never did tell him the real story.

But, even with our success at navigation and survival, we knew the Oke-fenokee was no more than a swamp. The real jungle was waiting for us in Central America. The Jungle Operations Training Center was located in Panama, and before any SF was considered qualified for jungle missions, he had to make it through the tough two-week JOTC course.

Jungle training was taking on a new significance. Trouble anywhere meant you were going to be reassigned, and more trouble was brewing in the world's jungles than anywhere else. January 1959 began with a band of insurgents taking over Cuba. Our government got blindsided real good when Fidel Castro set up his Communist regime. Suddenly, everyone in the Pentagon was waking up to the possibility of other Latin American countries coming apart.

Nine months after Castro began rattling everybody's cages, a bunch of us were airborne to Panama. We had a new word and a new mission to work on—counterinsurgency. That meant SF would be working with friendly governments to take out the insurgents—the guerrillas—who were eating up their countries. SF was going to train elements of those countries' armed forces to hunt down the insurgents and "neutralize" them.

It was one hell of a ride. The C-124 bucked and wheezed and lost an engine before we even left the borders of the U.S. On board was a full C-team that would be going through the school. That meant at least twelve A-teams. There were also small detachments from Military Intelligence and the Army Security Agency. We could only guess what their business was going to be once we landed.

We spent two weeks in the jungles outside of Fort Sherman, on the Atlantic side. There was a lot of one-on-one training by men who knew their stuff. I really took to the jungle. For me, it was as natural a place to be as anywhere. Toward the close, we were running missions all over the place. That's when we found some of what MI and ASA were doing—monitoring our radio links to Fort Bragg. The use of classified codes was part of the practice missions, and the white shirts were making damned sure we knew our business.

The other reason MI and ASA were there had to do with our final "mission"—to blow the locks of the Panama Canal!

The best six teams out of the twelve were given the targets. Two teams were to "destroy" the Gatun Locks on the Atlantic side, two others the Miraflores Locks on the Pacific side, and my team with one other was to take out the Pedro Miguel Locks in the middle.

Once World War II ended, the U.S. cut its Canal Zone payroll to almost one-third of what it had been, and that devastated a lot of Panamanians. Even before Castro, the U. S. was sure someone would exploit the poverty and unrest, so in 1957 the Pentagon started Operation Caribbean, secret war games to test the security of the Canal Zone. They determined that the government leaders of Panama couldn't be relied upon to wipe their hind ends, let alone help us protect the CZ. Worse than that, our own military defenses weren't worth a crap either.

The 1st Battle Group of the U.S. 20th Infantry Regiment out of Fort Kobbe had the responsibility of CZ security. It was our mission to infiltrate the CZ and blow them out of the water. We had a week to do it.

We were paired with a team whose team sergeant was Richard Meadows, an NCO who had the military in his blood. The team leaders and team sergeants were briefed extensively on the operation, but the actual methods each team would use would be determined only after a thorough reconnaissance of the target, and after synchronizing their plans with the teams hitting the other locks.

The trucks let us out in a jungle area east of the canal and a good day's walk from the target. Meadows and his team were taken to another jungle location on the opposite side. Just before dark, we had come to the outskirts of a tiny town that bordered on the canal. We stayed in the jungle and worked our way around to the south side of the town and set up camp for the night. Through our binoculars we could see a few houses very close to the locks. Our team sergeant sent two of our men who spoke the best Spanish into the town to check them out.

When they returned they reported locating the owner of one of the houses and striking a bargain to use it. We broke camp the next morning and walked into the village. Most of us wore "sterile" jungle fatigues and soft caps—no insignia or rank. A couple of the men were in civvies. Most of us knew just enough Spanish to bluff our way through the civilian population until we came to a small unoccupied house near the locks. We must have done our job well, since the Panamanians never questioned what these strangers were doing roaming around with weapons. We set up an observation post and brought the 77th Group headquarters up on the radio.

Group HQ had total operational control of the mission and was the communication nerve center. All our transmissions were encrypted Morse Code, just as if we were on a bona fide mission in the middle of the enemy. Everyone up and down the line was dead serious about this.

They patched us into Dick Meadows on the opposite side. His team had also plunked down in a civilian area. They had found native quarters in a good position on a hill alongside a road straight to the target. Both teams waited for nightfall.

From our position we could easily observe the locks through binoculars, but we still needed a much closer recon of the target. The team sergeant took me and a small recon element and we headed for the locks. We set up at the base of a hill across the road that ran along the locks' metal security fence. The security lights weren't very powerful and weren't placed very high. The locks were partially lit, as was the main gate. There were dark spots all along the perimeter and enough unlit areas inside to give us cover.

Through our binoculars we could see all the men on the target. The infantry unit from Fort Kobbe was on full alert. Even at that, the men gathered under the lights to talk, taking their attention away from us bad guys on the prowl.

A guard standing beneath a light can't see farther than the edge of that light. His eyes have adjusted to the area lit and he's blind to anything outside the light. The more powerful the light, the bigger the problem. BINGO!

On the night of our infiltration, we knew we could crawl on our bellies right up to the chain-link fence under the noses of the guards. There was a big tree against the fence totally in the dark. We could hide the whole team behind it and go up and over in a flash.

Over the next three days and nights we watched the comings and goings of the guards and had their shift changes and movements memorized. Our men in civvies had no trouble mingling with the locals up and down the road.

Dick's team radioed that they already had a plan to sneak in and place the charges. His operation had an advantage over us. We would have to cross more open area to get to the fence. On Dick's side, his approach was under more cover: the jungle went almost to the fence. And there was a lot less civilian traffic.

Our job, then, was to create a diversion—potentially the most dangerous element of the mission. We would be in contact with the enemy—the poor souls from Fort Kobbe, that is. And the enemy would have to be "eliminated." We calculated how long it would take reinforcements to arrive and felt we had a large enough window to maintain security while Dick's team got in and out of the locks.

Our plans and times were coordinated with the other teams through Group headquarters. As each pair of teams finalized their plans, the whole operation fell into place. All three locks would be blown simultaneously.

Now it was time to get really sneaky.

Our C-team commander, a sharp lieutenant colonel, thought it just wasn't fair for the Infantry detachment to be on full alert. Fort Kobbe had been made aware of our pending operation, although they didn't know when or that they were already under observation. The colonel thought that was cheating. So he grabbed the Canal Zone telephone directory and found the name of the head man who controlled the locks—a civilian. Then the colonel called the 20th Infantry's security officer-in-charge, who placed the men on the locks and, making like he's the head man himself, had the OIC scale back their security by 30 percent during the time we were going to hit it.

On the night of the operation, we sat there outside the fence and watched the standdown. At mission launch we moved to the checkpoint telephone next to the front gate. Thanks to their lights shining the wrong way, the first set of guards never saw us until we were right on them. We "assassinated" them.

"You're out," we told them. It was pathetic.

The fence sat on a dirt bank just above the level of the concrete surface that ran to the locks. We waited for other guards to show themselves. None did. If they had, they would have been "dead" before they made it to the top of the bank. Then we were through the gate and making our way in the shadows. Meanwhile, Dick Meadows and his team had scaled the fence on the other side with bamboo ladders laced together with parachute cord.

We reached the first guard location inside and started knocking them off.

Zap! Like so many flies.

Approaching one did not alert the others. When we got to the guy in the security shack, he was casually leaning back in the chair by the telephone—they had just changed the shift.

Zap! There went the whole security shack, telephones and all. It was easy. Then we stepped up the harassment with simulated bombs—whistle bombs.

That drew out the guard walking back and forth on top of the locks. We took him out, too. He never saw Meadows coming up from the other side, lowering his men into the locks.

If this had been an actual operation, I would have gone in with silencers and killed every guard with the first volley. There would not have been a lot of shooting.

Several of Dick's men were in the water inside both sides of the locks. Attached to ropes held by others in the team, they swam to the huge doors. They placed their charges and were quickly pulled back and up the slippery sides.

Using similar tactics, we destroyed all three locks right on the button. It was a beautiful operation. With time to spare, we made a fast exit back into the jungle.

Prior to the debriefing, we were all in isolation and still coming up with more ways to take out the canal—such as floating in a bomb submerged with a diver, or even attached to a ship's hull for remote detonation.

At the debriefing, the men from MI and ASA were impressed with our success. They were also a little befuddled.

"Colonel, tell us," they asked our C-team commander. "We could not break any of your transmissions—that's an A-plus. But we kept picking up this clear text—we couldn't understand it. Could you explain, 'Is you is, or is you ain't'? Please tell us what this is."

The colonel stepped up and said, "I'll tell you what it meant. One day the 77th Group CO says he's coming down from Fort Bragg and the next day he says he isn't. The day after that our headquarters transmitted again that he was coming. Then they called again, 'He's not coming.' "

The colonel had this big grin. "We finally got fed up and sent the message. 'Is you is, or is you ain't?' "

I didn't know if they accepted his story or not. It was more likely something the colonel did just to send them to the code books.

The man from MI had one final instruction for us. "When you leave here, you are to never reveal how you did it—or that you did it at all. It's highly classified. We intend to improve security and make your methods unworkable in the future."

We looked at each other and shook our heads. The Panama Canal was such a sitting duck.

chapter 4

Lighting the Fuse

Laos was a sticky situation for the U.S. The politicians had muddied the water, and when the French got their butts whipped, the Kingdom of Laos was divvied up by international agreement between three opposing factions of the same royal family. Laos was supposed to be off limits to everyone else, but, because it bordered on China and North Vietnam, the Communists were on their way.

Eisenhower sent in clandestine Special Forces A-teams as "advisors" on the side of the pro-Western prince, and Kennedy kept them there. That was in the spring of 1959. This highly secret operation was known as White Star.

The U.S. A-teams weren't supposed to be there at all. But then neither were the forces of Ho Chi Minh. His Viet Minh were supplying and training the Communist Pathet Lao. All the while we were both denying to the world that we were there.

The International Control Commission that was set up in Geneva to oversee this mess was made up of the only three countries the rest of the world could agree on—Canada, Poland, and India. So we had the West, the East, and the Third World represented.

While the Indians were meditating, the Canadians got the Poles drunk, and the Americans snuck in the backdoor. When the ICC finally woke up there were 115 U.S. in country teaching the Royal Laotian Army how to fight.

They wanted us long enough to take care of the Communists. Then they wanted us out.

The legendary Lt. Col. Arthur D. Simons—"The Bull"—put the first White Star Mobile Training Team together in November of 1958 to prepare for "Hotfoot 1," our first combined CIA and SF mission in the area. Simons was one of those rare men who gave his whole life to what he believed in rather than what would benefit his career track. An SF assignment for an Army officer was usually a two-year blip that interrupted his path to advancement in rank in his branch. We'd get men not only from the Infantry, but from Armor, Artillery, and even Signal. But Bull Simons stuck with Special Forces. It was in his blood. He was a member of one of the first Ranger battalions and CO of the 6th Ranger Battalion in the Pacific during World War II.

Simons didn't look like officer material. He was sloppy in uniform because of the way he was built—thick neck and big shoulders. He had this big Harley-Davidson hog at Fort Bragg and you'd see him on it, leather jacket and all.

I first saw Bull Simons in 1958. Asa Ballard, Howard Knussmann, and I were "playing" on top of this wood-board–covered rappelling tower next to our mess hall.

We were slack jumping. We made a regular rappel, and when we got three boards from the bottom we marked the rope. When we got back on top we'd pull all the rope up to that mark through our mountaineer snap links. Then we set ourselves with our brake hand behind our backs. We leaned off the tower and jumped. We would hang on for dear life, and when we came to the end we'd slam into the tower. We tried to hit as close to the bottom as we could without hitting the ground.

From the tower you could look straight across the parade field to 77th Group HQ. The commander's window was the closest to the tower and Asa would elbow me with "Bull's up there watching us."

This second lieutenant pops out from behind the mess hall and starts walking toward Group HQ. In 1958, a lieutenant in SF was a rotten apple in a barrel, he was so out of place. This one didn't have his hat on and didn't get ten feet from the mess hall when we heard a big growl come across the parade field. "Get your goddamn hat on, lieutenant!"

Ballard told me that was Bull Simons, and I looked over and saw this great big, ugly dude colonel come flying out the HQ door. He melted the lieutenant right in his boots.

That was the first time I saw Bull Simons.

By November, the rumors were flying about a big secret operation. About 125 of us had been sent to Pisgah National Forest for field-training exercises. They had moved us out of Fort Bragg for security reasons. We knew we were being prepared for something.

We were deep into survival training, and each team was running separate guerrilla and escape-and-evasion missions against units of the 82nd Airborne posing as "aggressors." One day Simons called everyone on CW radio to assemble at Point Alpha at 0500 the next A.M. Now, when the Bull called you, you damn well jumped. But radio security was very much a part of the exercise, and his Morse code was not encrypted. Some of the teams held their silence, fearing that it was part of the exercise and a trick by the 82nd "enemy" to direction-find their positions. Four teams failed to respond to Simons's call.

There was one common frequency that was our guarded frequency for emergency transmissions. Simons came up on the frequency. His voice was unmistakable, even over our AN/GRC-9s. "Damn it, where the fuck are you?" We all held our breath.

Simons bellowed, "Goddamn it, get your fuckin' ass in here or I'm gonna chop your fuckin' head off!" This was the Bull's favorite expression.

We were told we were going back to Fort Bragg for a special briefing. We climbed into trucks and headed east to Fayetteville.

The trucks lumbered up to the SWCEN theater, kind of an old World War II–style double-wide barracks building. The place was swarming with MPs. The security was tight. The doors were guarded, and inside the drapes were drawn. It was some scene.

Col. William Yarborough, the 77th Group commander, stepped forward on the stage. He let us know that there was to be a highly clandestine and very dangerous mission for SF and that once we left we would "cease to exist." He ended: "Anyone here that's not a volunteer for this mission has got the colonel's permission to leave."

There was a ripple of laughter. After all, what SF would do that? Two officers rose and took a walk—A-team leaders. We were all shocked that anyone would walk out on a covert mission.

Then Yarborough introduced us to a man from the State Department. He said, "I can't tell you where or when or even if you'll return." He left a long pause for it to sink in. "But I reiterate the colonel's desire that any man who's not a volunteer leave now."

Not a man moved.

"Gentlemen, the target is Laos."

From the back of the room, "Where the fuck is Laos?"

They brought out a map of Southeast Asia that had been covered from view, and the man pointed to Laos. The briefing was very general. We were going in to advise and train units of the Royal Laotian Army, who were fighting the Communist Pathet Lao.

The lights went out and the slide show started. The pictures had been made by something called the Program Evaluation Office in Vientiane, the capital. This was a disguised military mission set up by the State Department and made up of civilian "technicians," who were actually an advance team of Infantry officers—West Point types. "Ringknockers" we called them.

The slides showed the sorry state of the weapons, ammo, and tactics of the Royal Laotian Army. The Laotian king was getting $20 million in aid from us, but the stuff was rotting in the hands of the French, who didn't want Americans on their turf and had allowed everything to decay.

Our job was to fix the Army in spite of the "Frogs." The man ended by saying that none of the teams would be going into the two Communist provinces on the eastern frontier. We would not be working behind enemy lines. That answered the big question before we asked it.

The operation didn't have a name yet. We didn't have an exact destination and we didn't have a "go" date. All we knew was that we were going to take part in a super-secret mission, and we were no longer to talk to anyone on the outside about what we were doing. Not even our wives.

The two officers that walked out were taken out of SF, out of the 82nd, and out of Fort Bragg. God knows where they finally wound up.

The rest of us accepted our assignments to team FB-1 without any hesitation. On 11 November the team was alerted to go on the very first Special Forces mission to Laos. This was to be the first real SF mission that I knew of in peacetime. It now had a name—White Star.

But in the middle of our preparation M. Sgt. Edison Denton came up to me. "Joe . . . don't unpack, you're going to the NCO Academy."

Each unit had to send a certain number of people to the academy and the 77th picked me. The NCO Academy was a must for your career. They told me I'd be reassigned to the next team, FB-2, but I was really disappointed at being taken off that first team into Laos.

My place was taken by an intelligence specialist, and the first SF team departed for Laos in May of 1959. But I knew my time in Laos would come.

After the NCO Academy, I went through that jungle survival training in Panama, and had extensive medic and communication cross-training at Fort Bragg and Fort Gordon, Georgia. All of this was important to my career in SF, but it ate up two years and I watched team FB-2 leave for Laos without me.

By June 1961 Bull Simons was putting together team FB-3 for Laos. Ten twelve-man A-teams made up the B-team contingent. Laos missions lasted six months, and the 7th Group, as the 77th was now called, rotated with the 1st SF Group out of Okinawa. Laos was no cakewalk. We had already lost two men, including the man who took my place on FB-1. I always thought that could have been me.

In July, team FA-11 came together and was assigned to A Company of the 7th SF Group. The makeup of the team was based on MOS and experience, and FA-11 had some of the best in SF. In my case I knew they had made a good choice. I had excelled at Fort Gordon's commo school and was made the team's chief radio operator.

White Star was still highly classified, and SF had full control. We had our own cantonment area at Fort Bragg, and it was fully secured. Everyone in the company knew we were going to be deployed. As far as I was concerned, it was about time.

Most of the NCOs knew each other from either the schools or field-training exercises. M. Sgt. George Yosich, the team sergeant, had trained and led partisans in Korea and had an A-team with 10th SF Group in Bad Tölz, Germany. Yosich commanded everyone's respect.

The team sergeant is the main individual in all cases, because the team leader and executive officer— a captain and a lieutenant—just flew into SF for their two years. The next thing they knew they were on a mission to Laos. They didn't know anybody and no one knew them.

But we pulled together real fast.

Capt. Ed Frank was an infantry officer—a senior captain gray around the edges. He was level-headed from the start and fit in well with the team.

The XO was 1st Lt. Jimmy Jones. At thirty-three he was old for a lieutenant. Jones was just an old country boy from Beckley, West Virginia, who was an NCO with the 82nd Airborne in Korea. He came into the Group in 1956 and went through OCS. Jimmy was one of us and it showed. He loved to chew Red Man. If he couldn't get that, he'd chew on a big cigar. A cigar wouldn't last him long. Jimmy was the only bachelor on the team.

The White Star training was extensive. Captain Frank arranged all the study sessions at the SWCEN school. We had language training every day and studied the politics, customs, religion, terrain, weather, and whatever else we could about Laos and its people.

The biggest part of team training was getting to know each other real well and learning to work together by instinct. After all, who else were we going to rely on out in the middle of noplace halfway around the world?

So you'd think the first field exercise would throw the team into a survival situation. But higher headquarters had another task for us. They wanted us to stage a "mission" for photographers from *Life* magazine. I guess the people in the public information office were trying to counter some of the negative press the U.S. was getting from the situation in Laos and Vietnam. Remember, we were still only "advisors" there.

The setup was to blow up a small two-story brick storage building at Camp Mackall, a well-secured training area twenty-nine miles west of Fort Bragg. Our mission was to destroy the building using homemade explosives. SF are trained to concoct explosives from off-the-shelf materials that could be easily obtained anywhere in the world we might be. And you'd be surprised how effective and deadly that can be.

George Hill, our operations and intelligence sergeant, was a demolitions man with the first White Star teams to Laos and was back for more. He spoke with a slight Virginia accent and always smiled, especially when he was handed a chance to show his stuff. Bobby Gregory was our other demolitions man. He was usually quiet but was as eager as the rest of us to show off, since he had the latest training in explosives. Since I had taught demolitions early on, I offered to help.

We started with several twenty-five-pound sacks of flour. We followed Gregory's lead in filling one room plumb full of flour. Then we placed five 2.5-pound blocks of TNT on top of the bags and wired everything. The whole idea was to ignite the flour dust and spread a pattern of fire over the target. To create enough heat to ignite the flour we manufactured our own thermite, using garden-variety fertilizer. The timing had to be perfect. First we would blow the flour and then immediately blow the thermite for the heat and flash. For about twenty bucks you got a pretty deadly chain reaction.

After we set the charge we sealed the room with rags. All it takes is touching one side of a small battery. We blew out the building and had a little fire. The insides disintegrated but the building stood.

We were told it wasn't impressive enough for the camera. The homemade thermite wasn't hot enough to ignite the flour, so we brought out the real thermite, ground it out and rigged it to detonate the flour. The second time around took down the building. And that's the picture in *Life*, with the whole team running toward the camera.

We had an awful lot of skull sessions, going over weapons, demolitions, and communication. The first thing every morning I would check out my radio, then grab redheaded Clyde Ward, the other commo man, and be gone for the day. We'd take our radios home. We'd set them up in our backyards and we'd talk to each other all day. At times we would drive to the next town or go to the backside of the fort and operate back and forth, throwing up all types of antennae to see what worked best with the radios. We put our small generators to the test for reliability and durability and made sure we would have spare parts for everything that had a tendency to break down.

Every man kept himself sharp and prepared. We night-dropped into areas that went from dry to swampy, simulating the conditions we could expect in Laos. Our stamina and training were being put to the test.

But the medics didn't have the opportunity to show off what they knew. Charles Heaukulani, in particular, was one of the most highly trained medics I ever met. By the time he came into the 7th Group, he had already been through the military medical academy in Augsburg, Germany. Huk's view of being accepted into the team was simple. "How could they not take the best?"

We had one hell of a team.

After two months of training we got the word to prepare for deployment. This meant a mountain of paperwork. We had to settle all our personal affairs and give our wives power of attorney. Our paychecks were to be sent directly to the bank. In other words, we were preparing for the time when we "didn't exist." The mission was so highly classified even the wives weren't supposed to know where we were going. All we would say was that we were "going on an operation."

Each one of us was to have a top-secret security clearance for the mission. Top-secret to us meant "Don't say nothin'." Kathy and I were living off the base in a cracker box of an apartment next to Highway 401 when two men came to the door. They were in civilian clothes but had military haircuts. They looked like big SF men. "We're here on a security check," they said and showed their credentials. I made sure they were who they said they were because I was damned if I was going to give them spit if they weren't. They were from military intelligence and had come to confirm everything I claimed on my clearance forms.

All of the White Star teams traveled in civilian clothes and wore them for the entire mission, so we were given an allowance to buy a basic wash-and-wear wardrobe. Even our passports had us as civilians.

I never had a passport before, so when I applied for it I saw my birth certificate for the first time. I discovered that it said my name was Richard Garner, even though everybody called me Joe from the very first. It was a puzzle to me. All I could figure out was that after the midwife came to our house to deliver me, she went to the courthouse in Winchester, Tennessee, to make out the birth certificate, and unknown to all of us just put Richard Garner on the certificate, leaving out Joe. I guess she just forgot. And all this time I was using Joe R. Garner on my military registration and social security.

As the time got even closer, we read the latest CIA reports from the area and were briefed at the SWCEN by men from the first team FB-1 and others that had been back and forth. Laos was heating up. George Hill filled us in on working with the Meo tribesmen and what it was like to deal with the French.

The Laotian boy king had asked the U.S. to train his 25,000-man Royal Laotian Army to fight the Pathet Lao, something that was against the Geneva accords. Ike said okay but that we'd only send "technicians." Our job was to teach the technical part of weaponry. The French would teach the tactics and turn the men over to the U.S. in the afternoon. Then SF would say to the Laotians, "Forget everything the Frogs taught you, we're going to start fresh again."

JFK kept the pot boiling, and now Bull Simons was going back with ten A-teams.

We still didn't know our date of departure, but I knew it was soon. Kathy always knew it was only a matter of time before we were separated. She accepted that. We just looked at each other. It was "What are we going to do now?" time. Valerie was three and little Joe was one. I didn't want to leave Kathy alone for six months, so we decided the best thing was to send her and the kids to Missouri to stay with her folks until I returned. I moved back into the barracks.

The Army called the wives in for their own secret briefing. That's when the men knew the mission was close. The wives were told we were going to be in harm's way, and that if the mission was going to be blown it was going to be blown from gossip in that room.

"If you don't want your husbands to come back . . . go ahead and talk." The message was clear.

Then they pulled down the maps and told them where we were going. But nothing was said about what we would be doing there.

It takes a special woman. And the women who don't have what it takes to be married to SF soldiers are soon divorced.

Because of our missions, separations were frequent and sometimes long. That's just the way it was. Many men used their R&R time to mess around and made the excuse that if it wasn't for that they couldn't take being overseas. It was a two-edged sword. Fort Bragg was full of men, and the wives had trouble with their loneliness, too.

I was one of the lucky ones.

While at Fort Leonard Wood I was traveling all over Missouri to meet girls. Nothing seemed to be too important at the time until my bout with hepatitis made me think twice about my drinking and carousing.

A small PX sat at the backside of the fort near the barracks where the trainees lived. Most of us Engineer School instructors would gather there at the snack bar for bull sessions. There was also a little barbershop, where we socialized.

In August of 1957, I noticed that a new girl had been hired at the PX. From the barber chair, I could see her at a cash register. I asked the barber about her and found out that her mother and father worked on the post and got her the job. She had just graduated from high school. Her parents brought her every morning and picked her up on the way home.

I was already dating other girls, but this one was different. It was something you can't put into words. She was a beautiful little girl, and I didn't hesitate to walk up to her. Her name was Kathleen Williams, a farm girl from Waynesville. Right away I asked her if she would go out with me.

"My mother and father don't like GIs," she told me. "They do not want me to go with GIs."

The fort was full of stories about young women dating soldiers only to have their wives show up. One had gone so far as to buy clothes for her wedding.

I thought for a minute then said, "Would you go with me if I got permission from your dad to take you home?"

She wanted to go with me, and she didn't want to go with me. I almost knew that was going on in her mind.

"Yes, I'd go."

That evening, I waited for her dad to pick her up. I asked Kathy what he liked to do. "Hunt rabbit and fox," she said.

He pulled up in a dusty gray half-ton pickup. I went up to him and started talking about hunting—mostly about rabbit hunting because I didn't know a thing about fox hunting. He had a slew of dogs and that's all he did every weekend. I liked that. We talked for about thirty minutes, waiting for Kathy. I didn't get close to the subject of Kathy the whole time, letting him rave on about his fox and rabbit hunting.

Then, just before she got out, I popped the question. "Do you mind if I take Kathy home tonight?"

I waited for a No.

He said, "Okay."

That was the beginning of our relationship. We quit seeing anybody else, and I began spending all my free time with her. She lived way out in the country, and that made it all the better. Her mother and father were real nice to me. Before then, I really didn't have a place to go. All that changed.

It got to where I was taking Kathy home every evening. We were together every day and every night. We enjoyed each other—what one wanted to do the other did as well. But I knew that if I went back to Chattanooga, or even stayed in the Army, I would probably never come back to Fort Leonard Wood. I didn't spend a lot of time making my decision: she was the girl I liked more than any other.

After bringing her home from a date, I proposed in her front yard. "I just don't want to leave without you," I said. "Let's get married. Will you go with me?"

I really didn't expect her to say "Yes." But she was ready to go.

I never asked her father for his consent. We walked into the house and just announced it. They thought we were joking. I didn't think it had sunk into Kathy's head either that I was serious. But the more I talked to her folks, the more she realized that she was going to be my wife.

Her mama and daddy weren't shook up—just surprised. Her twin sister Jacqueline tried to talk her out of it. She told Kathy it was crazy to marry someone she'd just met—especially a GI. Kathy knew I was going to reenlist, and I'm sure she knew all the stories about what men did when they were away. But I knew she thought I was special.

I didn't have a ring yet. In fact, I didn't have any money to speak of. Kathy and I had to wait for my reenlistment bonus so we could have the wedding. As soon as that smiling recruiting sergeant handed me the money, I told Kathy to get a preacher and took off to buy a new car: a shiny new 1957 Pontiac. We were going to start our honeymoon in style.

On the night of October 22, four days after my reenlistment, Kathy and I were married in a small house in Laquey, Missouri: a groom of twenty-three and his bride of nineteen.

I had thirty days' leave before reporting to Fort Benning jump school and wanted to take full advantage of that time to be with Kathy. We left that night on a slow trip to Tennessee. Kathy told me her father had one last thing to say to her as they drove to the wedding.

"Did he try to talk you out of it?" I asked.

"Not really. All he said was 'Don't get married just to go somewhere else.'"

Kathy was a little nervous about meeting my mother. I was, too. When I wrote her I was coming home, I hadn't made up my mind about reenlisting. It was also before I decided to get married. I never told Mama about that, either.

When we drove up, Larry and Alan were falling all over themselves with excitement. But Mama just stood there staring at Kathy.

"Who's this?" she asked.

"My wife."

Mama had to catch her breath. All along, she had expected me to come back there to live. I guess she was counting on me to help her with Larry and Alan, who were pretty wild. She had fixed a room for me above the one-car garage behind the house.

Now here she sat, face to face with Mrs. Joe Garner.

Kathy and I already knew we would be separated almost right away. I was due to report to jump school the middle of December, so I left her with her folks and started a very lonely drive to Georgia.

At the end of the three weeks of jump school, I called Kathy and told her to get packed, hop a bus, and meet me at the Greyhound terminal in Chattanooga. She was so excited. I didn't tell her we didn't have anyplace to live off post in Fayetteville.

Fort Bragg had a guest house for noncoms and their families next to the NCO Club. We were there less than a week before we rented a tiny stucco house west of the post. It wasn't what I wanted for Kathy, but it was all I could afford on a corporal's pay. The inside was painted Army olive green. It had one big living room with a small gas unit in the bedroom for heat. You needed a towel or potholder to open the refrigerator door—otherwise you got a shock.

We were barely settled in when Kathy told me she was pregnant. We started looking for a nicer place, and three months later we moved to a bungalow that was in better shape. This was the first time Kathy had lived away from home. She had grown up in a place where she knew everybody, and now everyone was a stranger.

Up until the time she was six months pregnant Kathy didn't see a lot of me. I was gone practically all the time, either in the mountains of North Carolina or the swamps of Georgia. With yet another exercise coming up that would take me away from her, we decided it would be easier on Kathy to have her family around her as she got closer to having the baby.

I put her on the bus back to Missouri.

On August 17, Valerie Jo was born. A couple of days before, the Army cut me loose and I was with her for the birth. Leave was real short, then it was back to the field. When the baby was six weeks old, I arranged to meet Kathy in Chattanooga and bring her back. But, by the time I got there, I already had orders for another training exercise. It was sad news for Kathy, and she took another bus trip back to Missouri.

It wasn't until Valerie was three months old that Kathy and I felt it would be okay to bring her to Fayetteville. I had rented another apartment that was near a lot of other young military wives.

Joe, Jr., came along in August of 1960. But just before "Little Joe" turned one, my time with him was cut short. I had my orders for Laos and intensive team training had begun. Staring me in the face was the fact that once

I lifted off for Laos it would mean six solid months away from Kathy and the kids and the possibility I might not come back.

I felt it would be best for them to spend that time in Missouri. Two weeks before the mission, we loaded the car with baby beds and everything else imaginable. It was a tearful goodbye.

It takes a special woman.

chapter 5

Anything, Anytime

The alert came the night before we were to depart for Laos. We had been prepared for weeks and were anxious to go. It was actually exciting to get the word. Each of us had a full duffel bag of sterile civvies, jungle fatigues, and personal stuff, and our mountain rucksacks loaded with survival gear and lots of other field goodies. We took one set of identifying rank and insignia, but it was packed away from sight. The only weapons we took were the civilian types. Mine was a silver-plated .357 with a bone handle. Huk had his medical box that was like a mini-operating room and pharmacy. My commo box held the two Angry-109s, hand-crank generator, and antenna wire, and was filled out with spare parts and batteries.

We loaded a C-124 at Pope AFB and that's when we saw Bull Simons there in the cockpit. He was once again our commander, and we knew we were in good hands.

THE DON MUANG AIRFIELD AT BANGKOK GAVE US OUR FIRST GLIMPSE OF THE secret war. There were a lot of unmarked aircraft flying our military advisors around. This was Air America, the "civilian" contract operation run by the

CIA. We also noticed some Chinese pilots, Nationalist Chinese, I guess, flying cargo for the CIA. They had their own "company" called Continental Air Service.

We boarded an unmarked C-47. Up in the cockpit were two very military-looking civilians. We headed north.

There was a lot at stake in Laos. Hanoi had jumped the frontier at Dien Bien Phu, right on the border of Laos and North Vietnam. They started hacking out a trail to the south—a covert supply route that was principally a foot trail.

The communist Viet Minh had come across in large numbers in support of the Pathet Lao and were together threatening to overrun Laos with guerrillas and army forces. In Geneva the Pathet Lao was given the two northeast provinces of Phong Saly and Sam Neua, but they wanted a lot more.

The U.S. had been sending SF into the major Viet Minh travel routes to train Laotian soldiers and indigenous tribesmen. The tribal Hmong, cousins to the Montagnards, hated the Viet Minh. The Viet Minh had pressed them into service as forced laborers. The communists called them Meo, meaning "dog." The name stuck, but when they started fighting the Pathet Lao they didn't like being called "dog soldiers" so they renamed themselves Hmong.

Vang Pao was the strongest person with the most charisma among the Hmong, who were loyal to the king. The king made him a general with his own army to command. Vang Pao stayed away from the politics of the three princes that had divided Laos. As a result, he was trusted and supported by the CIA. A lot of SF worked with him near the Plain of Jars, a very hot area. Unfortunately, SF had also given him everything he needed to know to pull off a coup.

Ike had handed JFK a hot potato with Laos. Even the CIA and the State Department were at cross-purposes. The three princes and their generals shifted allegiances every time you blinked your eye. But for the U.S. the major headache was the massive military thrust of the Viet Minh–sponsored Pathet Lao. Laos was turning red.

We came in low over the Mekong River, which separated Thailand from Laos, and there was Vientiane, the political capital. Wattay Airport was busy with military aircraft, mostly unmarked like ours.

As we unloaded, Captain Frank and Lieutenant Jones were ushered across the airstrip to a large one-story plywood building sitting right at the edge of the field. It was MAAG-Laos and White Star HQ. That's where all the brass were, including Bull Simons.

Frank and Jones came out a few minutes later and began our briefing. Bull Simons had changed things by the time FB-3 was put on alert. Frank said White Star was splitting most of the A-teams in two. Where they used to send a full A-team they now sent half an A-team, with its other half staying behind doing the functions of a B-team in support. The two halves rotated at three months. But we were going to be split and assigned entirely different missions.

This hit us like a ton of bricks. We were an excellent team—we had trained and practiced as a team. Frank would take one-half of the team and Jones the other. The team breakdown would keep Captain Frank and M. Sgt. George Yosich together. George Hill, with time and grade in his favor, plus his O&I MOS, qualified as Lieutenant Jones's team sergeant. Frank took the older NCOs who had been cross-trained. Clyde Ward, the ranking commo man, would be with Frank while I went with Jimmy Jones. Heavy-weapons man Ed Clark and Bill Waltz, demolitions supervisor, also went with Frank. Robert Young, light weapons, and Bobby Gregory, the assistant demolitions man, would come with Jones since George Hill was also a demolitions and weapons man. Don Noe, the assistant medic, would stay with Frank. Huk, the senior medic, would go with Jones because there was less field experience between the lieutenant and the next ranking NCO.

And that was it. We were split. After four months' training as a team, we were being separated.

We stayed overnight in a Quonset hut–style billet. After breakfast, we said our goodbyes and moved out to our aircraft. The C-47 lifted off and swung back across the Mekong into Thailand and we followed the river northeast. We flew about ninety-five miles and crossed the river again, dropping down into Paksane, which sat just over the Mekong in Laos.

Paksane was nothing but a water hole. You could look over to the side of the plane and see a little ol' runway cut right out of the jungle, just big enough to set down the C-47. The plane kicked up a lot of dust as it hit the dirt runway and rolled to a stop. All along one side of the runway were stacks of ammo cases, the bottom tier sitting in water. Under a row of trees at the far end sat a lot of the locals. There were also several dozen native water buffalo roaming free in a grassy area.

We grabbed our gear and moved off the airfield to an adjacent large two-story frame building. This is what they called the MAAG district commander's hooch and headquarters, or embassy house. I guess, for that part of the world, it was the biggest house around. It was certainly the biggest one in Paksane. It had twelve rooms, a kitchen, storeroom, large dining room, and one small room upstairs for communications. The house had a section for SF and that's where they put us.

Lt. Col. William "Skip" Sadler was manning the house with his staff. MAAG had a presence in each provincial capital that was under pro-West influence. They were the only U.S. in uniform.

They told us not to unpack, that we'd be going up pretty soon. We thought this was unusual since we had expected a two-week overlap with a team we were replacing. There was a six-man split A-team already in the MAAG house supporting the other half of their team out in the jungle advising a Laotian unit. The two were rotating and supporting yet another six-man team—the team we were replacing. Between maintaining communications with both teams in the mountains, handling the operation at the house, and running shipments in and out of the airport, the men were spread a bit thin.

Radio operations were twenty-four hours and the operator slept by the radio. I went to the commo room to meet the operator and, sure enough, he was at his post and busy. There was traffic from both teams, but it looked like some flak was being transmitted from one of the teams in particular. The operator informed me that the team was in deep shit. I helped decode some of the traffic. Once it was decoded with a one-time crypto pad, it went to the MAAG staff and then they wrote another message and sent it on to White Star HQ.

We relayed White Star's answer to the team in trouble.

"Be prepared to be replaced tomorrow."

The team shot back, "We're not sure we're going to make it through the night."

"What the hell am I getting into?" I asked myself.

The morning was still dark when I heard Jimmy Jones shouting, "Eat and get your gear. There's a team that's about to get wiped out. We're going in to replace them. They've got to get out now or they won't live through another night."

About midmorning I saw an old H-34 helicopter landing at the air strip. Then all I heard was Jimmy yelling, "Let's go! Let's go! That's it! We're going in!"

We threw everything inside and climbed aboard. Our civilian pilots gunned the thing, and the old clunker shook and rattled into the air. We had one other passenger—a Laotian assigned as our interpreter.

The chopper took off to the north following a small creek. Five miles out there was nobody on the ground, no slash-and-burn areas being worked. I guess the indigenous had been scared of the fighting between the factions for so long that they all moved to the bigger villages.

We followed the creek for about thirty minutes, then turned west a short distance. I watched the terrain below, taking a good look at our exact path into the mountains in case I had to make my way back alone. I saw how the ravines came down and formed a little river that came right back to Paksane. Our route was along that small river, and we flew right up to its head.

Rising below us was Phou Tinpét, a tall mountain located about thirty-five miles north of Paksane. There were some hooches on top that marked the Laotian battalion headquarters and a tiny LZ in a saddle that connected that ridge with another. We flew into the rear area of the battalion down to the bottom of the hill. Near a small stream was a clearing that could only take a single chopper.

When we set down, all I could see was armed Laotian soldiers all around us. Because of the team's message we were anticipating some hostile action.

Then, racing out of the jungle, came three Americans in a panic. We could hardly get off the aircraft because the other men were frantically trying to board at the same time, that's how scared they were.

"Be careful . . . they're fucking trigger happy," one of the men told us in a voice that was strained.

They pulled our stuff off to make room for their own and hunkered in the back of the chopper, waiting to take off. Even the pilots were excited. They didn't want to stay much longer, either.

We stood there in the open looking at all these little men with long hair along the edge of the jungle watching us. Their weapons were in their arms, not slung on their shoulders. Some looked like kids, just staring at us. We weren't heavily armed and couldn't have defended ourselves. We were at their mercy, but we were just going to play it cool. If they accepted us, okay. If they didn't, okay, we would call for extraction. We didn't know how it would be.

We didn't want them to think that we were there to defend ourselves, so we set our weapons right on the ground and just casually looked around and tried not to show we were concerned. It was very tense.

One of the young officers finally approached us. "Follow us" was his simple instruction.

We just picked up our gear and headed into the jungle from where the other team had emerged. None of our men showed any fear. One young Laotian walked along with us, and after about four hundred yards pointed to a rundown bamboo shack.

"You stay here where the other team stayed."

This was obviously where the Laotian battalion CO wanted us to stay. We noticed two young soldiers watching our every move very closely. They couldn't have been more than fourteen or fifteen. Through the interpreter, Lt. Jones found out they were our "security guards."

I wasted no time getting on the radio with a situation report (SITREP) back to Paksane. Contact was good, and I reported our location and condition. MAAG had no new instructions.

Lieutenant Jones was meeting with Captain Leuders, the other team leader. God only knows what those boys really did to create all this tension. Their medic and commo man had also hung around to help us. They would be gone as soon as the chopper made its round trip back from Paksane.

Huk disappeared into the jungle with their medic. The commo man could see I had everything under control at my end and also went with Huk. Two Laotian "guards" hung behind them.

The old bamboo hooch was really sloppily built. The men broke out their knives and went to work on it.

We were interrupted by the noise of the old H-34 returning for Captain Leuders and the rest of his team. None of the Laotians lifted a finger to help them throw their gear on board. As the chopper shuddered into the air, Huk came over, shaking his head.

"These guys didn't do shit," he said. "There's no sanitation of any kind among the men. And we've got one hell of a medical situation down there."

Huk had found a lot of sick men and no hospital—no medical hooch worth a damn. There was a cook shed and a little hut next to it for the medic, but sick call was handled outside. In the hut was a bamboo rack for a treatment table.

Huk was very upset. "When I got there to the medical hut, the other medic says, 'I got guys in here dying—like six a day—and we don't know why. I reported it to Vientiane and they can't do anything.

"Joe, there were forty men lying there all bloated in the abdomen. I mean, really swollen—like they were pregnant. I used all the diagnostic equipment I had. I checked their temperature, blood pressure, and pulse. I looked at their skin color and eyes. While I was there two men died."

Huk wanted to go back, but Jones said it was just too dangerous right then. He felt that there was an assassination squad somewhere and wanted the team to stay together.

By sundown the team hooch was in livable shape. We had built a new bamboo house with a decent roof. We made split-bamboo beds about two feet off the floor, and a mess area with a roof, table, and bench. I made a table and chair for my communication gear, and the other men made more chairs out of rattan roots.

All the while the Laotians held their guns and watched. We knew they were still angry over the other team and probably wouldn't bury their feelings anytime soon, so we didn't know if we were going to make it through the night either. We picked defensive positions near the hooch and prepared to stay alert all night.

Throughout the night we heard a lot more than animal noises. We heard all kinds of moving around. They came right close to the camp and watched us all night, and I'm sure they had their weapons ready, because you could hear the bolts popping every now and then. We thought we were going to be their sacrificial lambs.

Huk was up before dawn making breakfast. By the time the rest of us were drinking coffee and eating, one of the Laotians had come to the hooch with more bad news about their sick men. Lieutenant Jones set Huk loose. "Get after them. Find out what that's all about and do what you can."

Huk grabbed the medical box and took off.

After a short meeting, Jones sent George Hill and Robert Young to check the Laotians' weapons and defensive positions and Bobby Gregory out to check their supplies of ammunition and demolitions. They were escorted into the jungle by some of our young Lao guards.

About midafternoon we heard the sounds of artillery way in the distance, followed by impacts near the battalion headquarters on top of the hill. I reported it back to Paksane. We were set up to transmit daily SITREPS to Paksane at 0800 and 1700, but we could come up on the air anytime. We also had the White Star frequency in Vientiane for emergencies.

It was very late in the day before anyone came back. Huk was the first in, and he was worried. "I have one man that's about dead right now. I've got to go back and help as much as I can. I'd really like to know what's killing so many."

Jones told him, "Eat first, then take the interpreter with you. If you need help, send word to us."

Bobby Gregory was the next in and reported that the Laotians were very short of rifle ammo, and some of the ammo appeared to be wet. Jones sent Gregory to help Huk in the medical hut.

Hill and Young returned right after dark. All Hill would say was "What a mess. What a mess." They reported that all the weapons were in bad shape.

"Looks as if most were never cleaned," he said. "Some even have bent barrels. That's great if you're shooting around trees."

It got worse. The defensive positions were laid out badly. In some cases there were no crossfires and in others the Laotians were actually positioned so as to fire at each other.

"Goddamn," Hill said. "When we left in 1959, they were in a hell of a better shape than this. Those other guys didn't do squat for them."

Because of the tactical situation, our work was cut out for us. Our 650-man Royal Laotian Army battalion was positioned between the Plain of Jars and Paksane. We were sitting on one of the Pathet Lao's major routes and, being thirty-five miles from Paksane, were situated to hold and contain the enemy. The other split A-team had Laotians on another hill to the west of us. Between the two battalions we were protecting Paksane. If the Pathet Lao ever got through to Paksane they would occupy a position right across the Mekong from Thailand, and create all sorts of hell for friendly river traffic.

I closed out the evening with a very long message back to headquarters. We had to order at least a dozen small-arms to replace the bent ones and ordered more ammo to replace all the wet rounds.

It was late when Gregory and the interpreter returned from helping Huk. "We've got some real sick men down there," Bobby said. "Huk's trying his damnedest but it doesn't look good."

We set up security again and slept a little better that night, but Huk didn't come in.

Huk showed up before breakfast. He really looked beat. He had lost another man. He came in for some food and his medical books.

We spent the rest of the day helping as many men as we could clean their weapons. We also changed as many defensive positions as we could, retraining the Laotians on their 4.2-inch mortars, but it would still take several more days, since the units were so scattered.

The battalion commander had put a couple of camps of four men each at almost a spitting distance away. These men were assigned to watch us and escort us everywhere we went. Jimmy Jones had been spending time talking with the Laotians and was slowly gaining their confidence.

"I made arrangements to go up and see the battalion commander in the morning," Jimmy told us. "I'll take Hill and the interpreter."

Hell, I was curious about these men watching us so I grabbed the interpreter and went for a visit. One young man was friendly enough. He told us he was the overseer. It was his job to report all our movements to the battalion commander. He gave us the story about the other team.

One of the SF on the team kicked some of the Laotians in the butt because they wouldn't unload supplies from the helicopter quick enough. They also hollered at them and cursed them. But one of the young Lao officers had taken some English, something the team was not aware of. The lieutenant couldn't speak the words, but he sure knew what they meant.

The battalion colonel ordered them out immediately. That's how those men almost got their asses killed, and if we hadn't got there when we did, they wouldn't have survived to the next day.

The Laotians and all the hill tribes have to be treated with respect. Their culture almost demands it. You would never take a hand to them. The Lao are the predominant group in the country. They're 70 percent of the population and live mostly in the northern part of the country. If you look at them closely, you'll see that they're more Polynesian or Burmese than true Oriental. They are very small. Males rarely reach five feet four, and that's tall. Lao women are under five feet. The Lao are one of five major tribes. The other major group, the Meo or Hmong, are more ethnic Chinese. They populate the mountains on the eastern side of Laos, Their reddish-brown skin and high cheekbones suggest both their Mongol heritage and an ancestry that can be traced back to Genghis Khan. Then there are the Black, White, and Red Thai along the Mekong River, which runs the length of Laos; the Kha, good tribal fighters spread throughout the region above the Plateau de Bolovens; and the Yao, along the southern border with Cambodia and on the plateau.

From White Star's beginnings, SF were charged with shaping all these ethnic groups into units capable of standing on their own against Communist domination.

We didn't see Huk all that day. He came in to eat and went right back to his patients. He hadn't slept in over twenty-four hours. But the next morning he was a new man. He came running up, excited as all hell. The news was terrific. Huk had managed to find what was killing the Laotians and had already saved two men.

"It's the simplest goddamn thing, Joe," he said, trying not to jump up and down. "They're not getting any vitamin B. They're eating junk."

I got on the radio and relayed the news to White Star in Vientiane with a request for enough Vitamin B shots to treat the battalion. Huk was on cloud nine, but through his excitement he explained how he did it.

"When I went down with the interpreter, I asked the soldiers a lot of questions, but I still couldn't determine what was making them sick enough to kill them. So I go back to the team hooch and grabbed my *Merck Manual*."

Medics carry three books: the *Merck Manual*, a combat surgery manual, and a medical dictionary.

"I looked at the chapter on symptoms and I find beriberi, the lack of Vitamin B. And the only thing that triggers my eye is the reference to Orientals and Asians getting beriberi. But I thought the Laotians should be getting vitamin B because they eat rice. But my guy died of beriberi and I was about to lose another man with the same symptoms. So I went to see how they were eating. A platoon would sit around this big cooking pot full of rice, reach in, make a ball of the stuff, dip it in a sauce made out of hot peppers and sometimes leaves, and pop it in their mouth. That was their meal twice a day.

"But they weren't eating their own rice, Joe. I look over and see a big bag of rice with 'U.S.' on it. My God, Joe. They're eating the same rice we're eating—polished. But at least we have protein. So I start to connect the whole thing. With no husks full of Vitamin B and no other source worth a damn, the poor beggars were dying of beriberi for sure.

"When I got back to the medical hut my man was sinking fast. His symptoms were right out of the manual. I didn't have any IV vitamin B so I had to do it with pills. But these guys couldn't hold anything down. People with a food imbalance can't hold anything in their stomachs, so you stick it up their rectum. You goo it up with petroleum jelly and shove it up, and the body will absorb it. But it'll only absorb about twenty-five percent of the dosage.

"I pumped my guy with a lot of vitamin pills, and I watched his temperature come down. Then his blood pressure came down, and I knew I had it nailed. I put him on a four-hour regimen, then I gave him water and he held it down. It was really a drastic change. I started on the other twenty men, and for a twenty-four-hour period no one died, Joe. No one fucking died."

Jimmy Jones was smiling like I hadn't seen before. He knew that this was the kind of news he needed for his first meeting with the Laotian battalion commander. Jones got Gregory to go with him, and a lot of the Laotians wanted to go along, too. From the second day we all started running around with our shirts off, and that's when the Laotians began tagging along with Jones. Jones had a lot of hair on his chest and the Laotians would come up and feel the hair. I could hear them laugh and giggle.

Jones decided to walk all the way to the top of the mountain. "I thought if I took a chopper up I'd look like any other MAAG advisor just collecting his pay," he told us. That was Jimmy Jones's style. Jones was an ol' country boy who was brought up polite like all country folks and was used to dealing with a man face to face. They never look down on anybody. I think country boys the world over are the same way. The Laotian soldiers picked up on this right away and took to Jones.

The rest of us went about our routine, wishing we could be flies on the wall for that first meeting.

It was late in the afternoon when Jones and Gregory returned. Jones looked pleased with their first encounter with the Laotian head shed.

"Hell, you should have seen their faces." He laughed. "I don't think they ever thought they'd see an American officer take his shirt off and come up the hill with only a pistol belt and canteen."

He pointed to the top of the mountain. "The distance to the battalion CP is two klicks—almost straight up. It was a damned four-hour walk. We got to the top by grabbing these two-inch-thick rattan roots and pulling ourselves up. Hell, those things run top to bottom.

"The commander is a colonel. Bou Noi is his name. He's got a bunch of young lieutenants up there as staff. I don't think they know shit about tactics. They're all in defensive positions and all they do is react to whatever the Pathet Lao throws at them. They've already heard about Huk's work. I think they're impressed. We're going to get along with Bou Noi real good."

Jones's good news was interrupted by distant artillery fire. Hill started yelling, "Incoming! Incoming!"

We hit the ground, and within six seconds the shells were landing a few hundred yards short of our position. I grabbed the radio, and Jones started dictating the message. We were counting the rounds. When the shelling stopped we had counted over fifty rounds and came up on the radio with our SITREP. Nobody was hurt. The rounds landed on the side of a ridge behind us.

"They already found us," Jones said. "Joe, you and me are going to build a bunker in the morning."

After my 0800 radio contact, Jones and I started digging out the bank right behind our hooch. For the roof we took axes to some big trees down the hill that were at least two feet in diameter. The chopping wasn't the hard part. Lugging those huge logs uphill was.

The enemy didn't give us a chance to rest, though. We got another fifty rounds in the afternoon. They were inching closer and knocking down trees that were just above us. The debris fell almost on top of us. Jones said, "All it takes now is a click on their tubes and they've got us."

By dinnertime the next day we had built the best damned underground bunker you ever saw, with palm brush and bamboo covering the logs and two feet of dirt on top of that. It wasn't big enough to sleep in, but if you heard the rounds coming in you could crawl in and forget about them.

Next, we heard small-arms fire real close to us, and all six of us were about to go into the defensive mode when the firing stopped. The Laotians had made little watch stations for themselves in the trees and we didn't know if they were doing the shooting or if it was Pathet Lao or what. Jones crawled over to me. "Take the interpreter and ask them just what the fuck is going on."

They politely informed us that it was a hunting party. They had hunting parties out all the time because meat was so scarce. Each recon patrol was also a hunting party, so now we had to be alert for that, too. There were several different types of wild animals around, but most of the hunting parties would come back empty-handed. If they were lucky they got a monkey.

White Star confirmed that Huk's medication was working elsewhere and had ordered all teams to administer vitamin B as soon as possible. We didn't know it at the time, but Laotians were dying of the same symptoms all over. It was a real epidemic. Huk had saved the lives of sixty men in our battalion alone.

But it didn't end there. Huk's findings about the Laotians' diet caused the MAAG commander to order fish oil to be flown in to all Laotian battalions. Within a week Air America was bringing in thirty-gallon clay jugs of fish oil to mix with the rice. There was only one downside to this. The fish oil had a distinctive odor that came out in the sweat. But we could live with that.

Hill, Young, and Gregory were out from dawn to dusk working with the Laotian units. They were so scattered, and there was such a lot of steep climbing involved in reaching all the units, that our men never saw more than thirty Laotians at one time. Huk and his Lao medics were also out with the units making sure all the soldiers had been shot with vitamin B and seeing that they were consuming the fish oil on a regular basis.

It took a couple of weeks before all the weapons were straightened out and defensive positions were set up properly. Their weapons were a ragtag collection of old Air Force–type M-1 carbines, some Garand M-1s and .30 bolt-action Enfields, real old air-cooled .30 machine guns, a few 60mm and 81mm mortars, 4.2-inch mortars, and a lot of 3.5-inch rockets with no launchers. There were a small number of regular hand grenades, old antipersonnel mines, and some World War II M-1 grenade launchers that would knock them down when they tried to fire.

Hill mentioned that because these men were so small they couldn't hold the very large M-1 rifle very well, so on his original FB-1 team, Sgt. Rocky Neasom had modified the weapon by cutting two inches off the stock so the Laotians could fire them.

We received incoming every day. The rounds sounded like our own 105s. Sure enough, when Jones returned from one of his meetings on the hill he confirmed just that. We put that in our SITREP to Paksane.

The Pathet Lao must have had a good supply of ammo because they sure did put a bunch of it on us. We had it timed out. Every time they fired the 105mm guns we had six seconds. You could hear the BOOM way off in the background. It was going to hit right where we were. After a while all the trees around us were blown to bits.

When we sent our SITREPS, Colonel Sadler refused to believe that we were taking 105s to the tune of fifty a day. "That's impossible" was his reply.

Well, the rounds kept falling and Jimmy said, "Fuck the counting and just guess."

So I would put down: "50 rounds."

Even with the 105s the enemy didn't try to overrun the Laotians or us during the first couple of weeks. I don't know why our supporting platoons and squads weren't touched once we got there, their stuff was in such bad shape. But we knew the whole situation could change in a snap.

We ordered a lot of weapons and had resupply choppers and C-47s flying in and out dropping bundles. We got all the machine guns in position and firing. Our men had to explain to every Laotian soldier why his weapon had to be clean—that if it wasn't clean, he wasn't going to kill anybody, and that he might be killed himself.

All the while we were strengthening the relationship between us and the Laotians. We were very polite to them the whole time. George Hill did the most to earn their confidence. He made sure their weapons worked and that they knew how to use them.

The Laotians were very proud of having stayed alive a long time with the battalion. They measured their stay in the jungle by the length of their hair. They never cut their hair while in the jungle, so you didn't have to ask a man how long he'd been there—you just looked at his hair. Short hair meant the man was a replacement. Almost all of the ones I met had very long hair.

It was hard to push the Laotians into a firefight. Every unit and element had a "high buddha"—the religious leader of the unit. The men turned to him for a "go" or "no go" on enemy contact. It was based on their religious superstitions. Sometimes their experiences were good, and sometimes not so good. We just had to learn to work with them.

One Laotian squad was on patrol with their buddha as point man. They walked right into a Pathet Lao ambush. The enemy got off the first shots at almost point-blank range. The point man took three bullets in the chest. But he just staggered, dropped to his knees, and came up firing, killing two. The rest fled with the patrol right after them.

When they returned, the patrol was convinced Buddha was on their side. They had phi—a good omen. Their high buddha kept showing off where he was shot and how the bullets "bounced off." We examined the man and found three blue bruises on his chest. He explained that the bullets lodged between his ribs but didn't break the skin, and he just pulled them out.

He also said the gun sounded very weak. To us that meant the enemy had wet ammunition. They were probably firing Chicom ammo that had bad crimping, letting moisture in to wet the powder. We were surprised the gun got off three rounds at all.

But the Laotians were convinced Buddha had come to their rescue. When the man pulled out the bullets, that was a big deal in their religion. It meant "you can't be hurt." When they realized they were going to win the battle, they overran the enemy position and wiped them out. They had no fear.

Of course, it could have gone the other way. If it had killed him, the rest would have turned tail. It would have been a sign that Buddha wasn't on their side that day.

That's the way it went. Most of their enemy contact was settled in the first seconds. It came down to whoever got off the first shot always being the winner. So we tried to do everything we could to increase their chances of successful contact and make them think Buddha was on their side.

Then there were the Buddha bags. They wore little pouches around their necks all the time. The bag held religious artifacts plus some smelly stuff, which turned out to be a piece of their umbilical cord. They thought the bag would protect them from being killed. They wore the bag as a badge of honor and that caused some friction.

Two of our security guards got into a heated argument. They challenged each other over the strength of their Buddha bags.

One of them yelled, "My Buddha bag is stronger than yours!" Then he stepped back and shouted, "Shoot!"

The other man raised his gun to fire when I stepped in to put an end to this before somebody got killed.

I told them, "Give me the Buddha bag. I want to show you something." The man handed me his bag and I walked to a tree and hung it on a limb. I took the man's carbine and tore that little bag all to pieces.

Huk was watching all this and almost wet his pants. He was sure I had screwed up and we were going to have a riot on our hands. But the men just walked off jabbering to each other. The interpreter turned to me and told me the man knew it didn't work and the other guy said, "No good Buddha bag. Buddha bag number ten. I find another Buddha bag."

On their scale of good and bad, "ten" means the worst—number "one" is the best.

Jimmy Jones continued his trips up to the battalion commander. He was establishing a good relationship with the colonel and his officers. But our

Laotian interpreter turned out to be too young and inexperienced and Jimmy found out that he was making up things. We sent him packing, and on the next H-34 from Paksane was "Joe," a tall, skinny Thai. Joe had trouble adjusting to the daily barrage of artillery, and was scared to death most of the time. When he wasn't with Jones, he stayed close to me for confidence.

Every morning the team would wake up to find breakfast ready. Huk was already gone. He was busy with his Laotian medics, building a proper hospital. In the evenings he would often return with freshly baked bread. There was an oven down near the medical hut. The commo man from the team we replaced had designed and built it and showed Huk how to bake bread in it. The oven had sheet-metal sides, top and back all covered with clay mud. It was heated with a gasoline-fueled squad stove. I could tell when the cook was going to bake. He'd send someone to "borrow" the gasoline I used for my generator. The bread was worth it. But I drew the line when the men started using my gas to fill their cigarette lighters, too.

After several weeks of watching us work, with their health improving, the Laotians' attitude toward us changed. They responded to our concern about them. They started coming around one at a time. They had accepted us. Around the radio I had all the company I wanted. They had a lot of old Korean-vintage banana-shaped walkie-talkies, which were always broken. They'd ask, "What can we do with this?" I ordered parts and tried to fix some, but I usually wound up telling them to dig a hole and bury the thing.

Sanitation among the Laotians was terrible until we got there. They were dropping all over their unit areas. Huk's efforts were working and he wasn't seeing as many intestinal cases at sick call. But we had our own sanitation problem. The team before us had built an outhouse with one seat. It was so full it was smelling bad. When you look down and can read the papers, you know it's getting full.

Huk, being the medic in charge of health, and Gregory, being the demo man, lifted the outhouse and there was the hole, probably blown. Six feet down was the goo pit. They decided to burn it out, so they poured in a mixture of generator oil and gasoline—my generator oil and my gasoline. Being good SF they applied a fudge factor—more of everything. While the stuff was soaking in, they forgot that gasoline burns on fumes—in this case, methane.

Gregory set fire to a ball of paper and dropped it in. They stepped back and BOOM! A ten-foot black column of shit rose into the air. At about one hundred feet it turned downward. I was in the hooch with my earphones on and heard what I thought was someone shouting, "Duck!"

It wasn't until I heard all the thumping on the roof that I realized something was going on. My nose told me the rest. When I came out, there was all this black stuff raining down from the trees. Some of it was hard, too, and really stunk bad.

Jimmy Jones and George Hill came up from the bottom of the hill. Jones looked around and asked, "What the hell are you doing?"

"Oh, we're burning the stuff, sir. No problem."

"What's that stuff all over the roof?"

"Oh . . . I don't know."

Hill sniffed at the air. "What's that funny smell?"

Huk and Gregory still didn't say a word. They put back the outhouse. Jones inspected the clean, round hole. "I like that. No smell in there."

But the rest of the place stunk for a whole week.

We had been in position a month when Jimmy Jones got back from another meeting at the battalion CP. He was just smiling and chewing his Red Man.

"Boys, we're going up on the hill. The colonel has 'invited' us to join him for the duration. And they're going to build hooches for the team."

Jones knew the only way to do a good job of advising and training was to be up with the battalion commander and his staff. It was cumbersome and inefficient being separated like we were. So he had made one of his "suggestions" to the colonel, allowing it to be his decision. Bou Noi was happy to have us. He liked Jimmy Jones. The lieutenant walked up the hill twice a week.

Jones told us, "They thought it was really something that an American team would come up and live with them. It was the colonel who said if we did that he'd build us hooches. I told him they'd better start workin' because we're on our way."

chapter 6

Anyplace, Anyhow

When Colonel Sadler got the word in Paksane that our team was moving up with the battalion HQ, he and his staff were critical of Jones's decision and radioed that we should stay back where it was safer. Jones replied that he thought the mission required us to be near the colonel to improve communication and that he needed to get to know the man better.

Jones got his way and also got Sadler's permission to send two of our men to Paksane so we could have someone from our own "family" in place to support us on the hill. The team back at the MAAG house was spread too thin to respond to our needs. So George Hill and Robert Young, who had already completed the weapons training, flew down.

By 0800 the next morning we were ready to go. All the Laotian soldiers living around our area came by to help us move our equipment down to the landing area. Most of them said goodbye in English, and those who couldn't shook our hands and said it in their own language. I actually thought that would be the last time we would ever see them.

We had laid on a helicopter to haul us and our equipment to the hill. The chopper pilots weren't too keen on landing there. Because of the shelling it was a hot LZ.

We lifted off and flew north almost straight up to clear the 8,500-foot mountain in front of us. We never quite reached the top but went around it and landed in a saddle right in the middle that connected two ridges. The LZ was so small it could hold only one chopper, and if there was a decent wind you couldn't land.

No sooner had we started to unload than artillery was coming in almost right in our laps. The pilot told us to get our stuff off fast because he was leaving. After we got the last piece out we found a big tree to get behind. We counted another fifty rounds.

The battalion commander was at the top of the hill way above us on the front line facing northwest. From this position we could see all the knolls below, where the Pathet Lao was. Our location was on the side of the LZ about fifty yards from the battalion headquarters, against the backside of the hill. The Laotians had three 4.2mm mortars on the headquarters side of the LZ just inside the edge of the woods.

The hooch went up pretty fast and then we hustled to build another bunker. This one was going to be stronger than before because we stood a lot better chance of taking a hit than down below. There was enough timber lying around from the shelling so that we didn't have to cut down any trees. But those babies were still big. We were chopping fourteen-inch-diameter logs and dragging them into position.

The bunker wasn't finished too soon. The enemy had the battalion locked in their sights and picked up on their daily shelling of at least fifty rounds or more. Of course, since Jimmy Jones was still pissed at Colonel Sadler, I wasn't doing an official count for our SITREPS.

Bou Noi was right, though. Our position was less of a target than the battalion headquarters. Many of the rounds would come over us and hit them. I don't think they cared. They had bunkers dug all over.

The Laotian 4.2s always answered but were no match for the enemy's 105s. The 105s were just out of range of the 4.2s, but they kept firing the mortars anyway.

The 4.2s fired over the helicopter pad, so anytime the chopper came in the Laotians would cease fire. The resupply chopper had to get away before they could fire, but that laid him wide open to enemy fire. When the helicopter flew around the mountain to the saddle, he was exposed to enemy fire. Then he had to lift off in the direction of the enemy, and to avoid being a sitting duck, he had to drop off the side of the hill at full tilt and make for the cover of the valley.

The attitude of the Laotians toward us was totally different from our initial reception at the base camp when we were on guard for the unexpected. Up here with the battalion headquarters they were coming around making friends from the start.

The first order of business was working with the battalion commander and his lieutenants on tactics. When we arrived they were just sitting there in a defensive mode hoping like hell nobody would attack them. We changed the tactics right away so that they would take the offensive.

That meant ambushes along known enemy trails and gathering spots. The battalion didn't have claymore mines, but we were surprised to find that they had a large number of 3.5-inch rockets. They didn't know what the 3.5-inch rockets were for because they didn't have the launchers. Gregory showed them how to conceal the rockets in the ground, and set them off with an electrical charge. They would be devastating to the enemy.

The Laotians were eager to learn, and we knew Buddha would be on their side with the 3.5s.

The first ambush was successful—a lot of casualties. After that we had them sneaking around booby-trapping more trails. They had the enemy spooked. Every time they blew a trail, we wouldn't see any more traffic for a while.

Even before we came to the hill the battalion had an ongoing operation trying to knock out a bunker complex where the enemy hid. The Laotians couldn't knock it out, and they couldn't advance past it. They didn't have anything to throw at it, and every time they tried to dislodge the enemy they were hit, so, of course, they turned tail and ran.

Jones just shook his head. "Joe, call down and get a goddamn 3.5 launcher up here."

The 3.5 launcher came in on the next resupply. Jones turned to Gregory. "Greg . . . do you know the 3.5?" Gregory nodded. "Get some key personnel and show them how to shoot it."

It was old and hadn't been used much. It didn't work. After half a day of cleaning and checkout, Gregory had it ready. He trained four men to shoot. They stood on the edge of the chopper pad and shot at the next ridge. For the rest of the day they fired from one mountainside to the other.

When the Laotians went on the same mission a few days later, they shot the rocket right through the bunker door, BLAM! They blew it to pieces and were just tickled over it. With their 3.5 launcher they could go after more bunkers and just bury the enemy in them.

I don't think Colonel Bou Noi was educated. He owed his position to political pull, and we all knew it. The five lieutenants got their rank the same way, but they were educated. All the operations were run by the lieutenants. When the colonel would order an operation, the lieutenants had to use their own initiative to make it work. The officers could be the dumbest knuckleheads in the world, but they were never blamed for the failure of a mission.

Jones excelled in tactics, and he would start with a "suggestion" to the colonel, with the staff and lieutenants in attendance. Jones just took it slow and easy. He was careful not to "tell" Bou Noi what to do.

"Hell, he's been fighting half his life and I've been here a month," Jones said. "They'd resent anybody from the outside telling them what to do. So you discuss options." Jones suggested almost all of their missions and was always able to make the colonel think it was his idea. Only a country boy could pull it off.

Getting water to the battalion was difficult. In a deep gorge a thousand meters below was an underground spring. The Laotians had taken bamboo, hollowed it out, and run it a half mile from the spring. Then they had to hump it almost straight up, grabbing onto the long rattan roots. They offered us their water, but we couldn't chance it. Their systems might be used to the bugs, but ours weren't.

All the water the team used was flown in from Paksane. It came from the Mekong River, which wasn't the cleanest either, but it was heavily treated. Every two weeks we got two five-gallon cans of water. That's not very much. Jones rationed the water—one quart canteen per day for drinking (including coffee), washing, shaving, and brushing our teeth. On Saturday, he got generous. We got two to take a bath. Huk got the best of the deal. He was the cook and would tell Jones, "I have to wash the rice." But I knew he didn't wash it clean.

We had set up a .50 machine gun on a point covering a trail that the enemy could use to sneak up to the battalion HQ. We looked across at the enemy position and we could see this one Pathet Lao. He'd get up every morning, do his face, and put on a clean white T-shirt. Here we were with green Army fatigue pants that had turned brown—we hadn't had a bath, only sponged down, and we'd start getting real angry at the man. The range of the .50 is 2,700 yards and this guy was within 1,500. So, we locked the .50 on him, looked down the sights, pressed the trigger—and nothing happened. Shit.

Gregory and I tore that sucker down, got it all fixed up, and still nothing. We figured it was an improper head-space adjustment, but we didn't have a gauge to use, so we improvised a fix. Then it fired one shot. One stinking shot. We took it apart again and again, but it would only fire one round. It just sat there looking beautiful.

Since we could never get it to fire on automatic, I made sure the one round it did fire was a tracer. The next morning I had that soldier zeroed in, but as soon as I shot, he'd dart out of the way and it would hit where he had been standing. He played games with us. I didn't hate him; it just irritated me because of his white T-shirt and all that water.

Now that we had the .50 firing—even one shot at a time—we gave the Laotians their own shooting gallery to play with. With field glasses you could see the enemy crossing a small clearing about twelve hundred yards away at a thirty-degree angle, probably blown open by our 4.2s. You could see them go across with their light khaki uniforms; our people wore drab green.

They zeroed it and invited me, "Come up and get some Viet Minh." If you sat there for an hour, you would get a shot. I don't think I ever hit one, although I tried. They had the gun locked in to shoot at the same area. It was more a scare tactic. The Pathet Lao knew where it was aimed; they just had to run fast. Sometimes they would grab their AK-47s and return the fire. Nobody got hurt at this game.

Payday for the battalion was something to watch. First, there was a lot of grousing because the pay was so little. The colonel and the other officers seemed to get a lion's share of the pie while the troops got shortchanged. There was also supposed to be money issued to battalion commanders for rations, but it stayed in Paksane and bought almost nothing. To us, it appeared that there were a lot of hands in the till, and by the time it filtered down to the men there was almost nothing to distribute. So the men were always poorly paid and hungry.

But they still used payday for fun: they just forgot about working. They'd play cards at the battalion CP and drink a lot while playing. Bou Noi was a damned card shark, sometimes winning back all a private's pay at poker. Out in the field, the battalion high buddha had a game going all the time. The games were played with their own type of gambling cards. Now, these religious men were supposed to have no use for money, but this high buddha had a duffel bag full of his winnings. Every time we saw him he was laughing.

Jimmy Jones was always invited to battalion HQ when they were drinking. The first time he took them up on the offer, he came staggering back about half snockered. The battalion commander had offered him a few swigs from a bottle of Lao Lao—a foul-tasting liquor that had a picture of a swinging monkey on the label. Jones took a few pulls on the bottle and said to them, "This tastes like monkey piss." The men got a kick out of it and started calling the drink "Monkey Piss." But it didn't stop there. From that time on, Jones himself had the nickname Monkey Piss. And it spread through the battalion.

Our standing order from White Star was not to accompany any unit on a mission, and Jones made sure we never made enemy contact. "We didn't come in to kill anybody," Jimmy reminded us. "We came in to help them kill." We could have helped them more, but we understood the underlying reasons we were to stay back. Jones visited some of the areas of operations (AO) to advise the units, even though Bou Noi would rather he didn't since he was responsible for our well-being.

We were finally getting a decent night's sleep now that we had the colonel's assurance that he was taking care of our security. But it wasn't long before the colonel's security went all to hell.

My radio gear was at one end of the team hooch, which put me almost in the saddle at the head of a little draw. From my radio position I could look out through the space between the bamboo wall and the roof. Off to the right sat the 4.2s. Over to the left sat the battalion HQ. I had a good view down onto the landing pad about fifty yards away.

Late one afternoon I was transmitting one of those long supply messages and was real busy. Suddenly, I heard the damnedest screams from the interpreter Joe coming through the earphones. I looked up and he and Gregory were running toward me from the landing pad. Joe had his pistol raised and was yelling like hell. I turned around to my left and there stood four Pathet Lao about ten feet away, just looking at me. They were in their cream-colored uniforms with the funny little hats. I told the people on my radio to hold on and grabbed for my .357 sitting on the table.

Joe let off a shot, POW! The four men looked at Gregory and the interpreter running at them then looked back at me and took off, turning tail and dropping off the side of the hill, down the draw, and out of sight.

The Laotian soldiers around us reacted to Joe's screaming and emptied out from their dug-in positions all across the mountain. Before I could get a shot off, bullets were flying everywhere. They ran over and started shooting down the draw. I think every Laotian on that hill was firing at them.

When everything settled down, the battalion sent out a patrol. They combed the area but found nothing. How they managed to escape without getting shot is beyond me. That was the first time any enemy had come into the camp. I don't know if they were lost, or wanted to turn themselves in, or were just on patrol. Anyway, they were quite a distance from their HQ.

I think the most dangerous thing about our position was that there were so many dense covered areas around us. You just did not know when someone might appear and shoot you. We had Laotians behind us and on the other side of the helo pad, but no one was guarding the draw.

The Pathet Lao obviously had a little trail in there they used for a number of incursions. There's no telling how many times they came through there. They could still come up any time at night and pitch a grenade into our hooch. That night we didn't sleep. We dressed and armed, ready to defend ourselves.

That's when I asked Jones, "Are there any mines around this godforsaken place? We've got to close the routes to the camp."

The next morning, one of the lieutenants showed Jones a whole bunker full of mines. There were cases and cases of them. God knows how long they had been there. Like the 3.5s, nobody in the battalion knew what to do with them.

Sure enough, they were the kind I taught back at Fort Leonard Wood. Jones made a "suggestion" to the lieutenant that they ought to mine the trails. The Laotian lieutenant nodded his head.

At about 0900 their men showed up with trip wires and fuses ready to go. I took them down into the draw, where I almost got ambushed, and started "school." I showed them how to place and hide trip wires. I went over the different types. Some of them are pull-and-go. When the wire tensed it armed, when it relaxed it went off. The enemy walks through and breaks the wire. BOOM!

There were also the "tomato cans." They were about the size of a can of tomatoes and had a pressure release mechanism. When you stepped on the small prong at the top, you armed the device. When your foot was lifted it flew up in the air about five feet and went off. The thing was full of corrugated metal pieces and exploded into tiny fragments that just tore up a victim.

We showed them how to set the mines on trails and on avenues in and out of the camp. We booby-trapped the hell out of them.

Our security remained tight. The colonel assigned someone to stay near us. We also tried to keep at least one man alert at night. During the day whenever one of us left for the Laotians, guards went, too. Because I was by myself a lot they also made sure there was a man with me who spoke a little English.

Jones came away from a meeting with the colonel and told us Bou Noi wanted us to mine the entire valley because it was just too large an area to guard. Well, I couldn't be gone from the radio that long, so I took three key men and spent several hours showing them how to set the mines. They loaded their bags with mines and with ten more men went down to the bottom of the mountain to place them all over the area. The rest of their men were left to guard the trails.

Two nights later, at about midnight, we heard the mines go off, and we thought we had had it. There were explosives blowing one right after another, and the boys that were guarding down there were firing wildly in the direction of the explosions. Jimmy Jones, who slept with all his clothes off, jumped out of bed and started running to battalion headquarters buck naked. Gregory yelled, "Wait . . . put on your pants!" Jimmy stopped dead in his tracks. The rest of us knew better than to laugh.

The firing below stopped, but we thought for sure that the enemy was preparing to attack us in full force. We stayed up all night long waiting for them to come up the hill so we could have a battle and get it over with. The rest of the night was quiet.

In the morning, one of our men from the bottom of the hill came running up. He was so excited and winded that we couldn't understand him at all. Finally, the interpreter was able to get the story straight: "We killed some elephants!"

It was a herd of elephants moving down from the north into that valley that had stepped on the mines. Once a year the valley was an elephant run, and this was the time. They went all through that mine field.

A few of the men guarding the trail came up with two huge tusks about eight inches in diameter. We had killed the lead bull.

To the Laotians that meant meat—lots of meat. They offered us a chance to go down and retrieve some meat for ourselves. I looked at Huk and asked, "How do you cook a damned elephant?"

Huk just shrugged and said, "All I know is that you eat it one bite at time." We politely turned down their offer.

The Laotians ate every ounce of that elephant. One bull was all we found, although we found a lot of blood. The whole battalion got pieces of the poor beast.

It wasn't three days before another mine went off—one that was very close to us. I said to Gregory, "Oh, my gosh, I'll bet one of our men got that, the way it sounded." And sure enough, here they come, dragging him up through the woods. It was the big-time gambler, the high buddha for our group. He had gone to take a dump, and while he was out there, security had set out the mines. He came back in and they went off.

He had a dozen holes all over him, but nothing vital was hit as far as we could tell. I don't know why the mine didn't kill him right away—maybe the jungle protected him. We didn't want to move him too much, so we made a lean-to right next to the chopper pad. Huk took out what shrapnel he could and cleaned him up. I called for evacuation.

He didn't act like he was dying, lying there not complaining about the pain. All he would say was "I want my duffel bag. Where's my duffel bag?" Joe kept telling the men, "He wants his duffel bag." We persuaded them to find the bag. They returned with it, plumb full of Laotian money. He was all smiles.

The next morning he went out on the chopper holding that duffel bag and laughing.

THE SEARCH FOR NEW SOURCES OF WATER WAS ONGOING. ONE OF OUR PATROLS reported, "We found water a lot closer, but the Pathet Lao is using it. They're swimming in it."

I said to Jones, "Why don't we just mine the damned thing?"

Jones asked, "How are we goin' to do it?"

Gregory and I put our heads together and came up with putting tomato cans under the surface of the water and detonating them remotely like we did with the 3.5s on the trails.

Our idea was to take out the firing mechanism and replace the pressure cap that usually protrudes at the top with an electrical blasting cap, then place the nasty little things under the water and in the sand. We hid the leads and ran the wires back into the jungle. Then we sat and waited. As soon as the enemy was in there taking a bath, we blew their asses off. Buddha smiled on us again.

Battalion morale eventually came down to food—the lack of it. The Laotians had a resupply system of their own, too. At the base camp below, an Air America C-47 would drop out all of their rice, fish oil, ammo, and other supplies.

The C-47 would come flying in at treetop level. It was so close you could see the man at the door. The plane was supposed to be flown by "civilian" crews, but their hair was too short, and they wore military boots. The rice was dropped in three fifty-pound burlap bags kicked out in a free drop. One Laotian ran out to grab one of the bags when another one came down on him and took his head off at the shoulders like a blade. They didn't know they had to clear the area for the drop and had been very lucky before. Well, that was one thing we didn't have to give a class on.

Even our own basic diet continued to be rice. Huk couldn't bake like he did at the base camp. We couldn't get a resupply of flour. Nothing came in fresh. There were no C-rations, only civilian-style canned goods from Vientiane. At times the Laotians tried to trade some of their food for ours until they tasted our canned stuff. They hated the canned food. When they got meat they always brought us some because they felt sorry for us. Sometimes we were offered monkey, but when they killed one there were so many to feed we didn't want to take it from them.

The battalion commander and his staff ate very well—better than the rest. They had meat at almost every meal. Once when they flew in a slaughtered cow and dropped it on the pad, they wanted to show their appreciation to us by offering us what was the best part of the cow to them, the tongue. I said, "No, no. We don't want to take your best. Give this to the colonel and give us that ol' piece that ain't no good along the backside."

The next time around we were presented with a large piece of water buffalo hindquarter. When I saw the man bringing it I thought, "Hey, fresh meat!"

But Huk had a different opinion. "This animal really smells, Joe. It's been lying in that awful muddy water and is really rank." We had a lot of faith in Huk to make it edible, and after soaking the meat in a strong marinade of soya and cooking it thoroughly, it didn't taste too bad. At least Jimmy Jones and I never complained. But Huk swore that was the last water buffalo we would ever have. After several days, he could still smell it on his hands.

All C-47 drops were made below the mountain at the base camp because they would be too exposed flying up where we were. So the H-34 resupply chopper was our real lifeline. Because of the daily shelling, our pad remained a hot LZ. One time we came mighty close to losing the chopper. On his approach the enemy zeroed in. We hadn't got him unloaded when the shells landed. He took off and just fell off the other side, and it looked like he was going right to the bottom. But Air America pilots had the feel, and our man pulled up just above the treeline and off he went. That was the only way to do it.

I had to be near the radio all the time. I was especially alert when the helicopter was coming in. Someone had to direct the aircraft in case it was a new man who couldn't find us. If he flew past us, he'd be shot out of the sky.

I was out on the pad intending to flag this one in. I left Joe, our interpreter, near the radio just in case. Suddenly, the chopper started going on by. I shouted, "Joe! Get on that radio and tell him not to go up there."

Joe's English was more a mix of Lao than anything and he was excited. He broadcast, "Mai bai whop whop. . . . Mai bai whop whop. Please don't go up there. They shoot you!"

That ol' plane just peeled off and came right in to us. I ran to the radio just as the pilot came on.

"Who in the hell is your radio operator?"

I was proud of Joe. "Hell, that's a good radio operator—my main number one man."

Joe had a lot of time on his hands once Jimmy Jones found out that some of the officers spoke English, and he didn't have to take Joe with him all the time. Huk didn't need him either, since he had already trained his Laotian medics. So Joe hung around me and the radio. I had checked him out on the basics and it paid off.

Those young officers were eager to learn more English and often came down to the hooch for lessons. Gregory and I obliged, and I'll bet there are now three Laotians speaking with a southern drawl.

Living in close quarters for so long a time, a team has to get along. Your mission—and lives—depend on it. By this time we all had this silent communication between us. We knew each other's moods well, so we knew when a guy was moody or upset. You just shut up. It was worse than being married.

Mail was always a big morale boost, especially with Jimmy Jones. He sometimes acted like an officer and sometimes acted like a nice guy, depending on the mail from his honey, Jane. They had seen each other every night and day before we left Fort Bragg, and they had written each other every day since. The team always hoped that each resupply brought letters from Jane, so that he would be in better spirits. She really loved him because she would send him packages with Red Man chew.

"She used to hate my chewing," he would say, "and refused to kiss me unless I stopped."

Now he would get it in cases. He kept a big wad in his mouth all the time, and the Laotians thought that was hilarious, too. Jones would spit from his plug and take another swig of Monkey Piss.

My vice was cigarettes. I couldn't survive without one. The Laotians were heavy smokers, too. But they smoked all kinds of hard stuff—so harsh none of us could smoke them.

Drugs were never a problem in our team. Huk pushed vitamins, quinine, and antibiotics, and got really upset when we wouldn't take our daily doses. He was like a mother hen to us, but that's what he was there to do. SF travel with a pharmacy of drugs and all of us carried speed—amphetamines—to stay awake, but we never needed any. Our team was too tough.

The Laotians had a problem with one man that reported for sick call. The man really looked bad—he was vitamin deficient, he didn't eat worth a damn, he was all skin and bones, and his eyes were bad. As Huk checked him out, one of his Laotian medics said, "There isn't anything wrong."

Huk was ruffled. "What do you mean? Just look at him."

The interpreter named something in Laotian and went through the motions of smoking and puffing, making like his lungs hurt and breathing was hard. Huk was still having trouble with it when Joe asked Huk for his lighter and made like he was cooking something with it. Bingo! Huk realized that this guy was a dope head. Huk had his first opium addict.

The Meo tribes brought the stuff down the trail from the area of the Plain of Jars in the form of large balls the size of a basketball. The Meo tore off the poppies and crushed them into a brown and gooey ball that they could easily carry. The battalion officers told us that General Vang Pao was up to his neck in the trade along with our CIA. The CIA had built a secret landing strip for him called Lima-Lima up against a hillside near his Long Cheng headquarters and was bringing in supplies and taking out opium.

Colonel Bou Noi ordered the man tied to a tree. When we asked for how long, one lieutenant shot back, "As long as it takes." It was hard for Huk to watch it, and he would visit the man, trying to get him to eat and to take vitamins. He would just scream and scream. After six days they stuffed his mouth with rice and tied it shut to keep it there. He'd shit all over himself and they'd clean him up. After ten days they took him down. We didn't know where he went. So much for Laotian cold turkey.

The battalion fired their 4.2-inch mortars almost daily, mostly to support the men out on operations. They'd fire almost directly over our heads. Our bamboo outhouse was an open-roofed hut that just happened to be straight in line with this one mortar on a firing mission. I was using the facility, just sitting there listening to them throwing the rounds out—ten, fifteen, twenty. And then there was a dull "thoomp." I looked up and saw the round going up. It was a "cookoff"—a short round!

"Oh, shit." I came flying out of there with my pants around my ankles. The round landed right by the outhouse, but it didn't detonate.

When the Laotians fired the mortars, they didn't know to quit before the tube got too hot. The round would just be blown out of the tube about a hundred feet and land out near the chopper pad or near our outhouse. It happened every now and then without harm. In a cookoff the shell probably doesn't get enough revolutions to arm itself or land on its head. But it could have landed smack inside the latrine and blown it to kingdom come.

We had been in Laos several months when I received the message: "The President has approved the green beret for headgear. It will be dropped to you tomorrow. Put on your rank along with the green beret for the remaining time you are there."

I guess the world must have known by then that we were in Laos after all.

They parachuted the green berets to us by chopper. They were made out of cheap material, and none of them fit, so we put them in our bags and continued to wear our regular soft hats. Jones had this Australian-style bush hat that he wouldn't have swapped anyway. We pulled out our stashed rank and other insignia and stuck them on.

The battalion was shocked at our ranks. They had all along thought they were dealing with officers. Jones was the biggest surprise to them. I heard one of the Laotian officers say he thought our team leader was at least a colonel because of his age. I guess Bou Noi treated Jones the way he did because he thought he was a colonel. The officers saw that three of us were only sergeants, including the "doc," and they showed resentment over it. They didn't know what to make of the situation at first. Their first response was to shun us. They stayed away, thinking we had been playing a game with them.

The Royal Laotian Army also considered the enlisted man as second class, so when the officers we were helping with English saw our ranks they didn't want to continue learning from "these men of low rank."

Whoever came out with the order to be in uniform had their heads up their butts. They didn't realize all the work we had done to establish rapport in the first place.

After a week they invited Jones to battalion headquarters and gradually the officers and men started coming around again.

WE PROBABLY RECEIVED A THOUSAND ROUNDS OF 105S IN FIVE MONTHS AT Phou Tinpét. And we didn't get a scratch until one late barrage of some 120 rounds.

Jimmy Jones was up near the battalion CP when he heard the unmistakable sound of incoming rounds. He dove for the nearest bunker, colliding with somebody else running in. He hit his head in the collision, jamming the prongs from his new captain's bars into his forehead. After the shelling he came out of the bunker bleeding from the puncture wounds.

At first, he refused to let Huk treat them. They argued for a couple of minutes then he let Huk patch him up. Jimmy was a little peeved. "If they hadn't made me put this stupid brass on, I would never have been wounded in this war."

I offered to put him in for a Purple Heart.

Near the end of our tour the battalion commander requested that we stay longer. They felt safe when we were there and they knew our time was running out. We knew HQ would never let us stay.

The day we left, men came in from all of the outposts, with hair down to their waists and some down to their butts. Some came to see us for the first time and others to say goodbye. The pad was absolutely full. It even spooked the chopper pilot. He didn't know what was going on.

To show his appreciation the colonel took one of the elephant tusks and sawed a big piece off the tip. It was pretty scarred, either from fights with other bulls or from the mine fragments. The colonel took his knife and inscribed his name and the date on the tusk. We told him we couldn't get it through customs, but he said, "You can get it through if I sign it and say it's a present." He gave it to Jimmy.

Parting was very sad but we had no choice. It was like leaving family. We were not replaced because the battalion commander didn't want anybody but us.

We arrived in Paksane and greeted George Hill and Robert Young like long-lost brothers. You could tell who had been in the jungle. We were so dark and they were so white.

They had pretty well taken over the team house. Young's responsibility was the house—food, cooks, and finances. Hill took care of the airstrip, supplies, and communications. The half team already there at the house was able to break loose to train a Laotian battalion defense force on the outskirts of Paksane and rotate with their other half in the jungle.

We all contributed money to run the team house even when we were on the mountain. The money went for room rent (MAAG rented the whole facility to begin with), a food fund, and bar stock. The bar stock was an investment, according to Hill. He bought cases of booze from the embassy commissary in Vientiane, sold it by the bottle at a profit, and threw the money back into the bar fund. At the end of our tour we would split it six ways.

We were brought back to Paksane to help support new A-teams coming in and acting as a small B-team when they were deployed. Jones stepped in to coordinate operations at the house and I took over communications.

COLONEL SADLER WAS IMPRESSED WITH THE WAY FOUR MEN COULD DO THE work of six in the mountains and with our two men handling the jobs of six at the team house. He threw a party in our honor. It was one heck of a greeting. They roasted a big ol' hog for us.

Three planeloads of MAAG people came in from Vientiane, and I knew we had Air America pilots and CIA there, too. There were quite a few local women. We could dance with them but that was all.

Huk was one of the few men entertaining those girls because they looked so bad. "Hey, after four straight doubles, they all looked good," he said.

The commo man had a ham license, and from time to time we sent up a signal for anyone in the world to pick up. A couple of times we called the U.S.—just searched through the frequencies—and found someone we could talk to in Morse Code. We talked a lot with a ham operator in South America—some good ol' boy from Peru or Colombia.

He asked, "Where are you at?"

"Oh, we're in Hawaii."

"Hawaii? Wait a minute."

He came back on in a few minutes, "I oriented my antenna toward Hawaii and couldn't pick you up. But I oriented it toward the Far East and picked you up. Where did you say you were at?"

"We're from Hawaii."

Military Intelligence was always monitoring U.S. radio traffic and tried to find our transmission, but they never found us. I heard some rumbles about it. Hell, you're out there for six months and dying to talk to people.

Huk was not only responsible for our medical needs, he took on the added responsibility of the MAAG personnel and their Laotian counterparts, as well as the local villagers. He spent a lot of time teaching them sanitation and hygiene. The people lived in houses built on stilts for the monsoon season. They kept their pigs and other animals underneath. They never used the dung for fertilizer, and they were sick all the time with parasites and intestinal problems. The sick call ran all day long, with pregnant women and babies.

At the end of the main drag in Paksane was the hospital, but it was for the Laotian military. It was manned by Thai volunteer doctors, and there was a visiting Scandinavian team with nurses. Huk spent what free hours he had at the hospital trying to absorb all he could about medicine in the outside world.

It was at the hospital that Joe, the interpreter, showed Huk this fat, pudgy little guy. "Do you remember this soldier?"

Huk said he didn't.

Joe goes into his opium-pipe act from the mountain. This healthy little man was the same one they had tied screaming to the tree. Huk told me later, "That cold turkey really works."

A Chinese shopkeeper had opened a whorehouse with girls imported from Thailand. At 300 kip ($3) he had a booming business. The Laotian Army was going to raid the place because the Pathet Lao were going in there, too.

But it never came off. I guess they thought they would have a mutiny on their hands.

The first "victim" of the place was one of our SF. He had encountered a prostitute the men called Iron Jaw. He sheepishly showed up one day at sick call. The poor idiot's organ was a sorry, swollen mess. "She bit the hell out of me," he confessed to Huk, who gave him a tetanus booster, other antibiotics, and a stern lecture.

The Mekong River ran almost parallel to the main street in Paksane. On the other side was Thailand. We were in the "dry" season, even though it still rained a lot. The river was down and real muddy. We would blow up our air mattresses, roll up our clothes, put them in a waterproof bag, and paddle across to the village on the Thai side. We fit right in.

The mayor of the village invited the whole team for the wedding of one of the MAAG interpreters. This time we got into a dugout canoe to cross the river. During the big party I noticed that Jimmy Jones was enjoying one of their delicacies. At least I thought he was.

As we were leaving, Jimmy showed me two coat pockets full of chicken heads. "Goddamn, Joe. I picked up something cooked and bit into it. I took it out of my mouth and suddenly saw eyes looking back at me." He didn't want to upset our hosts and snuck them into his pockets. The waitresses thought he was really scarfing them down and kept shoving more at him.

The Air America pilots were an amazing, and crazy, group of men. They were incredible flyers, who put their butts on the line every time they took off. They were also good to the locals, hauling villagers, livestock, and bloody pieces of freshly slaughtered water buffalo to places that weren't on any map. The Laotians would herd the buffaloes to one edge of the airfield and then ask George Hill where the next chopper was headed. If it was back to their people, one would grab his M-1, run over, and shoot one of the animals. In a matter of minutes it was quartered and the pieces wrapped in burlap sacks. When the chopper came in, they threw the whole bloody mess on board.

Choppers came in and out at a frantic pace, and it was easy to confuse deliveries. A lot of times there were no map coordinates for the pilots, and they were given visual references for their drops. Once, a helicopter was delivering a load to a unit at a particular intersection of streams. They landed and a bunch of men jumped in and unloaded. The chopper returned to Paksane, then made another delivery to the same location. On the third delivery one of our Laotians climbed up to the cockpit with a note that read,

"Please do not land here anymore. We do not like you. You deliver two loads to the Pathet Lao."

In Paksane we saw firsthand why our men in the jungle never had enough food or pay. Laotian commanders up and down the line were keeping the money. The Mobile Group Commander, who was a Laotian general officer in Paksane and Lieutenant Colonel Sadler's liaison, would draw the money for every battalion under his command. The funds came via Air America in special wooden lockers. The general would pick up the money, take his "share," and divide it among the battalions. The battalion commanders would take their "share" and divide it among the companies. By the time it was doled out to the troops, what was left was pitiful. George Hill and Robert Young had once seen a Mobile Group commander take ten out of twenty lockers as his "share."

Battalion food money was taken the same way. Rather than risk an incident, Sadler would buy food with American money and have the stuff brought in by Air America.

Before coming to Laos we were drilled in the customs of the area and told to be sensitive to all their religious beliefs, but I think we went too far. Once a year the King would come down the Mekong on a barge from the ancient royal capital of Luang Prabang. Every night he would pull off to the side and all the people would offer all the virgins in the area. He would choose one and the girl would try to become pregnant by the King. As a royal child it would be taken care of the rest of its life.

When he came to Paksane we were forced out to greet the King. We were told we would have to kneel, and all of us Americans were really up in arms. "We don't kneel for the President so why do we have to kneel for this jerk?" Sadler ordered us to conform to their customs. They put out a red carpet from the airport to Mobile Group headquarters. The whole town was there, forming a mile-and-a-half corridor. Nobody walked on the carpet. We didn't kneel, just squatted. The King made it a point to greet all the SF that were there. He looked like a young boy.

By the end of March a lot of teams were coming into Paksane, mostly from the 1st SF Group out of Okinawa. We had not been briefed well when we arrived, and we wanted to prepare the next group so they wouldn't stumble through things like we did. We wanted to share, but these new men didn't want to listen. The team replacing us had their stupid radio operators transmitting classified stuff in the clear. I thought, "My God, how the war's changing." That was the last team to come in on White Star.

As we readied to leave Paksane, we said our goodbyes to the MAAG staff. Joe, the interpreter, took our departure very hard. He cried when we released him to go back to Thailand.

As our C-47 lifted off for Vientiane, my parting feeling was that all us plainclothes "advisors" didn't fool anybody. Who were we going to fool? Almost everybody knew we were over there—the Chinese, the North Vietnamese, the Russians. This was no secret. The politicians were just trying to keep the families in the U.S. from getting upset—just a game they play.

Our whole team came back together in Vientiane. Captain Frank's part of the team had gone south near the Bolovens Plateau to new training centers outside of Saravane. They had spent their six months working with hundred-man Kha tribal shock companies called the "Kha Maquis." We weren't the same team though. Because we had been separated for six months we didn't jell as a team anymore. So we continued to act as if we were split.

Ol' Bull Simons called us together and asked, "Boys, where do you want to go for R&R? You can go either to Bangkok for three days or to Hong Kong for three days." We all chose Hong Kong. Jimmy Jones was excited over it. "I want to get me a Suzie Wong. I'm gonna get a Suzie Wong."

I tried to save as much as I could from the extra $19 a day the Laotian government paid us as "advisors." But I was willing to part with some of it for some R&R. We checked into a big downtown hotel reserved for Americans. Jimmy Jones wanted to stay to talk with Ed Frank, so it was just me, Huk, Gregory, Young, and Hill.

Vientiane had this steambath and massage parlor called the White Rose. A woman owned the place and knew exactly what Americans wanted. We called it "detigerization." Here was a bunch of guys just coming out of the jungle happy to be alive. The place was already full of SF. We took our place in line and one of the women offered us a beer.

These women had body massage down to an art. By the time I walked out of there, they had wrung all the layers of jungle crap from my bones and muscles. I felt terrific.

The streets were full of rickshaws—"cycle-o's" they were called. If you gave the man more money, he'd go faster. So we hired two rickshaws and had a race through town. George Hill pulled off his belt and started whipping the puller like he was a horse.

We said, "C'mon, George. Give the guy a break."

"Hell, no, I want to win!"

We started betting on the outcome and offering our pullers more and more money to go even faster. The guys were laughing at each other and playing the game, too. One would slow down and the rider would offer more kip. Then he would speed up. Then the other would slow down until he was offered more. Those boys probably made a month's wages off us.

We flew to Hong Kong and took a whole floor in a big hotel. We asked the porters for directions to the "best place to buy a suit and a pair of shoes."

Jimmy Jones found a place with alligator shoes and went berserk. He just loved alligator shoes and ordered a bunch. He must have spent $1,400 on those flashy shoes.

I bought one little ol' suit, something to replace the khaki I wore in the jungle. Shoot, those tailors will make one in no time. The shops had beautiful Chinese girls with skirts slit almost to their butts.

"Come over here and let them take your measurements," the shopkeeper said. So I did.

We left Jimmy at the tailor shop. He was having a good time getting measured, too.

Huk hadn't gone with us. When we got back to the hotel we found out why. Huk and Don Noe, the other medic, had reserved a big suite for a party. When we walked in, there was Huk with eight girls wearing skirts slit up to the hips. Noe was at the door charging $10 to everybody who wasn't part of our team.

I walked over to Huk and asked him what the deal was.

"What do you think, Joe?" he asked, pointing to the girls. "Not bad for fifty bucks. We've got them the whole night. Noe thinks I'm a pimp."

"What are we going to do with the girls, Huk?"

"I had to promise their boss that there would be no fancy stuff. But, hell, the guys can work out the rest on their own."

By now the word had gotten around. There was a big bar downstairs and men were coming up, bottles in hand. We already had twenty-five.

Jones showed up with a girl from the tailor shop. She was a beauty. He took me aside. "I got me a Suzie Wong, Joe. While she was measuring me I thought, 'Shit, I'll just ask her to party with me for the night.' And I did."

Some dancers showed up, too, and the party was on. At about three A.M. the phone rang. It was a Thai Airline stewardess complaining about the noise. We invited her to the party. Then there was a knock at the door and there stood this beautiful Thai girl and everybody said, "Wow, another one! Come on in!"

"No, no," she said.

Then her girlfriend came up. "Please, we must get up early and go to work. We fly. Could you hold the noise down?"

Two guys left with them.

For guys just out of the jungle, who never saw a women except in Paksane, we behaved ourselves. We were real pros and never treated the women like whores.

We stayed in Hong Kong three days. We didn't leave the hotel very much because we had to be cautious moving around. Because of the work we did, we never knew who might be gunning for Americans on the streets.

Going home wasn't on our minds in Hong Kong. We had been isolated from civilization for six months, and had to taper off before going back to the States. Hong Kong was our release.

But at the airport that final day, I never thought I would be so happy to see a C-124.

chapter 7

Save the Banana Republics

While the U.S. was getting the job done in Laos, it was having one hell of a bad time right off its own shores. Fidel Castro had come out of the hills of Oriente to establish a Communist state a hop and a jump from Florida. The concern was that Cuba would soon be crawling with Russians, so the CIA started recruiting Cuban exiles as an invasion force, and SF was right in the thick of it. And, as always, the SF did their job to the letter.

Twenty-seven top NCOs from the 7th Group were requested by CIA operative Richard Drain for training special teams of the Cuban brigade. The CIA and the Secretary of the Army didn't see eye to eye on the invasion, called Operation Zapata, so the Army dragged its feet on sending the NCOs even though Eisenhower approved it. After a CIA appeal to the President in December 1960, the twenty-seven SF, all now "official civilians," arrived in Homestead, Florida, and in Colombia and Guatemala.

In Guatemala, the SF set up shop at Helvetia, a five-thousand-acre coffee plantation high up in the Sierra Madre Mountains near the village of San Felipe—a spread owned by Roberto Alejos, brother of the Guatemalan ambassador to the U.S. There were soon about fifteen hundred Cuban exiles there, some of whom would be handpicked by SF for clandestine operations.

To the west, by the town of Retalhuleu near the country's Pacific coast, a large airstrip was also built for training pilots of the Cuban brigade's air force. The U.S. pilots had southern accents. They had been recruited from all over the Southeast, and from the Alabama Air National Guard in particular, to train pilots of the invasion force. They flew World War II-vintage B-26s, the aircraft chosen for the bombing runs because that's what Castro's Air Force flew.

The SF set up a top-secret communication net, with Eglin AFB in Florida as the hub, and waded in to train elements of a free-Cuba army in weapons and guerrilla tactics. The idea was to infiltrate from the air and sea, link up with anti-Castro guerrillas in the hills, take over an area, and pretty much copy what Castro himself had done to overthrow the dictator Batista.

But the SF suddenly found their command choices replaced by some politician's son, and when the units infiltrated they got their butts wiped out. The SEALs, who controlled the waterborne portion of the operation from Puerto Cabezas in Nicaragua, lost nine motorized assault boats filled with infiltrators. They found the boats belly up.

The anti-Castro underground was told to come out about twenty-four hours before the invasion and link up with the infiltrators. Somehow they came out early, were exposed, and were wiped out. By D-day, 17 April 1961, Castro knew all he needed to know about the invasion. The U.S. had to back off its promised air support and eventually told the Cuban government-in-exile that we would wait for a better time because the whole operation had been exposed.

The Bay of Pigs invasion was a military and diplomatic screwup. As a result, the U.S. was expecting a flurry of activity in Cuba and had to prepare for the spread of Castro agents throughout the Caribbean. Two months before the landings JFK had ordered the creation of a force to deter guerrilla warfare. Now that timetable was being moved up.

Unconventional-warfare teams of SF, Air Commandos, and SEALs were running secret exercises between the Hurlbert training areas at Eglin AFB and Navy installations in Key West. By November of 1961 several A-teams were standing by at Key West for missions against Cuba. One team had arrived to attend the Navy's underwater diving school. Even the Navy didn't know this was a cover—the SF were already Scuba-qualified. The school was never aware of the team's mission.

When JFK came to Key West to boost morale, he went to the diving school. Everyone was lined up to greet him. At the end of the line were twelve men with green berets. JFK walked by and just smiled. He knew why they were there.

I WASN'T HOME FROM LAOS A WEEK BEFORE I HEARD WE MIGHT BE GOING TO Panama. But it was just scuttlebutt in the team room at the time and I didn't pay much attention to the possibility. Kathy and I were busy moving into our first house in a new Fayetteville subdivision. Even with all the chores that went with it, I still managed to get in some fishing along the Cape Fear River. Our fishing spot was full of mosquitoes, and I guess I made a good meal for them. When I got back to the house I was sicker than hell. Alan, my youngest brother, was staying with us. He took one look at me and said I was real yellow. I passed out.

Alan and Kathy took me to the base hospital. During my examination I passed out again. They didn't know what I had, so I was put in the contagious ward. I was in quarantine and nobody could see me, not even Kathy. Alan was really disappointed. He had hitchhiked all the way from Chattanooga and was looking forward to having a good time with me. So we let him drive our car around town. Alan was fifteen and didn't have a license, but what the heck.

I would get the chills, shake real bad, and ask for more blankets. But the doctors didn't know what was wrong. After three days of this, an orderly came in while I was shaking. He lit up.

"I know what you got!" he said, and went flying out of there. He came back with a nurse, who took a sample of blood, and before the day was up I had medication. The next morning I felt like a new man. I had gotten malaria.

Laos had reached out and given me a parting shot. I never came down with it there, but I remember Huk getting angry when I didn't take my quinine. I had the bug in my system all along and the mosquitoes at the river finished the job.

The Army must have been satisfied with my recovery, because the orders came down sending me to Panama for three years. Bull Simons had gotten the call again and we were going down as an advance unit for a new full SF group that would be a springboard for clandestine operations in Latin America.

Once we were put on alert, our drill was similar to the preparation for Laos—area studies and a short course in Spanish given by one of our Latino SF. Although our families would follow in about two months, secrecy was to be maintained as to our mission. This was the first time Kathy and the children would be with me in a foreign country, and there was a mess of paperwork that had to be finished before I left. We had to turn around and sell our brand-new home, dispose of most of our furniture, and prepare what was left for shipment, including the only other touch of the U.S. we would have down there—our Chevy Impala.

On 10 July 1962, Simons, his staff, and a contingent of forty-eight hand-picked EM and eight officers from the 7th Group took off from Pope AFB aboard an Air Commando C-130 loaded down with gear.

Until our arrival, the only activity at Fort Gulick besides SF jungle training was field training for the School of the Americas, a U.S. training program for military officers from friendly Latin governments. But that was going to change real fast.

We quickly formed committees by expertise to put together all the training and work areas for the main body of men, who would start arriving in three months. Within six months, a new SF group would have to be trained and ready for deployment.

M. Sgt. Dick Meadows was our NCOIC for training and in charge of jungle navigation. Meadows was the elite of the elite when it came to training and conditioning and was a walking example of the best that SF put into the field. That's the kind of person I made close friends with. I was in charge of the mountain climbing and rappelling and laid out the course, while river operations were in the hands of other skilled SF. To make sure everything would work, Dick and I ran the course over and over again.

After a month I started itching to jump again. I had brought my competition parachute, and I didn't want to waste it. There was a small parachuting unit at Fort Clayton to the south. It had an Airborne element that did sport jumping. They called themselves the Atlantic Sport Parachute Club, but they only jumped every now and then. We got together and organized jumps on a more regular basis, getting planes from Fort Kobbe every Sunday.

Dick, M. Sgt. Earl McIntosh, and I whiled away whatever other off-hours we had fishing. We had an open fishing invitation from the civilians working in the Canal Zone. The more American faces, the better, as far as they were concerned. They'd take us out for tarpon in the waters outside Limón Bay. The scene looked like a postcard.

By September, the C-team headquarters was gearing up for the arrival of our families. Quarters assignments were being made, and post facilities and civilian services had to be martialed. We had already Americanized the commissary at Fort Gulick with a snack bar, which we had the post build adjoining the PX. There was some grumbling from them about having to cater to us so much. I think they saw us as a bully taking over the neighborhood. Even our routine was hard for them to accept. Here they were, mostly instructors for the school, and here we were, a bunch of gung-ho SF taking PT at dawn and running strange training missions in and out of the jungle. But, once they realized how serious our business was, they swallowed hard and got along.

Kathy and the kids arrived in September—a terrific reunion. Our new home was on the Fort Gulick compound, three blocks from the barracks— a small three-story stucco house with cement-block walls and cement floors. The windows were just openings covered with screen with louvers halfway up. The backyard ran right up to the jungle. At least the street in front was paved.

By early October, we had a full SF company in training. We also had a Military Intelligence element assigned to C-team headquarters. That meant we were moving closer to something hot.

That something got even hotter; our regular routine came to a screeching halt. At one minute past midnight, 20 October, all SF were placed on alert status DEFCON 5. We weren't the only ones. U.S. Armed Forces worldwide were also on alert. Intelligence had confirmed that the Russians were building missile launch sites in Cuba. In fact, some would be operational before the month was out.

We began picking up fragments of information. The 1st Armored Division was on the move from Texas to Georgia, and five more divisions were placed on alert. Four tactical air squadrons were also placed on readiness for an air strike.

By Sunday, 21 October, everything SAC had was in the air fully loaded.

On Monday, our alert was raised to DEFCON 3. SAC was upped to DEFCON 2. Nobody that I knew of had ever been on this high an alert in peacetime. We'd already heard that our old faithful training submarine, the Sea Lion, was on its way down the Atlantic coast full of SF and Navy SEALs.

Fort Bragg was emptying out. The 82nd Airborne was being transported to a staging area in Key West.

That night, Kennedy addressed the nation and demanded that the Russians dismantle and remove the missiles. He also announced his decision to stop all foreign vessels—that meant the Russians—and prevent them from delivering offensive arms to Cuba. The first interdiction could come in a matter of days.

On Tuesday, the 101st Airborne was at DEFCON 2. By now, everyone knew this was definitely no bluff.

The task for SF in any kind of Cuban invasion made the mind reel. Under the cover of darkness, the SEALs would go in first to clear all water approaches to a beachhead. SF would follow by sea to secure an area and link up with friendly locals to locate and identify targets hidden from the air and set up radio beacons for guiding in aircraft. Air Commandos would support SF, dropping in and engaging in air-assault operations against enemy installations. All this would precede any formal invasion or full-scale air attack. The men involved in special warfare are trained to operate on their own in the middle of enemy territory. Cuba would be no walk-through. The island had been transformed into a fortress.

At the UN, our ambassador was busy showing our U-2 photographs to the world and calling the Russian ambassador a lying son-of-a-bitch.

At 1000 hours Wednesday, the quarantine of Cuba began. Things were going to get nasty. There were twenty Russian ships closing in on the five-hundred-mile barrier. Activity around us had stepped up. Air Commandos from Howard AFB and some Navy SEALs were over near Fort San Lorenzo diving around the limestone caves. Apparently, U.S. intelligence had reports that nuclear warheads might be stored in similar caves in Cuba. The Caribbean was full of these formations.

That afternoon we heard that some Russian ships had changed course short of the quarantine line and some had stopped dead in the water. We held our breath. The words were flying between Washington and Moscow.

On Thursday we waited, still at DEFCON 3, all the while trying to piece together what bits and pieces of information our SF network provided. SF on the *Sea Lion* were practicing night landings along the Florida coast, and A-teams were already in Key West.

Early on Friday, 26 October, the first ship was stopped and boarded. It wasn't Russian, but it was a merchant ship chartered by the Reds and carrying cargo from the Soviet Union. Then our intelligence reported more bad news. Aerial photos of Cuba revealed that Russian IL-28 bombers were being uncrated and assembled. There were thirty of them.

Up to this point, we didn't know if the Cubans could shoot down any of our high-flying U-2s. The Russians had sent in surface-to-air missiles (SAMs), but were they operational? On Saturday, 27 October, one of our spy planes was shot down over Cuba, a real shock, killing the pilot. Now, everybody was talking about an all-out invasion. All off-post personnel were ordered back to Fort Gulick.

We didn't have to wait any longer. The order came early Sunday morning. Everybody was jumping. We were at DEFCON 2! I was assigned to an A-team and full combat equipment was issued. There was no briefing. We weren't being told a thing, except that we'd be given our mission en route. I knew we were headed for Cuba.

There were two C-130s standing by at France Field. Almost all the A-teams from Fort Gulick were on board when we took off. The wheels were barely in the well when the pilots laid it out for us. A full-blown air strike was coming. Photo analysis had counted a total of twenty-three launchers and thirty-three missiles at six identified SS-4 MRBM sites. There were three SS-5 IRBM launch pads but no missiles had been identified yet. Nuclear warheads were probably present, but not confirmed.

There was a major obstacle. With the downing of the U-2, the Air Force had to contend with twenty-three operational SA-2 SAM sites. Our mission was to go in and destroy as many SAMs as possible in order to give our aircraft a fighting chance at the ballistic missiles.

If an air strike could not guarantee that the U.S. would be able to destroy all the missiles, that might leave enough to kill millions in the U.S. We had to better the odds.

Ours was a direct-action mission. Just go in, hit our target and get out. The mission was to prevent the missiles from being fired. We would jump on top of them and first try to destroy the electronic guidance systems and then the triggering mechanisms.

We would come across the sea right on the deck, then climb to about five hundred feet just before reaching the target. Once we got to our missile we would bail out on top of it. Jumping at five hundred feet instead of twelve hundred made for a tough landing. Teams would exit at the same time from opposite doors—two teams on a target. The aircraft would leapfrog from missile site to missile site until all the men were out. We might even be dodging SAMs ourselves.

IT WAS A VERY BAD-LOOKING SITUATION. ESCAPING OR SURVIVING WASN'T PART of it. You just had to do the best you could. We knew to expect 99 percent casualties. There wasn't a lot of talking among the men. We were busy as hell getting our gear ready. Concentrating on the mission kept any anxiety from clouding my mind. I also knew I was good enough to be that 1 percent to make it.

We circled over the Caribbean for several hours waiting for a go signal. The C-130 carried enough fuel for twelve hours, but we didn't have to stay airborne for nearly that long. We received orders to stand down and returned to Fort Gulick before dark.

It was over. Khrushchev had agreed to terms.

On Monday, 29 October, a graduated stand-down began for U.S. forces around the world. That was as close as we had ever been to taking a missile in our backyard. Of course, Castro wouldn't have had an island left to command.

It turned out we weren't the only SF with a Cuba mission. I talked with SF who said they were part of a clandestine U.S. force that had infiltrated a swampy coastal area during something called Operation White Swan. There was trouble from the start. Intelligence had said the ground was not swampy, but it was and they lost some armored vehicles in the ooze. They could see U.S. aircraft flying out over the ocean but couldn't radio for air cover. As they moved inland their advance was stopped when they encountered a busload of Communist Chinese women. The women were captured and the force withdrew. That's all they would say.

I believe that if the Russians had not backed down when they did there would have been a full-scale invasion. SF, being the first in, would have definitely sustained a major loss. Some teams would have been completely annihilated. Some might not have been successful in stopping the missiles. We'll never know.

chapter 8

Blue Sky Men

The primary tactic of Special Forces is infiltration, which means being the first into a hot spot. In most cases, that's accomplished by dropping out of the sky at night. That's why a man has to be jump qualified to enter SF.

My very first week with SF gave me a good idea of what to expect in all the training to come. We jumped. It came about the middle of the week in pitch darkness—midnight. That first jump in SF was called the "cherry jump," and even though you made five jumps in jump school, those day drops didn't count for squat. There we sat in that lumbering C-123 with no prior instruction on night jumps. I didn't know what the ground at Sicily DZ would look like, what the trees would look like, the rivers, the roads—anything.

I wasn't really scared—I hadn't been from the first jump at Fort Benning. Hell, jumping a hundred feet into a rock quarry as a kid didn't faze me. I was disappointed I couldn't go higher. So to me dropping from 1,250 feet was just another hill to climb. I was filled more with expectation than doubt. Everyone was tense, but only because they wanted to perform well.

The plane slowed for the jump, but it was still doing over a hundred miles an hour when we went through the door. It was early February, and the winter air over Fort Bragg was heavy, making for an easy jump—easier than jump school. I was imagining everything that could happen—landing in water, hitting a tree, busting my tail. It didn't really matter. I knew I could take it. Hell, worse had already happened in my life.

I landed and did a soft roll. As I gathered up my parachute, I noticed there were no trucks for us. It turned out that the jump was the easy part of the exercise. We walked forever before we turned in the parachutes. Then we were given the big hike—fifteen miles back to the unit.

Jumping was a technique we had to perfect. On the way to perfection I landed in a lot of trees. If I could see them below me, and couldn't get out of it, I would pick a live one to land in, and one with lots of branches. A live tree, especially a pine, had limbs that were limber. At night, though, you just guessed and took your best shot.

The strain of jumping must have aggravated the old injury to my left wrist, because after my first thirty days in SF, it hurt like the devil. It got so bad I couldn't even open a car door. I had it X-rayed and they found three broken bones. One of the three was the navicular—the one that supports the thumb. I returned to my unit with the wrist in a cast. I wore gloves to hide the fact from anyone who could throw me off a jump. I had the cast three months and never missed a jump.

Special Forces wasn't content to stay at 1,250 feet. They figured, "Hell, let the Airborne do that." There were men at Fort Bragg who, on their own time, were already going as high as some of those old planes would fly—dropping out and falling free for a while before opening just above the ground. It was called skydiving, and it was about to change SF forever.

SF had its own word for it, HALO—High Altitude Low Opening—a term created by Major Lucien Conein, a man whose days in the OSS made him an ideal unconventional-warfare officer. HALO was actually the Army's own version of free-fall, jumping out of an aircraft at altitudes of up to 12,500 feet and delaying the opening until around 2,000 feet. Jacques Istel, a Marine Reserve major, and his partner Lewis Sanborn became the true pioneers of free-fall.

Istel's claim to fame was the ability to drop in a stabilized and controlled position without tumbling wildly and having to pull the parachute in a panic. He and Sanborn jumped spread-eagled in what they called the "French

Cross" position and managed to stay flat and horizontal for up to a minute of free-fall. This was a far cry from the old tuck-and-tumble daredevil style that skydivers used.

When Istel tried to sell free-fall to the Marines, they passed on the idea, but some of our top commanders at Fort Bragg saw the potential of free-fall to be part of SF's unconventional-warfare mission.

In December 1957, Istel trained and qualified a small group of SF volunteers in military free-fall. They were a very special bunch and were also expert riggers—since one of Istel's main requirements was that the free-fall jumper had to pack his own parachute.

The Army still didn't officially adopt military free-fall. It wanted more testing and analysis. But free-fall was allowed to continue as a sport. Skydiving clubs started to mushroom at Fort Bragg—at the 82nd and 101st Airborne and at the 77th Group.

The Special Warfare Center (SWCEN) head shed encouraged our men to continue their weekend jumping, knowing that was the kind of experience vital to HALO. But with no funds to throw around, they couldn't do much more than that. The club was always scrounging for equipment and aircraft, and all the basic expenses came out of the pockets of the men.

Their skydiving was done on sheer guts. They had no instruments to give them altitude or to deploy automatically. They would just start counting off seconds and watch the ground. They always managed to open in time. Their first decent new piece of equipment was a stopwatch to activate as they fell.

Even with all the hassles, the men of the SWCEN Parachute Club were getting ready to make history. Well, fate works in strange ways and, in the spring of 1958, 1st Lt. James Perry connected with the club. As a Marine, Perry had trained with Istel and Sanborn, and free-fall was in his blood. General James Gavin had seen him jump and offered Jim a regular Army commission to replace the one he had in the Marine reserve. Perry saw the career he wanted and jumped over to us.

He was given a free hand to experiment and develop free-fall techniques that SF could incorporate into its various missions. HALO was still operating in fits and starts, so Perry concentrated on the ongoing activities at the club.

Perry encouraged the men to come up with ways to improve their control in free-fall—to try to "fly" before they deployed their canopies. Loy Brydon had stumbled onto a froglike position for his arms and legs and, along with the likes of Danny Byard, Jim Pearson, and Dick Fortenberry, took Istel's crude style of stabilized flight and started to replace it with true aerodynamic control. Under Perry's eye, these frog arm and leg positions became the trademark of the Parachute Club and enabled our jumpers to move themselves around with the kind of control and precision never before achieved.

Harry Denny, who had been with me in jump school, was in the original Special Forces A-team selected by the 77th for HALO training. I had missed out, but always felt it was something I would really want to do. That first team was conveniently made up of men from the club, the only really experienced free-fall jumpers around. Harry talked it up every time he saw me. "Joe, you gotta do it. It's the only game in town."

Denny's enthusiasm and my continued curiosity got the best of me. I joined the Parachute Club in the fall of 1958, and was hooked immediately. It was a different crowd. These men liked the danger and they were the kind of people I wanted to run around with.

Danny Byard was my instructor. He was one of the first four certified by Jacques Istel to teach. I spent my first three days lying on a parachute packing table learning the positions for stabilizing my body, from the French Cross and arching with the legs upward to let you rock with the wind, to bringing the arms and legs into the more relaxed frog positions for controlling body movement.

It was hard to stay on the ground, I was so eager to get in the air. It was just before Christmas when Byard finally let me go up for my first jumps. There would be five jumps from 2,800 feet—static line jumps, but with a twist. Even though the parachute would automatically deploy at five seconds, you had to pull a "dummy" ripcord to simulate going for the D-ring in free-fall. You left the aircraft spread out in the French Cross and the jumpmaster watched you stabilize and "pull." You had to master these basics before you did anything else.

Out I went. I did everything that Byard told me, caught the wind just right, flattened out and "flew" for five seconds. Lord, it was fun.

My progress had been slowed by fourteen weeks at the NCO Academy, but I made up for lost time. Three months out of that school I was jumping on my own. The training called for you to work your way higher and higher, with longer periods of stabilized fall. I did so well in my first four dummy rip-cord jumps that the club said I didn't need a fifth and gave me thumbs up to go without the static line and try for five seconds of delay. From that point on, the static line would be a thing of the past. I jumped free for the first time in the spring of 1959.

We used an old Army L-20 single-engine aircraft. We would stand on a little strut built out from the door—like a little step. We would assume our first body position and push off. Ahead of me were jumps from eight thousand feet with thirty seconds of free-fall and several stages leading up to almost sixty seconds at over twelve thousand feet.

We wore stuff that was simple—and cheap. A helmet from the local motorcycle shop and $12 painters' coveralls from Sears, Roebuck. The wives dyed them for a more professional look. Mine was blue. Long johns underneath kept our butts warm. At first, we wore goggles, only because men like Istel and Sanborn wore them. We tried different styles, from the heavy desert tankers' goggles to the fancy plastic bubbles used by skiers. They were uncomfortable as could be and we tried jumping without them. When the air at 125 miles an hour hit your eyes, the irritation made your tear ducts gush, messing up your vision. But we soon discovered that, after several jumps without goggles, your tear ducts dried up, and we did away with the goggles.

Skydiving in the U.S. had its own national organization that issued licenses as you reached a certain number of free-falls. I didn't waste time coming up to twenty-five and my B license. I was playing catch-up. Most of the other men already had hundreds of jumps under their belt.

Learning meant making many jumps. When you made a mistake, you talked it out on the ground and went again, jump after jump. We packed on the spot. A man would land, gather up his chute, take it to the packing mat lying on the ground, pack, and stand by for an available seat. We could pack one in ten minutes and be ready before the plane was back on the ground. That way each man might get six or seven jumps a day from 7,000 to 12,500 feet. The Army pilots saw how dedicated we were and got interested enough to volunteer to stay for a few more lifts. We never had any trouble getting an aircraft on the weekends, and we had it up to fourteen hours a day.

In late spring, Fort Bragg held the first National Invitational Sport Parachute Meet with parachute clubs from all over the U.S. The 77th Group sent ten from the SWCEN Club as its official entry. There were so many in the three-day competition that each team had only one try at the target, and our men were among the last to jump. Up to that time, if you got within fifty yards of the target, you were doing real good. Thanks to the body-control techniques created by Brydon, our team skunked them all.

The parachutes we used in the club and for HALO were regulation-issue Air Force T-7s—the same as used by the Airborne. They were crude and not steerable, except by pulling on a riser to tilt the canopy to expel air. You always wanted to land into the wind, and the T-7 made it very difficult.

We had one modification—a single open slot made by cutting open a vertical panel section between seams, called "gores," in the rear of the canopy. The opening was referred to as a "single blank gore." The irony was we were copying what the Russians had done. The Russians were killing everybody in world competition, and Jacques Istel had brought back one of their parachutes for us to study.

A lot more had to be done to make the parachutes more controllable for greater accuracy in landing, and when Jim Perry got back from Laos, the SWCEN opened up a whole new chapter in the history of skydiving.

Perry returned late in the spring of 1960 and found Brig. Gen. Joseph Stilwell, Jr., waiting for him. The SWCEN had formed the U.S. Army STRAC Parachute Team, strictly as a demonstration unit for public appearances and to represent the Army in worldwide competitions. Stilwell handed Perry the reins and told him to do what he had to do to make the parachute team the best in the world.

Fortunately for the Army, the nucleus of the team had come from the SWCEN Sport Parachute Club, many having upwards of a thousand jumps by this time. In fact, if you weren't in the club, you weren't eligible for the Army team, either. That's how the men kept it all in the family. Perry's first act was to acknowledge the STRAC team's real roots and rename it the U.S. Army Sport Parachute Team.

Stilwell sent Perry to Charleston to pick up a boxcar load of surplus Air Force bailout parachutes. There were five hundred B-12 orange-and-white twenty-eight-foot canopies for us to work on in order to build a good, steerable parachute. We began cutting experimental slots, or turn windows, out of the parachute. By attaching control lines from the suspension line to the corners of the turn windows, we gave the canopy a faster turn capability— true steering.

The Sport Parachute Club building became the headquarters for our modifications, complete with special sewing machines "requisitioned" from various sources at the 82nd and 101st. Once cut and stitched, the parachute was put to a stress test in the parachute loft. If it didn't hold, we threw it away and started cutting a new pattern in another. The height, width, and position of these windows were largely determined by the weight of the jumper and the amount of trade-off between steerability and speed of descent.

Sometimes we would take twenty-five of them at a time out to the DZ along with two rolls of parachute repair tape. One man would say, "I've got a brilliant idea about this thing."

"Okay, " Perry would answer. "Cut your holes in the damn parachute . . . tape it up . . . and take it up."

The jumper often came down with it streaming above and on his reserve. "Hell, that's no good," he'd say, and toss it away. "Let me try another one."

It took a lot of nerve to do what we did. Some of the men might have been a little crazy. Maybe that's what it called for. Ron Brown was one of those characters. He had bought a brand-new T-Bird right after he got married and wanted to go down the road as fast as he could to see if a parachute would stop him like the drag racers. He tied it to the back of his car, supposedly to the bumper. Then he put a man in the trunk—helmet on and everything—to open it. His idea was to get up to speed and bang the side of the car to signal the man to deploy the parachute.

Right after a jump he took off from the DZ, barreling down Manchester Road at one hundred miles an hour in his just-bought T-Bird, his new wife beside him and that kid in the trunk. All at once, the parachute popped and we heard the engine roar. It was the awfulest damned noise, but the car kept going. When Brown stopped to see what happened, he saw that the parachute had pulled off the bumper and the entire dual exhaust system along with it.

Another time, one of our younger jumpers went flying down the road on a motorcycle wearing his parachute. When he released it he just stopped in midair and the motorcycle went on without him. He was dragged all along that hot asphalt, burning the hide off him. He wound up in the hospital, skinned from head to toe.

Crazy or not, it took people with those kind of guts to be the Army's first skydivers.

As the U.S. involvement in Southeast Asia heated up, it became harder and harder to round up aircraft for the weekends. General Stilwell often came to our rescue. We'd be shooting the bull, packing at the club, and Stilwell would come in with a big smile. "Hey, I got an aircraft," he'd announce. "Anybody want to jump?" We'd all run to the DZ. The general jumped right along with us.

I had three parachutes of my own out of the boxcar load and had them at the DZ so I wouldn't miss a seat on the next flight while packing from the last jump.

By June 1960, I had my C license—seventy-five jumps—and was getting pretty good at controlling myself in free-fall, jumping higher and higher with delay times between twenty-five and thirty seconds. However, I had a minor glitch when I pulled to deploy. The D-ring was on the left. Reaching across with my right hand disturbed my position and reduced friction with the air, almost as if I wanted to go into a dive. After a hundred jumps, I thought, "Shit on this." A couple of the men had moved theirs onto their right side. Since my right hand was the strongest, too, I remounted my ripcord pocket to my right as well. But I went the others one better. I put the ripcord handle in a vise and bent it up, so instead of lying flat on my chest it curled out a bit. That way, I could keep my arm to the side already positioned in a modified frog, then slide it down a bit, hook my thumb into the D-ring and push it out in one movement. It was an outside pull and Jim Perry standardized it within the team. A man could have it either on his right or left side.

In the middle of our modifications we had jumpers entering competitions all over. The rest of the world didn't know what we were up to, and the men were anxious to show off on behalf of the U.S. Army. The Russians and Bulgarians found themselves completely out of luck that summer when the brand-new U.S. team went to France for its first international competition and beat their butts.

The competitions gave us a boost, and we worked even harder to come up with the right canopy design. We would meet at the club once a week and sew like madmen to get ready for the weekend. Even with that, every day when we got off at 1600, most of us ran over to our little building and worked on our parachutes before going home to eat. We wanted to glide to a pinpoint landing standing up. And, up until that point, that was unheard of.

Stilwell kept scrounging aircraft for us and we were making ten to twelve jumps in a day. Flying by the seat of our pants, we experimented with patterns cut into the parachutes that looked like a W, a T, a double T, and a U. Finally, we arrived at the combination TU. We had something that really worked. Cut across a total of seven gores, the TU became the standard jumped by the Army Sport Parachute Team.

My first taste of competition came in September when I was part of a four-man team from the Sport Parachute Club representing the Army in the Southwestern Conference Parachute meet in Houston.

There were two categories of competition—style and accuracy. In the style event, you left the aircraft at 7,200 feet. The scorers on the ground knew that a jumper doing the French Cross would take ten seconds to accelerate through terminal velocity. They started the clock when you left the aircraft, and at ten seconds large panels on the ground signaled the style, or type, of movement to perform. There were a number of types involving 360-degree turns to the left or right, end over end back loops, and multiple combinations of all moves. You never knew what the judges would ask for. They watched through high-powered binoculars and graded on execution and position along a prescribed flight axis laid out on the ground. Other points were scored on how quickly you executed the full series.

We arrived with several aces up our sleeves. We had refined our arm and leg positions to increase or decrease the rate of fall at will by throwing more resistance into the wind or pulling resistance out of the wind. We also had the "delta." We had found that if you got to terminal velocity as quickly as possible you had more control when you were flashed from the ground. So when we jumped, we closed our legs a bit, swept back the arms, and put our heads down at a thirty-degree angle. Cutting through the air, we were bombs!

We beat the crap out of anything that resembled the French Cross and went to terminal several seconds before the ground opened the panels. Our movements were really sharp, and we shot all the old records to hell.

In the accuracy event the jumper landed as close as possible to a six-inch disc on the ground. That was the bull's-eye. It was inside a one-hundred-foot-diameter chalk-mark circle placed on a giant orange panel. The jumper scored one hundred points if he touched that disc and less the farther away. You had three chances at it. With our new modifications, I hit it the first time standing up.

The team came in first, and I was concentrating so much on making the team a winner I didn't know I had come in second in the individual competition. I found out when they called me to accept the trophy.

When we returned to Fort Bragg, we had an invitation to the Canadian Parachute Championships in Alberta. The Army wanted to keep a winning thing going and asked us to go. Now, you never "had" to do it. As with Houston, it was all at our own expense. But you didn't refuse that kind of request.

We again took four men, loaded parachutes and gear into a little Renault, and started for Canada.

At these meets you're given a day to practice, but we went right into the competition. I did very well in the style event, but on my first accuracy jump disaster struck. As I executed a radical turn into a real strong wind it started forcing me away from the target disc. I tried to recover by stretching my legs out to try to gain on the target, but when I was fully extended I slammed into the hard surface of the airstrip, heel and butt, using my hands to break my fall. My left wrist couldn't take it and gave.

I thought, "Shit-fire . . . here we go again." Sure as hell, it was broken again. I must still have landed close enough because my combined score had me thirty-eight points ahead.

The wife of the head man at the meet drove me to the hospital. The doctor looked at the X-rays and shook his head. "You've got five scaphoid fractures—two new breaks and three old," he said. "And the navicular has never fully healed."

I was dumbfounded that my wrist was still in such bad shape. But my main concern was the team. "Well . . . just wrap it up the best you can," I told him. "I'm going back to the jump."

The doc just frowned and wrapped the wrist in a couple of layers of Ace bandage. Hell, that was all I needed before.

I returned to the DZ at the meet. Since there were so many jumpers, my second accuracy try had not come up yet. The team was sweating our point standing. "Joe . . . you gotta make this last jump. All you've got to do is land inside the circle and we've got first place."

I ran to my parachute. The blasted thing wasn't even packed. I don't know how I did it, but I did—mostly with one hand. I took a "rider"—that meant an extra person in the plane. It was something they didn't like doing because they needed all the space for the other jumpers. All I wanted him to do was throw me out.

I went up and spotted for the pilot—you have to do your own spotting— lined it up real good and yelled, "Kick me out!" They shoved and out I flew. Everything went fine until I opened. You had to reach way up high to grab the steering toggles, but with that heavily bandaged wrist I just couldn't get my left hand up high enough to grab the left toggle. So I had to handle both toggles with the right hand—first, pull the ones on the right, then reach high over the back of my neck for the others. If I hadn't, I would have been spinning around.

I landed in the one-hundred-foot circle, but just so far out that I lost first place. I took fourth, but the team won first place overall.

The docs at Fort Bragg put my wrist in a cast. I was supposed to wear it five months, but after three I took the thing off myself. "Well, if it ain't knit by now," I figured, "it'll never knit." I still wanted to continue sport jumping, so I had the orthopedist at Womack Army Hospital make a steel and leather brace to support that weak navicular bone. I told him I couldn't afford to lose my jump pay—$55 a month. I really didn't want to lose out on any time with the club.

Jim Perry was pulling the best jumpers from all over the Army for special duty with the Army Sport Parachute Team. I wanted to be part of it, too, but my C-team commander had a cooler head. The old colonel gave me a fatherly talk.

He said, "Joe . . . If you go with the Parachute Team full time, you're going to be reassigned out of Special Forces. I know you can't jump like you used to because of the injury, and it's going to take some time to heal. You're going to have to make a decision. A career in Special Forces or SD with the team."

I knew the colonel was right and just looking out for my welfare. "Sir, there ain't no decision," I said. "I didn't reenlist to join the parachute team. I joined SF and I intend to remain with SF."

I had given up being in the first group of the Army's crack new Golden Knights demonstration team, but there would still be a lot of weekends for me to jump my tail off.

When Bull Simons began putting together the FB-3 teams for Laos, I was nearing 250 jumps. I still hadn't closed in on a sixty-second delay because most of the aircraft we commandeered had trouble getting to 12,500 feet. The most we could get was 11,000 feet and a delay time of fifty-five seconds. Whenever we took up General Stilwell's Huey, he was right there jumping with us. Like the rest of us, he wanted to get to over 12,000 feet in the worst way. He'd sit with his feet dangling out the door, watching the ground and calling to the pilot to get higher. That poor old chopper just vibrated.

The pilot leaned back and said, "General, I don't think we're going any higher; we're plumb out of power."

Stilwell shot back, "Before you get to the damned release point, I want six hundred more!"

We topped 12,500 and the pilot was shouting, "It's gonna fall, It's gonna fall!" Stilwell wasn't satisfied.

I thought for sure that chopper was going to drop before we had a chance to jump. I asked the pilot, "If it starts to fall can we get out?"

"Yeah . . . but dive out quick!"

At 12,800 feet Stilwell knew that was it, and we jumped. It was the longest delay for me—sixty-three seconds.

When I got to Panama in the advance party of Bull Simons, I found Fort Gulick had the Atlantic Area Sport Parachute Club, made up of jumpers from the Airborne unit at Fort Kobbe, the Navy at Rodman Naval Base, and Infantry at Fort Gulick. They were using old single blank-gore parachutes, but when they saw what I was jumping they "hired" me to modify theirs. There weren't any riggers around who could pack our parachutes, let alone cut and sew them, so I told Kathy to get her old trusty Singer portable ready.

I showed Kathy how to do it and we were in business. When she finished one, I would stick the repair tape around the cuts for reinforcement. Over several months she modified a couple hundred for the club.

I had more than enough jumps for my D license, the highest level awarded by the Parachute Club of America. But I didn't have the required jump into water. Simons took care of me and arranged for a helicopter for that one jump. I took it up to 2,200 feet above Gatun Lake, just off the bluff from Fort Gulick's headquarters at Quarry Heights. There were two sixteen-foot Army assault boats waiting below—a marker boat as the target and another running around to fish me out if I had a problem.

I considered landing smack inside the marker boat. I had that kind of control. But the requirement was a water landing. As I maneuvered toward it I decided to have a little fun and made like I was going to land in it, anyway. The four boys in the boat weren't so sure, though. I was coming right toward them and I could see their eyes widen. As I swooped over the boat I came around to face into the wind, made a quick adjustment, and dropped alongside, hooking the side of the boat with an arm as I hit the water. My head never got wet. But I had used my left arm and hurt it again.

The C-47 was our workhorse, getting us up for delay times well in excess of sixty seconds. We would climb fast so we wouldn't be exposed to the rarefied air too long. If our heads got foggy, that was okay as long as we could see well enough to get out the door. By the time we fell down a ways, we'd come out of it.

The name of the game in free-fall is altitude and delay time. Records were being set in the U.S. and elsewhere, and we wanted to get in on it, too.

We began looking at twenty thousand feet.

At those altitudes we always made sure the flight crew carried walk-around oxygen bottles with a twenty-minute charge. Not for us—for the jumpmaster. We wanted his head clear, since he had to do the ground spotting for our release point. This was particularly critical when we jumped at night. When I spotted at night I gave myself a simple test. I'd lean back from the door and look at the light above me. If there was a ring or haze around it, I'd suck on some oxygen and watch the ring around the light disappear. Then I'd put the bottle down and continue my job.

It was standard procedure for anyone using military aircraft above twelve thousand feet to go through an Air Force high-altitude simulator. Each individual has a different reaction to hypoxia—lack of oxygen—and we had to know our symptoms. In the chamber, we were taken to 42,000 feet. They dropped us back to 30,000 feet, and we were asked to take off the mask and write something on a tablet. You really bore down on what you were writing and thought you were doing real well. Then, just before you passed out, they slapped the mask back on. After a few deep breaths you looked down and saw that the writing was all over the page.

BY MID-1963, WE WERE ROUTINELY JUMPING FROM TWENTY THOUSAND FEET with a ninety-second free-fall. But all that on-duty practice had a price tag. U.S. Southern Command headquarters at Fort Amador pulled some of us out of the 8th Group to represent the U.S. in demonstration jumps all over Central and South America. It was a public-relations stunt as well as a selling tool to interest friendly governments in buying equipment and training. We jumped from three thousand feet to twenty thousand feet into parade grounds, playgrounds, golf courses, and airfields.

My buddy Dick Meadows wasn't jumping with the club on the weekends. I wanted him to join and talked him into making a jump with me. Dick had received his skydiving experience in England as part of the first exchange program between the British Special Air Service and U.S. Special Forces. Theirs was a lot different than ours. They just jumped out, fell, and opened at a predetermined altitude. That was the extent of it. There was no attempt to control themselves in free-fall.

We went up to 7,500 feet above the Fort Gulick parade field. I was the jumpmaster, and after I sent the others out I kicked Dick out. Then I went. Once I was satisfied that we were right where I wanted to be over the field, I went into a Delta and dove on him. I came down right above him and hovered a little bit. He had no idea I was there. Then I swung right in front of him and startled him good. I grabbed his hand, shook it, gave him a high-ball salute, and ZOOM, dove away from him.

HALO had finally become an official component of SF, but it had taken the perseverance of Joe Stilwell to convince nonjumping generals that free-fall was a military necessity.

He had some heavy ammunition. Loy Brydon had exploded every negative argument the airborne-development brass had about free-fall in the military. At the Yuma, Arizona, test site, Loy had shown how fast and with how much control a man could drop. He jumped from thirty thousand feet in one of our modified twenty-eight-foot canopies, hitting a glide ratio of 1 : 1.8, meaning for every 1.8 feet he fell, he moved forward 1 foot. It was like he had a rocket up his tail. Loy took his muscular body, went into a head-down position, pulled everything in—feet together—and literally covered his balls. He threw his neck back and was calculated at 250 miles an hour! Since the readings came at 18,000 feet and were an average figure for the whole jump, Loy's actual speed was faster than that. Then he flared out to 107 miles an hour and into perfectly stabilized and controlled flight. At least one hundred military followed him and his yellow jump suit through high-powered glasses. That's when they all became believers.

Hell, we wanted to jump that high, too. So our next objective was to set a South America high-altitude record. We really didn't know what the existing record was, but we knew we could break it, anyway. Along with Jim Perry and me were Dick Meadows, Capt. Jesse Ramos and Lt. Chuck Fry. We took off from France Field airstrip in our Air Commando C-47. After an hour, the airplane struggled to 23,000 feet. We jumped, but that wouldn't do. The next day the pilots were able to coax that son-of-a-gun to 24,500 feet—enough to free-fall 128 seconds. We wanted more, but the C-47 was all we could get and that was all it could manage.

The pilots thought we might still get higher if conditions were on our side, so we suited up the following day for a third try. It was November 22, 1963.

The pilots showed up full of confidence. "We're going to do it today. I think we can stretch it to twenty-eight." We were sitting outside the aircraft, just talking, while the crew completed their flight check. The pilot slid back his cockpit window and leaned out. "John Kennedy just got shot in Dallas."

We were stunned and agreed to delay the jump until we found out how he was. The pilot kept his attention on the radio while we waited, still with our heavy parachutes on. "What the hell's going to happen, now?" we wondered. Castro came to mind right away because Kennedy had stared him down during the missile crisis.

"Maybe we'll finally get to fight Cuba."

"Maybe we'll have that mission to run after all."

After an hour, the pilot hung out the window. "Kennedy died."

Our faces changed to sadness. We quietly pulled off our parachutes. No words were spoken—none needed. Special Forces had lost its friend.

A HALO school was operating at the 1st Group in Okinawa, and all of us doing free-fall wanted our own in the 8th, too. Sending men to Fort Bragg for four weeks meant separating them from their teams, and we wanted the men to train with their teams.

Chuck Fry sent in a request to 8th Group headquarters. At first, the response was lukewarm. But we were determined and sent in request after request until Bull Simons had "this idea" to create a HALO school at the 8th Group.

That was exciting news. We would have all the equipment: new parachutes, automatic openers, our own rigger, and our first C-130 to play around with, complete with a bona fide oxygen console for us to suck on when we went over twenty thousand feet. Newly promoted Capt. Chuck Fry, fresh from Fort Bragg's HALO jumpmaster course, appointed me, Meadows, and ol' Harry Denny as primary instructors and jumpmasters. There was one minor problem. Except for Fry, the rest of us weren't officially HALO qualified and, as far as the Army was concerned, all our Parachute Club experience and competition success didn't count. We still had to be certified in HALO.

"I've got the authority to issue certificates," Fry told us. "I'll take you, Meadows, Denny, and Ramos up for one jump, qualify you, and we'll have the HALO committee."

That's how I got my basic HALO. But each of us still needed another flight to qualify as a jumpmaster and instructor. In my case this was just so much bull since I had been in the very first group certified by the Army as a Sport Parachute Instructor. But it wasn't HALO.

Jim Perry went up with us. He had to comply with Army regs, too. Every time a man was reassigned to a new Group, he had to requalify in HALO. Jim might have been a little rusty, because he almost met his Waterloo on that jump. Certification required that we jump with full field gear, rucksacks and all. We were at 20,000 feet over Río Hato, a seldom-used military location along the southern coast, about sixty miles southwest of Panama City. We weren't in communication with any control tower, so we were pretty much on our own.

Six of us were sandwiched, waiting at the door. Chuck Fry was our "unofficial" jumpmaster, sighting down the edge of the C-47, lining up our release point. He signaled and we bolted out. If you don't want to be scattered all over the place, you don't waste time leaving an aircraft. It was a HALO-style team jump and we were going to assemble in the air about two meters apart.

On the way out the door, Perry snagged a section of the nylon tie-down straps securing his rucksack. Unlike a cotton strap, nylon has a tendency to slip, and Jim was falling with a loose rucksack. We went through the normal buffeting getting out in the slipstream. Then, as we all flattened out and started to form as a team, Jim's rucksack got caught with the wind and it went down around his ankles. He went into a spin, and centrifugal force whipped him out of control.

At the same time, we had an intruder in the form of a big-ass Constellation. There was no tower to tell him to look out for us. He was close enough so that I could see the pilot's eyeballs. He was making 400 knots toward us and we were making 125 miles an hour down. WHOOSH! Right through the formation.

As we were all fighting to stay stable, Capt. Jesse Ramos was on Perry's back, helping him get rid of the rucksack. It was a hellish job, since the straps were hooked to the reserve in front. Ramos wrestled with it for twenty seconds and then pulled it free from Jim. We recovered as a team and landed together. It was a reminder to us that, no matter how much training and experience you've had as a jumper, disaster can be just around the corner.

The wind over Río Hato was very strong from the north. Our release point had been well inland to allow us to drift with the currents and not be forced over the ocean. Dick and I thought about that while we waited on the ground for our pickup aircraft. Cuba had the same strong winds and we figured it might be possible to fly to the edge of Cuba's twenty-mile limit at night, drop out at thirty thousand feet, unseen by their radar, and eventually drift over the island, free to land anywhere we wanted. We couldn't wait to give the idea a try.

A few days later we took a C-47 to twelve thousand feet over Río Hato and had the pilot ask the radar operator at Albrook Air Force Base to scan for us. We jumped, and opened at two thousand feet. The operator reported that he saw the aircraft but nothing else. We were too small to have a "signature," and the parachutes were transparent to the signal. We were damned invisible.

Dick and I knew we could jump from the bomb bay of a B-57 or B-52 jet, free-fall in a tight ball to withstand the 250-mile-an-hour wind we'd find, pop and drift the twenty miles to infiltrate Cuba undetected. It was just a matter of getting a better canopy. At Fort Bragg, the Golden Knights were experimenting with something very radical—a parasail. It was like a wing and highly maneuverable. We couldn't get one, so we had to just dream about interrupting Castro's dinner.

A lot of the units in Panama continued in a stand-down mode, so we organized jump meets for excitement. Our parachute club sponsored the South American Sport Parachute Championship. To spice up the competition we came up with a "donkey jump." As a jumper came down, two men held a donkey about one hundred feet from the center of the target. He could sense that parachute coming in and get spooked, so you had to be careful he didn't kick you. We knew you couldn't land on the donkey, so you had to land as close as possible, get out of your parachute, mount the little ass, and ride him into the scoring circle. Your total jump time included the time it took to get the donkey to the target. Half of the jumpers fell off. We had more fun out of that shit.

The club put together several more competitions, but even this wasn't enough to satisfy our desire to set a high-altitude record for South America. It was near Christmas of 1964 when we decided to go for the record again. We got lucky. The Air Commandos brought us a big C-130. Our goal was thirty thousand feet or better,

We shot north over Colón and circled out over the Atlantic, gaining altitude in a steep climb. We were in a pressurized cabin for the first time and in more comfort than we were used to. We headed back to land, climbing all the way full bore. As jumpmaster, I had worked out the flight path with the pilot before we left the ground. We both had the route memorized.

We had been in the air less than a half hour when the pilot reported we were climbing through thirty thousand feet. We were ten minutes out from release and the wind readings at that high altitude were relatively calm. I hadn't been this excited about jumping in a long time. We went through a final equipment check.

In a few more minutes he radioed, "We're at 31,800 feet. That's all she's got."

I told the crew chief that I was ready to spot. We grabbed the masks from the oxygen console as he notified the cockpit to depressurize. I fixed my helmet and goggles and signaled the crew chief to open the door. I leaned out and damned if I couldn't see almost the whole Canal Zone!

By my calculations, we were six minutes from our release point. We were going into the Gatun DZ, a tiny area near the French Canal about five hundred meters long and four hundred meters wide. From our altitude, it was hard to see, even with the marking panels and smoke put out by the ground team. I knew the place well. It was a sugar-cane field before Dick and I and a bunch of other SF cut it down by hand to make a safer landing spot for the 8th Group.

At two minutes out I told the men to go to their bailout bottles. This was a first for us since we hadn't been at this altitude before. The men lined up at the door and I checked them carefully to make sure they were getting oxygen and that the masks were tight.

We gave each other thumbs up and I waved them out. It was a fantastic fall—two and a half minutes of maneuvering all over the sky. I tracked at least halfway around the DZ and came back to join the others in a tight formation. We closed on the DZ and pulled at eighteen hundred feet for a bullseye landing—on our feet.

We didn't have a big celebration. We were going to save it for the jump we would make from even higher.

chapter 9

"Unwelcome Mat"

From every angle Panama was a beautiful country. I enjoyed it from the air, hunting in the jungles, and SCUBA diving in the ocean. The place was full of small game and I had never caught so many fish in my life. And there was lobster. It was as if the good Lord had stocked the Atlantic just for us.

It was almost a paradise. Almost.

The country was a stewpot of Spanish-speaking Roman Catholics, English-speaking blacks from the Antilles, and Central American and island tribal Indians. The wealthy ran the country, and the poor ran in the streets. A French company was the first to try building a canal here but went bellyup. There were tens of thousands of workers from Jamaica, Haiti, and the Dominican Republic that were stranded. Most of them didn't go back, and they became the second-largest culture in Panama and very poor.

World War II brought money back into everybody's pockets. But when that ended, most of the jobs ended, too. Colón's beautiful tile streets turned into one of the worst slums in the world. When you looked past the well-scrubbed little Front Street shops you saw shit. I mean real shit.

The six or so Indian tribes went about their own business isolated on their own lands, mostly in remote areas. The Cuna Indians were the only ones we had any contact with. They came from the San Blas Islands along Panama's northeast coast. They were good people, intelligent and hard-working, and had jobs at our mess halls and commissary. We got along with the Cuna on one point—we both disliked the Panamanians.

We had almost eight thousand Panamanians living in the Canal Zone earning Yankee dollars, and we thought they were lazy and ungrateful. Outside the Zone there was poverty everywhere, along with jealousy and discontent with the government. It had already caused a lot of trouble.

In 1958, Panama City university students tried to plant a bunch of their flags, but the Canal Zone police pulled them up. They demonstrated for a month against the U.S. It turned nasty and nine died in a clash with the Panamanian National Guard. About a year and a half later, during the Panamanian Independence holidays, the unrest boiled over again, with bigger anti-American demonstrations caused by a lot of lies printed in newspapers owned by former president Harmodio Arias, who wanted his family back in power. The mobs came to raise their flag in the Canal Zone again and the U.S. called out the troops. The Infantry at Fort Kobbe laid down barbed wire, but several hundred crossed the barricades and fought with Canal Zone police. A second wave was pushed back by the National Guard and the troops.

There was a lot more violence going on in the streets of Panama City. Windows of the U.S. Information Agency library were smashed and the mobs ripped the U.S. flag from the ambassador's residence. After things died down the U.S. was afraid that there would eventually be more trouble and put up a fence along the entire border of the Canal Zone and beefed up the infantry presence in Fort Kobbe.

Back in 1959, we proved that none of these security measures were worth a damn. One of the favorite "missions" of SF continued to be sneaking in and out of the Canal Zone. Our teams would take it upon themselves to mount these exercises to test themselves, using every trick in the book, and they always succeeded in "knocking out" a lock. They went in with cameras, dressed as civilians, and left their crap all over the place like calling cards. There was no telling how many packages were left with little notes on them that said "Boom."

We just shook our heads over it.

The Panamanians never forgot the incidents in 1958 and 1959, and continued to stew over them. The State Department wanted to let them raise their flag in one spot as a gesture of "good will," but our generals were unhappy as hell because they wanted the Panamanians and the rest of the world to know who was really in control of the Canal Zone. They finally stopped their squabbling and allowed the Panamanian flag to be flown side by side with the U.S. flag at one location in the CZ. The flags were raised in a ceremony in 1960. The Panamanians knew we had thrown them a bone and they went away with a real hard-on for the U.S.

That hatred was still stirring when SF arrived to build the 8th Group. The wives were warned about going into the towns to shop, but many of them were so anxious to get out of the confines of Fort Gulick and the American sector of Coco Solo they went anyway. Some of them got hurt as their purses were grabbed. The police didn't give a hoot—they just looked the other way.

The Pentagon big brass finally stepped back and allowed the Panamanian flag to fly next to ours at several sites, including the American high school in the Balboa section, just inside the Canal Zone. But U.S. citizens living in the CZ got angry and balked. Students of the high school raised the American flag by itself in front of the school. Egged on by the adults, they did it again the next day.

When the news hit across the border, two hundred Panamanian students took to the streets that second day, January 9, 1964, and marched into the CZ ready to hoist their flag. The Zone police met them and agreed to allow six of them to put the flag in front of the school. About five hundred Americans were waiting there with other ideas, and the police knew they had stepped in shit. They asked the Panamanians to leave and all hell broke loose. Panama City came unglued and thirty thousand Panamanians came down Fourth of July Avenue toward the CZ. They stormed the border fence and the fight was on. Zone police pushed back the first wave, but it took troops from Fort Kobbe to handle the rest. They dug positions in front of the Tivoli Hotel and spent the time ducking small-arms fire from all over. They were first ordered to use birdshot, because our government didn't want to hurt anyone. U.S. commanders didn't put up with this nonsense very long and sent in sharpshooters to kill the little jerks. The Panamanian government accused us of aggression and broke off relations. At that point I don't think any of the U.S. troops really gave a rat's ass.

The news of the rioting spread like wildfire. We got word of the shooting in Panama City and that it had just spread to Colón, four miles north of us. A lot of the men were nervous. They had families living in Coco Solo, the American sector just across the Río Folk inlet from Colón.

We knew what had to be done. Bull Simons knew what had to be done. It was the U.S. government that didn't want us to do anything. Washington was telling Southern Command brass not to create another ugly "incident" with the Panamanians. Just as we were preparing to leap in, the Army refused to release ammunition to us, so there we sat with empty rifles. That was bad news for Dick Meadows. His wife, Pam, was in their house in Colón. We had to get her out.

Our B-team commander gave us the okay to use our own shotguns as long as we only used birdshot and only in self-defense. "Bullshit!" was our answer. I called Kathy and had her bring my shotguns to the team room with all the .00 buck she could find. Dick and I climbed into a borrowed car and we started up the road to Colón.

We could see the clouds of smoke up ahead, and Dick was running that car as fast as he could. As we got to the outskirts of town, we turned up the back alleys, trying to avoid any confrontation. We could hear occasional shooting. The sounds were distinctly of M-1s firing, probably from the Fort Davis infantry units that were ordered in. At least *they* had ammunition.

Dick lived in the old section of Colón, which was mostly slums. Every now and then a fancy house as big as a mansion would pop up in the middle of a bunch of shacks. These old homes had tall iron fences around them and were left from the days of the construction of the canal. Canal officials or land barons probably owned them before everything was given back to the Panamanians.

We weaved in and out of these slum areas until Dick pulled in front of another big house. It was owned by an old Panamanian woman, who had divided it into apartments. We drove by a big iron gate to the rear of the house, where Dick and Pam lived. Dick didn't see his little blue Renault, and when we got inside Pam was gone. Dick cleaned out some of his stuff, then we ran through a few more alleys to the home of one of Pam's friends, the wife of a civilian oil-company worker. Their house was empty, too. We knew we couldn't stay any longer if we wanted to get out safely, so we headed back for Fort Gulick.

When we got back, Dick breathed a sigh of relief. Pam had gotten out in the early hours of the riots and wound up at Harry Denny's house at Fort Gulick. Pam wasn't a bit scared by the rioting. She had been through a lot worse in the jungles of Malaysia with her father, an NCO with the British SAS.

Meanwhile, angry crowds had started to move on Cristóbal, just south of Colón. Jim Perry had been sent in and his team had positioned themselves on the fourth floor of the Brown Hotel. They had bayonets on their empty rifles, gas masks, and canisters of CS (tear gas) and CN (nerve gas). Other teams were running small operations as diversions. There was a plan to send an A-team across Limón Bay to Colón and set fires behind the rioters. While they were putting out the fires, SF would put out the riot. That plan was knocked out of the water when the SF received a radio message that said, "No bayonets." The SF had to settle for being spotting teams for the infantry units, relaying crowd movements. That was really a crock.

Perry wasn't about to just sit on his butt. He sent a couple of his men back to Fort Gulick to make slingshots. The men worked on a band saw and cut rough slingshot handles. Back in the barracks, they whittled them into decent weapons, while other men collected surgical tubing from B-team medical kits and the post dispensary. The ammunition was wicked—steel ball bearings from the .00 cartridges used in their own twelve-gauge shotguns. You could haul back on the tubing and whistle one of those little devils two hundred yards.

They got back to the Brown Hotel just in time. The mobs were closing in and the team had already given one rioter a good whiff of CN. A couple of hundred had gathered below and were screaming. The man who was hit with the gas came back, running across an open area with a flaming Molotov cocktail. One of the SF hit him between the eyes with a ball bearing and down he went—for good. But, the rioters still set fire to the hotel and the team hightailed it down the back stairway, making it back to Fort Gulick.

Throughout the night, mobs in Panama City tried to burn any building they could find that was used by the government or the U.S. In Colón they set fire to a beautiful bank, a library, and a new USO building.

By late the next day, the mobs in Cristóbal had been dispersed, but trouble continued in Colón. Just south of town, infantry from Fort Davis had set up a barbed-wire roadblock across Las Cruces Road, the main route out of Colón. But some of the rioters now had guns and had holed up in a house, firing on the troops.

The first news that the U.S. had taken casualties came that night as Kathy was on the telephone to her close friend Barbara, wife of our B-team commo supervisor, Bob Ramsey. They lived in one apartment of a four-family stucco building on Limón Bay near Colón. Barbara had heard her American neighbor screaming. She looked out her window to see a U.S. Army staff car outside. The woman was told her husband had been killed by a sniper.

Two men from Fort Davis had been hit. One died on the spot and the other had been taken to our hospital in Coco Solo. He wasn't expected to live. The Infantry commander put out a call for SF to neutralize the snipers. Simons passed the word down to our B-team. "Get rid of them" was all he said.

Most of us hunted, and by this time almost all the men had their shotguns and .00 buck. Our commander picked several of our Spanish SF to take out the snipers.

At the roadblock, the troops were dodging Molotov cocktails as well as .22 rounds coming from the windows of a small two-story stucco house across the street. Our men worked their way into Colón and easily mingled with the crowd. Suddenly, we heard the BOOM! of a shotgun from the sniper location, and a body came flying out the window into the street. The other sniper kept firing. Every so often he would rise to the window, shoot, and go back down. When he rose to shoot again, BLAM! He didn't shoot anymore. They blew the hell out of him.

The boys from Fort Davis gave us a cheer, but our quick success scared the SOUTHCOM commanding general into ordering all SF restricted to barracks. The Army already had its hands full and was afraid to set us loose anymore. We were forbidden to go into the Canal Zone or into any civilian areas. They thought that if we were shot at we'd shoot back, and a lot of Panamanians would be killed. Hell, yes, we would have! And they were right; it would have been a damn massacre.

The worst of the rioting lasted three and a half days. Four American soldiers were killed along with about twenty-five Panamanians, mostly on the Pacific side. With the exception of a few lucky shots from American troops guarding buildings, the U.S. didn't employ any crowd-control techniques worth a damn, so the majority of civilian casualties came from the mob action itself.

With so much unrest, the facts weren't worth dirt. The Arias newspapers and television had been grinding out propaganda from the beginning of the riots, and the locals ate it up. Arias dragged out pictures of every Panamanian who had died over the past two years, whether they were killed by cars, sickness, or whatever. That was the stuff Kathy and the other wives had seen on TV. The reporters pointed to each body and charged the U.S. with their "murder." The Panamanian government went along with this crap and re-named Fourth of July Avenue "Avenue of the Martyrs."

From the start we couldn't depend on the National Guard to help us. Even though the U.S. had trained them, they disappeared when the riots began, refusing to fire on their own people. I could hardly blame them. The Fort Kobbe Infantry units were fully detailed to guard the locks—that was their mission. The men from Fort Davis were protecting government build-ings and blocking approaches to the CZ. So SF was called on to secure other sensitive American sites.

We flew a whole B-team to the Pacific side and set up combat fighting positions around a Nike antimissile launch site and a large ammo storage dump. We were alert to the possibility that the Panamanians might try an assault at any time.

Back at Fort Gulick, it was very quiet—largely because no Panamanian civilian workers were allowed in. In fact, no Panamanian workers were al-lowed back into the whole Canal Zone. Wives took over the commissary and the PX. Even the San Blas Indians were kept out, and soldiers had to do their own KP.

We stayed on alert for two weeks. By the time we returned to Fort Gulick, Panamanian workers were trickling back into the CZ, but all areas outside the fence were off limits to the military. Washington and Panama City were trading charges back and forth, and it was an unstable situation.

The Pentagon was expecting more unrest and sent FBI experts to train us in riot control. In Coco Solo, they had cleared out a section as a mock Panamanian village. We learned techniques for going house to house and room to room, clearing out the bad guys. We learned how to wield billy clubs and use rifle butts to subdue rioters. Then the different B-teams would switch roles between being rioters and army forces. We'd throw eggs and tomatoes and then the army forces would try to capture someone in the crowd. We'd beat the crap out of them, and the next day they'd beat the crap out of us.

It was kids' play on one hand and tough training on the other. We knew that, with the slightest provocation, the Panamanians could go off again.

They were crazy with hate.

chapter 10

Tough Times All Around

The Panama uprising in January of 1964 caused us to be confined to Fort Gulick and the other U.S. military facilities in the Canal Zone. That cut into our ability to roam the jungles to train. Bull Simons always wanted us fit and ready for anything, and was looking for an exercise designed to keep us razor sharp.

Halfway around the world, Americans were in the mountains and jungles of Southeast Asia, facing an enemy as ruthless and cunning as any. All SF in Panama knew it was a sure bet that our next stop would be Vietnam. There were rumors and suspicions about what we would face. It wasn't a pretty picture. It meant trying to survive in an incredibly hostile place and it meant training like never before.

In November, all Special Action Force A-teams were put on a mission alert. My team was alerted and put in isolation. In our briefing we were told that we were going to infiltrate a jungle area, link up with "friendly" guerrillas, and help them in their cause. We were given an advance story about where we would be meeting the guerrilla chief and told that he would then lead us to the mission site. We were given an escape-and-evasion (E&E) network to follow through the jungle to friendly contacts. That's all we got.

We didn't know what we were to do to help the guerrillas in the area or what the target was.

Well, I knew that there was more to this than we were told. My natural senses were alert. As a kid, I learned not to get caught off guard or from behind. I owed that to my father. Thanks to him I never relaxed my guard again.

MY CHILDHOOD WAS WAR. DAD SET THE TONE.

He had dropped out of college to marry Mama, who was just sixteen, while his brothers and sisters went on to finish. In those days, there was nothing to fall back on but manual labor. From the first day I can remember, he led a life that ate at him, and all his frustrations and failures were vented on Mama and us kids.

They were married in 1924, and he built Mama a little one-room cabin in Sherwood, Tennessee, a small limestone-mining town at the base of the Cumberland Mountains, about thirty-five miles west of Chattanooga. To his credit he was an excellent carpenter and had promised mother to add a room for each child that came along.

Vera Jean Garner was the first. Mama said she was beautiful and looked just like Dad, with coal-black hair, dark brown eyes, and beautiful olive skin. She barely made it a year and a half before taking sick with pneumonia. Brother Lewis had just been born and, for some reason, Dad didn't take Vera Jean to a hospital or doctor. Before they knew it, she was dead. Dad always blamed himself. I don't think he ever got over it—Vera Jean looked so much like him.

Lewis had blond hair from Mama's side of the family. This added to Dad's bitterness, and he often took it out on Lewis. Sally was born eighteen months later, followed by Roger. And then, on May 6, 1934, it was my turn in the world.

It was my luck, and my fate, to look just like Dad. I guess he took a shine to me at the expense of the others. But that wouldn't last for long.

Dad worked with explosives in a rock quarry of the Gaugert Lime Company, the main industry in that small town. Grandpa Wells, Mama's daddy, also worked there. When the mine suddenly played out, all the jobs went, too.

And now, brother Jerry arrived. So here we were, a poor mother and father and their five small kids. I was two and a half when they sold the house to move to Winchester, another mining town fifteen miles northwest on the other side of the Cumberland Plateau. Dad had rented an old house on the edge of town. Everything was packed into a borrowed pickup truck and off we went. I didn't know it yet, but we would be moving a lot.

The yard was so small that we didn't have a decent place to play. But that didn't matter, because no sooner had we settled in than the landlord sold the house. Dad moved us two miles farther out on Liberty Road. It was a real pretty place. It had an apple orchard, pear orchard, and grape vineyards.

By this time the family was already under stress. Dad had never planned for this kind of life, but he had a lot of mouths to feed. He again went to work as a blaster in the quarry nearby.

Sally had just entered first grade when she took sick with diphtheria and was unconscious for two days. Mama kept everyone out of her room. When she finally came out of it, Mama burned all the bedclothes along with the mattress and springs. No one else caught it.

Mama didn't have an easy time with me, either. From the first, I was sick with stomach problems that really hurt. The druggist had her put me on paregoric, an opium derivative and a very common remedy in those days. It kept me quiet for almost all my first three years.

But Mama had already lost her ability to handle me and the others, too. That first summer she sent me to Grandmother Garner back in Sherwood. Dad's brothers came over and gave me a lot of their time and attention. Grandma and Grandpa still had two teenage children living there, and we played together in the Sewanee Mountains behind the house.

Up on a ridge, my Uncle Ken had a steel cable hooked up that ran down to a tree in the backyard. A metal bar was attached to a roller and you held on to ride. It was a long ride and you couldn't drop off. Near the end you touched the ground, slid your feet and ran until you stopped. If you didn't you would hit the tree. Since I was only three, I always came awful close to the tree.

Grandma put me on a diet of buttermilk and other good food. Soon, I was rid of the stomach troubles. No more paregoric. This was more of a home than I had ever had, and I didn't want to leave.

Dad's temper was worse than ever. Unfortunately, our German shepherd became an easy target. He was a good old dog and was very protective of us. He wouldn't let anyone come close to the house. The dog sucked some of our neighbor's chicken eggs and Dad took him out to the apple orchard and blew his brains out with a shotgun. The shot echoed up to the house.

It didn't stop there. Sally had a black cat with kittens. He drowned the whole litter.

All of us were nervous. We never knew what would set him off. Whatever he did, Mama had to go along. And she often bore the brunt of Dad's anger. Even taking her out on a Saturday night eventually led to abuse. But Mama was so starved for a life outside the house that she grabbed onto the chance whatever the outcome.

They would leave us kids alone and walk to town. The gathering place was a grocery store where people drank and danced. When they returned home, Dad spent the rest of the night cursing and threatening Mama, waving his gun around. We'd wake up and just keep out of sight.

Sure as hell, the house was sold from under us. We had been in it only two years and Mama was happy there. She had a garden out near the groves and loved picking all the fruit. Now we had to leave it behind. We moved closer to downtown Winchester, but it was still on the edge of town. A graveyard was going in right next to us, and we made it our playground.

Dad would sometimes drive home in his demolition truck with a pile of apples. We ran like the devil to get them. He seemed to actually enjoy this. Then our life turned upside down.

There was an accident at the quarry. Dad was caught in a blast and was badly injured. A small piece of rock had lodged in his lung. For a long time he coughed uncontrollably, until one day he came home from work and began spitting up blood—gobs of it all over the porch. It was awful, and mama called the doctor. He had tuberculosis. All those years breathing in lime dust had done the damage. The rock in his lung had simply aggravated his condition and hastened his TB.

He stayed home and Mama tried to take care of him. But he couldn't handle being dependent on her. He would sometimes scream and throw his food at her. He once bloodied her nose.

We became isolated from the other kids in the neighborhood. Nobody would play with us. It was an awful lonely feeling.

The sickness made him meaner than ever. On Christmas Eve he brought his pistol out again and started his same routine of threats. Mama called the police. They came out to get him, but he said, "I don't know what you're talking about. Why are you questioning me?" They looked around for the gun, but couldn't find it. No wonder. He had buried it outside. Sally saw him do it, but was afraid to talk. There were no presents that year.

The resentment and bitterness grew worse. Dad was now unable to work and couldn't pay the rent. We had to move.

The new house was a tiny, rundown sharecropper's shack five miles out in the country. It was the only place we could afford. The shack sat in a field that was part of the landlord's farm. There were three rooms and a big, long kitchen with a chimney. It had a front porch and a tin roof. There was a well and an outhouse. We were surrounded by farm animals, fields, and fences.

Dad was very sick and stayed in bed most of the time. All of us kids tried to help out as much as we could. Mama wanted a vegetable garden. We located a plow, but didn't have a horse to pull it. So we pulled the plow.

We also worked for the farmer that owned the house in exchange for the rent. We didn't do a whole lot of work. Hell, the lousy house wasn't worth that much.

Kids can always find some fun, even under the worst circumstances. There was a river several miles away, and we would spend the whole day there. Lewis and Sally taught us to swim so that it was as natural as walking. Even Jerry was a good swimmer by the time he was three. We were swinging on a rope tied to a tree that went out over the water. The rope broke, and Jerry fell into the middle of the river. We couldn't see Jerry, so we all jumped into the river to find him. We thought he had drowned. We looked all around, and there he was sitting on the riverbank. "Hey, what's y'all looking for?" he asked with a big grin. After that, you could never keep Jerry out of the water.

Playing all over the countryside had its hazards, too. A creek branch ran behind the RC Cola plant and continued on through the farm property. At that point it was overgrown with vines and hidden. Jerry and I didn't know we were playing right at the edge when I slipped and fell face first into the creek. I put out my hands to brace myself and landed in a creekbed filled with broken bottles. Both wrists were cut wide open. The nearest help was an old black woman who lived in a shack near the farm. I ran to her house gushing blood. Jerry was frantic. That old lady grabbed her broom and ran all over her cabin collecting every cobweb she could reach. She had gobs of them and wrapped them around the cuts. Then she wrapped rags tight around my wrists. The cobwebs acted like gauze. I never saw a doctor, and the wounds never got infected. She saved my life, for sure.

As a family, we were just barely making it. Mama put us on relief and Dad sank deeper into his frustration. Just before school started, some welfare organization brought us a box of old clothes. Both sides of the family also helped with hand-me-downs and food. We were the poorest of the lot.

Mama just couldn't handle us, and Dad, too. That's when Sally took it upon herself to "raise us right." I don't know how she knew to do it—it was just instinct with her. It started the day we left for school. With no transportation, we walked the five miles. That was nothing for us since we were used to walking to town to buy what food and supplies we could afford.

It became a daily task for her to correct things we did. "Pull your shoulders back!" she'd bark. "Don't stoop over. Walk straight! Walk straight!" She made us walk that way the whole five miles. All the boys in the family grew up with straight shoulders and straight backs.

Sally was three and a half years older than I was, smart as a whip and very strong-willed. She had to be. If we didn't do our homework, she was the one who got on us. She straightened us out good—even our table manners and the way we dressed. All we learned during childhood—stuff a child learns at home—came from Sally.

Most of all, she made us stand up tall and be proud. "We're not poor," she drummed into us. "We're just down on our luck, that's all."

But it was Dad who was dragging us down. He was sicker and meaner. He got to beating Lewis bad. One day, Dad decided he didn't like Lewis's blond hair and ordered him to stay under the bed so he wouldn't have to look at him. When Lewis would try to come out, Dad kicked him in the face. I never saw Sally so angry. I think she would have killed Dad if she had been older and stronger.

Roger and I suffered, too. He would beat us boys at the slightest provocation, blaming his family for his misfortunes. We could never do anything right.

After one really bad beating, I started to run whenever I got on his bad side. I had the dodging maneuver down pat, and I could move like a deer. I knew that, if I stayed away from the house long enough, one of the other boys would get him riled up, and by the time I returned, he would have forgotten.

It wasn't a home as such. It was just a place to sleep. And I even began to hate that, too. Dad got ahold of me once, and put me in the cellar of the shack. It was a smelly hole just under the floor. The moment he pulled the floor back to let me out, I ran for the woods. I stayed out overnight and didn't return until late the next day.

As the family situation deteriorated, I stayed away more—sometimes for several days at a time. I could walk for miles through the woods, never getting lost. I spent hours playing as if I was an Indian—I always thought I looked just like one. It was nice being alone out there.

School had started again, but Lewis would never enjoy it. Dad made him quit eighth grade and go to work. That was a sad day. Lewis really liked school and was very smart. Dad told Lewis he didn't need an education, that it hadn't done *him* any damn good. Lewis moved out and went to stay with Grandma and Grandpa Garner, who were now in Chattanooga. Grandpa had a successful barbershop there. Lewis went to work for a company making airplane parts.

The Second World War was going on, and Mama was pregnant. This was against the doctor's orders. He had cautioned Dad not to get Mama pregnant again because of his tuberculosis. But Dad didn't give a damn about her welfare or the baby's because he thought it would keep him out of the military. Before he got TB he had begged the doctor to give him a document saying he was unable to serve, but the doc refused. Dad was just plain afraid to go in. None of us had ever seen him afraid of anything before. He thought another baby would for sure guarantee him an exemption. I guess it did.

The mining company paid for his sanatorium treatment, then gave Dad five hundred dollars from his medical insurance. As soon as he got the money, he took off for Florida. We had all been counting on that money, but now we had nothing—not a penny. Mama got a postcard from him. Sally tried to control her anger as she read it to her.

When Mama was ready to give birth, she sent us boys to the RC Cola bottling plant just down the road. Sally had called for the doctor, but he didn't get there in time. Sally and the midwife tended to the delivery—another boy. Sally gave our new brother, Larry, his first bath. The men at the bottling plant gave us all we could drink in celebration. By the time we got home we were sick as hell. Sally had cooked a big meal, and we turned green.

Dad was gone six months. When he returned we figured it was because the money ran out. He tried to make himself useful by helping Sally wash clothes on the scrub board. At least he was going through the motions.

Dad was able to find work as a security guard at Northern Field, an Army Air base to the north of us in Tullahoma. But his TB got the better of him, and he couldn't work anymore. He went into a sanitarium in Chattanooga, but after he was released he still spent most of his time lying on the couch.

Then we had to move again. Grandpa Garner found a place for us in Chattanooga, and we started packing. It was a particularly sad time for Mama. She could have really been happy in the country. She loved the place. She had planted flowers and made a garden.

Cooley Street was in Avondale, a very rough part of town. I hated it. I hated school, too, and was in and out a lot that first year. I got into plenty of trouble—mostly fighting with the other kids. People say things to you because you're a little country boy, and I wasn't about to take any shit off anybody. Sally was in junior high and wasn't there to ride herd on me.

I was fighting at home, too. All of us were fighting. We fought over clothes, food, space, everything. Our situation was so miserable.

Dad was running round on Mama and she took it, catering to his every whim. That pleased him, and he did whatever pleased him. There were many nights when he would dress up and head toward town. Sometimes he'd take a streetcar, but more often than not a woman who lived beside us would hop in her car and follow him down the street. We figured out the rest.

Spending time with his lady friends didn't soften his violence toward us. The last beating I took was because Jerry and I got into a fight. Hell, kids do that all the time. Mama helped Dad tie me to a post in the bedroom, and he whipped me pretty good—for nothing. I was more angry than hurt and vowed this would be the last time my father, or anybody else, would beat me up.

The fact that Mama sided with Dad was hard to forget. I thought she resented me because I favored Dad so much—much more than my brothers. I held that against her for a long time.

Dad was still beating my brothers, but not me anymore. I was gone in a flash at the sign of trouble. I was worse off here in Chattanooga than I ever was in the country, so I decided to run away. I had help from some of my buddies in the neighborhood.

I ran off to a barn outside of town and hid while the others brought me everything. We put together a getaway bag. It was a poor neighborhood, but each buddy gave me something. One, a blanket, one gave me a bicycle he had stolen. All I wanted was to get back to the country. It was, I guess, fifty miles to Winchester. I figured I could live in the old farmer's barn with the cows until I found a place.

My family searched for me, but I stayed hidden. All my buddies lied and said they hadn't seen me. I was gone for almost four days. That last day was going to be my sprint. I had snuck way down into another part of the neighborhood and was pushing my bike along when I spotted the police heading my way. My folks had called the cops on my butt. I dropped everything and ran. They chased me for an hour until they trapped me in an alley with cars at both ends blocking my way.

They got me. All they said was "You sure are a fast little bastard, ain't you?" I was filthy and tired and hungry, and they never hurt me. Off I went to jail. The police weren't worried about a little kid and left the cell door unlocked. I could open it and walk around the jail.

Dad didn't show up until the next day. "C'mon, let's go" was all he said. He didn't say much else all the way home. There was no beating or anything. I vowed that this wasn't going to be a one-time thing. That's when the woods became my real home.

I began spending a lot of time away from the house, thanks to an old man who took me under his wing. He lived behind us across the alley. I had seen him in his backyard working on a fishing pole and went over to him. "Where are you fishing?" I asked. Hell, there was no place around us to fish. He told me he fished along the banks of the Tennessee River and offered me a chance to go with him on Saturdays. We would follow the railroad tracks almost five miles to where it crossed the river just below Chickamauga Dam. According to the old man, that's where the fishing was best. I used a little ol' pole that I cut off the bank. We dug up worms, and he supplied the hooks. It was real crude, but that's all we needed.

He showed me how to cook fish and field corn on the riverbank. He taught me to forage for food, and soon I had learned what was edible in the forest.

Food was scarce, so I caught all the fish I could carry, came home, and cooked them myself. The family lined up when I started cooking. There wasn't anybody to do it but me.

My time with the old man soon came to a screeching halt. Even though Dad continued to see other women, he was still very jealous of Mama. The old man's son once started up a conversation with her in the alley behind the house. Dad reacted in a rage, accusing her of flirting. He picked up a board and broke Mama's arm, then attacked the neighbor, sending him to the hospital. Mama was deathly afraid to cross him again and went to stay with her sister Bessie for four days. She left him several more times, whenever the abuse became unbearable, but always returned.

As soon as I returned to school, I started fighting again. This time, it spilled over into our neighborhood. My brothers and I didn't like it when the bigger boys beat up on the smaller ones. That's when we waded in against the neighborhood bullies. But I guess I did most of the fighting. It wasn't that I was the meanest in the family, just that I was the one who wouldn't take any shit.

Sally was always fussing at me about fighting so much. I didn't like it because I was just trying to defend the little guy in those fights. I got real tired of her scolding me and we had a knock-down drag-out fight on the front porch. She popped me good and I decided that was going to be our last bout. Sally was one tough girl. When Dad told her she'd have to quit school after the ninth grade, she stood up to him. "No!" she snapped. "I'm going to school until I get good and ready to quit!" He never again said anything to Sally about it.

My brothers and I started getting along a little bit better, doing more things together. Those few times we had any money, Jerry and I would go to the public swimming pool in Warner Park. We won all the swimming and diving competitions there. We had the advantage because of all our river swimming.

You might say we kept in shape the hard way. During the summer we would walk two miles to the Tennessee River. We had fixed big swings to take us over the river. We dropped into it and had to fight a very swift current back to shore, so the pool at Warner Park was a piece of cake.

Diving came naturally, too. I can't ever remember being afraid of heights. There was a rock quarry at the top of a hill about two blocks from the house. It was the neighborhood swimming hole. No one ever checked on us, so we could do whatever we wanted, and I sure as heck did. The sides of the quarry were blown-out rock and almost straight up. I started scaling the sides and jumping into the water. I began at twenty feet, and that first jump knocked the breath out of me. I didn't hold my hands together tight enough, but I fixed that and started going higher, ten feet at a time. I just pushed off and turned around in midair. Once I got to the top of the rock that protruded, I figured I could stand on it and do a swan dive into the water a hundred feet below. The water was about eighty feet deep. Nobody would do it but me. The dive was just too dangerous—for them.

By the time I was twelve, I was also jumping off the high bluffs at Chickamauga Lake, and that was after a four-and-a-half mile walk to get there. Sometimes we ran. Diving into the lake was a little different. I had to run real hard and dive out as far as I could to clear the rocks. On weekends, people would picnic along the banks. They were watching us, and that gave Jerry an idea.

"Let's make a little money," he said. Jerry would approach people with "You pay and Joe will dive." We charged a nickel. After Jerry collected the money, off I went. I did the same thing back at the quarry. If Jerry wasn't there, I'd climb to the rock on top and sit, waiting for other kids to show up. "Put your nickel on the ground," I'd tell them. "When there's enough nickels, I'll dive off." They were as poor as I was and usually had to go home for the money.

That's how we went to the movies. The movies were a dime. I was really taken in by the first Western Sally took us to. When the cowboys came out shooting, I dove behind the seat. "Those fools are shooting at us!"

We loved to explore, and it didn't matter how far away a place was. The municipal dump was four miles from the house and some of my buddies and I found enough old roller skates to make five good pair. As soon as we had them in working order, we took off for the Chattanooga airport five miles east. The highway to the airport began less than a mile away and ran through a tunnel under Missionary Ridge. We skated all the way to the terminal, messed around for a couple of hours, and headed back. Just before the tunnel, one of the boys got heat stroke. We dragged him into the tunnel and got him cooled down. By this time the skates were shot. We had worn the wheels down to the ball bearings. We walked to the quarry to cool off. Our only concern was being able to find new wheels.

At home, it was still a matter of keeping out of Dad's way. I made a slingshot and went back into the woods for hours on end. I got pretty good with it and could hit anything. Sparrows were my favorite target. At night I kept on shooting, this time popping out streetlights. Marbles from Jerry's winnings made the best ammunition. Jerry was real good in marbles and always had a slew. My buddies came along, and we all had at the lights. The police would chase after us. Actually, we liked getting their goat.

Both Sally and Jerry thought it was wrong for me to run around with poor boys. They thought I ought to play with a higher class of kids. But I was comfortable running around with boys as poor as I was. They made more sense.

Mama just couldn't handle me. Sally told me Mama wanted to put me in a boys' school. That meant reform school. Dad had said no. It was the first time he had ever come to my defense—probably just to fight with her.

My mischief prompted Dad to take me to his folks. That was okay. I liked it there. It was a big, two-story house in a nice neighborhood. I was given a room off the kitchen that was once a maid's room. They never would talk to me much, so I just stayed out of the way and had at the refrigerator.

Then the inevitable happened. Dad left Mama for good. He moved in with Grandma and Grandpa and took my room. I was sent back home. Mama was expecting again. She put us on welfare, and we tightened our belts even more.

Alan, my youngest brother, was born, and Mama found herself battling the welfare people. She was told, "Give up the children and go to work." Mama resisted and applied for an apartment in the East Lake housing project. She was denied a place because of a technicality: Mama wasn't making the minimum $45 a month. "What a blessing to be poor," Sally said with some relief. The project was the last place any of us wanted to be. A lot of real trash lived there.

Times were really tough on Cooley Street. Lewis had just turned seventeen, and Mama had him quit his job to go into the Navy. She signed the necessary papers, and Lewis was gone. Since Dad had pulled him out of school, Lewis had no hope of a good-paying job. Now Mama would receive his military allotment, which would be a lot more than what he could earn in Chattanooga.

At school, Jerry and I cleaned tables in the cafeteria to earn our lunch. Then a chance to deliver newspapers came along. All I needed was a bicycle. The municipal dump again saved the day. We went back and forth until there were enough parts to make one. It was just a frame and wheels, but I was delivering the *Chattanooga Free Press* and making money.

I was doing chores for Grandma Garner, and I would see Dad a few times. We didn't have much to say to each other. Nobody would hire him because of his medical problems, so he lay around a lot. He finally got a job working for a brother-in-law. That's when he moved in with another woman.

The divorce followed. Shortly after, the Garner family abandoned us and never came around anymore. Dad had spread a lot of lies about us, and we were now treated as outsiders.

The struggle to survive was made worse because Dad never sent the alimony he promised. To help fill our table I would hunt down pigeons with my slingshot. I could always find plenty in vacant lots and at the rock quarry. I cleaned and cooked them.

Mama did what she could to bring in money. Our house had a separate bedroom-and-bath arrangement in the rear with its own door. We rented it to a woman and her little daughter. Mama also took in children for working people in the neighborhood.

Even that wasn't enough, and it wasn't long before we could no longer afford the rent on Cooley Street. I couldn't believe we were being uprooted again, but had to accept it. It was a pitiful move into another poor section—Oak Grove.

Going to a new school didn't change me one bit. I was in the sixth grade and still fighting for the underdog. We had a real big dumb-looking boy in class. He was two years older than the rest of us. He had attacked a younger, smaller boy and slapped the fart out of him. I broke it up and told him to stop. He picked up a rock and tried to throw it at me. When he did, I decked him. He sprang to his feet and charged. It scared me, so I grabbed him around the neck and had him on the ground. I wasn't going to turn him loose because I figured he could whip me, and held on until he almost passed out. A man from next door pulled me off him.

After talking to everybody, Mr. Claybaugh, the principal, called me into his office. I just knew that was the end of my school. But he patted me on the back. "I'm proud of you," he said, "proud of you taking up for that little boy who couldn't defend himself." The bully was suspended.

Mama had another surprise for us. One day, right after school, she broke the news. "Tomorrow, don't come here after school," she told us. "Go to East Fourteenth Street because we're moving there." It was to another small house just blocks away.

That first summer in the new house wasn't even over when the landlord sold it lock, stock, and barrel. We moved to the Ridgedale section of town, less than a mile away. The house on Buckley Street was nicer and in a better neighborhood. It had a separate bedroom and kitchen on one side, and Mama rented it out real quick. No sooner did we get the money than it was spent.

Life was still a struggle with six kids to feed. Sally was working after school at the Kress ten-cent store. Mama even told Roger to go to work. That really hurt. Roger was a terrific pitcher and wanted to play high school baseball. We played sandlot ball, and he was throwing smoke. So, when Mama told him he couldn't be on any team, he was devastated. She got him a job after school, right when the team was playing. He was bagging groceries at the Red Food grocery store, owned by one of dad's brothers-in-law. Roger brought groceries home every night. He resented it.

Jerry and I capitalized on every opportunity for money. There was a big water-drainage ditch, about four feet deep and ten feet across, that ran along the side of our yard next to the street. About one block away was a beer joint called "Bud's." The drunks would leave Bud's, come down by our house, get down in the ditch, and sleep under the bridge. Well, they were in our ditch, so Jerry and I went down there and "collected rent" while they slept. We dried out the money in the kitchen. They finally found another place to sleep. They didn't like paying rent.

I was scrounging whatever odd jobs I could from the neighbors. It was an area full of pigeons, and I was getting five cents a bird to rid them of the nuisance around their houses. Jerry got upset with me for using his marbles and that ended that. I started mowing yards for a dime. That was enough for the movies. When I brought the money to Mama, she turned around and gave it to Jerry. The only thing I could do was go back out and find another lawn to cut. This time, I kept the dime.

Mama had her hands full with Jerry, Larry, and Alan. I was definitely more than she could handle. I did poorly in school and being behind a grade didn't help, either. I was headed for a bleak future when my life got turned around. All that wildness, all that aggression, and all that misplaced energy found an outlet—sports. Athletics were consuming practically all my free time, and I quit getting into trouble.

When I wasn't in school, the recreation center became the center of my life. At fourteen I won the city championship in horseshoes doubles. In the fall there was volleyball. I was the youngest on the team when we won the city championship. For the first time in my life I was winning. Shit, it felt good. I wanted to play on every team they had. I was growing up.

Seventh-grade football was terrific for me, too. I got a kick out of hitting the bigger boys. Contact meant nothing. The harder I hit them, the better I felt. I was gutsy and strong from all the sandlot games and all that swimming and running, and wasn't afraid of anybody. I made the first-string football team. We went undefeated and I was picked for the all-city team and the all-star game.

Right after football, Coach Summers approached me. "I want you to go to the track meet with us," he said. "I want you to enter the mile run." He knew how I ran the football and I guess he thought I had a chance.

I ran every event at the meet, and when it came time for the mile, I looked at those tall, slim ninth graders and thought, "How in hell am I going to run against them?" I was the smallest one. Coach Summers gave me very simple instructions. "Run like the dickens until you're way out in front of them," he said, "then cut back and coast in." I ran off and left them the first half mile. I had got about fifty yards in front when I slowed to a cruise, and when I crossed the finish line they were still a couple of yards behind. It was a school record. All that mountain running had paid off.

Eighth-grade football was even better. I was captain of the team. We never lost a game and scored at least thirty points every time. Our games were written up in the newspapers, and I was always mentioned for outstanding plays and made the all-city team again. Mama and the kids came to the games to cheer and then brag on me at home. Sometimes I saw Dad in the background. He never approached me, and I never let on to him that I saw him.

My success in sports didn't spill over to my classwork. I wasn't doing very well, but I didn't hate school as in years past.

Being a football star had its advantages. People noticed me, and I made friends. If I had any homework, I never did it. The girls at school started following me home and they did it. I wasn't learning anything.

Roger, on the other hand, was doing well in high school, but he never got a chance to finish. He was in the eleventh grade and in the Marine Reserve. Korea had exploded, and his whole unit was called up. They were undergoing training in California and Mama was receiving his allotment. The money couldn't have come at a better time. Lewis was out of the Navy and was thinking of getting married. With his own family to consider, he couldn't help us much.

That summer was the best one yet for me. I was approached by the football coach from Hixson High School, six miles away on the other side of town. He offered to get me tutors and advance me one grade into the tenth so I could play first string for him. He promised to pay all school fees and guarantee me free food. Since he lived past our house, he offered to drive me to and from. He discussed it with Mama, too, but it was my decision to make.

I was leaning toward Central High School. It had a more recognized athletic program, led by the legendary football coach Red Etter. They had also promised to bump me up to the tenth. And I had a lot of friends at Central—all the boys I played ball with over the years. Their football program was hurting, too. The Marine callup all but destroyed it. Most of the team were in the same unit.

I had the whole summer to make up my mind. And my mind was on baseball. The local post of the American Legion sponsored a team in the seventeen-and-under category. Red Etter was our coach. Under him we won the state championship and went on to the six-state Southeastern Regional championship games in North Carolina.

Central High School was my choice and I was excited about being part of a winning football tradition. Life was never better for me, but the good times were about to end.

Roger was scared to death to go to Korea, so he had Mama get him out on a hardship deferment. She did it reluctantly. The steady allotment money was important and it was hard to give up.

It was August 1951. I was one week into football practice and two weeks from starting classes when I came home to find Mama with a guest—a recruiter for the Air Force. Mama handed me some papers and said, "Joe, sign here. You're in the Air Force."

I shouldn't have been surprised. Lewis was out of the Navy and his allotment to Mama was gone. Roger was back and he wasn't working. Sally was out of school and working at the DuPont Company. But she had gotten engaged and needed to save for herself. So there wasn't enough money to take care of Mama and the rest of us.

I was seventeen and I guess it was now my turn to help. I signed.

AFTER A CHILDHOOD SPENT KEEPING MY GUARD UP, I WAS READY FOR ANYTHING and afraid of nothing. It was really a short road from Buckley Street to Bull Simons's guerrilla exercises.

During our team isolation, I knew we were being set up. The Bull had something up his sleeve. That was for damned sure.

Our movement began at night. We were transported to the old air and sea base on the water at Coco Solo, next to Fort Sherman. We were put into an old World War II assault boat, one of those things with the ramp that came down in front. On the boat was another SF, who briefed us on our contact with the guerrillas. Our infiltration point was a small dock just inside the mouth of the Río Chagres. We would be met there.

The boat circled out into the Caribbean and came back a little to the west of Fort Sherman. The mouth of the Chagres was right ahead of us. All I could think about was what was under the surface. Where the river met the sea was considered to be the world's most infested shark haven. In those waters was right where the world record was established for a mako shark—eighty-seven inches in girth and almost two thousand pounds.

In daylight you could see those big mothers in there. We had to be extremely careful when making our troop jumps. We didn't want a strong wind. On the other side of the isthmus near Howard AFB was the Red Devil DZ. Across the little bay we could see the sharks tooling around below—whole schools of them. In order to jump the Red Devil DZ we had to have a motorboat standing by in the bay. In fact, Gatun Lake was the same way—you had to have a boat.

Farther up the Chagres we had a cable slide for life from one bank to the other. You had to hang on to the slide until you got to a submerged shark net. The big sharks swam there, too, and if you didn't drop inside the shark net your ass was food. A couple of years before, two of our men had stripped down to their underwear and tried to swim a hundred yards across. As one made it he heard his buddy scream, and the guy was gone. We dragged and dragged but never found a trace.

We made our way into the river. The dock was barely visible up ahead just behind and below Fort San Lorenzo. Then we saw a light blinking from it. It was a prearranged signal for us to approach. We came alongside the dock. Our guerrilla contact was waiting.

"Follow me," he said in Spanish.

I recognized him as one of our Spanish SF—a master sergeant from Texas. My senses were more alert than ever. They weren't fooling me one bit.

The guerrilla led us away from the dock into the jungle and to higher ground. We came to a halt and we sat. Still speaking Spanish, the man gave us a well-rehearsed spiel about the situation. He was trying to get us to follow him to another location.

The guerrilla finished and moved away to let us talk among ourselves.

The team sergeant was not buying it, and neither was I. The captain wasn't convinced either. "Well, let's go with him to this next location," he said. "If we don't disagree with anything else he says, we'll go into the E&E."

We followed the guerrilla to a spot near a road. He stopped and told us to wait while he went a little ways to talk to another guerrilla. The team sergeant and I looked at each other. Something about the rehearsed speech—this whole thing—gave him away.

The team sergeant said to me, "Joe, I know you hunt out here all the time. Can you get us through the jungle to the Gatun drop zone?"

I just smiled. Our E&E route was supposed to be the jungle between the Chagres and the French Canal, but none of the others on the team had been there before. I knew every inch.

"I don't believe this fuckin' guy," he said. "Let's move before he gets back."

We left the area before the guerrilla returned.

The exercise was at night because they were counting on us being afraid of the jungle and not wanting to escape through it. I never did mind being in the jungle. It didn't scare me a bit. Some men got real spooked. They could feel the jungle closing in on them. I thought it was home.

The men didn't say a single word as I led them. I could tell some weren't really sure they would make it out and not get lost. There was nobody else out in the jungle, so I didn't know if they were afraid of the snakes, or animals, or just having to survive.

Well, it always seemed that if you were going to be in this part of the world, you should be out learning all you could about it. But only a handful of us ever went out. When we weren't jumping we were hunting, and eventually we learned the entire jungle in the Canal Zone. And we never got lost. That was unheard of.

I kept the team moving quickly through the third-growth jungle. If you didn't know your way around you could go a few meters into the real thick stuff and be completely lost. Then you would have to wait for the sun to come up.

We walked for several hours. There were no trails or anything. I followed the streams because I had been in there so many times. The men were still not sure they would come out of this. I could hear them muttering about snakes. That was always a major concern. In Panama, there were more snakes than you could imagine.

It was a long trip through the jungle and it was morning when we finally broke through at French Canal, which ran parallel alongside the regular canal. A truck was waiting there. That meant we were out of the E&E.

He carried us across the Panama Canal and back to the barracks at Fort Gulick.

We had just unloaded in front of the team headquarters building when a second truck pulled up with another A-team. The men were full of stories about escaping a POW camp stark naked and making it to a fire station to get some clothes. Some had gone to a housing area where dependents of JOTC instructors lived and grabbed clothes off their clotheslines. Some of the families even took them in and fed them.

"We even had them driving around looking for more POWs," the men said. "There were MPs all over trying to find us."

We didn't know what in the world they were talking about. We didn't know anything about a POW camp. Suddenly, an officer came running out of the headquarters building screaming at the men in the truck.

"You ain't supposed to talk to these men. They ain't supposed to find out about this!"

Then he turned to us. "You men get on the truck!"

We grabbed our gear and loaded up. We knew we were in big trouble. The truck took us back to Fort Sherman. When we pulled to a stop there was another truck and twenty men with guns.

"All right . . . you're prisoners. Get in there!"

They shut us in under the canvas.

That was the whole plan. The first guerrilla was supposed to set us up for an ambush, probably one that we couldn't escape from. Then we would be transported to a POW camp. What I had done was lead the men to a part of the E&E net set up to receive men who had already been through the POW camp. The man waiting there thought we had come from the camp.

I knew what to expect.

Early in 1958 I was on a team at Fort Bragg putting a bunch of young Air Force pilots through a POW camp exercise. The camp was run by a group of older NCOs with World War II and Korea experience. We were treating the pilots as if they had been shot down behind enemy lines, and the civilian resistance underground had set up an E&E net to get the pilots back to friendly lines.

We had rigged the E&E net as a trick to guarantee they would be captured. Then we took them to our POW camp. We wanted to give them a taste of what could happen to the mind in a POW camp and how easy it was to manipulate the mind. We put them through all kinds of agony. Stripping them bare was the basic technique. That alone was mental harassment. We placed them in a steel CONEX container and beat on the thing. While a man was tied so he could not move, we would throw a water-soaked rag over his nose and make him think he was going to drown. Some just broke down and bawled. And some of them were so tough we couldn't control them at all.

WE COULDN'T HAVE BEEN RIDING MORE THAN TEN MINUTES WHEN THE TRUCK stopped. The driver put it into reverse, and we slowly backed up a ways. When the truck stopped again the canvas was thrown back.

We were inside a POW camp.

The place was an old shore-to-sea artillery battery set partially underground into the mountainside. There were armed guards all over the place.

"Get the hell out of the truck!" they shouted. They must have thought we were scared to death. Well, I knew what was coming, and all of it was baloney to me. Besides, at that point in my life, being scared of those men was a joke. I already knew what being scared was. Scared was being a little kid and having your father tie you to a bed and beat the living dogshit out of you. You can't run and you can't hide. You can't beg for forgiveness because you haven't done anything wrong, and you can't fight back. Then, if that wasn't enough, you'd be shaking from fear as you watched your father beat the hell out of your brother, over and over, until his spirit was broken.

There certainly wasn't anything at the POW camp to scare me.

"All right . . . strip down!" the guards yelled.

They took our clothes. One by one we were taken to a small room. The cell door closed behind us. Then they stuck a fire hose through the bars and hit us with a high-pressure stream. Shit, it was cold sea water.

Once we were hosed down they took us through an empty room that led to a holding area, an old gun position with at least a fourteen-foot-high wall with a walkway on top, which ran three-quarters around the holding area. The one open side was full of barbed wire, with guards on the other side. The wall at the backside had a steel-bar door that made a clanging noise as if you were in a real prison. Four guards stayed with us.

As soon as they put us in there they pulled our team leader and took him away.

The Bull had built a POW camp to see if he could break us.

Rusted steel rails ran from outside into the middle of the room. They had probably brought ammunition to the old guns. The guards made us kneel with our knees against them. We stayed there for several hours. It hurt so bad. If you tried to get up the guards would swat you with a billy club.

I never lost my cool. I always had a high tolerance for pain. Jumping with a wristful of broken bones didn't faze me, and I knew there was nothing they could throw at me that could be any worse.

We still didn't know where the captain was.

Each one of us was isolated from the others and put through a series of "torture" chambers designed to inflict enough mental stress to break a man.

They put me on a rack—two small logs secured to trees about four feet off the ground and three feet apart. With my feet and hands tied, the guards lifted me up and laid me across so that my chest was against one log, with my thighs pressed against the other. It was extremely painful. That was the kind of stuff that was calculated not to cause physical damage—just mental.

They pulled me from the rack and marched me up a set of concrete steps to an upper-level interrogation room. There was one chair in the middle of the room. One interrogator stood in front of me and one behind. The one behind ordered, "Sit down!"

The man in front was dressed like a young officer. He started by trying to intimidate me with threats. Actually, I was relieved to be away from the rack. I gave my name, rank, and serial number. The interrogator kept trying to scare me. He'd scream in my face. Every once in a while the man behind me would slap me in the head. I must have been grinning at them, even though I tried not to show it. I considered myself tougher than they were, and just knew they weren't going to get anything out of me.

When they were through with me, I was shoved into a barbed-wire cage just big enough to stuff a man. You couldn't scratch your butt without the barbed wire cutting into you. But that wasn't all. The cage was set next to a fire-ant mound and the little devils were all over me. Every time I tried to get them off, the barbed wire cut into me. They left me there for a couple of hours. I was bitten and all cut up, but I was holding my own.

I was finally thrown into a great big cage with steel bars. It was about thirty yards back into the mountainside and set alongside the rails. Some of my team were already there. There were also men from another A-team. Loudspeakers were blaring a squealing noise at maximum volume. "Boy, that's one hell of a good trick," I thought to myself. It was like nothing I had ever heard before. The squeal went up and down, up and down. It would make your hair stand on end. All you could do was sit and hold your ears.

One at a time, the rest of my team was brought in. That's when we saw the captain again. But the guards were all over to keep us from talking to one another.

After about six hours of this, I began to suspect that they were going to do something to get us out—to let us "escape" back through the E&E net to complete the exercise.

That's when the commotion started. We heard screaming from a little room on the other side of the rails. We could see a man struggling and fighting with some guards. Then four guards came out dragging a POW who was kicking and shouting.

They pulled him up to our cage and threw him in. Lo and behold, if it wasn't Capt. Jim Perry.

He looked like hell, like someone that had been in there a while and had been tortured a lot. His face was all cut up and he was bleeding. Perry managed to sneak around and finally got off in a corner with the captain and team sergeant.

I knew that this had to be it. Perry was a plant to gain our confidence and show us how to "escape." The captain and team sergeant slowly worked their way to the other men to pass on the word. Perry's story was that he had picked a fight with the guards in order to steal the key to the cage. He had the key and knew when the guards changed. We would have just a few seconds to make a break for it. He added a kicker that there was even worse torture in store for us if we stayed. Perry knew just how to work on the mind. The prisoners hadn't had any food, water, or sleep in twenty-four hours. They were light-headed, disoriented, and ripe for a setup. I thought Perry was doing a magnificent job.

It was midafternoon when Perry gave us the "go." The guards had moved away and Perry got the cage door open. He led us across to the room he had been dragged out of. We found our clothes there and grabbed them on the fly. I thought this was real convenient. We followed him through the room and into the holding area, where we had come in the day before.

The guards on top of the wall started shouting and firing into the air. We jumped over a section of barbed wire that was partially down and ran bare-ass naked into the jungle. Perry stayed behind.

As soon as we got out of sight of the POW camp, we put on our clothes. To make it through the jungle, we had to cover our skin to protect against the thorns and all the other stuff.

I headed east back through jungle trails with the men following me. We got to French Canal before dark and came upon the same place we had found the day before. Sure enough, the same ol' boy was waiting with the truck.

It gave Kathy quite a shock when she saw me. I was very dirty, bleeding, and bruised all over. "You look like you've been in a bad car accident," she said.

I told her what I had been through, and her eyes got big with amazement. Then she doused my butt with iodine. That really stung. "Oh, you're not so brave," she remarked.

The next day there was another surprise waiting for us at the team building. The same truck was back.

"Load up in the truck!"

"Wait a minute," I said. "We just did this. Ain't no way I'm goin' back."

"You're going out to replace the goons. You're going to be running other teams through."

"That's good," I told him. "Now I won't have to whip your ass."

Perry had his own private room at the POW camp. The man was living like a king. Being a skydiving buddy from way back, he gave me a tour of the camp and filled me in on the whys and wherefores of the POW exercise.

Bull Simons had turned to Major Pat Milantoni, a survivor of a Korean POW camp, to make the camp as tough as possible. It was a real hush-hush deal. No one outside the Bull's staff knew what was going on. Senior officers from Intelligence (S-2) and Operations (S-3) were there along with men from the MI unit attached to Group, who did the interrogation. Other elements from the 8th provided support, all operating in total secrecy. The NCOs at the POW camp ran it. They did the physical work. One team was picked to run the camp, another was the capture team.

Since our team had successfully evaded capture and had done so well through the POW camp, we were picked to run the compound. So we were essentially doing to the next teams what was done to us. As a POW I figured that, if I was ever captured, I would use all my brains and brawn to escape. Now that I was on the other side I was definitely going to learn how to keep a man from escaping, and how to make him talk. That was the Bull's idea all along.

I asked Perry how he got to be the inside man. He leaned back in his chair and took a long drag on his cigarette. "Hell, I volunteered. No shit, I did. I took the very first team in. We came across Gatun Lake, paddling canoes with M-1 rifle butts so we could outrun a couple of steamers bearing down on us. We were going to infiltrate by the yacht club at the spillway, but we had to change our plans quick and landed near the Gatun DZ. Well, I knew what the scenario was but the men didn't. But I still went through all the shit, and when they finished interrogating me they pulled me out and said, 'We need a fink in the jail. Somebody has to tell these guys how to get out.' So I had Major Milantoni punch me out a few times—I took some good licks. Then I took a razor blade and cut up my face. Then they threw me in the cage."

Perry said that I should be glad to be the compound team. He told me that the capture team turned out to be a dangerous assignment. While my team was in isolation, the team ahead of us got into one hell of a fistfight when they found out the guerrillas had set a trap for them.

"The Bull is dead serious about this thing," Perry said. "The word is that if a man breaks he's gone."

The first team we faced was the one that had hit us with clubs. We got back at them good.

Some men were shoved into a metal cage that had about two feet of water in the bottom. It was so small that standing was impossible. The man had to remain in a crouch. You didn't dare sit down because you had no clothes on, and you didn't know what was in the water. The thing had a big steel door and every once in a while one of us goons would come by and beat on the door with a sledgehammer.

Then it got worse. There was another cage, a real steel box with diesel oil in the bottom. We dumped green horse manure in there and made him sit in it. We took a sledgehammer to it, too.

We put a guy in a dumpster and shoved a loudspeaker right against the thing full volume, blaring, "Lollipop, lollipop . . . oh, lolli, lolli . . ." all day long. The guy came out almost a vegetable.

We would also leave a man alone in a small enclosure with a boa constrictor. We also had guys strapped with chains out in the open—all the time naked. The key was isolation—twenty-four hours of containment with most of the time spent naked and alone.

We had this one master sergeant, Al Solis, from 8th Group S-3. It was Major Milantoni's idea to dress him up as a woman and parade him in front of a naked POW during interrogation. He got some of the wives at Gulick to dress him up, and they even taught him how to walk in high heels. They doused him in perfume and sent him on. When he showed up Perry and I did a double take. Solis looked beautiful. He was from Guam and had a baby face—real smooth light-brown skin with no wrinkles.

One of our prisoners was a young officer—a West Pointer. You could tell he was embarrassed over being naked. MI noticed all of this. They took him in front of Milantoni, who was dressed as a Gestapo officer. Milantoni walked back and forth in front of him with his jackboots clacking on the stone floor. Every now and then the major snapped him with a bullwhip. But the guy didn't break.

Then they got Al Solis. They took hold of the lieutenant and straightened him up. So there he was, exposed for all the world to see, and they marched Al in. The guy didn't see him at first because he had his back to the door. Al started to talk in a woman's voice and the poor dupe almost died. Al walked around him making a lot of "kissing" noises.

"Oh . . . he looks so sweet, I could eat him."

The lieutenant strained to get loose and began screaming all this stuff about the Geneva Conventions. It was going to be a good lesson for the lieutenant. The Geneva Conventions didn't mean diddly-squat in war.

With one team we made police-style ID photographs of each man. After we let them escape late at night, we posted the pictures all over the neighboring civilian area and offered a reward. One sign read: "500 balboas for this man, a known Communist and Cuban sympathizer." We had farmers out looking for them with shotguns. Six men from that team did real well: they evaded us for four days.

No team was treated exactly the same, but we tried hard to break every one of them. We never inflicted physical harm even though they felt it was physical harm.

There was only one man who was reported to have broken under the strain. He had been put in one of the concrete storage rooms and locked behind a solid steel door. It was downright tiny, three by four by six feet, with six inches of putrid, smelly water on the floor. After ten minutes, there wasn't a sound from inside. We quickly opened the door, and there he was, passed out. The doctor was summoned, and he determined the guy had hyperventilated from fright. The doctor put a sack over the man's head to revive him. When he came to, he was scared to death and pleaded, "Just don't put me in there again!" The man wasn't SF, but rather from one of the support units. It was a pitiful sight.

The POW camp did its job real well because Bull Simons had gathered volumes of notes on POW camps, interrogation, escape and evasion. Then he let his NCOs run the show.

He knew all his men by their first names. But the relationship was strictly business—no small-talk sessions. Simons was a very physically active man and always stayed in shape. He also saw to it that the men had facilities to keep in shape, too. He loved handball and had a handball court built. And that's how I came to spend time with The Bull.

Dick Meadows showed me how to play handball in return for showing him free-fall techniques. Dick and I practiced until we got good enough to challenge Simons and his handball partner, Lt. Col. Duncan Naylor, the 8th Group chaplain. After a few games, they started sending challenges to us. We never played just one game, we always played at least two hours in all that heat and humidity.

We were playing Bull one time and he was a real Bull just like his name. He would hit the ball and stand in front of it so you didn't have a fair shot. He did that just one time with me. I hit him in the back of the head so hard he saw stars for five minutes.

"That was a damn good shot," he finally said.

The greatest lesson I learned from Bull Simons was "Don't get captured—alive!"

chapter 11

Stay Ready

SF didn't go to places like Laos and Panama without the kind of preparation that allowed us to run missions the very second our feet touched foreign soil. SF had to be trained and fit for reassignment anywhere in the world, and orders could come quicker than a blink. Even before White Star, we had already spent many months practicing the counterinsurgency and direct-action skills we would need wherever the President sent us.

On each exercise we were told that, no matter where we were sent, we were to use whatever means necessary to accomplish the mission. We took that very literally, and if you were an SF worth a damn, your operations would be described very simply: "If you ain't cheatin' you ain't tryin'."

We were good at it, too.

The Pisgah National Forest of western Tennessee was a big training area for us. We jumped into its rugged terrain a lot and set up month-long exercises in guerrilla tactics and survival.

It was the fall of 1958, and it was cold. I had drawn a team that was going to instruct younger SF. My CO was Capt. Jake Clements, a feisty nononsense type of SF, who I respected. Master Sergeant Burgess, another old SF, was our team sergeant. He, Clements, and Sfc. Sparks set up the survival phase of a two-week round-robin course that rotated the students through several training sites. I was the lowest-ranking NCO on the team and was doing the grunt work, setting up animal snares and traps, all the while happy to be learning from the best.

The last two weeks of the exercise was guerrilla-warfare training. Each team was assigned an AO, and after we kicked them out of the truck they had to set up a radio link for receiving missions. Then they would go cross-country, chased by "aggressors" who were always one of the other teams. The aggressors operated in a team's AO for harassment and to keep them from reaching the target. All they had to do was wait for stupid mistakes.

Our team participated in the guerrilla exercises, too. We were always in training, keeping sharp, so we had aggressors on our tails as well. But the aggressors weren't the only ones looking for us in the woods. The hills were full of mountain men—good ol' boys who were running "businesses" hidden far from the rest of civilization.

Moonshine was all over the North Carolina mountains. The bootleggers always knew when we were in the woods—their woods. We always ran into them because they made it a point to visit. They took a liking to us—the way we operated in civilian clothes and all. When SF had started using the area, the moonshiners had been enlisted to play our "games" with us. They liked it, and sometimes made up our intelligence and escape-and-evasion networks.

But there were some hard and fast ground rules. You didn't dare get near one of the stills. That was a real big no-no. If you wanted some 'shine, all you had to do was ask, and they were happy to bring you quarts of it.

We were on a recon patrol up a mountain when we came to a small dirt road. There sat two good ol' boys on the fender of an old car. One gent had a shotgun across his lap, and as we approached, he slowly moved the barrel in our direction. We understood the signal perfectly.

I recognized the old man from another meeting. He seemed to recognize me, too. He smiled, but that didn't mean a thing.

"Hi, boys . . . where you goin'?" he asked.

"Oh . . . we're tryin' to get over to the other side and run into an old logging road." It was the best route for us.

"I wish you wouldn't stay on this road. I don't think that's a good idea." He pointed out another route. "You probably could go down . . . there, and go around . . . there, and get . . . there."

We knew right away that he was the lookout for the still. Ain't no two ways about it. When he asked us our business, we were real open about it. He liked that. That probably saved our asses.

After we made camp, all Captain Clements and Master Sergeant Burgess talked about was getting into some moonshine. They loved the stuff. Sure enough, a couple of the local mountain boys came out of nowhere and sat down. All they wanted to do was shoot the bull with us. Just to be friendly they brought a "present."

It was definitely the good stuff. It was pink and real smooth. It had been aged. One moonshiner put his booze in redwood barrels and buried them for six months. He brewed the stuff on special order for customers in Asheville and Atlanta and only for them. The liquor was delivered in time for Christmas and New Year's celebrations. After his sales he would buy a new car for running the moonshine, and he had enough money left over to last the whole year. He was in his forties and, like most of the others, had very little contact with people outside his business. He didn't have a birth certificate, and, as far as the government was concerned, he didn't exist on paper. He wanted to keep it that way.

One quart of the pink stuff got us all so drunk we were lucky the aggressors didn't find the camp. Jake thought he could handle it, but after four shots he was off his feet, and I could hardly walk. It was so smooth when you drank it, but in a few minutes you were pretty screwed up.

We still managed to be on our way at first light. The cold mountain air was good for the head. By the end of the day we had moved to the top of a hill and made camp in some real thick brush, mostly mountain laurel. At daybreak, we determined it didn't provide enough concealment, and we needed to find a secure place to set up a base of operations for whatever missions we would be given.

We could see there was only one paved road. It zigzagged around the mountains from one little town to another. It would be advantageous to be hidden near the road. Down in the valley was a big farm. There was a barn on the backside and it looked like a good place to set up. We waited until just before dark and snuck down. From the barn we had a good view all around and could see any aggressors a long way off. In the morning, Clements planned to ask the farmer if we could stay.

The whole attic was full of apples. Some of us slept below, others climbed up there and pushed the apples aside to make room for their sleeping bags. A family of owls kept us company.

It was an old man and his wife, just the two of them in their seventies. They thought it was quite thrilling. In fact, they invited some of us to stay in the house, but the captain wanted us together in the barn.

The farm was a perfect cover. We ran our missions at night and helped the old couple farm their land in the daytime, careful not to expose more than two men at a time. The highway was just down a little way from his dirt driveway. A lot of times the aggressors flew over us, but we just stayed inside. Our missions were to disrupt aggressor communications and interdict convoys, and the enemy never knew where we came from. The old man even made his truck available to us. We would put on our civilian clothes and go into town. We just fit right in with the locals. That was the whole idea.

Even though we had supplemented our C-rations with food runs to the town's general store, the exercise called for a night resupply drop. We set up the DZ and the bundles came down. When we got the order to move out we had fourteen cases of C-rations too many. The nice old couple didn't have much of an income, and we knew they were poor. When I asked if they would like the C-rations they were delighted.

We returned to Fort Bragg, and started preparing for Laos. That's when Master Sergeant Denton said, "Garner, you're going to the NCO Academy."

THREE MONTHS OUT OF THE ACADEMY, I WAS RUNNING TRAINING EXERCISES IN the north Georgia mountains near Dahlonega and running the boots off Army Rangers. By late summer I had returned from Panama with my "Jungle Expert" certificate and was on a month-long exercise inside the Pisgah National Forest—in the hills west of Morganton, North Carolina. This time there was a twist. After two weeks of round-robin training, two weeks would be spent marching 180 miles up the old Appalachian Trail, running missions along the route.

It was a big exercise involving a whole C-team. We had eight SF A-teams and two Marine SEAL teams to put through stiff courses in intelligence, communication, navigation, mountain climbing, rappelling, medic practice, and survival. Survival was my portion.

We had something new for the men. The Army wanted us to test some new rations. The food was dehydrated and was made to conserve weight on long patrols, where resupply would be difficult. There was one big problem.

We quickly found out that you needed an awful lot of water. At the camp that was easy. We just walked down to the stream and got a canteenful of cold mountain water. The food also tasted better if it was cooked in hot water for ten minutes. Hell, we had a big campfire and plenty of time to heat the rations.

On a long-range patrol, there wouldn't be such an easy supply of water or the time to heat the rations. Besides, in enemy territory, we couldn't even have a fire. The rations needed to be tested under the conditions for which they were intended, and to see how long we could go before requesting water resupply. But we weren't supposed to take the rations out on the Appalachian Trail itself, so the test was for the dogs.

And we told the Army just that.

I was winding up the survival phase when the woods finally got me. I knew there was a big ol' bass in this stream, so I was going to catch it and show the men how to cook it. I went into a bush to catch a grasshopper for bait, but instead I felt the sting of a snake. A copperhead had struck! He bit me on the finger, and I jerked back so hard it broke his teeth off in my finger. I pulled the teeth, sucked out the poison with my mouth, then put my belt around my wrist and cinched it tight. I grabbed a stick and killed him, then took my knife and cut off his head.

I carried it to the C-team medical tent and pushed it right in the face of the NCO medic.

"Hey, doc, do you see this? This little son-of-a-bitch bit me."

It startled him good. "We're taking you to the hospital in Morganton for an antivenom shot."

At the hospital the doctor told the medic, "I don't think he's got any poison in him. But if you insist, we'll give him the shot."

On top of the antivenom shot the doctor gave me a tetanus shot. "You gotta stay here overnight," he said.

I flat refused and went back to the camp.

That night I started getting little welts all over my body. I was having a real bad reaction to the damned antivenom shot. I ran back to the medic mad as all hell. "You idiot," I called him. "You had the doctor give me that shot and now look at me."

So back to Morganton we went. The people in the emergency room just shook their heads. "Yeah, you've had a reaction to the venom in the shot, all right." I spent the night in the hospital.

The next morning I was perfect and ready for the trail march. The medic didn't want me to go. "Hell, if my team's going, I'm going," I said. So big, burly Captain Garber had to step in.

"If Joe wants to go, Joe's going."

We figured the trek would take about ten days, so rations were a big deal. "We can resupply you," we were told, "but not before six days."

"Now how in the world are we going to carry that many C-rations?" we asked. We decided to carry enough for two meals a day. To lighten the load further we took just the meat, fruit, and powdered soup, and left the rest.

A West Point captain was leading one of the teams. The guy was showing his ignorance. He had a bright idea about taking even less food. He announced, "If a dog can live on dry dog food, so can a human being."

And that's all he packed.

The captain wasn't the only officer with crazy ideas. One of the Marine SEAL team leaders thought a 180-mile hike would be easier in tennis shoes.

"Educated idiots," we all thought.

Each team departed, four hours apart. Our turn came at 1000 hours the second day. The trail wasn't marked too well, so we had to keep a map handy.

Our second day out, we came to a gully to cross. Our mountain rucksacks had a little loop in front, and you could either tie a line through to hold it against you when you jumped, or you could hook your thumbs in to hold it. But for some reason I didn't bother to grab it at all, and when I hit the other side of the ditch the rucksack slammed into my kidneys. My urine ran red, and the pain was so bad I couldn't bend over for two days. My team had to pick me up and lay me down. At night they heated big rocks and placed them on my kidney area. In the morning, they picked me up. Once I was in an upright position, I could do as well as any of them. By the third day I was as good as new and a lot wiser.

Our resupply by air got fouled up, and we were told to meet a couple of trucks on a blacktop road where the trail crossed. It was at about the halfway point in the march. We found the trucks in the parking lot of a beer joint and restaurant. The resupply had to wait. We took over the place, gobbling up hamburgers and beer. Big Tom Bottom and some of the other men carried away a bunch of six-packs. They decided to carry beer instead of water the rest of the way. They were more worried about not finding beer along the trail than not finding water.

About twenty miles into Virginia we came upon a little town that was way down in a valley, just like a picture in a magazine. We said to the captain, "Hell, it's not too far off the trail. Let's go down and have a decent meal." We were so tired of those lousy C-rations. Tom Bottom liked the idea. He was running out of beer. "Okay," said Garber. "We can come back up onto the trail tomorrow and continue the march."

When we got to the town there was nothing but women. They watched us from behind the windows. Some even shut their doors when they saw us. Then, this real old man came up to us. "Where are all the men?" we asked.

"They all work up in Roanoke," he said. "There's no work of any kind here. They come back on the weekends and go out again."

Now we knew why the women were hiding. Here we were just walking out of the mountains, a whole damned team of men. And the only thing between us and them is this one old man.

"Are you it?" we wanted to know.

"Yep. The men put me to take care of the women."

"How old are you?"

"All of ninety."

One way or another, I guess, he was "taking care" of them. We kidded around with him about sex and about his claim to be ninety. We didn't necessarily believe him but we went along with it. He gave us an empty building at one end of the town to stay in overnight. Nobody got out of line, and nobody propositioned any of the women.

The next morning he wanted to walk up the mountain with us. I'm talking about a mile climb, full of ridges. "I'm going up on top for some wood," he said.

"You're going all the way to the top of the mountain for a load of wood?"

"Yep. I'm going up there and carry it down." He got this big smile. "I do it every day."

Now that took some doing. If you've ever carried an armful of wood, it's the most uncomfortable thing in the world. And, on top of that, walking a mile up then a mile down.

He started walking along with us.

Every A-team carried a forty-pound hand-cranked generator to power the AN/GRC-9 radios. Each man was already carrying fifty pounds of gear, and you couldn't also carry that heavy an object and still be comfortable. On other training exercises we usually swapped the load around as we moved. This time the team had a young Hungarian SF who was built like a wrestler. He had a big, muscular neck and volunteered to be our "G-man." He hung the strap of the generator around his neck and dangled the bulky thing in front.

The old man saw the loads we were all lugging and the generator in particular.

"Let me carry that for you," he said.

We just looked at the little guy. He was dead serious. So the Hungarian handed him the generator. That was a mistake. The old coot walked off and left us behind. He disappeared up the side and we thought we had lost our generator. When we got to the top of the mountain, there he was, just waiting for us.

"You boys are kinda winded, ain't you?"

We thought about that all night. We had to accept the story about his daily mile climb for a load of wood, he was so strong. But it was still hard to believe his age. We reached another conclusion. Maybe it was taking care of all those women that had him looking ninety.

When we finished the exercise it was the morning of the ninth day, a good twenty-four hours early. None of the other teams had showed. We had passed the teams that left before we did. The only one we actually saw along the trail was nursing their feet as we passed. According to them, they were "temporarily dislocated." They had to double back and pick up the trail again. In other words, they got lost.

We were the best navigators, staying on the Appalachian trail even when there were miles and miles without markings whatsoever. We found signs that the others didn't. There were a few places used by Indians to go north and south. You could see imprints where they used horses. The locals told us all about these trails, and we knew to trust the Indians.

We had a high old time greeting all the other teams as they dragged themselves in. Two men were missing—the dog-food captain and the Marine SEAL team commander with tennis shoes.

On his fifth day things had gotten grim for the dog-food captain. He came around the campfire asking if anyone could spare any soup rations. The men started baying at him like hounds. The following day he had to be taken out for medical and "other reasons." The poor fool was so sick.

The Marine SEAL team leader was the next casualty. He had made it a little over a hundred miles in those tennis shoes, but his feet were completely torn up. He was a tough guy, but he couldn't walk any farther. They took him out, too.

"Just no common sense," we said.

FORT BRAGG WAS GETTING A LOT OF FEEDBACK ON THEIR PROBLEMS FROM OUR White Star teams in Laos. Even with the training from the JOTC in Panama, there was still a lot to learn about jungle operations. Some of the best jungle fighters were the British, so the U.S. and Great Britain worked out an exchange program between SF and their British counterpart, the SAS—the Special Air Service.

The 7th Group had sent two of our best SF, Captain Elliott Sydnor and my old friend M. Sgt. Richard Meadows, to the 22nd SAS Regiment in Herefordshire. The regiment sent us a captain and a sergeant major who had just come out of four years fighting Communist insurgents in Malaya. They were in the squadron that tracked down and captured the terrorist Ah Hoi in the steamy Telok Anson Swamp on Malaya's western coast. These men were just plain tough.

The Group S-3 and the SAS set up a training program for jungle tactics. The British soldiers were experts in tracking, and we were all ears as they gave us the details of how they tracked the CT—that's what they called the Communist terrorists—how they located their overnight camps and contained them.

Their real trick was how they kept the enemy from tracking *them*. In a heavy-underbrush area of Fort Bragg, the SAS taught us how to fade into the jungle—moving quietly into the thickest and thorniest area, then closing it off by pulling back in all those bushes and branches we moved, covering up anything we disturbed on the jungle floor, and placing a security watch for our overnight stay. You had to remember that the enemy was more familiar with the jungle than you were, so as you traveled you had to be careful not to break off any foliage or disturb the wet jungle floor.

After a week of class it was time for the real test—a ten-day mission in the Green Swamp training area—thirty square miles of ooze on the North Carolina–South Carolina border. This was always my favorite part of training—the jungle didn't scare me a bit.

Each team moved into the area with a specific direction of travel, but not a given distance. We had to remain in the swamp and evade detection and capture. M. Sgt. Earl McIntosh, our team leader, knew I was a good navigator and put me at the point. The compass man was right behind me and Earl took the third position as we moved out.

Earl brought a machete and almost right away I heard the blade whoosh through the air and slice into something. I looked over my shoulder and saw he had cut through a snake. It was a cottonmouth—a real mean sucker. Earl moved up behind me and motioned for me to keep going. I took a few more steps and . . . WHOOSH! THUMP! Earl had another one. The damned things were hiding under the mounds of grass sticking out of the water, and when I stepped on a mound it roused them.

As we moved on I made it a point to step aside every time I hit a mound of grass so Earl would have an easier time of it. Earl was a real expert at this. Every stroke was executed in such a way that it blended in with all the swamp sounds. The thickness of the jungle also worked to our advantage. That's how it went the whole day, WHOOSH . . . THUMP! I'd turn around to see a snake's head go flying. At one little water hole, Earl killed four. He saved my butt a bunch of times.

The aggressor force was under the direction of the two SAS, so we knew we had to be real sharp to evade them. Our plan was to go as deep into the swamps as possible that first day, so it would take the aggressors the majority of the next day to find us. That would give us more time to look around and change our route for additional evasive action. That was a page right out of their book.

We managed to go right through to the other side—five miles through the jungle, zigzagging all the way. We stopped a little ways from our first target, a small bridge. It was getting dark and we used the cover of night to recon the target. We walked along the edge of the old narrow asphalt road and stepped right onto the bridge. The aggressors weren't around. They hadn't expected us to cover so much ground the first day. We determined the best places for our "charges" and planned on blowing the target the next night. WHOOSH! THUMP! Earl was at work again.

Not too far from the bridge we found a good place to RON—remain overnight. We straightened up the foliage around us to cover our tracks, providing a blind spot so that, if anyone was tracking us, they would go right by. We built our little hooches like the SAS showed us, taking vegetation and a short length of parachute cord and tying it together like a fortress. We made off-ground beds, using small limbs tied with cord. All of us carried nylon parachute cord. One string alone had a tensile strength of five hundred pounds. All it took was one loop around each tree and a simple knot. Once the bed was secured, we added a layer of branches and threw on a poncho. Then we blew up our air mattresses, and we were ready for the night.

Besides targets, we were given a secondary mission—more damned new-fangled rations to try. The Army had been working to improve the dried trash they gave us in the mountains. We were told the new stuff was being prepared for our men going into space and that we were the first to give it a real test.

It was still based on the old dehydrated rations, but this time we didn't need to soak any of it in water. Most of it was actual food compressed into what looked like a candy bar, but a lot harder. You needed a good set of teeth to chew the stuff. There was no meat. The scientists were still working on that one.

We were forced to rely on these rations; that was all we were going to have for our ten days in the swamp, and according to the briefing, we couldn't get out of the swamps because they had the roads patrolled.

The next day we watched the bridge for signs of the enemy. Nothing. They were probably still trying to find us back in the swamp. Late in the afternoon, we moved toward the bridge. That's when we heard a vehicle approach. We hid down below the bridge as an old beat-up pickup rattled out of the woods. It stopped halfway on the bridge, and an old man got out. He walked to the carcass of the snake Earl had killed the night before. It was a big sucker.

We watched the old man. He was poking at the snake with a stick. We climbed onto the bridge and walked up to him. "What are you doin' there?" Earl asked.

"Who in the hell killed my snake?" He was very upset.

"Your snake?" Earl shot back.

"Yes . . . my snake. All the snakes in here are mine."

The old man told us that every February he went into the swamp and captured all the poisonous snakes he could. Then he took them north to sell to a laboratory that used the venom for snake bite shots and other stuff. That was how he made all his money for the year.

"I hate to tell you this," I said, "but it looks like you're going to be out of business this year."

He knew we messed up his living. I could see it in his face.

"We've got ninety people back in there training. I know they're going to kill a bunch. We've already killed twenty-one."

Boy, was that old farmer angry. We told him it would be dangerous if he stayed around. He drove away calling us all sorts of names.

We placed the charges and simulated blowing the target. We radioed a quick after-action report and surprised the hell out of everybody.

After the second day of eating those terrible-tasting rations we decided enough was enough. There were farms running up to the edge of the swamp, and we took a chance that we could find something else to eat. We moved within a short crawling distance of one big farm and, lo and behold, there was a cornfield that came up to the edge of the jungle. And it looked like awful good corn. We snuck in and gathered a load.

Stuck inside our rucksack were some of our most important items of survival—a new roll of aluminum foil, a bottle of hot sauce, and a block of C-4 plastic explosive—items we never did without in case we found some fish. The people monitoring the rations experiment never knew we had the stuff.

Drop your C-ration can in a canteen cup of water. Cut off a slim piece of C-4, like a slice of cheese. Put it between a couple of rocks, light it with a match, and set the canteen cup on the rocks. By the time that thin piece burned up, your rations were nice and hot.

The C-4 wasn't a potent explosive until it was zapped by a special fuse or blasting cap, creating a specific amount of compression. It was pretty harmless otherwise, and would just burn with a blue flame. It gave off a smelly odor that could be a beacon in a real combat situation, but on a training exercise we were willing to chance giving away our position for a hot meal.

We rolled the corn in the foil and stuck it inside the hot ashes of C-4. The steamed fresh corn was so good we ate it for the rest of the exercise. Our only problem would be explaining our gain in weight.

It was a busy ten days. We ranged all over the swamp, monitoring roads and enemy activities. We did the job and they never detected us in advance or tracked us going away. We used every trick the SAS showed us about doubling back on our own trails and tracking enemy trails to their own camp. Even the SAS men, who were out looking every day, never spotted us. At the end of the exercise, they asked, "Where were you?"

We just set our minds to thinking it was a real mission in enemy territory and did everything possible for survival. If you didn't do that, there was no way you were going to live through the real thing, and with more teams headed for Laos, you couldn't play games.

It wasn't long before we had a brutal reminder of just that. Late in the summer of 1961, Special Forces lost its first three men in Southeast Asia. These brave soldiers were captured by the Communist Pathet Lao and never made it back.

chapter 12

In Country

In February 1966 we landed in Nha Trang. We were an entirely new B-organization, beefed up with extra communications personnel for what we knew would be around-the-clock radio operations.

I felt lucky to be on the team. Just six months earlier, back from Panama, they put me in the 3rd SF Group and I trained for missions in Africa. I didn't cotton to going to that part of the world. The jungles of Vietnam were more my style.

So, right out of the E-7 promotion board, I asked for Vietnam. A lot of us back from Panama did the same. For those three years we felt we had been left out of the Vietnam War. In November 1965 I was given a commo slot on a B-team just going into premission training.

The men came from all over, brought together from scratch. For four months we ate, slept, and lived Vietnam. We buried ourselves in the history of the conflict: how the French got their butts whipped, and how much new stuff was going on between the Americans, the South Vietnamese, and all the other people running all over the countryside.

We spent two, sometimes four, hours a day attached to earphones in the language lab. I had tried learning Laotian before and I didn't think it would work any better this time. Imagine Vietnamese as spoken by a poor country boy from Tennessee.

I took advantage of our stay overnight in Nha Trang to visit everyone I knew, especially the senior NCOs. These men knew all about what was going on. Over a few beers at the NCO Club, it was possible to get the kind of "intelligence" that would make life easier and a whole lot safer.

The upshot of all the talk that night was that, at least in Vietnam, the role of SF had changed. When I came into SF, we were advisors to the locals in guerrilla operations. The whole idea was for us to win the confidence of the people in the villages and show them how to subvert the forces that had taken over their country.

But the word had changed. SF was now involved in "direct action," something that was costing us a lot of SF who had spent many years in guerrilla warfare. The 5th Special Forces Group was running a whole bunch of small special-action units that were inviting enemy contact on purpose. The A-teams that were the original backbone of SF were being sent to clear and secure known enemy areas, then, along with ARVN special forces known as LLDB, to recruit hundreds of local tribesmen to do the dirty work.

The next morning when we landed at C-team headquarters in Pleiku, I had a surprise coming. Fred Davis, the team sergeant major, approached me with the C-team's commo officer. "You've got too much rank in your commo section," said the lieutenant, "and you've got one more commo man than any other B-team.

"We're losing our area communications supervisor in Ban Me Thuot," he said. "Navarro's heading home in two weeks. Would you mind taking over as B-23's communications supervisor?"

I "volunteered."

Right after breakfast the next morning, I was on a chopper to Ban Me Thuot, about a hundred miles south. Our C-team covered the Central Highlands with three B-teams, each with a minimum of four A-teams. Each A-team had at least four companies of indigenous hill tribesmen (CIDG), with a total of five hundred or more men in each camp.

As we approached Ban Me Thuot, I had regrets that I wouldn't have a chance to apply all my jungle training in an A-team of my own.

There were about fifty bamboo-and-thatch hooches lined up along either side of the road from the airport. Cattle and water buffalo were tied up out in the grass behind the huts. Most of the hooches belonged to lowland Montagnards, cousins to the mountain tribesmen running with our A-teams.

The roads in Ban Me Thuot were hard-surfaced, probably paved by the French years ago. There was a lot of activity. It was a crossing for Highway 21 from the coast and swinging south, and Highway 14 from the Cambodian border swinging north.

The B-team was right in the town, surrounded by hooches. It was a very small compound, no more than one hundred feet on a side, secured by a wall of sandbags all around. If you knocked down the sandbags, you'd be in the hooches. Coming off the street, all personnel went through the HQ building to enter the compound. The one gate opened only for deliveries.

Sgt. Maj. Tom Panchism greeted me with a slap on the back. "Have a cup of coffee, Joe," he said. "You're about to get busier than shit."

The HQ was small with offices for Panchism, Lt. Col. Robert Gillette, the commander, and his staff. We walked out the back and into the compound. The radio shack was a little elongated, one-story building. It was split, with a bamboo partition separating the teletypes from the radio gear. The radio operators had quarters right in the building—three men assigned by the signal unit supporting us from Nha Trang. The men worked in eight-hour shifts, handling commo from five A-camps: A-232 Tan Rai, 75 miles south; A-233 Ban Don, on a plateau 22 miles to the northwest; A-234 An Lac, 35 miles south, just below Lac Thien; A-236 Lac Thien, 20 miles southeast on Highway 21; and A-237 Luong Son, 125 miles southeast near the coast off Highway 1.

Sfc. Bobby Navarro ran a good network. There were several different antenna towers oriented toward all the different A-sites in our area of responsibility. Along with an auxiliary thousand watts of power, we could wrap an AM signal well around the horizon in any direction.

The radio room was starting to hum. It was full of the latest high-powered Collins gear. We were handling CW and voice. The bulk of the transmissions from the A-camps was CW using one-time crypto pads. There was a pad for encryption and a pad for decryption.

CW decryption can be cumbersome, so I got the Signal Company in Nha Trang to give me another man. That way I had a man to receive and another to decrypt, so an answer wouldn't be delayed.

Each radio man had a distinctive way of sending his dots and dashes. It got so we could tell who was transmitting by this "fingerprint." There was a downside to this, though. The enemy, who monitored all our transmissions, could also tell who was transmitting. Not necessarily the man, but they could connect the fingerprint with a particular A-team or recon patrol. That way, they knew who was where.

Our teletype scrambled and unscrambled messages to and from Pleiku. Once you turned an alphabet knob that encrypted each letter, the KY-38 Coded Burst Device automatically transmitted the whole message in a high-pitched "burp." It was a highly classified device, and the radio operator had to be careful to identify himself with his secret code so that the man at the other end could verify that the unit was still in friendly hands.

The three units we had were similar to ones Saigon used to transmit to the Department of Defense in Washington. Even the White House had one.

Panchism was right. I got busier than hell. The A-teams were seeing a lot of action and I had to keep them on the air. That meant keeping their AM and FM radios in working order and supplying them with one-time pads. The pads came from Nha Trang via armed courier, and I signed on the dotted line for them. My butt was now on the line. The pads and radio parts had to get to the camps even when they were under attack. Since my radio men always had their hands full, I was the delivery boy.

The A-camps were usually built on a rise. Some were constructed on the sites of old French artillery bases. Once an area was secured our combat engineers went to work. Some of the camps looked like "stars" from the air. Some looked like huge snowflakes with the points designed for overlapping fire. A dozen or so small corrugated steel-roofed buildings were spread out inside the compound. The Montagnard companies had long hooches set on stilts. Within easy reach of all positions was a system of bunkers and other fixed defenses. The perimeter was usually a fence of concertina wire. Some camps also had an outer perimeter of barrels of homemade napalm that could be blown to repel an enemy assault.

A Montagnard village was usually at the outskirts. Some thirty to forty hooches on stilts formed a loose semicircle around a slash-and-burn area. That's where they farmed. They were really nomads, moving to new areas every several years. Buildings were flimsily put together with bamboo and straw. In the center of the semicircle was a big, long building that was the home of the village chief and the center of tribal activity. Animals roamed nearby under the watchful eye of a handful of the villagers. They had a few weapons—mostly bows and arrows—probably for monkeys. What guns they had were usually antiques, crude as hell, like our old black-powder rifles.

Things didn't always go well between the Americans and their companies of Montagnards. There was a lot of bad blood between the Montagnard tribesmen and the ethnic Vietnamese in the camp. The Yards hated them from way back, and the hatred began to fester with American SF in the middle. Vietnamese LLDB were usually commanding the companies of largely Montagnards. That didn't sit well. But the Yards were very loyal to the Americans. They probably saw us as the only friends they ever had.

The pot boiled over in 1964 with a major Montagnard uprising against the Vietnamese, FULRO. It was a bunch of fancy French words that stood for a movement to separate and liberate the Yards from Vietnamese "oppression."

The Montagnards had hoped the Americans would side with them, but we were dancing around some very hairy politics and butted out. In the process, we had to close many A-camps where the Montagnards were hostile to us, too.

Buon Brieng was the first problem A-camp for the headquarters B-23. It was forty miles north of Ban Me Thuot on Highway 14 and was taken over in July 1965 by Rhade forces, who were running with the Montagnards. Our SF were imprisoned along with the Vietnamese. The Rhade withdrew several days later with almost two hundred CIDG who rallied to their side.

The 5th Group shut down Buon Brieng early that September. Other closings followed. This was really screwing up the mission of the A-camps, so the U.S. started working to get the Vietnamese government to recognize Montagnard grievances. We started building back the camps, but for the SF it was like walking on eggs.

Then A-233 at Ban Don killed a village elephant and had a whole Montagnard rebellion on their hands. The village was a hub of commerce, and the economy relied heavily on pack elephants running goods all over. There was a big possibility the villagers were Viet Cong sympathizers. Montagnards had not been on the side of the VC until their tribes rose up against the South Vietnamese government. That made many allies of the enemy.

Our pilots had reported that the villagers were transporting military equipment and that there were NVA with them. Gunships went in to shoot up the place. An elephant belonging to the village was killed and that was all they needed to start a firefight with a Vietnamese company from A-233 who went into the village area on patrol. The little suckers were mad.

Once the company was engaged, the camp couldn't send reinforcements and still maintain camp security. Only ten or twelve U.S. manned an A-camp and two were already involved in the engagement. Others were out on patrol, too.

Lieutenant Colonel Gillette ordered a company from each of two other A-teams to go in as a reaction force and help settle the dispute. He put his S-3 captain in command, and I volunteered as radio operator, something I much preferred to running the commo section. We rounded up the companies and headed for Ban Don. Our choppers landed on a small airstrip near the camp, and we moved out through the jungle toward the village and the besieged unit. There had already been a considerable amount of VC activity in that area, so we were on alert all the way.

We linked up and faced the Montagnard village ready to attack. I thought we were going to have to fight them for sure. They were certainly ready to fight. Then they stood down. I guess the village chief got them to cool off. The captain asked me to take out a patrol to find the elephant, examine the area that got shot up, and verify what actually happened.

It was a good half day from the village when we came upon the poor dumb animal. He was a young one, about ten. They're not fully grown until forty. There were chain marks on his hide, so he had been carrying a load. It could have been for the NVA but there were not enough signs to point to the enemy coming through the area in force. No large trail. It was a hill tribe's old slash-and-burn area with chest-high grass that stretched a couple of hundred yards. It was real pretty, almost manicured. I thought it might be grazing land for the elephants.

The area was reported to be infested with NVA, and the chopper crew was probably shooting at anything they saw. Stuff like that happened every day. People in the rice fields, farming, would be shot from helicopters. Maybe the villagers were involved with the NVA. It's possible they were playing both sides, and that was my conclusion. But the hill people were just doing what they could to survive in the middle of a war. The SF were trying their absolute best to be the good guys in their eyes, so the helicopter should have been more careful about its targets. Destroying the village elephant just ruined our relations with the locals.

My patrol cut off the three-foot tusks and wanted me to have them. We were back at the village about dusk to see about our other task—soothing some ruffled feathers. It was a crying shame to have the Yards angry at us. I liked them a heck of a lot better than the Vietnamese. They were easy to get along with and work with. With the Vietnamese, you spent most of the time pushing them to save their own butts.

Tensions eased by the time we finished our powwow with the village chief and elders. For them, it was time to celebrate. I had offered them the tusks, but they wanted me to keep them. Then they gave all the SF little metal bracelets and passed their rice wine. It was potent as the devil and tasted like hell, but I had to go along with the ceremony. The last thing I wanted to do was insult them. I was dizzy all the way back to Ban Don.

When I returned to Ban Me Thuot, the S-3 told me to give him the tusks. "What for?" I asked.

"Because I was the one who directed you into the area." The captain was serious.

I wasn't having any of this. "You didn't get the tusks. I got the tusks. It was my ass in the sling out there. They ought to be mine."

"You're either going to give them to me or I'll confiscate them and return them to the village."

I thought quick. "How about I give you one and I'll keep one?"

"Okay, I'll go for that."

I was really upset I couldn't bring both home. I really should have left them to the village.

THE SF IN THE A-CAMPS WERE SMACK IN THE ENEMY'S BACKYARD AND LARGELY on their own. They had a small cadre of LLDB as team leaders, but the rest of the men were to be recruited from local villages and farms. When it came to winning hearts and minds, the SF were the ones who did it.

CIDG recruiting was always a dangerous business. SF never knew who they really were. There were twelve of you and there might be four to six hundred of them. You were their commanders and saw to their indoctrination, training, rations, and pay. Except for coming into the B-team to draw their pay, the only other Americans you might see for a whole year would be the aircraft overhead. Supplies would be dropped—sometimes not too successfully. Over Tan Rai, the plane came in low and threw out a cow. The animal didn't survive, so the men had beef instead of milk.

There weren't many breaks from the constant tension in the A-camps. Every day they sent out patrols with two U.S. and a dozen or more CIDG to ascertain hostile enemy intentions and ensure that the area was safe.

Sometimes the recon would stay a week, thinning out the camp's ability to defend against assault. The men in the camp were always on pins and needles. There was always a potential to be overrun.

The NVA and VC knew what weapons the camp had for defense and how to get around them. In the middle of the night, they would sneak in and stash armaments for later use. That's when they would infiltrate again, attack, and run like madmen through the "fan" of defensive fire to get out of range.

Each SF was ready for an assault. In fact, the teams never tried to hide their camps. "C'mon, NVA," was their attitude. That's just what they wanted—for the enemy to start something and expose themselves.

Even though the camps were well set up to repel the enemy, some were still overrun despite the heroics of the SF. One camp's last stand was in a commo bunker. The enemy was throwing hand grenades inside as the men closed it off with sandbags. By the time the NVA was routed, there were still Americans alive in the bunker. But the NVA paid one big price for every camp they attempted to overrun.

We had an aircraft called the Dragon Ship by the Air Force. We called it "Puff, the Magic Dragon." It was a C-47 with ports for a battery of Vulcan machine guns. Each of these cannons had six 7.62mm barrels that fired six thousand rounds a minute.

To prepare the defense of a camp, the pilot walked around recording all the data he'd need to cover the camp from the air—the location of all buildings, bunkers, and defensive positions. He'd finish up by marking the metal roof of one of the buildings near the center of the camp.

When the camp called in Puff, the pilot would fly in low and use the building in the center for guiding on, aim his wingtip, and bank into a continuous tight circle, firing at the enemy. It was a sight to behold. Every tenth round was a tracer, and the fire was so rapid it looked as if someone had taken a red pencil and drawn a straight line from the plane to the ground. They claimed that with one dip of the wing one burst could cover an area the size of a football field with a bullet every twelve inches.

Bye bye, NVA.

The radio shack monitored everything, and as the action heated up, my radio operators sometimes came out from under their earphones and speakers in a daze. I would take over while they relaxed with a cigarette. Not only were we handling all commo from our A-teams, we were coordinating transmissions from forward air controllers (FAC) flying over the combat areas in support of the camps and patrols. FACs, jet pilots in their own right, hover over the battlefield, sending in the big boys to lay waste.

The A-camps were being encouraged by the 5th Group to transmit their SITREPS by voice, calling out their "Alpha-Bravos" off the one-time crypto pads. We quickly found out how many had weak signals.

An Lac was often the weakest. I went out there one day and saw that their antenna wires ran almost the length of the compound, but were only five feet off the ground. "Our mama-san puts her wash on the antenna wire like a fucking clothesline," the radio operator said. "That's when my transmission is interrupted."

The mama-san couldn't be talked out of it, and the camp didn't have the poles to get the wires high off the ground. I wasn't concerned just for the security of our men. The An Lac indigenous needed to be protected, too, and radio contact was vital.

I made a suggestion. "The next time she hangs out her wet stuff, come up to full power." The commo man gave me a big grin. I think he had already decided to whip it on her.

Two days later, he came up on the radio and asked for me. He was laughing. "Remember our clothes hanger?" he said. "I burned her good. I thought I killed her, but she went through the camp screaming." His signal was loud and clear.

All the camps needed tall poles for their doublet antennas, and that was a job for the B-team supply sergeant. Let me tell you, a supply sergeant can make or break an operation. Ours was a marvel. He was tall, lanky, and real country. He was old for his rank, so we called him "the old E-7." But, if there was anything to be got, he got it.

The first time he showed his stuff had to do with replacing one of our 50KW generators. Two ran the whole camp. A Vietnamese was on the payroll whose sole job was to keep those suckers running twenty-four hours a day. They'd run for weeks at a time without being cut off, and they were showing their age. When the communications started flooding in, I wanted at least one new generator on line.

Knowing the right people was the key. Our old E-7 had a pilot friend who knew of one generator sitting on an airstrip somewhere. But to get it, he had to help out the officers' club at the C-130 base. They needed a case of whiskey. In less than two days the old E-7 showed up with a case of booze. His pilot friend came into Ban Me Thuot with his C-130, picked up him and the whiskey, and flew to wherever this generator was. Those boys down there were so happy they loaded that half-ton unit on the aircraft for him and back it came, no paperwork whatsoever. The kicker was, it didn't belong to the Air Force.

The barter started when the old E-7 dipped into his stores of captured weapons and traded them for the liquor. He also had a large collection of Montagnard bows, little bamboo arrows, and some of those old guns of theirs. These were his biggest trading items—hot in demand.

And that's how we had steaks galore on the table, as well. He would go to the beaches and wait for the ships to dock—then start wheeling and dealing.

If an A-team was lucky with enough time, you'd find their supply sergeant at the beaches, too. But, more often than not, those SF ate out of a can. It was rough. Nobody gained weight on an A-team.

Except for the pilots themselves, nobody in Vietnam flew as much as I did. It was part of keeping all the radios going. All that flying narrowed the odds of being shot down. But it wasn't enemy fire that almost did me in. Flying back from one of the A-camps, we came off a plateau real high above the plains where Ban Me Thuot was. The VC were everywhere and we were losing helicopters at a rate of one a day. With that going through their minds, Huey pilots would rapidly drop the ship down in an evasive maneuver and skim the treetops back to the city.

This time, we had a very young pilot, who pushed the nose way down, and I knew we were dropping too fast. I was sitting on the left side right behind the pilot, holding on for all I was worth. The gunners on both sides were pulling at their straps and preparing for a crash. He tried like hell to pull up, but it was too late. There was a giant tree right in front of us and I braced myself for the end. BOOM! We hit it doing about one hundred miles an hour. Limbs came all through the chopper, flying by me along with chunks of Plexiglas. But we were still flying!

I was amazed. The prop had cleared the tree, and we managed to fly right through the top of it. A couple of feet lower, and we would have met our Waterloo; the rescue team would have had to peel us off the trunk. The gunner on the left caught hell—the limbs almost jerked him out of the aircraft. The hot-rod pilot got the worst of it. A limb went through the bubble and right through his leg. The copilot took over and we began tossing out branches and pieces of the plastic nose as we approached Ban Me Thuot. The chopper was a mess.

The shook-up gunner gave me a ride to the B-team. He seemed in a hurry to get me away from the airfield. "Please don't say anything about this," he said. "We've got to cover our ass somehow."

It was pilot error, plain and simple, but I felt sorry he got hurt. I was glad it wouldn't be me trying to explain it all.

THE 5TH GROUP HAD A NEW COMMANDER, COL. FRANCIS J. "BLACKJACK" KELLY. Colonel Kelly was one aggressive CO, and from day one we started doing a lot more to make the enemy miserable. He sent into our area 150-man quick-reaction mobile strike force companies (MIKE) in support of A-camps in trouble, as well as six-man Apache recon teams to roam the jungle finding NVA and VC units. I was "wired" to all of them.

The MIKE forces were real bad dudes and were sent into areas of heavy enemy activity for periods up to two months to put the fear of God into them. The Apache teams really had the nerve. They'd sneak up under the noses of the enemy and just listen.

It was a few hours after dark when I got called into the radio room. A very weak transmission was coming in from an Apache team. The man was whispering and barely audible. The team carried a radio designed for this purpose, the URC-4. In fact, it was called the Whisper Radio. It hooked next to your throat. Even at that, we had a hard time trying to figure out what he was saying. We cranked up the volume and still had trouble. One of the radio men ran to his bunk and came back with a little tape recorder. He pushed that up to the speaker, and played it back, raising the volume another step. I had a direct telephone line to the sergeant major and the colonel, and called them in, too.

The Apache team had found a place to remain overnight. Right after they settled in, an NVA unit came in and put down in the same place. Our men literally froze in position.

"They're just a few feet away." That was the first thing we made out. "A big NVA unit . . . right on top of us." It was like he was exhaling it.

He whispered to us all night. An NVA had walked to within touching distance of one of them and pissed on a bush he was hiding behind. It was that heart-stopping close.

In the morning, the enemy picked up and moved out. *That's* how to gather intelligence.

Under his code name "Blackjack," Colonel Kelly created special search-and-destroy operations to deny the VC their secret bases and freedom of movement. He launched his first full operation, "Blackjack 21," in October 1966 in the Plei Trap Valley, southwest of Kontum. "Blackjack 22" followed in December, and that brought in my commo section.

On top of all our A-team activity, we were monitoring and coordinating transmissions for about two hundred men, including a dozen SF and a Pleiku MIKE force that were operating in the Buon Mi Ga area, thirty-five miles west of us.

After four weeks, the VC attacked them with a vengeance. We lost an SF and the task-force commander was wounded. The leader of the MIKE force took over and saw to the medevac of all wounded.

Colonel Kelly came up on the radio from Nha Trang, wanting constant updates on his men. We relayed everything we heard. We were also communicating with the C-team in Pleiku. They had a forty-man search-and-destroy strike force out as well. The FAC pilot radioed that they were suddenly in a world of hurt, too. He could see the enemy massing to surround them. We were getting CW from them at a ferocious pace. Their commo man was one of the fastest in country. He had memorized the one-time pads and I had to put two on him to receive and decode. I was also getting transmissions from the tactical air element (TACAIR) supporting them and Blackjack 22.

My men were falling behind the incoming transmissions just as one of my other radio operators walked in off his sleep period. I was relieved to see him. Under normal circumstances the men got sixteen hours to rest, but this was a desperate situation for the teams in the jungle.

With two men on the CW and a man just getting to sleep, I didn't have anyone to work the vital teletype link to Pleiku. I finished relaying the current situation to Colonel Kelly and turned to the man. "I'm sure glad you're here," I said. "I've got a team in heavy contact and I've got to get messages out."

"I ain't doin' a goddamn thing," he spit back. "I'm still off. I don't have to go back on for another eight hours."

I got madder than four hells. "You son-of-a-bitch!" I yelled, and belted him right through the bamboo wall into the teletype room. He just said the wrong thing at the wrong time. The man picked himself up and ran out of the shack.

In about ten minutes someone from the HQ came in and asked, "Joe, what the hell happened? That kid came into the orderly room, crying."

"He was no good to us here," I said. "That's all."

"Well, he spilled his guts to Panchism and Tom gave him five minutes to get the hell off the compound. Gillette backed him up and the kid's gone."

About three days later an investigating officer showed up from Nha Trang. The little radio operator had gone to his Signal Company CO and they lodged a complaint with 5th Group HQ. Panchism and Gillette flatly denied the officer access to me.

The lieutenant had to spend the night until he could get a return aircraft. He showed up in our club. Panchism signaled me to go back to the commo room, but the man had already spotted me and walked over.

"I've received word from your CO not to interview you and not to record any statements," he said. He paused for a minute, then leaned closer. "Off the record . . . what happened?" The lieutenant was trying to be nice and at the same time trying not to return to Nha Trang empty-handed.

"He refused to assist when I had men being killed. Some were my friends."

"Did you hit him?"

"No comment."

I never heard a single word about the incident after that.

Panchism and Gillette rotated out and were replaced by Sgt. Maj. Leland Ashcraft, and Major James Jones the new CO. Ashcraft was a familiar face from Fort Bragg, but Jones I had questions about.

Lac Thien had put out a CIDG company of about a hundred. They were short SF for a control element and the B-team sent a couple of NCOs, including weapons leader Henry Cardinal, a big Indian and a good buddy. Near Buon Ea Yang they got into a skirmish with the NVA. Several CIDG were killed, and Henry took a bullet in the left wrist right through his Rolex. "Sarge is wounded!" the radio said. We could hear the cross-talk between them and the FAC. Henry didn't want to leave the contact, but they called for medevac anyway. He also didn't want to leave until he had scooped up pieces of that damned watch of his.

Colonel Kelly called us to take a reaction force and relieve the pressure on the Lac Thien company. We couldn't pull a commo man from our other

A-teams, and being the only one not tied to a set, I would be radio operator for Major Jones.

We picked up two other companies from another A-camp, and flew on to Buon Ea Yang. We put down at the edge of a slash-and-burn area and moved east toward the skirmish. Major Jones stopped and ducked down. "We're being fired on," he said. "Did you hear that go overhead?" I didn't hear a thing. If there's one thing you can't miss, it's a bullet whining overhead. I just shrugged.

Major Jones did that several more times.

We continued east until we got to one side of a valley. There was a small village on the opposite side. The Lac Thien force was east of the enemy and had made contact on the mountainside at the edge of the village. We were at the edge of the other mountain, about four hundred yards from the action and moving parallel to it.

One of the A-team officers took a CIDG company and moved in a hurry to the far end of the valley in an encircling maneuver toward the west to cut off any possible enemy escape. The rest of us backed up on the hillside to the north to look down on the fighting and set up team control. The company we were with set up ambushes behind us.

Major Jones thought we had the enemy between us and directed me to call an air strike before it got dark. I called in the strikes to drop just ahead of the company on the move. But it was too late.

At daylight the blocking unit and the Lac Thien company found that the enemy had broken contact and fled. As we linked up we found their trail right over the top of the mountain and down the other side to the south.

When Cardinal got back from the hospital in Pleiku, he sent the watch pieces to Rolex. Rolex sent him a brand-new one at no charge.

Henry really earned that new watch. But it seemed to me Major Jones tried to get something he didn't earn—a Silver Star. He put in for it, claiming enemy contact.

One of the last A-camps we put in was Duc Lap, almost a spitting distance from the Cambodian border. A Blackjack operation had secured this particular area, and the combat engineers were building on top of a hill. The camp had been receiving action every day, so we weren't flying many aircraft in and out.

Even vehicle travel was very hazardous. The enemy was always out placing mines in the one road to the camp. I was a radio operator again, this time escorting some of the engineers. The camp called and said that their executive officer was on the way to lead us in. We had just driven through a neighboring village and were about a quarter mile from the camp when we heard this BOOM! We looked down the road and saw a Jeep going up in the air and turning over. Two men were thrown out in opposite directions, one blown completely over the treetops and one falling beside the road.

The Jeep landed upside down and we sped to it, careful of any more mines. The XO, a lieutenant, was hanging under the steering wheel. We dug him out and he was still alive, but all his insides were ruptured. From the size of the crater, we figured it was about twenty pounds of explosive. The lieutenant had been sitting on top of the gas tank on sandbags. That saved his life.

The other two men weren't so lucky. They were still barely alive, but were missing limbs.

Duc Lap gave me something else to remember it by. Soon after the whole camp moved in, it was given a recon mission near the border. As the team was checking a large knoll covered with tall grass, they found plenty of enemy signs. They found something else—a large bundle filled with smaller packages wrapped in Chinese newspaper. I received their radio call and relayed the report via teletype to Pleiku.

The team soon reported that several unmarked helicopters had swooped down on their location. The men inside were in civilian clothes and confiscated the bundle. Our men were told not to talk about what they had found. Well, that threat never stopped anyone.

I found out that the bundle held raw opium. The stuff was probably destined for NVA units. A lot of times, before they attacked, the NVA would get high, so they would charge without hesitation. They had to be stoned to do what they did in their attacks.

The scuttlebutt put the value at $5 million as it sat. But the dope never made it to Pleiku or Nha Trang. From my friends in S-2, I was told the choppers went to Saigon and the opium was divvied up between U.S. and South Vietnamese "officials." Duc Lap continued to report flyovers by unmarked planes.

By February 1967 I was back at Fort Bragg. I got two letters from Ban Me Thuot. In the first, Ashcraft wanted to know the whereabouts of a missing radio. He also wanted to know if I could verify the incidents in Major Jones's application for a Silver Star. I gave him the whereabouts of the radio and told him that, to the best of my knowledge, not a single enemy bullet ever came our way.

The second letter arrived before Ashcraft received my answer to the first. He said they had found the radio and that Major Jones had received his Silver Star.

What a bunch of bunk.

chapter 13

The Dirty Work Begins

Special Forces is a triple-volunteer unit. First, you volunteer for the Army—you can't be drafted and then go into SF. Then you volunteer for Airborne. And then you volunteer for SF.

I always considered myself a "quadruple volunteer." I volunteered for combat in Vietnam. I always felt I had all my training for a reason, and that if there was a job that had to be done I was there to do it.

That's why sitting out the war for almost a year was a hard thing to do. After I got back from Vietnam in February of 1967, there were field-training exercises and a lot of time in classrooms. Sure, I got a lot of training under my belt, but all of that was a poor substitute for the real thing.

SF NCO assignments came from a special office in the Assignment Branch of the Department of Army presided over by a wonderful lady, Mrs. Billye Alexander, who worked seven days a week assisting SF no matter where we were in the world. Well, Mrs. A let the word slip that the Army was looking for thirteen top-ranked NCOs to volunteer for special missions.

I knew immediately what this meant. MACV—Military Assistance Command, Vietnam—had been secretly running SF teams into Laos, Cambodia, and North Vietnam under a clandestine operation known as

MACV-SOG—SOG, the Studies and Observation Group. SF were normally sent to the 5th Group in Nha Trang, and from there given assignments in country. SOG was the only group taking men directly from the States. So these were for sure SOG mission assignments Mrs. A was talking about.

Dick Meadows and I called Mrs. A about putting our names on the list. "You got it," she said. "You'll get your orders in a few days."

I didn't know who was the happiest, Dick or me. I didn't care to go back to Vietnam as a commo supervisor. I felt I could do more leading patrols. Hell, the mountains and the woods were in my blood. The whole idea of running teams for SOG was right up my alley.

I touched down at Tan Son Nhut Air Base late in the afternoon of 26 May 1968 under a set of very plain orders sending me to MACV. The orders said nothing about SOG—only that I was assigned to "Special Operations Augmentation," 5th Special Forces Group. It was all a cover to make it look like we were a special bunch assigned to the 5th, when we were really under secret orders to MACVSOG. I even traveled in civvies—khaki trousers and a short-sleeved shirt.

I stayed in a big hotel in the middle of Saigon. The place was run by MACV and was an intermediate staging area for men on their way in and out of Vietnam. It had a big mess hall on the main floor. There were soldiers there in all kinds of uniforms and a lot of civilian "contractors." No one really identified themselves.

My room was on the top floor. From the balcony I could see most of the city. There were some small fires burning in the distance. I could also hear a lot of noise and the sound of small-arms from downtown. Because of the January Tet offensive, there was still a lot of action going on. American units were still mopping up after the largest coordinated enemy attack of the war and there I was sitting around with no weapon. I didn't like that at all. From the time I was a kid, I didn't like being unarmed.

The mess hall was packed for breakfast with other men in civilian clothes. I was met at the checkout counter by a soldier in a sterile uniform—no rank or insignia. He knew my name. We climbed into a black unmarked Jeep and headed downtown.

Painting vehicles black was very appropriate for MACVSOG, which ran the "black" stuff, using clandestine teams made up of Special Forces "agent handlers" and a combination of LLDB along with mercenary teams of Vietnamese, Cambodians, Montagnards, and other indigenous tribes. Their operations were considered "officially disavowable" by the Department of Defense.

For the most part, SOG took over from the CIA's Operation Tiger in January of 1964. The CIA really hated giving up its hold on covert operations in and out of South Vietnam, but the Army had the hot hand. The original idea was to give SOG a year of operation, but as the war went on SOG was given more to do.

SOG ran out of three operational bases. CCN, Command and Control North in Da Nang, ran teams into North Vietnam; CCC, Command and Control Central in Kontum, put teams into Laos; and CCS, Command and Control South, was in my old area of Ban Me Thuot, sending teams into Cambodia. These teams were commanded by the cream of SF and I was sure I was going to run with them.

We made our way downtown, dodging all the little people on their bikes and mopeds. MACVSOG headquarters was on Pasteur Avenue, and sat right up to the street. There were no markings, of course, but it looked like a military compound. It was a two-story cement-block building topped with all kinds of commo antennae. It was surrounded by a five-foot cement wall with a twenty-foot chain-link fence and barbed wire on top of that.

Most of the men inside also wore either civilian clothes or sterile uniforms. There might have been CIA types running around, but that was none of my business. It was a paperwork formality. They assigned me to Long Thanh, a camp about thirty miles east of Saigon. I wasn't told what my job was or what I might be doing. The first sergeant just told me to go there and wait for the project officer to brief me.

I had the same driver on the way out. I was his only passenger. The road ran to Long Binh, headquarters of the 25th Infantry Division and III Corps. The driver said most of the roads were safer since Tet, although some stretches through the jungle still had VC.

The Tet offensive was a disaster for the NVA. They got the living hell kicked out of them, but for some reason, we didn't pursue them and bring them to their knees. I thought that was a big mistake and that it would come back to haunt us. By the time I arrived, most of the NVA had pulled across the border to regroup and lick their wounds.

Long Thanh was a small, well-set-up camp guarded by U.S. and a few Vietnamese LLDB and very well secured, with quad-50 gun emplacements on the corners. Just to the west to one side of the camp was a good-sized airstrip with a hangar. Beyond the airstrip was a small village. I liked having the open airfield between us and the village. The NVA would have to cross in the open to get to the camp.

Once we were through the gate I saw some very familiar things. There was a thirty-four-foot jump tower and a parachute landing fall platform. This was obviously a jump-training facility for SOG teams, and I was very anxious to find out what my duties were going to be.

There were also familiar faces running the camp. I was greeted by Sgt. Maj. Sam Bass, the camp's first sergeant. I had last seen Bass back at Fort Bragg. When I asked what my job was, all he would tell me was that I would be working on a certain POW project. Other than that I would have no duties.

"The commander doesn't want you to be tied up with anything," Bass said.

Long Thanh was officially a Vietnamese Airborne Ranger training center, but SOG was also training a lot of their cross-border mercenary teams there. It was a highly classified operation run by SF Detachment B-53, the resident team.

The camp was well fortified. In addition to the quad-50s, mine fields were set up in the blind areas that were hidden after dark. There also was a field that been purposely cut down to expose an area between the camp and the jungle.

About a rifle shot to the west was an Infantry unit. They were a quarter mile away between us and the thick part of the jungle. They had armored personnel carriers and a lot of other vehicles running up and down the road between us and the airstrip. They were hit hard during Tet and had been on alert ever since. Every now and then we could hear them shooting their mini-guns at something. It made our compound more secure, and it hadn't been probed at all.

Sfc. Elmer Hubbard ushered me to the camp warehouse where I checked out an M-16. That was the first time I had felt comfortable since touching down in Saigon. The weapons room was manned by Philippine armorers. Hubbard said the camp commander considered them some of the best he'd ever seen. The Filipinos were more of SOG's civilian contractors. They maintained the camp's generators and took care of the mess. At one time there was a Chinese cook at the mess. Some of the Cambodian mercenaries didn't like the food and shot up the kitchen with their Swedish Ks.

My room was right down the hall from the office of the camp commander, Major Stanley Olchovik. We hit it off right away because he loved hunting and fishing, too. Over the next couple of days we got to know each other real well.

Olchovik was a muscular six feet with short-cropped blond hair and steel-blue-gray eyes. He was born in Czechoslovakia and at fourteen he was forced into a German labor camp in Bavaria. During the confusion of a bombing raid, he killed his Nazi supervisor with a hammer and fled. He escaped German patrols, picked up odd jobs in the coal-mining areas and eventually made his way into occupied France. He was captured by the French Maquis resistance, and because he looked like a German to them, he had to do a good job of convincing them he wasn't a blond, blue-eyed Nazi, but a poor Czech on the run. The French put his looks to good use. For two years Olchovik fought alongside the Maquis.

When the liberating American Army came through, he followed them east as far as he could, then picked his way back into Czechoslovakia, where he found that the Russians were taking over. He stayed to go to school and got a degree in Forestry Engineering at seventeen. All the while he continued as a resistance fighter against the Russians. It wasn't long before the old Czech government was replaced. Olchovik and his friends crossed into the American Zone of West Germany. It was touch and go for a while but once in American hands, they were handed over to the United Nations Refugee Organization.

The U.S. wanted them, and they were recruited by the OSS to work in secret operations deep into Czechoslovakia. One of the skills Olchovik learned was flying gliders, a great way to infiltrate. As a reward, he was promised he could come to the U.S.

He joined the U.S. Army and went into SF as part of a special program. He was an NCO for seven years, then went to OCS at age twenty-eight. In 1955 he was the very first second lieutenant assigned to SF—the 77th at Fort Bragg.

SERGEANT MAJOR BASS GOT THE WORD TO ME THAT I WAS TO REPORT TO MAjor Bert Spivy at MACVSOG. I grabbed one of the black Jeeps and hit the road. The name sounded awfully familiar, and I was thinking that I wouldn't be surprised if I knew him, too.

Like everyone else, Spivy sat behind his desk with no insignia or rank. Major Berton E. Spivy IV—and we did know each other. In 1964 he was the CO of the MI detachment in Panama, part of the Special Action Force of the 8th Special Forces Group. "Hell, I used to watch you jump all the time," he said.

He had come to SOG to take over a project that was already set up by the CIA. He was very quiet and businesslike and did a quick briefing on what our job was. SOG was running an operation picking up NVA prisoners from U.S. units and holding them for interrogation in the POW stockade at Long Thanh. MI would try to turn them around to be intelligence "agents" for us. Then some of them would be inserted back near their old units. The men would be instructed to either contact another "controlled American source" or return to U.S. positions as a *chieu hoi*—voluntary surrender.

"You're the new NCO in charge of the POW stockade," Spivy said. "You'll go with me to our combat units to pick up the POWs, and then you'll see to their care and handling in the stockade. We'll tell you who goes back, and you'll get them ready and then insert them on my orders."

The very sound of "POW stockade" set off bells in my mind. The bells were clanging, "Bull Simons . . . Bull Simons . . . Bull Simons." Then I thought, "I hope to hell they don't want me to torture these damned people. That might get us secret information, but it's no way to get the poor prisoners on our side."

I was very uneasy about the assignment. I didn't like it at all. I really wanted to be in the jungle running intelligence missions with a team, not baby-sitting a bunch of scared-to-death little prisoners. What we were doing didn't seem proper, and I knew it wasn't what the Geneva Conventions had in mind for prisoners of war.

At General Westmoreland's daily intelligence briefing, MACVSOG would be given the word that a U.S. unit had a POW. Depending on what kind of intelligence that unit's S-2 got from the man, SOG would make the decision as to who was valuable enough to pick up.

SOG had its own aircraft, and we could get anything we needed for our missions—choppers, L-20s, Otters, or even the unmarked C-47 Gooney Birds flown by Air America.

"All I do is pick up the phone and it's there," Spivy said.

He told me to go back to Long Thanh and get familiar with the stockade. Other than that, I was to wait for his orders.

The stockade was inside an eight-foot solid wood wall with a row of concertina wire at the top. There was a small exercise area and an outhouse. The prisoners had their own shower sitting under a tank of water. The stockade building was crudely built and sat at the backside of the POW compound, up against three of the walls. There were small windows near the top of the front wall facing the center of the stockade, just enough for ventilation and light. There was one main room where the POWs ate and slept. Large wood beams supported the walls and a rough ceiling. There were twenty single bunks, and each POW had a foot locker. I saw a couple of other small rooms that were locked.

There was time for a little hunting, and Major Olchovik and I took advantage of it. Near the cleared area between us and the infantry unit were several draws with heavy underbrush. That particular area was full of little red Vietnamese deer. The area was also hot with NVA, so we had to be careful we didn't become the hunted. We saw deer signs all over. Vietnam had a large deer population, which ranged from the "barking" deer about the size of a dog to giant ones about the size of a horse. The red deer we were after weighed about fifty pounds.

I found a little guy and trapped him between us. Since all we had were M-16s, we needed a clear shot. So, I started to flush him out of the draw toward Olchovik. I was moving along the edge of a little ditch when a gunship suddenly zoomed overhead. He darted out of sight behind some trees, and I could hear him circling back. He came back fast and I found myself looking straight into his cannons. He thought he had himself a damned NVA kill, what with my green fatigues and dark skin.

"Oh, Lord," I thought. "I'll be splattered to pieces."

I yelled to Olchovik, "Take your hat off and wave at those guys!"

I sure as hell wasn't going to take off my hat with all my black hair. The pilot was looking right at me and I could feel his hand getting tight on the button.

"Olchovik, take your damned hat off now! They're fixin' to blow us to hell!"

I didn't think the major ever heard me yelling, the noise of the chopper was so damned loud. He was right on top of us—cannons, missiles, machine guns, and all.

Olchovik stepped out of the bushes on his own and waved his hat, showing off his blond hair. The gunship pulled away. If I had been there by myself, I would have caught hell. I thought about what I would do if I ever met that pilot. I would slit the man's throat, or hug his neck. I didn't know which.

The whole camp tasted deer that night.

The first call from Spivy came after a week. "We're taking a trip tomorrow," he said. "I'll see you at the plane at 0900. You'll need a weapon to carry at all times. I'll bring a couple pair of handcuffs."

I elected to leave the M-16 by my bunk and checked out a 9mm Browning automatic with a wooden grip—standard SOG issue.

When Spivy drove in the next morning a C-47 was already waiting for us at the airstrip. He was in civvies. We were both sterile, but I preferred to wear fatigues. I felt better in military garb in case the plane went down. And planes were going down every day. The uniform was tough and made for the jungle.

Our first pickup was from a Marine unit near Hue. From the air, Hue looked like one big mess. Everything was shot to ribbons from Tet. The last stronghold the NVA had was a monastery. You could see big holes blown through the walls. Remnants of the enemy were still being chased, and when we got there the Marines had some corralled and were trying to wipe them out.

The unit S-2 addressed the major as "Mr. Spivy." Spivy introduced me as "Mr. Garner." The Marine officers accepted us without any more discussion. They must have guessed who we were from the unmarked aircraft. It was a strange feeling.

Spivy then showed them what looked like a fluorescent light. I hadn't seen it before. I had the feeling that I was getting my own OJT at the same time, so I watched very close. The major explained to the S-2 that we would be putting some POWs back into the field and that we expected them to try to come back.

Each POW would be marked under the fingernails and around the cuticles with an invisible dye that would shine blue under the light. Whenever they took a prisoner or a *chieu hoi* they were to shine this light on his hands. If the fingers responded, they were to notify MI in Saigon and either he or "Mr. Garner" would come out and pick the man up.

I overcame the language barrier with the POWs by pointing where I wanted them to go. In the aircraft I handcuffed their hands behind them before I sat them down. The safety belt was fastened from the front, and this ensured that they couldn't get to it. But we didn't shackle them. There was no need to treat them that way if you were trying to win them over. Still, I didn't know their state of mind. They could try to jump out of the plane, or go nuts and do something to make us crash. I had to be very, very careful.

Once in the stockade, they were guarded night and day by some of Ol-chovik's Vietnamese LLDBs manning the four turrets.

I went with Spivy on the next couple of pickups. He would go through the same briefing drill with each interrogating officer or unit S-2. I was introduced to each one as working with Spivy on the project, and as one who would be picking up the prisoners. I still couldn't get used to being called Mr. Garner by the NCOs and MPs. They didn't know who I was, and a lot of times they addressed me as "sir," but I couldn't say anything.

Then it was up to me. Spivy began sending me on my own to infantry units in the southern part of the country. Sometimes I would show up unannounced for meetings with the S-2s just to show them how to work the blue light to identify a *chieu hoi* as ours.

I saw a lot of units in bad shape. The men would tell me stories about the NVA coming in and hitting them right in their base camp. One division headquarters to the south of us in IV Corps was in total disarray. When I got there they were still running around screaming and all. The night before, sappers came through the wire, penetrated deep, and dropped satchel charges in their bunkers. They sustained a lot of casualties. There was debris all over the place.

If you were squeamish, all the blood, bodies, and body parts would be overwhelming. It didn't faze me. I had seen my father, sick with TB, puking up blood all over the house. The walls and floor were covered with it. The sight of blood and death never bothered me after that.

The pilot didn't want to stay long. It was still a hot area and everybody was on full alert. We got no results out of that unit, so we took off.

Some outfits were just plain ragged from doing a lot of jungle work. Their headquarters compounds looked like trash dumps—barrels and ammo scattered all over. If they were concerned about the war, then their approach was one-dimensional—they didn't think about anything else. When you're sloppy and disorganized, you're wide open to the enemy. A lot of other units took what the enemy had and still stayed sharp and together. Some of the best organized were Airborne and Marine units.

After several pickups, a big, burly redheaded MI out of MACVSOG showed up at the stockade. He was built like a football player. He said he was there to interrogate the prisoners and monitor the listening devices.

Well, Major Spivy never told me about bugs in the stockade. But I had an idea there were some somewhere. When the POWs were out in the yard, the MI showed me how they had expertly embedded listening devices in the beams and walls of the whole building so you'd never know it. The four-by-six beams had been grooved out from the top and microphones were placed inside. The POWs could not get to the devices unless they had a knife to cut away to the bug.

Spivy called a halt to the pickups after we had fourteen locked up. He drove from Saigon every day for the interrogation. The POWs were debriefed in a small room in the back of the stockade. The redhead also got involved in it, but spent most of his time in another little room that had the recording equipment. He recorded everything that went on.

For all our dealings with the prisoners we had an ARVN officer as an interpreter. He was with Spivy for all the interrogations. But I often saw the other MI talking to the POWs himself. He was obviously bilingual.

I wasn't involved in the interrogations. I was never in the room with them. Up to that point, my job was to care for the prisoners. We fed them well and clothed them in their regular NVA clothes. I supervised daily exercise, and even played volleyball with them when I had time. I liked spiking the ball. When I got ready to spike it they would run off the court, I hit it so hard.

There were times the MI picked up bits of conversation that alerted him to possible trouble. He told me he could tell that some of them knew they were being monitored by the way they were acting. "Watch to see if they're looking for them," he instructed me. "And whenever you come in here I want you to check carefully to see if any of the devices have been tampered with."

Sometimes you could see where they had tried to peel the wood back with their fingernails, but they never got into the hollows where the instruments were. The MI was able to pick out which POW had the intelligence to figure out stuff like this, and he would isolate the man.

"I think I'm going to have a little trouble with that one," he would tell me. "See if he's doing a lot of talking." But some that he thought might be trouble were, in fact, quiet.

I never carried a weapon inside the stockade. I saw no need because none of them was near as big as I was, and they had nothing they could make weapons out of. We made sure of that. But I always checked. You didn't get but one mistake, and then you were dead. I would sometimes bump into them on purpose to see if they had made anything out of a stick. If they had been American POWs, someone would have for sure made a weapon. But we never had a problem. It was like dealing with children—they were young and inexperienced and did what they were told.

I was always curious about the prisoners, and Sam Bass gave me an interpreter whenever I needed one. The POWs talked freely about themselves. They'd tell some of the weirdest stories. Most of them confirmed that they got their butts whipped during Tet.

There was one real young prisoner. He said he was glad the war was over for him, and that he was told he'd be going home. He was just seventeen, working in the rice fields with his family, when the NVA picked him up. He thought he was taken because he looked old enough and big enough to be in the Army. They sent him to a training camp for thirty days. After that, the recruits were marched for a month all the way into Laos. They walked from North Vietnam down the Ho Chi Minh Trail alongside many vehicles on the road.

They linked up with others in Laos, but it took another three months to form a unit of about nine hundred to a thousand. Then one day they walked across the border into South Vietnam and were hit by our B-52s. Three hundred were killed instantly, and over three hundred more were wounded. The rest who could still walk had to carry the wounded back across the border. It took them six months to get the unit's strength built back up to come across again.

The very next time he crossed back into South Vietnam his unit was hit again, this time by one of our infantry units operating between Kontum and Pleiku. He was captured by a brigade from the 4th Infantry Division near Plei Mrong.

It was Major Spivy's job to determine which ones were worth putting back. They weren't harassed or intimidated. Making them feel comfortable and safe opened them up. We were always able to get information on the strength and location of NVA units. Unlike American soldiers, these men didn't have a code of conduct to guide them.

Those POWs we couldn't put in the program were sent to the Con Son

Island "Correction Center" off Vietnam's southern coast, in IV Corps area. If we got any of our men back from insertion, they'd eventually be sent there, too. The hard-core uncooperative POWs went to a much tougher facility.

The interrogation lasted two weeks. Then SOG gave us the go-ahead to reinsert the POWs. I was to take each POW, one at a time, to the U.S. unit nearest the last known location of the POWs old unit. It wouldn't be easy. Since Tet there had been a lot of NVA movement into Laos and Cambodia. Major Spivy started with the capture location and compared that with the latest intelligence on NVA positions.

Spivy then coordinated with the S-2 of the U.S. unit as to the best place within their AO to insert. We wanted to make sure the U.S. unit didn't have any force on the ground in the area where we were going to place an NVA.

The MI rehearsed their cover stories, even though there was no assurance any of them would ever get back to their units. We had all the necessary NVA uniforms and equipment at the camp, so they were given back as much as we could of their original field equipment, including weapons but no ammo. We were careful to wipe the men clean of any suggestions of having been a POW.

Spivy marked them under the fingernails and around the cuticles with the identifying dye. I guessed SOG expected to see them again. They had it explained to them. "When you *chieu hoi*, you identify yourself by your fingernails."

They understood *chieu hoi*. The clever boys in Psychological Operations (PSYOPS) had done a good job of dropping "safe passage" leaflets into NVA areas promising that they would not be harmed if they surrendered.

Spivy showed them on a map right where we were going to put them. They were also told which way to travel to get back to their units. Even with all of that none of them looked too eager to go back in the jungle. Only a stupid fool would.

The insertions would be one at a time. I would transport the man to the U.S. unit nearest his NVA buddies. Then we'd launch from there in an H-34 King Bee. Our reinsertions would always be into South Vietnam. Hell, no need to take them home!

Once away from the launch site, we flew at treetop level to the insert location. We were never more than a hundred feet above the ground, flying as fast as the aircraft would go. The ARVN tail gunner kept his eyes glued on the jungle.

There was very little conversation with the POWs. I could tell they were very tense and worried. They had been safe for a while back at the stockade—fed well and treated well. Now, they would have to return to a war they didn't want. The MI told me that each POW knew that if his unit was ever able to break his cover story and find out about how he got back, they'd shoot him. That news made me very cautious, and I tried not to take my eyes off the prisoners.

We tried to find a tall grassy area to set down in. Those openings in the jungle were slash-and-burn areas that had been cleared for planting long ago by the mountain tribes and abandoned after four or five years of farming. The grass that took over could grow as tall as a two-story building. The area was usually about half the size of a football field and more secure than a truly open area. The vegetation provided some cover for us.

We usually came in on the high part of a slope so the enemy couldn't look down on us. We'd hover about six feet off the deck and let the prop-wash push down the grass. The POW would hesitate a bit because we were still off the ground, but I knew the grass would support his fall. So, I often "nudged" them out of the chopper. If I had to, I sometimes picked the man up and threw him out. Then we rose fast above the top of the trees and got the hell out of there.

On almost every trip we got a lot of small-arms fire, but the ARVN pilots stayed low and got out without being hit too badly. The damned things were so noisy I never knew we'd been hit until the pilot announced it. Sections of the chopper often looked like Swiss cheese, but we never went down. Just the thought of it kept the adrenalin flowing on every flight. Being the only American on the chopper, I was a little paranoid and mindful that, if need be, I would shoot them all just to stay alive.

One of the hottest areas we flew into was near the tri-border area west of Kontum. It was a long trip and we arrived in Kontum late in the afternoon. I locked up our POW for insertion the next morning. CCC had a lot of cross-border teams out and the whole place was on alert. Kontum took a pounding during Tet and the enemy was still active from there to Laos.

I saw some of the men carrying the CAR-15, a shortened version of the M-16 and a lot more deadly. Along with a shorter barrel it had a sliding stock so you could comfortably sling it over your back—a perfect weapon for long-range recon patrols. I found the CCC supply sergeant and asked how I could get one. He shrugged and said they were all issued out to the teams. I was disappointed.

IT WASN'T THE FIRST TIME I MISSED RUNNING WITH THE GUN I WANTED. IT WAS my first gun—a BB gun. I never got to use it. I was twelve and already real good with a slingshot. We had moved from the Avondale section of Chattanooga to Ridgedale. We were next to a rich neighborhood and a bunch of us kept in practice by shooting out the streetlights. Hell, we loved to get the police to chase us.

There were also a lot of pigeons in that part of town roosting in the eaves. A couple of old ladies asked me to shoot them out from their house. But I needed good, solid ammunition of the right size, and that's when I took younger brother Jerry's marbles. I was knocking off pigeons right and left.

Other old people asked me to get rid of their pigeons, too. I was getting a nickel a bird. But the marbles hit the houses with a terrible noise and the people suggested I find something different to use. Jerry was also angry at me for taking his marbles, and Jerry would fight in a heartbeat.

The idea to use a BB gun was a natural. Anyway, I had always wanted one even though I never shot one before. I went to work mowing yards and doing other odd jobs to save enough to get one.

I brought it home, still in the box, unopened. I left it there and went out through the neighborhood getting verbal contracts from all the old people who had pigeon trouble. Hell, at a nickel each I could have paid for that gun in one day.

When I returned home the gun was busted into a hundred pieces. My sister, Sally, had found it and took it out in the back and beat it to pieces with an axe. I guess she thought I was going to shoot out more streetlights. But I hadn't done that for a year, and all I was doing was thinking of ways to make money for the family.

I came after her with a poker. If I hadn't been held back by my brothers, we'd have had a funeral. It took me a long time to cool off. Damn, I never fired a single BB.

THINGS WERE HEATING UP IN KONTUM. CCC WAS TAKING A TOLL ON THE ENemy but was getting their people killed left and right, too. One team sergeant just coming out of the jungle remembered me from Fort Bragg. He knew I had a friend running Bright Light patrols into Laos—rescue operations aimed at finding downed U.S. pilots. He gave me the sad news. My friend had been killed along with his entire team. A strike force was just going out to recover the bodies.

"I know you liked him," he said. "His stuff is being brought in. Joe, I'm sure he would have wanted you to have his weapon. It's a CAR-15."

It took three weeks to insert almost all our POWs—except for one older POW who was left at the compound. I asked Major Spivy and the other MI why we didn't have a mission for him.

"We just have something else planned for him," I was told.

Our redheaded MI spent a lot of time with the POW. While I was running the insertions I had noticed the MI taking him out in a Jeep. After a short time they would return and he would talk to him awhile. Then they would go out again, and when they returned he would sit the man down and talk to him some more.

I was real curious.

It wasn't a day after my last insertion when Major Spivy came to me. "Joe, I want you to take half a day over the next week and train this man to parachute from an aircraft in flight."

"Jesus Christ," I thought. "What the hell do they have up their sleeves?" We had the jump tower and the landing-fall platform in place—just right for this type of training, but taking on a POW was something I never expected. I tried to hide the fact that I was nervous about it.

I had him in the morning hours, and the MI took him the rest of the day. I could see them. He was training the POW to observe and report intelligence. They would drive out on a road with an armored vehicle purposely placed at the edge of the woods. When they got back to the stockade the MI would ask the POW to tell him what he saw that would be of intelligence value.

Every afternoon there would be a different setup for the man to see. They would go back and forth all afternoon, It was as if he was being trained as a spy. And that's exactly what was happening. Geneva Conventions, my ass.

The prisoner was as good a student as I had anywhere. But there was a big difference. If the man refused to jump from the aircraft, I would have to forget how I handled students back in the U.S. and kick him out the door.

He kept saying how glad he was that he was going to be taken home and would be out of the war. He was also told that if he was contacted by a certain person he was to give him information about things that he saw, and that he was going to be paid for his services. He would find his first payment under a certain bridge on his way home. That was all he was thinking about—going home.

At the end of the week, just before dark, a C-130 Blackbird arrived at our location. I didn't know where we were headed, but with a C-130 you could fly pretty far. The Blackbird got its name from its paint job. It was charcoal on top, and the underbelly was light-colored like the clouds. It was the Air Force's "Sneaky Pete."

We were going right into North Vietnam. The mission was to jump our man into a prearranged location fairly close to Hanoi. They didn't tell me the exact location of the DZ, only that when the green light went on I was to jump him. That was it.

This was going to be extremely dangerous. We would have to be at five hundred feet to jump the man and that meant being up inside enemy radar. My mind went on instant alert. Crashes were an everyday event, and I for sure wanted to pick my ground route back from the North. The navigator gave me a route so that I could set up my own E&E just in case.

In a few minutes, we roared into the sky. I wasn't alone with the prisoner. Master Sergeant Paradis, an old air-commando buddy I jumped with in Panama, was in the back with me. Next to us were a couple of large bundles strapped to parachutes. "What are you doin' with these?" I asked Paradis.

"Hell, I'm goin' to throw these out behind your man."

"Oh . . . you are?"

The bundles held supplies for a unit—a unit that did not exist. The bundles were a diversionary tactic to make it look like we were supplying mercenaries in the North and to get the NVA to commit forces into the area to look for them. It was all a setup. The POW didn't know the bundles were coming out after him or anything about the bundles. He only knew he was going out when the green light came on. That poor little guy was a dead man.

We flew high over Laos, safe from any ground fire, and crossed the North Vietnamese border, then dropped down into the mountains. The pilot informed us each time we were being hit by radar, and once he thought some planes were after us. We stayed on the deck through the mountains, and the bogeys didn't pursue us.

The pilot knew where the missile sites were and avoided them. The Blackbird was filled with classified communications gear and outfitted with radar deflection and terrain-avoidance radar. TAR let the plane fly right down between the mountains. Radar deflection made it very difficult for the enemy to lock its radar on us because the system absorbed and regenerated the signal, shooting it out the other side. The enemy received no return and no aircraft signature. But once we rose to five hundred feet it was possible for the enemy to put two radars across the aircraft and pick us up.

We flew a long time into North Vietnam, staying in the valleys and just above the treetops. We had been in the air seven hours when the pilot announced he was climbing to jump altitude. We made a big circle up to five hundred feet. I received a few minutes' warning to prepare the POW and got him up and ready. We dropped the tailgate. He didn't freeze, though it wouldn't have mattered to me if he had. I held him as we walked out toward the tailgate. I wasn't going to let him change his mind.

I held him until the green light came on. Then I just tapped him on the butt and out he went. I watched his parachute open, then I ran back to Paradis and we shoved the two bundles out after him. I felt sorry for the POW because I knew he would never get back home.

The route back would be much more dangerous because of all the radar installations. Paradis and I asked the crew chief to leave the tailgate open for the return trip. We both had our HALO parachutes and could jump in a second.

As we headed back, three rockets were fired at us. Paradis and I leaned out the tailgate, hanging onto the edge of the fuselage. We watched the oncoming missiles looking like so many flying stove pipes sitting on a ball of fire.

My muscles tensed as I prepared for a hit.

"If those sons-of-bitches start to come in here, I'm going out!" Paradis shouted.

"And I'll be right with you!" I yelled back.

I was ready to take my chances in the jungle. I had a belt full of survival gear, and two hundred rounds of ammo. If it came to it, I could hunt and trap for ten years down there.

Suddenly, the Blackbird took evasive action and dropped quickly into the valley below and flew behind a hill. I was hanging onto the right side of the aircraft and Paradis was across from me. We were prepared to bail out the tailgate in an instant if the maneuver failed. It was very, very scary.

The missiles went by us.

We started to giggle. It was like a magnificent roller coaster, and it completely took our breath away.

The NVA launched missiles at us two more times, and each time the pilot took the same diving evasive maneuver behind a mountain. The missiles would go flying by.

We returned to Long Than about daylight.

A day later Dick Meadows sent word for me to join him in Da Nang. He was sending Floyd Payne down to replace me because he needed some help running cross-border teams. That was the best news I could have had. I wanted to work with Dick since leaving Fort Bragg.

I had mixed emotions about leaving Long Thanh. The assignment was exciting, all right. But putting those pitiful POWs back into the war just wasn't right.

In Da Nang I tried to find out about the man I jumped. The news was very sad. According to reports he was observed getting his money under the bridge and then was intercepted by the NVA. That was the last anyone saw of that poor, dumb country boy. He was probably killed. He was just an MI guinea pig.

I also learned that within thirty days of that mission a C-130, with Paradis on board, smacked into a mountain. There were no survivors.

chapter 14

The Shadow Soldiers

Ever since I volunteered for SOG, I wanted to go across the fence, and now I was looking forward to running in the woods. I could only guess what my part would be. The exciting thing was that Dick Meadows and I would be working together.

Da Nang sat on the South China Sea about a hundred miles south of the 17th Parallel. It was characterized by a mountainous hook of land, called Monkey Mountain, which swung into the ocean and provided an excellent harbor for a number of clandestine operations, including the Navy SEAL teams. It was also headquarters of the 3rd Marine Division. CCN was based here, running teams of U.S. and LLDB into northern Laos to gather intelligence and play havoc. They did some mean stuff.

Dick was not involved with CCN. He was the S-3—operations officer—for the STRATA team project. SOG was split up into eight commands, going by names such as OP-31, naval-studies group; OP-32, air-studies group; OP-33, PSYOPS; OP-35, ground-studies group; and OP-34, the cross-border intelligence-studies group.

OP-34 ran the covert STRATA teams. STRATA stood for Short Term Recon and Target Acquisition. The teams were largely made up of Vietnamese and Cambodian mercenaries, who were paid big money to insert into North Vietnam and watch the NVA. Meadows was perfect for that kind of stuff. In 1966 and 1967 he had been a team sergeant running a lot of SOG cross-border recon and rescue operations into Laos and North Vietnam. He earned a battlefield commission to captain.

The STRATA teams bore the stamp of the CIA. The men had been recruited as "civilian" mercenaries and sent to Long Thanh to train with SF. They received salaries and got big bonuses for good results on their missions. The SOG mercenary program was put together so as not to expose a lot of U.S. troops by sending them across the fence when they weren't really supposed to be out of the country. Even right out of Long Thanh, the teams were able to gather sufficient intelligence to justify the program. These were not direct-action missions; they were reconnaissance missions only. The teams had ten days to get information and get their butts out.

The whole thing went by the code word "Footboy." The OP-34 and STRATA names came up on the official organizational charts as "Monkey Mountain Forward Operations Base." Even Dick had a cover—Combat Operations Advisor to ARVN 11th Battle Group. It all looked good on the books.

Dick met me at the airfield. He was driving the usual sterile black Jeep, a SOG trademark. "I'm damn glad you're here," he said. "Climb in, you old son-of-a-gun." We headed east along a dusty road that ran south of the town. We crossed the bridge over the Song Cau Do inlet and, way up ahead, I could see China Beach and the sea. We ran past rows of little shacks and huts, mostly full of women and children. "They belong to the men at the camp," Dick pointed out.

Dick explained that STRATA was made up of ten ten-man teams: eight Vietnamese and two Cambodian. Their performance in the North was disappointing. "Really horrible," he said. "In fact, we're losing too many men in there. Long Thanh sends them to us only half trained for our kind of missions. I need you to turn the whole camp around and get these men trained. I mean, really trained."

"You're going to be the camp commander," Dick said. "You'll be the ranking NCO out there. You are the training officer and their agent handler. You will be responsible for everything that goes on."

The term "agent handler" was straight CIA. Plain and simple, it meant I would prepare a team for its mission, button them up for three days of isolation, brief them along with the S-3, and escort them in a sealed "blacked-out" vehicle and sterile aircraft to NKP—Nakhon Phanom, Thailand. After a final intelligence briefing, I was to accompany them on the mission launch and insert them into the North. Then I would extract them and confirm that we got the same men back.

On paper, it was a basically sound proposition. But a lot of them never came back. Their missions were very dangerous. The teams would have to walk a long way to their targets, and that meant extended exposure in hostile territory. They were told to keep away from water points because the enemy could be watching, so SOG aircraft dropped black water bladders into preselected locations. That was their only supply for the ten days, and it wasn't very successful.

STRATA had even trained a team to jump into the North, but it became one of their early disasters when the crew of the Air Force C-130 Blackbird turned on the green jump light over the wrong location. The team landed right by a North Vietnamese village and were all captured and killed.

When a team was on the run, which happened all too often, communication and extraction became very difficult. They often missed their pickup locations, and SOG had to search outside their AO, putting the pilots at risk.

One team felt it had been compromised and moved into Laos for extraction. In their last contact they were given the route to take and the extraction point, but the team was never heard from again. SOG searched to no avail. They were declared a lost team.

Another failure involved a team of Chinese nationals (CHINATS). They were busted apart and Da Nang lost communication. "When that happens, we never know if we'll ever see them again," Dick said. "But we always keep flying the area. Usually, after four days with no communication, you can sure bet they're gone."

This time, one man made it back. He kept traveling south until he could hear the big U.S. guns and followed the sounds. They were in front of him, and he kept moving toward the firing, all the while avoiding the enemy. To sustain himself, he ate the bark off trees. It took him a week and a half to reach the U.S. position. He came in and "surrendered" as a *chieu hoi*, but the Marines had taken so many casualties any Asian was fair game. They beat him up. The poor fellow finally persuaded them to call Da Nang.

"The news was terrific," Dick said. "We flew out to pick him up right away. His clothes were torn all to shreds, but, except for the bruises from the Marines, he was very healthy for the ordeal."

You couldn't write off all this trouble to bad luck. It was lousy preparation. And Dick was counting on me to transform the program.

Dick hung a left and we headed north up a sandy highway that paralleled the beach. In a few minutes, we passed CCN headquarters, sitting smack on the beach. Even behind a tall metal fence, the place was exposed. CCN used to be at Marble Mountain, a sharp peak of white rocks on the beach several miles south. They never got hit there, but VC sappers snuck in with satchel charges as soon as they moved to their new location. We lost two good SF to the little sneaky asses. One took a satchel charge right in his bunk and was blown to pieces. Another man lost his life trying to clear the fence of demolitions. Since the compound was right off the highway, the VC came right out of the jungle and placed C-ration cans with grenades at the compound gate. Sfc. Audley Mills would grab the cans and throw them in the ocean. One grenade had a short fuse. It went off in his hand and killed him.

I was hoping STRATA wouldn't be that wide open.

Monkey Mountain was dead ahead. Rising from the top, over six hundred meters up, were a lot of radio antennae. "Ours and the Navy's," Dick said. "SOG runs a lot of stuff out of here."

Right on the coast, at the base of Monkey Mountain, was a small, highly secured Navy compound known as Camp Fay. It was home to the Naval Advisory Detachment. NAD ran clandestine interdiction and infiltration operations into the northern Gulf of Tonkin with LDNN South Vietnamese Navy Commandos. Their calling card was a patrol fleet of very deadly Norwegian PTF "Nasty" boats.

Once through the gate, we passed a couple of service buildings, which included the Navy mess and a small barbershop. Dick rolled up to a one-story white building sitting at one end. This was STRATA.

Our HQ section was at the front, with Dick's office, the CO's office, the first sergeant's office, and the office of the Vietnamese colonel, a political figurehead. Two rooms made up the communications center. One held the teletypes—coded messages to and from MACVSOG. The other was full of long-range CW and voice radio gear to monitor teams in the field, as well as radios for talking to USAF air controllers.

The rest of the building was just a shotgun house, like the kind I grew up in. The bedrooms ran back on either side of a hall. Dick's was up against the radio room. He pointed to the one next to his. "This is yours," he said. "We both need to be on top of the radios."

The one creature comfort was a little "club" set up at the very end. "When the commo man has time, we open the bar," Dick said. "We eat with the Navy. You'll never want Army chow again."

Dick introduced me to the other officers and their South Vietnamese counterparts.

The next morning Dick and I left for the STRATA team camp. The camp sat about a mile to the east and south, along the shore at the base of Monkey Mountain. About a hundred yards farther south of the camp were the SEAL teams. Dick mentioned that the SEALs had become a sometime supply source. Occasionally, STRATA personnel would "commandeer" one of their Jeeps. Our Filipino help would then paint the Jeeps SOG black with SOG "serial numbers."

After CCN got hit, security was on everyone's mind. Even inside the heavily guarded NAD compound, I didn't feel totally safe. It wasn't far from the wall of our compound to the villages, and VC sappers could easily come along the edge of the wall and throw a satchel charge over it. They might even get into the camp and throw one up against the wall where I slept.

I had talked to some of the POWs in Long Thanh, and they said that sometimes they'd run as many as twenty miles a night. They had a network of "high-speed" trails and fixed their sandals so as not to fall off. They'd wear only their skivvies, run in, make a hit, and run until they were outside of the artillery fan before they'd quit.

Not all the teams were in the camp. Several were out on missions to the North. Except for the two Cambodian teams, most of the mercenaries were Vietnamese from all over South Vietnam, obviously from the rice fields and farms and tiny hill villages. They looked a little different than your city-type Vietnamese, who were a bit lighter-skinned and a little more educated. I had a word to describe most city Vietnamese: "cowboys." They put on a good show, but that's all there was. Many of the STRATA enlisted men were probably ARVN, although I wasn't told who. The young team leaders had been ARVN and the Vietnamese camp commander definitely was.

Dick and I stayed for dinner in the one big mess hall that served all the teams, then we visited each team building. There were two teams per building. Each was no more than an unfinished shell—open wood structures with metal roofs. The walls came up chest high, and there was screen all around from that point. There was a small dispensary that was used by our medic to take sick call. The camp had a tiny supply area, but all the major stuff, including weapons, came from our STRATA supply back at NAD.

I asked about the training. There was no training worth a dime. They'd get up to take a little bit of calisthenics in the compound under the Vietnamese camp commander's direction—something I wouldn't recognize as real PT. There were no special training areas of any kind. They didn't even have live-fire training. "My God," I said. "You're taking weapons into combat that haven't been tested? Well, we're going to change that real damn quick." I turned to Dick. "How far can I go with this?"

"As far as you want," he answered. "I want these men in shape and combat ready."

I didn't need to hear anything else.

From that point on, every morning at daybreak, I'd be there. I'd run their butts up and down the beach and give them all kinds of exercises. Only then would I turn them loose to eat.

It was my desire to train all the time in the camp, from PT at first light to weapons after breakfast and on through team movement, tactics, and recon techniques. I would take a team out daily for a two-hour run of a live-fire rifle course that the Vietnamese camp commander and I set up at the edge of the mountain—crude stationary targets to check weapons and accuracy. Then I grabbed another team and ran them through.

It was a difficult task because there were teams always coming and going—teams on alert, preparing, while other teams were returning from missions. I couldn't mess with the men, so I sometimes didn't have many left to train. But we trained nevertheless, and by the end of the first week they had more training than they had since the beginning of STRATA.

The mission orders to put teams into the North continued while I was trying to train. Missions were still our top priority, and it was my job to prepare these teams.

Dick would notify me of a mission and put the operation plan together. I picked the team, and Dick and I would discuss how many team members to run. Then I alerted the team leader, who got the men into the isolation building—sealing them off from all outside contact for three days. That first night we brought the weapons and ammo and began the briefing. Dick would leave us to work out team details. The next morning, we gave him a briefback on the team's conduct of the operation and what each man's role in the mission was.

Their mission was pure intelligence. We gave them PIN-EE 35mm cameras to confirm their sightings. Radio frequencies were assigned and their escape-and-evasion routes set. If they wanted to come out early, they'd transmit on CW and we'd respond with an aircraft. A FAC would be dispatched to talk to them on FM and bring in the ships to pick them up.

MACVSOG had an elaborate commo net set up, employing AWACS as a flying relay platform near the border. The team had a long-range radio plus an FM radio for talking to FACs and helicopters. Long Thanh had already given them extensive radio training. They knew Morse Code and used a version of our five-letter-group encryption system—characters from our alphabet to stand for their own words and phrases. OP-34 would also set up a code system strictly for them and for that particular operation, and they were to transmit their situation daily on CW.

The team was flown in an unmarked C-123 to NKP for final briefing and mission launch. The men were inserted into the jungle on a nylon line we called a "string" holding three at a time from a CH-53 Jolly Green Giant helicopter. The agent handler who inserted them also had to be there to extract them. You never knew who you were getting back as they came through the canopy. My time to insert a team was coming up, and another agent handler, Sfc. Larry Rader, warned me, "Joe, when you put in the team, you better memorize every face, because you're going to be standing in the door with your gun when you pick them up, and you damned better be sure who you take into the chopper."

The teams preferred to run in the North with the AK-47. We always issued the weapons, including ones with silencers, best suited to the mission. The AK-47 was a good jungle weapon. When you shot somebody, you for sure wanted him to stay down. The weapon's 7.62mm round flat did the job.

Whoever designed the M-16 never walked the jungle. Its smaller 5.56mm round spit out with a muzzle velocity of 3,200 feet per second. That meant you had this little bullet going faster than quick down range. That was real good unless you were fighting in Vietnam, where there was heavy foliage. Anything it hit was going to deflect it.

On the other hand, you really knew you were in trouble when an AK-47 fired, followed by the CRACK! the bullet made going through the sound barrier, and then little bushes and branches fell on your head. The round was not deflecting. It was cutting right through things. You didn't get that with an M-16 or a CAR-15.

The AK-47 had a thirty-round mag that held and fired a full thirty rounds—

not a twenty-round mag that would carry eighteen. When we put twenty in an M-16, within three days there was usually a malfunction caused by jamming from the magazine. If the mag spring got weak, it wouldn't present the round properly. The M-16 also had a very weak extractor and, when the humidity caused the cartridge case to swell just a tiny bit, the extractor wouldn't throw the round out. Some U.S. forces had lengths of cleaning rod taped to the forward grip on the barrel.

You could grab an AK-47 by the barrel and drag it several hours through the swamp, shake big pieces of mud from the barrel, take out the mag, blow the stuff off the rounds, reinsert the mag, and be ready to go. Do that to the M-16 and you're going to hurt yourself. The M-16 was a nice piece of gear if you were shooting varmints—the tolerances were very tight and well made—but it definitely was not a military weapon. The AK-47 was like the old .45. You could shake it and count the parts. It was a breeze to strip and clean. It was always ready to fire and cheap to make.

When DOD directed that the M-16 replace the M-14, which also used 7.62 slugs, the Marines did it right. They told everyone, "Get stuffed, you can't have our M-14s." The rest of us just needed a folding stock, not a new weapon.

The M-14 was paid for and in huge quantities in warehouses. And the primary reason it was replaced was that the M-16 inflicted casualties, but not deaths. The think tanks at DOD figured that was enough to slow down the enemy by stretching his logistical chain with wounded. But they forgot who our men were fighting. Charlie was a ghost. He was a fog. He had no logistical chain. All he had was some fish heads, some rice, four magazines, and his AK-47.

A major reason the STRATA teams wanted the AK-47 was that they would resemble NVA if spotted by a local villager. Also, the 7.62 ammo was everywhere. It fit three different types of weapons the NVA used. But I always sent the men out with a warning not to use captured ammo or NVA weapons. The CIA would put faulty ammo into the NVA supply system. When the firing pin slammed forward, the doctored powder would ignite so fast it would cause the cartridge to explode inside the chamber and the gun would blow up in your face. It wreaked psychological hell on the enemy every time he thought about firing his weapon. That split second of hesitation saved U.S. lives.

After a mission, each man was thoroughly debriefed, taking it step by step from day one until the time they got on the aircraft for extraction. A polygraph test on a whole range of things was standard procedure. The guy doing the test was CIA and was concealed behind a wall.

Soon after my first few weeks in the camp, one team failed the test. Even though they failed, they didn't prove to be bad guys. They just didn't accomplish the mission, and they tried to lie about why. If they didn't accomplish the mission, they wouldn't receive mission pay. There were times we got only a few back from the team. The men would be hurting because of losing the others. They shared the same feelings of loss as we did. I could see it in their faces. Somewhere along the way they had made a mistake and the enemy caught up to them. Something went wrong and we didn't know what. They would try to cover it up during the debriefing.

It was difficult to take people like that and put them into enemy territory and expect them to perform like U.S. troops. So you had to take care dealing with them. My STRATA men might have been uneducated hill people, but they were still men deserving respect.

There still had to be discipline in the teams. If I didn't approve of a man's performance on a mission, I would most likely drop him from another mission, because that's where they made their money. I did that with men that failed the polygraph. The first time it happened, I was asked, "How come I'm not going out any more?" I thought about my answer for a while. "Well, we haven't had a mission suited to you." I tried not to insult them because I had to work with them every day.

I knew stationary targets and classes alone wouldn't adequately prepare these men for their missions. I had to put them out in the jungle and observe them. Several teams were running in the North, but I was able to muster four teams of Vietnamese and a team of twelve Cambodians. SOG wanted more of our NCOs and officers to train with the teams, so Dick pulled them from behind their desks and we flew three hundred miles down to Da Lat for ten days in the jungle.

Right from the start, I had the teams show me combat formations, how they read maps, how they covered their trails, how they set ambushes, and how they maintained security. There were a lot of deficiencies, but the Cambodians were in better shape than the Vietnamese. The Cambodians seemed a little more knowledgeable about maneuvering in the jungle and were led by men who impressed me.

1

Eighth-grade football
at Eastside Junior High in
Chattanooga, Tennessee.
Dick Sherrell (*left*) was our
quarterback and kicker. I was
team captain and played
offense and defense.

2

My first photograph in a
military uniform. Taken
at Lackland AFB in 1951.
I was seventeen years old.

3   On the deck of the submarine USS *Sea Lion* during 1958 waterborne assault training at Little Creek, Virginia. From the sub, SF practiced clandestine night infiltration of areas around Camp Lejeune, North Carolina.

February 1958, right after reporting for duty with Special Forces. I was twenty-three years old.

December 1958 graduation from Fort Bragg's NCO Academy.

6   Outside of the team house in Paksane, Laos, just before leaving for
    the U.S.A. *Top*, left to right: Capt. Jimmy Jones, Sfc. George Hill,
    Sgt. Bobby Gregory. *Bottom*, left to right: Sgt. Robert Young,
    Sgt. Charles Heaukulani, Sgt. Joe Garner.

Certificate for
White Star
service in Laos.

Fort Bragg, September 1960. We had just won the team championship in the Southwestern Conference Parachute Meet at Houston, Texas. *Left to right:* Joe Garner; unknown officer; Sgt. Bruce Baxter; Colonel Jones, the JFKSWCEN commander; Sgt. Edgar Vickery. Two weeks later we won the Canadian Team Championship. Our fourth team member, Keith Jorgenson, is not pictured.

France Field, Panama Canal Zone, 1963. Sgt. D. P. Bechtel and I present the baton that was passed among three jumpers in free-fall. Receiving the baton is the commander of a newly arrived Air Commando unit. Looking on (*far right*) is M. Sgt. Dick Meadows.

10 Me leaving an aircraft 16,500 feet above the golf course at Fort Davis, Panama Canal Zone. The photographer hung out of a window above the wing.

Over Fort Gulick, Panama Canal Zone.
One of my many jumps from 1962 to 1965.

A walk-through SF demonstration area set up for VIPs visiting Fort
Gulick. Second from left is the legendary Col. "Bull" Simons. I'm
barely visible standing between the two display easels.

Certificate for MACVSOG service given by the Republic of Vietnam.

One of our captains requested that his team operate in an area just north of Da Lat. The maps showed a large trail that ran over the top of a mountain and down into a deep valley, continuing toward the town. He wanted to ambush the trail. Dick gave him the mission but told him to just sit and observe what came down it and not engage any NVA.

Because this was purely a practice mission, there was no intent to make contact to see how many KIAs or other casualties we could inflict. This was strictly to learn about the men and see how they would operate as a team.

I started noticing a lot of stuff that didn't go—uniforms, for instance. All of the U.S. had jungle fatigues with wide pockets that made far too much noise. Some of them were also throwing pieces of paper around—candy wrappers. One or two were using C-rations, also noisy. We also had metal canteen cups that sounded like cowbells in the jungle. I knew the NVA were around and we were lucky we didn't get hit.

After ten tiring days I was glad to fly back to Da Nang. There was a surprise waiting for me. It was Tadeusz Gaweda, the first sergeant of our operation at NKP. We all called him Ted, which was a lot easier to pronounce than his Polish name.

He grinned when he saw me. "I'm here to make things easier for you and Dick," he said. Ted was STRATA's new sergeant major and he had that twinkle in his blue eyes that signaled he had already settled in and was making his presence felt.

From the first day he arrived in SOG, Ted started making waves. Like all the others in sterile uniform, Ted wore no insignia in MACVSOG HQ. There was a Navy lieutenant commander decoding a classified message. He wadded up the paper and tossed it into an open wastebasket. Ted proceeded to chew him out over the breach of security. He told the officer to pick up the classified material and dispose of it properly. Then Gaweda ran him out of the room. SOG quickly reassigned Ted to Long Thanh before the flak hit.

Gaweda's first task was to help Dick handle an unfortunate incident that occurred during our exercise. Some people had actually come down that trail that had been covered by the captain's team and they shot them all to pieces. When the smoke cleared, it turned out to be a bunch of poor civilians. It was a very dumb thing to do, and the Army had to defuse a very sticky situation by making monetary reparations to the families.

It was a colossal lack of training—in particular, a lack of training as a team. And it certainly didn't work with a bunch of headquarters people running with mercenary teams that did things their way. Dick and I were probably the only ones qualified to lead a team, but SOG also wanted others. And this was the result.

chapter 15

Special Permission

No Americans had ever been on the ground with mercenary teams running in North Vietnam. It was forbidden. So it was kind of a surprise when Dick Meadows asked if I would run a mission to the North if he could get approval.

"You bet" was my answer. On the outside I may have been calm, but on the inside I was thinking, "Hell, yes!" I knew any STRATA team could perform better with me along than any Cambodian or Vietnamese mercenaries without Americans. Besides, surviving in the jungle was second nature to me.

In the beginning, Americans couldn't even go on SOG insertions, let alone be on the ground.

Meadows was being coy. "It's a highly sensitive mission and I don't think a mercenary team can do the job unless an American goes with them. I want you to put a team together. You can have anybody you want. This is going to be your team."

My first thoughts were the Cambodians. I was impressed with them coming off the Da Lat exercise. I chose them for physical ability. I thought they were the best of the STRATA personnel among the ten teams. In my book, they had the best grades.

I dismissed the idea of running with any of the Vietnamese teams. Some of them had been ARVN. They were very independent and commanded by former ARVN NCOs and officers who I felt didn't want their jobs taken over by an American. The officers tended to be a bit headstrong, and I wanted to do things my way.

Compared to the Vietnamese, the Cambodians were more friendly toward me when I went to the camp. They were easy to talk to. They also kept themselves in a state of readiness and were a close-knit group. The two Cambodian teams were the only ones who stayed together in the same hooches.

Up until now, when an American was made a SOG team leader he was given his people. He had no choice. I was the only one who had the opportunity to handpick his team from a pool of almost a hundred STRATA mercenaries. The real ball game had just begun.

Early the next morning I went to the camp. The interpreter was waiting at the gate as I drove up. He was so tiny, no bigger than a boy. He might have weighed in at ninety-five pounds sopping wet. His name was Binh. He was from Da Nang and was just out of school when SOG hired him for team briefings and debriefings. When he signed on, he wasn't a hired mercenary, but still got in on any team bonuses that were handed out.

Right after putting the men through PT, I sent the Vietnamese on to chow and gathered the Cambodians at their hooch area. I told them I was going to choose ten to be on my team. They buzzed with anticipation, but they didn't jump with excitement.

Most of the Cambodians had been involved in some type of conflict almost their whole lives. There had been so much strife in that area, what with the French, NVA, VC, and all. I'm sure it was difficult for them to accept outsiders coming into their area and showing them how to jungle fight and all that.

As far as I could determine, the Cambodians had not been ARVN. I didn't know if they had been recruited in Cambodia and brought in, and I never asked. I never wanted to embarrass them. In my opinion, they were better soldiers and more honest than the Vietnamese.

They reminded me a lot of the Montagnard hill tribes I encountered around Ban Me Thuot. Even back in 1966 I liked the Yards better than the Vietnamese. The hill people suffered much like the Indians did in the United States. They were definitely the underdogs in the conflict.

My Cambodians were close in makeup to the Montagnards. They were built stronger than the Vietnamese. They had a more pleasant disposition, too, and seemed to have a personality all their own. All the Vietnamese in camp seemed the same to me. Also, they'd just as soon tell a lie as not—whatever made them look good at the time. The Cambodians always told it the way it was—good or bad.

Even though I reserved my final decision on who would be my Cambodian team leader and assistant until we completed additional training, my gut feelings were strong about two men who looked real good during our Da Lat maneuvers. I wanted them to help me pick the team. One was Tranh, in his thirties and the oldest man of the group. He also was the strongest built. He had been fighting many years and was quite battle-scarred. He knew a lot and let me know he felt safe with me. Tranh had no family. He was already leader of one of the teams. His assistant was Quon, a lot younger, and the only one with a real personality. He was very good in the jungle, especially at shutting the door when his team stopped to rest or RON. I planned to test him as my tail gunner.

I selected ten men, mixed from the two teams. That meant splitting up the teams. Taking my team leader and assistant team leader from one of the teams left no complete second team. The remaining ten men were put on stand-down and instructed to train with the other teams in camp and be available to me at a moment's notice. My team was assigned their own building at the camp.

My men were good-looking—not a one had bad teeth or health problems. Binh, on the other hand, looked like he was sick all the time, he was so scrawny. When I told him I needed an interpreter for the team on missions, he thought a minute and said he would go. Then I told him, "If you want to go with us, you'll have to train with us." He looked at me and nodded. But I don't think he had any idea of what was in store for the team when they got back.

Dick had his initial briefing ready for me. "Joe, here's the mission." He spread out a map section of North Vietnam. "Two years ago, SOG put in a stay-behind team here." He pointed to a little village near the Chinese border, twenty-five klicks from the northern frontier of Laos, a tri-border area. "They were supposed to blend in with the locals and supply intelligence on Chicom and NVA movements."

Dick moved his finger north along a trail and stopped. "We're going to go in there to observe them receive a resupply drop at night. MACVSOG doesn't know if they're still ours, if they've gone over, or if they're all NVA. We need to identify them and initiate action against them, if necessary."

This had definitely been a CIA operation. The white shirts put them there and were in charge of the resupply. We had to find out if the NVA were getting our supplies.

SOG had a lot of misgivings about this team. They had been living with the North Vietnamese for two years, assigned to blend in with the local community wherever they were. Every so often they would receive an air drop. SOG was concerned about the team's being compromised since we were still running other teams in the North.

The tip-off came from their own communications. Messages during the first several days on the ground were short and often—SITREPS of a team moving to their target. Then, the team stopped transmitting for a long period. When they finally called, they gave very suspicious explanations about the delay and flimsy reasons why some of their assignments couldn't be met. The icing on the cake was their request for expensive stuff they could slip village leaders to gain favors. MACVSOG knew this was all bull and that the team was probably in the NVA fold.

In the past, SOG dealt with the problem by sometimes booby-trapping resupply drops to explode in the face of teams intelligence knew had been compromised. There were also times when teams in the North couldn't be resupplied or extracted for security reasons—the area was just too hot. Olchovik was a major with OP-34 when he received a message from a team that said, "If you don't pick us up we'll defect." Colonel John Singlaub, one of SOG's first commanders, shot back: "Tell them we'll pick them up—then burn them!" According to Olchovik, the order was never carried out. But I got the distinct feeling they came close to doing it.

After two years I certainly wouldn't risk lives to find out if they were still in there, but we were just following orders from MACVSOG.

Trying to identify faces from a distance in the dark was going to be a real chore. "How about the starlight scope?" Dick suggested.

The starlight scope was a light multiplier that allowed you to pierce the darkness to see. But you still had to have a tiny bit of light for it to work. I had lots of experience with starlight back at Fort Bragg. It was part of our operations and intelligence training.

Communicating with SOG was my next concern, especially while running so close to the Chinese border. Even though we had Cambodians trained as operators, I wanted another American on that lifeline.

Dick put out feelers, but there were no volunteers. Even the man in our radio room refused to run with the mercenaries. Dick was prepared "to volunteer" someone, but I wanted a man to come on the team who really wanted to do it. Otherwise, I was concerned that he wouldn't have his heart in it.

That's when Larry Hunt came forward. Larry was a tall, lanky young staff sergeant from California, a clerk with S-1. He heard that we were looking for another American. "I'll go with you," he said. He told us he wasn't doing anything, and that they really didn't need a clerk, since the S-1 first sergeant took care of all his own paperwork. Larry had a communications MOS and worked shifts in the commo room.

The whole idea of Americans on the ground so close to China was such a sensitive issue that the okay had to come from very high up. This kind of operation had to have approval from the Joint Chiefs of Staff (JCS) on down. MACVOG would send the request to General Westmoreland, the MACV commander. Dick knew the General personally—Westy had handed Dick his battlefield commission to Captain. From COMUSMACV it probably blew through the hands of Commander-in-Chief-Pacific (CINCPAC) on its way to Washington. SACSA, the office of the Special Assistant for Counterinsurgency and Special Activities—the black operation inside JCS—would sign off on it and send it back to Westmoreland. We would still need political clearance from the American ambassador in Saigon, twenty-four hours before mission launch. If he said, "Go," Saigon would then notify JCS that we were going to proceed. JCS would inform the office of the Secretary of Defense, the office of the Director of Central Intelligence, and the Secretary of State.

The word came down in less than three days. "I've got special permission for you and Larry," Dick announced. "The drop goes in two weeks."

Dick and I went over the mission again, this time with the purpose of laying down our own survival escape-and-evasion plan. Even though I would have a team E&E in case we got split up by the enemy, we were never certain how the team would react to being busted by the NVA in the North. We couldn't count on their loyalty when everything started turning sour.

One CCN team had already been wiped out—we were convinced at the hands of their Vietnamese. Before closing down for RON the night they were killed, their FAC reported that another team was in trouble, but he didn't want to pull himself out if there was NVA around. The SF reported no enemy sightings in the area and FAC and TACAIR were then released. The next thing anyone knew, they were dead. Four of their Vietnamese had signaled for extraction at a point away from their scheduled exfilt. A special rescue Hatchet Force was alerted and rappelled in, to find the three Americans shot in the head by their own CAR-15s. It was a mess.

Our weapons were always ready. The whole deal was: "You just can't trust anybody."

If the team came apart in the North, Larry and I would leave together and go dead west into Laos and call for extraction. From the map we'd have small clearings picked out for extraction. E&E routes and extraction points varied depending on where we were in the mission when we split up. Dick and I coordinated all the rally points and the time we'd be there. Dick was the only one in OP-34 who knew where Larry and I were going to be along our survival E&E network, and it was up to him to put the FAC on us.

Larry and I had the tiny URC-10 FM survival radio with our getaway gear. The Cambodians would never know we had those radios.

The Air Force had AWACS always in the air flying up and down the borders. We called the plane "Moonbeam," and it had the team frequency and the secret frequency of our E&E survival net. The mercenaries were not provided with this kind of survival net. We couldn't give them everything. If they got captured, they either talked or died. And, if they talked, they still might die.

I always thought it was more difficult for indigenous—the Cambodians in my case—to trust you than for you to trust them. It wasn't the ordinary kind of trust. It was their trust in you to take them into combat and bring them out safely.

That's one reason I wanted to do all the training: show them that I was no fly-by-nighter and that I meant business—that I wasn't going to get their head shot off. I certainly didn't want mine shot off. Their safety was as important as my safety. I also knew that if I took care of them they would take care of me.

PT before breakfast always began the day. After the meal, I trained the men in use of the M-16 with stationary targets at the base of the mountain. They had been running in the North with AK-47s, but I wanted them to carry the lighter M-16 on our mission. The M-16's ammo was also lighter, allowing them to pack a lot more bullets, something I felt was needed as well. There was another big reason not to have AK-47s. We might have to run back across the border into South Vietnam. Most American soldiers would take one look at us and figure we were the enemy for sure.

When I handed Binh his M-16, he told me he had never had one before. He only wanted a pistol, but I made him take the rifle. In the jungle, you can't defend yourself worth a flip with a pistol. It's good for a backup, if that's all you've got left.

The men took to the M-16s quickly, but I noticed they didn't sling the weapons properly. They wanted to shorten their slings and wear the guns on their shoulders, and that could prove fatal.

In Ban Me Thuot, a friend who had been wounded told me, "Joe, you just cannot believe the impact that AK-47 has. I got shot in the leg and it knocked me head over heels. My rifle went ten feet from me. This NVA came up, and if it hadn't been for one of the other men killing him, he would have killed me."

I impressed on my men the danger in being separated from their weapons when they were down. I had them make the strap long enough to wrap around the neck. If the strap was only on the shoulder, you could get hit and, whoosh, the weapon would be gone. If it went behind the neck and across your body, it would stay with you. We used the D-rings we had attached to our shoulder harness for extraction. The suspenderlike harness held up our equipment-heavy webbed belts. The ring was usually on the side opposite the one you shot from, and we ran the weapon sling through it and behind the neck.

I carried my CAR-15 around my neck all the time. I could do that because I was stronger than the men were. Even the M-16 got heavy as you trudged through the jungle, and because of the weight, the men would put it under the arm, a practice I got them away from. It took too long to bring the weapon up to fire from there. In those precious few seconds, you could be dead. We kept the weapon in front and in our hands, ready to shoot.

The training was about to get tougher. I thought the time would come on a mission when we might have to insert or extract on a string because the jungle would be too thick for a chopper landing. For all their time in Long Thanh, my mercenaries had very little training in being pulled out or rappelling in, so I laid on a helicopter and, for several days, ran them through day-long training.

In STRATA, we didn't burden ourselves with either McGuire or STABO rigs—special harnesses for extraction hookups. Instead, part of the equipment every man carried was a fourteen-foot nylon "sling" rope. We made what was called a "Swiss Seat" that did double-duty for both rappelling and extraction by helicopter. While in the chopper, you wrapped your sling rope around the thighs one time like a seat and around the waist twice and tied it through your mountaineer snap link with a loop.

Rappelling ropes were rolled up in the chopper inside a sandbag. We threw out the sandbag, and the rope unravelled as it fell. Before we hooked up, we stood on the skids with the rappelling rope to our side. You inserted the trailing rope into the snap link, then grabbed the portion of rope in front of the snap link and pulled up enough rope for a loop which you brought into the snap link and secured with a square knot. That way a man could not accidentally fall free of the rope. You put the trailing end of the rope in your rappelling hand, placed it behind you as a break, leaned back from the chopper, and waited for the command of the team leader to leave the aircraft.

Rappelling in was always dangerous. Extraction by string was even more hazardous. You did it in an extreme emergency only and then only through a thick canopy—no clearing. I can tell you that is no thrill. You're exposed to the world and in one tough bind while the chopper carries you, dangling, to a place to set down.

If we had the time and luxury of being put in or hauled out by a Jolly Green, it had a winch and a seat for three men. Even then we wrapped our ropes around our waists a couple of loops and hooked ourselves to the cable with a snap link, so if we were shot we wouldn't fall off the rig.

We couldn't rely on this ideal kind of situation. What we were most likely to face was a thick canopy in a hot area. That meant rappelling in fast. The big thing was not to come loose from the rope before you got to the ground. The chopper rope was 120 feet long and we had to make sure there was enough below us so we didn't run out of rope ten feet off the ground.

There was a lot of coordination with the flight crew. The rope disappeared through the canopy below, so a lot had to go right. The closer the chopper could get to the canopy, the better it would be for us. When we landed for insertion, an enemy had to be right there to shoot us. If we rappelled above the canopy, a man could shoot us from anywhere away from the LZ.

The Cambodians did very well. Poor Binh had the worst time of it. He burned his hands on the rope pretty bad—enough to where he couldn't do it anymore. I took pity on him and let him sit it out.

Jungle maneuvers were next. It was our task to train them away from what they learned in Long Thanh. That training was completely different from my concept of a recon team. We used Monkey Mountain. It was mountainous with jungle—a lot of vegetation on the back side of it. We cut trails and designed a live-fire reaction course that closely approximated running a live mission through the jungle. The trails zigzagged up the mountain and were full of hidden pop-up targets that Larry and others from the camp would pull to spring on the men. We planned on running the team through a lot and would change the target locations every time.

On the beach, I first walked the men through different formations used in traversing and moving through the jungle, then we'd go to the mountain. We were in full mission gear and fully loaded with ammo, grenades, and mines.

Binh was another story. Larry had trained him on the PRC-25 for talking to the FAC, and we had him loaded with that. He was so small that we didn't want to load him down much more beyond his quart canteens of water, so he could only carry about a third as much ammo as the rest of us—one hundred rounds.

I got them to simulate recon patrol formations walking through the jungle. Then we sprang the targets on them. We had long cords tied to them. Larry designed them so that, at the pull of a string, they would swing from behind a tree or out of the thick jungle into the trail. At times it was comical, but it worked well.

The first time I took them on the course, I let them do whatever they wanted to do. I told them, "Do what you do on your patrols in North Vietnam. Show me what you do."

When we popped targets on them, they fired from the hip like a bunch of cowboys. Bullets sprayed all around the target. They wasted so much ammunition I thought they were lucky they ever came out of North Vietnam alive. They could withstand only one attack, and then they were tapped out. They would have to run from the enemy as hard as they could. Hell, you have to conserve ammo during contact. That way you can withstand several attacks and continue to move at the same time.

During my critique, I told them, "If you can kill what you see instantly, it'll put the rest of them in a confused state. They'll be stunned and hit the ground, allowing us plenty of time to get away."

It's very important to kill the first people you see. Kill the first three, and the rest will hit the dirt and start shooting everywhere. "You just can't shoot up the damned bushes and miss all that you see," I warned them, "because they would be able to tell what was there. They'll say, 'Damn, it was just four or five of them.' And then they'd come after you."

Ammunition conservation was absolutely essential, especially when you were going for ten days and you might not be able to get resupply. We went in with three hundred rounds apiece and it certainly wouldn't take long to expend every bullet in contact, if you didn't have any discipline.

I introduced the men to "point-and-kill." From the hip you can't direct the end of the barrel toward the enemy because of the density of the trees in between. You can see only from eyeball level. So I made them shoot from the shoulder, with both eyes open, no squinting through sights. Just point and aim. I had them set their weapons on semiautomatic and ran them through the course three more times, but they still didn't get it.

I was really concerned about this as we came down from the mountain practicing team positions. That's when I heard a bunch of monkeys chattering away in a thick-leafed tree up ahead to our right. A bell rang in my head. I thought it would be a perfect time to show them how effective the technique was. There was one big monkey on top. You could see about twenty others through the thick leaves inside the tree.

I got in front of the men and told them, "When we get even with that tree, I want every man to turn on my command and shoot from the hip into that tree. The monkey on top is mine. The rest belong to you. I'm going to shoot from the shoulder and I'm only going to use two bullets. Set your weapons on semiautomatic and load one magazine each. We'll see how many you kill."

We came abreast of the tree and I yelled, "Fire!" We all spun to the right and fired. I got my monkey with the second shot before he could react to all the firing. The men were laughing and cutting up. "Let's go and see what we killed," I said.

We searched all through the tree and found only one dead monkey— mine. The men had shot their wad and just killed the tree. I used that as an example. "That's going to happen on a mission with no resupply." From that time on they didn't even think about shooting from the hip.

I was looking for a good point man because the most valuable man on patrol was the point man. When you made contact, it would be head to head, quick and decisive. Then it's over. The point man had to be awfully quick and had to have a killing instinct—kill without even thinking about it. Just do it!

Each team member had a specific job whenever the point man made contact, so we spent a lot of time practicing doing things instantly, by reflex. The targets were also set so that most of the team had cleared them when Larry popped them up on the flank. We tried to recreate all situations, such as the enemy firing from all sides.

We practiced setting out security when we stopped. Security on patrol in enemy territory was critical. I usually moved two hours after dark before RON. Wherever we spent the night was a place I had picked in advance. We usually set up a circle. If it was an open area the circle was wider—how wide depended on the density of the jungle. We always faced out. The tail gunner always faced the direction we came from so we wouldn't forget our path. I wouldn't have a problem with it, but that's what I wanted to teach them to do. Even if you're traveling cross-country following a half-assed azimuth, you could always find the direction you came from. The point man faced the forward point of travel. The tail gunner "shut the door" with booby traps and kept an eye on our back after we closed in for the night.

I really didn't pick a tail gunner, he chose himself. Quon, the assistant team leader, turned out to be a natural as tail gunner. He knew a lot about setting mines to cover our back, especially the nasty little toe-poppers. I gave him the assignment almost from the start.

Before dawn we pulled the booby traps and moved off, putting at least two hundred yards between us and where we spent the night before daylight.

I put the team through a lot of exercises rigging ambushes with our claymore mines. The claymores spewed death in a pattern and you had a distinct killing zone. When the teams spotted NVA they wanted to kill them. They were still a little trigger happy, and a lot of times that initiated the ambush before all the enemy was in the killing zone. And then they would be in deep trouble. STRATA was a recon force, not a fighting force. That's what we were trying to impress upon them—that we were not out there to kill all the NVA. We were set up for defense. It took a lot of discipline and a lot of practice.

We staged mock ambushes, using the other Cambodians from the camp as the enemy patrol. We'd set out dummy targets and set off the charges to see what effect the ambush would have: how many bullet holes were in the dummies and what was the best place to be standing so you didn't get crap blown all over you from the back flash of the claymores. I'd set the example and the little people followed suit.

We went ten miles in ten days, zigzagging all around Monkey Mountain. And there we were, speaking two different languages, using a Vietnamese interpreter who didn't speak very fluent English. The Cambodians had been around Americans long enough to pick up a few words but couldn't put them in sentences. However, there were hand and arm signals that we all could understand. The Cambodians watched my facial expressions and passed their perceptions along to the others. If one did something wrong, and I gave him a really angry look, it was almost like an insult. So I had to be careful how I reacted to what they did or said. Calling them names was a bad idea. Even in English, they could pick up the meaning very quickly. Never strike them, especially with an open hand. The only time I raised my voice a little was when I was one on one. I wouldn't do it as a whole team. If I wasn't satisfied with their performance, I'd try to keep my voice low, demonstrate what to do, and run them through again. I had learned a lot in Laos about treating our indigenous. It was the only way I operated.

By the time we were wrapping up the exercise, my STRATA team had a Cambodian expression for me. I wanted them to call me Joe, so they called me "Dai Wee Joe." Binh said that meant "Commander Joe." I doubt that any of them knew my name was Garner or even what my rank was. I also heard them refer to Dick as "Dai Wee Meder" for Commander Meadows, who stayed at the "Bo Chi Wee," the HQ.

It was a good exercise. Tranh and Quon didn't disappoint me a bit. I had made good choices in them. I also wound up selecting my point man, Sang. Like Tranh, Sang was one of the older men. He was lightning quick and light-footed on the trail. He was tall for a Cambodian, almost as tall as I was, and that gave him a good sight line. When I told him of my choice, he gave me a big grin.

I brought him a Swedish K 9mm automatic rifle. The weapon had a folding stock and slung easily under the arm. It was short enough to allow him to swing it up to fire without the bushes interfering. It fired from a forty-round magazine while the M-16 had a twenty-round mag. I wanted the Swedish K on point, where the man could get maximum effect instantly. He would carry the weapon with the safety off while the rest of us traveled with our safety on.

Sang was so proud of it he went into downtown Da Nang and with his own money had a special camouflage vest made that would hold a bunch of the clips. Before that we really didn't have any way to carry a lot of those long Swedish K clips. His new harness looked a bit like the NVA type that held a number of AK-47 magazines in front. Not to be outdone, Nim, my M-79 man, had his own vest made for all his 40mm grenades. The two of them showed up in camp proudly displaying their new equipment.

While we were roaming Monkey Mountain, the STRATA staff had been busy finding a training location that matched our mission AO in the North. I was just bringing the men in when Dick came to me all excited. "You're not going to believe this," he said, "but I found a place near Da Lat that looks exactly like the area around the target."

On his maps Dick showed me the drop location in the North and a little village along a trail to the south the stay-behind team was supposed to be working out of. "The area in Da Lat is identical to what you see on the map. I looked at maps in Saigon and got photos from NKP, and when I compared the terrain you could almost overlay the two. Even the DZ matches. So we'll take you in the way we'll do it in the North. You'll work your way to the target, stay to observe and then we'll extract you."

The next morning, we took all our briefing materials and called the team into the isolation building. I told the men to prepare for a ten-day mission. The rest of the briefing was very short. Dick handed Larry one of the starlight scopes and we left him to bring the team to Da Lat.

Dick wanted me to recon the training area with the FAC to get a first-hand look, so we flew down that morning. The starlight scope was stuffed into my rucksack inside its carrying case. It made a big bulge.

Da Lat was the garden spot of South Vietnam. All the fresh vegetables that fed the SF camps in South Vietnam came from its rich farmland year round. It was headquarters for II Corps, and the U.S. had a big landing strip there that handled a lot of C-130s constantly flying in and out on supply missions.

Of course, the NVA tapped the same resources as well, hiring indigenous to shop for and transport supplies in caravans of bearers and elephants. II Corps had no active units engaged to intercept and disrupt this activity. I guess they didn't want to screw things up by rocking the boat. As far as I was concerned, that did not make Da Lat a very secure place.

Da Lat is up in the Central Highlands. It's a really beautiful place—almost like Switzerland—sitting on a high plateau with mountain streams running all around the edge. It was a resort when the French were there in force, and all the big food tracts were under their supervision. That's why vegetables grew better than anywhere else.

A lot of French still lived there in big, fancy houses. I didn't know what jobs they had, but they probably remained because they had roots there. You could see in a lot of the young women that they were part Caucasian and part Vietnamese. And I don't mean part American. They were already grown.

The first stop was Air Force flight operations, so Dick could lay on the FAC for our recon that afternoon. Then it was over to II Corps HQ to inform their S-2 and S-3 that SOG would have a team operating in their area and to make sure there were no other Americans in our AO. Sitting behind the first sergeant's desk was Charles Ferguson, II Corps command sergeant major. "Dirty Charlie" was an old SF and happy to see me. He hated being out of the action and did everything he could to help all SF that ran in his area.

The FAC plane, a Cessna O-1 Bird Dog, could carry only one passenger, so Dick and the FAC went up first, leaving me at the airstrip to wait. Dick was gone less than an hour when Ferguson came running over from II Corps to tell me Dick had crashed.

"We've picked up his beacon, and I've already had planes in there," he said, "but the goddamn fog bank blocked them so they couldn't see the crash site."

Ferguson took me back to II Corps. "Give me a map and the coordinates," I told him. Charlie handed them to me and I went right to it. "I can tell you right where Dick will come out," I said.

"No shit?"

"No shit." I showed Charlie the crash site on the map and where Dick would go for extraction. Dick knew the jungle as good as I did and it was easy to guess where he would pick an LZ. Charlie called the air controller and after a short conversation said, "It's still too foggy over the crash site, Joe. When the fog lifts, we'll use the II Corps commander's aircraft. We'll try for two hours."

That was frustrating news. I didn't know if Dick or the FAC was injured, and I didn't know how much enemy activity was in the area. "Meanwhile, you can rest at my place," Charlie said. He pointed to a billet next door.

I took his offer and headed over. On the way I could see the general's helicopter sitting on the backside of the compound. I said to myself, "Well, if

Outside Da Lat during a 1968 training mission. I'm measuring an NVA trail using the CAR-15 as a reference for the intelligence guys analyzing the photograph. This trail led to the "lost" NVA battalion we were to find on a later mission.

At Hill 1044, March 1969. Jerry "Mad Dog" Shriver beside an NVA artillery piece, victim of our B-52s.

The desolation on Hill 1044. At far right is my Cambodian point man, Sang. The wounded and disoriented Marine sitting on a log was a good example of the condition of the whole company. The fog remained at treetop level the whole time. We called the place "the hill of death."

March 1969, en route from Hill 1044. Dick Meadows interrogates the wounded NVA prisoner we "rescued" from some very angry Marines. My team made the stretcher and we carried him to Tam Boi, the Marine battalion CP.

Hill 1044, March 1969. S. Sgt. Larry Hunt, my radio operator, looking for a place to rest on "the hill of death." Under almost every footfall was a body part. The rest of my team is in the background.

March 1969, on the hill overlooking Tam Boi. 19
Left to right: Capt. Dick Meadows, me, S. Sgt. Larry Hunt.

Celebrating the end of a successful mission at a Da Nang restaurant.
Tranh, my Cambodian team leader, watches with amusement as the
establishment's pet monkey examines the back of my head.

20

Tam Boi, March 1969. Quon, my Cambodian tail-gunner, "shutting the door" outside the Marine battalion CP.

21

22   The dam at Lake Tillery, North Carolina. My SADM civilian target.

The Pentagon, February 1972. We presented ceremonial paddles to commemorate our successful retracing of the route of Lewis and Clark. *Left to right*: Secretary of the Army Robert Froehlke; Captain Lewis; me; Army Chief of Staff General William Westmoreland.

Batujajar, Indonesia, 1975. Inside a C-130. I'm training members of the Indonesian Army's paratroop battalion in jumpmaster procedures.

SECURITY TERMINATION STATEMENT AND DEBRIEFING CERTIFICATE	DATE
(AR 380-5)	1 0 APR 1968

PART I - BASIC INFORMATION

FROM *(Originating Headquarters)*   HQS, 7TH SFGA, FT. BRAGG, N.C   DOSSIER NO.   *H 300 35 14*

LAST NAME - FIRST NAME - MIDDLE INITIAL   GRADE *(Mil or Clv)*   SVC NO. *(Mil)* - SOCIAL SCTY NO. *(Clv)*

GARNER   JOE   R.   *SFC E-7*   *RA-14401901*

DATE OF BIRTH *(Day, Mo, Yr)* *6 May 34*   PLACE OF BIRTH *(City, State, Country)* *SHERWOOD, TENN.*

PART II - REFERENCES

a. APPLICABLE TO ALL PERSONNEL WHO HAVE HAD ACCESS TO DEFENSE INFORMATION:

  (1) ESPIONAGE LAWS: TITLE 18, U.S. CODE, SECTIONS 793, 794 AND 798 *("temporary extension of Section 794")*.
  (2) INTERNAL SECURITY LAWS: TITLE 50, U.S. CODE, SECTION 783.
  (3) AR 380-5

b. ADDITIONALLY APPLICABLE TO PERSONNEL WHO HAVE HAD ACCESS TO *RESTRICTED DATA*:

  (1) ATOMIC ENERGY ACT OF 1954: TITLE 42, U.S. CODE, SECTIONS 2014, 2162, 2274, 2275, 2276 AND 2277.
  (2) AR 380-150
  (3) AR 380-157.

c. ADDITIONALLY APPLICABLE TO PERSONNEL WHO HAVE HAD ACCESS TO *CRYPTOGRAPHIC* MATERIAL OR INFORMATION:

  (1) ESPIONAGE LAWS: TITLE 18, U.S. CODE, SECTION 798.
  (2) AR 380-40

d. ADDITIONALLY APPLICABLE TO PERSONNEL WHO HAVE HAD ACCESS TO INFORMATION SPECIALLY COMPARTMENTED BY DOD OR DA DIRECTIVE:

  (1) LETTER, AGAM-P *(M)(16 Mar 64)* ACSFOR, HQ DA, 8 APR 64, SUBJECT: "SPECIAL SECURITY POLICY FOR THE NIKE X SYSTEM".
  (2) LETTER, AGAM-P *(M)(23 Dec 63)* ACSI-AS, HQ DA, 2 JAN 64, SUBJECT: "SECURITY POLICY FOR MILITARY SPACE PROGRAMS".
  (3) AR 380-34.

e. OTHER: *(Specify)**

PART III - SECURITY TERMINATION AND DEBRIEFING STATEMENT

1. I acknowledge that I have read the applicable material for the level of classified information to which I have had access, and I understand that the revelation of classified information to an unauthorized person or agency is prohibited and punishable by law. My initials below attest to the level of access which I have had and to the applicable material, as identified in References, which I have read.

INITIALS

EXTENT OF ACCESS

  a. TOP SECRET - SECRET - CONFIDENTIAL defense information *(Reference a)*.

  b. RESTRICTED DATA *(Reference b)*.

  c. CRYPTOGRAPHIC material or information *(Reference c)*.

  d. Information specially compartmented by Department of Defense or Department of the Army directives. *(SPECIAL ACCESS Information)*

  e. Other: *(Specify)**

2. I do not have classified material or documents in my possession.

3. I will not divulge classified information orally, in writing, or by any other means, to an unauthorized person or agency.

4. I will immediately report to the Federal Bureau of Investigation, my supervisor/commander, or other military authority, as appropriate, any attempt by an unauthorized person or agency to obtain classified information.

5. I received an oral debriefing, immediately prior to the execution *(i.e., signature)* of this Security Termination Statement.

* Can include access to information covered by treaties involving the U.S. *(i.e., AR 380-15, AR 380-16, or AR 380-17)* and access to critical stockpile and production information *(i.e., AR 380-157)*, plus any travel restrictions.

DISTRIBUTION:	SIGNATURE
FIELD 201 FILE *(Military)* CO, USACRF *(Civilian)* LOCAL SECURITY FILE	

DA FORM 1 APR 65 **2962**

25

The type of document we had to sign upon reassignment or service separation, where we promised to be real good boys and not give out any of the classified secrets entrusted to us.

THIS IS AN IMPORTANT RECORD
SAFEGUARD IT.

1. LAST NAME-FIRST NAME-MIDDLE NAME	2. SEX	3. SOCIAL SECURITY NUMBER	4. DATE OF BIRTH		
			YEAR	MONTH	DAY
GARNER JOE RICHARD	M	412 46 2227	34	05	06

5. DEPARTMENT, COMPONENT AND BRANCH OR CLASS	6a. GRADE, RATE OR RANK	6b. PAY GRADE	7. DATE OF RANK		
			YEAR	MONTH	DAY
ARMY-RA	SGM	E-9	76	09	21

8a. SELECTIVE SERVICE NUMBER	8b. SELECTIVE SERVICE LOCAL BOARD NUMBER, CITY, STATE AND ZIP CODE	8c. HOME OF RECORD AT TIME OF ENTRY INTO ACTIVE SERVICE (Street, RFD, City, State and ZIP Code)
NA	NA	1808 S. Beech St. Chattanooga, TN 36404

9a. TYPE OF SEPARATION	9b. STATION OR INSTALLATION AT WHICH EFFECTED
Retirement	Fort Bragg, North Carolina 28307

c. AUTHORITY AND REASON	d. EFFECTIVE DATE		
	YEAR	MONTH	DAY
	78	06	30

e. CHARACTER OF SERVICE	f. TYPE OF CERTIFICATE ISSUED	10. REENLISTMENT CODE
HONORABLE	DD FM 363A	

11. LAST DUTY ASSIGNMENT AND MAJOR COMMAND	12. COMMAND TO WHICH TRANSFERRED
CO C 3d BN 5th SFGA FORSCOM FC	RCPAC 9700 PAGE BLVD ST LOUIS MO 63132 USAR CON GP (RET-RES)

13. TERMINAL DATE OF RESERVE/MSS OBLIGATION	14. PLACE OF ENTRY INTO CURRENT ACTIVE SERVICE (City, State and ZIP Code)	15. LAST DUTY ASSIGNMENT THIS PERIOD		
YEAR MONTH DAY		YEAR	MONTH	DAY
NA	FORT BRAGG, NC 38207	76	07	16

16a. PRIMARY SPECIALTY NUMBER AND TITLE	b. RELATED CIVILIAN OCCUPATION AND D.O.T. NUMBER	18. RECORD OF SERVICE	YEARS	MONTHS	DAYS
11B5S INFANTRYMAN 780301/NONE	NA	(a) NET ACTIVE SERVICE THIS PERIOD	1	11	15
		(b) PRIOR ACTIVE SERVICE	24	1	24
17a. SECONDARY SPECIALTY NUMBER AND TITLE	b. RELATED CIVILIAN OCCUPATION AND D.O.T. NUMBER	(c) TOTAL ACTIVE SERVICE (a + b)	26	1	9
12Z5P COMBAT ENGR SR SGT 751006	NA	(d) PRIOR INACTIVE SERVICE	0	8	21
		(e) TOTAL SERVICE FOR PAY (c + d)	26	10	0
		(f) FOREIGN AND/OR SEA SERVICE THIS PERIOD	0	0	0

19. INDOCHINA OR KOREA SERVICE SINCE AUGUST 5, 1964	20. HIGHEST EDUCATION LEVEL SUCCESSFULLY COMPLETED (In Years)
☑ YES ☐ NO VIETNAM 680525-690518	SECONDARY/HIGH SCHOOL 12 YRS (1-13 grades) COLLEGE 0 YRS

21. TIME LOST (Preceding Two Yrs)	22. DAYS ACCRUED LEAVE PAID	23. SERVICEMEN'S GROUP LIFE INSURANCE COVERAGE	24. DISABILITY SEVERANCE PAY	25. PERSONNEL SECURITY INVESTIGATION	
				a. TYPE	b. DATE COMPLETED
NONE	30 Days	☐ $15,000 ☐ $5,000 ☒ $20,000 ☐ $10,000 ☐ NONE	☒ NO ☐ YES AMOUNT	BI	660224

26. DECORATIONS, MEDALS, BADGES, COMMENDATIONS, CITATIONS AND CAMPAIGN RIBBONS AWARDED OR AUTHORIZED

National Defense Service Medal
Combat Infantryman Badge
Armed Forces Expeditionary Medal (Laos)

Master Parachute Badge
Vietnam Service Medal
Republic of Vietnam Campaign Medal with 60 Device

27. REMARKS

Republic of Vietnam Cross of Gallantry with Palm
Navy Parachute Badge
Air Medal
Army Commendation with V Device
Bronze Star Medal with V Device
Joint Service Commendation Medal
Republic of Vietnam Cross of Gallantry with Gold Star
Army Commendation Medal (2d Oak Leaf Cluster)
Presidential Unit Citation
Meritorious Unit Commendation
Republic of Vietnam Honorary Jump Wings
Good Conduct Medal (6 Awards)
Indonesian Parachute Badge
Meritorious Service Medal   Individual requests a copy of DD Form 214

28. MAILING ADDRESS AFTER SEPARATION (Street, RFD, City, County, State and ZIP Code)	29. SIGNATURE OF PERSON BEING SEPARATED
Rt. 1 Box 58 Waynesville, MO	

30. TYPED NAME, GRADE AND TITLE OF AUTHORIZING OFFICER	31. SIGNATURE OF OFFICER AUTHORIZED TO SIGN
ROBERT E. LEE 1LT AGC Asst AG	

DD FORM 214 1 NOV 72	PREVIOUS EDITIONS OF THIS FORM ARE OBSOLETE.	THIS IS AN IMPORTANT RECORD SAFEGUARD IT.	REPORT OF SEPARATION FROM ACTIVE DUTY

26

My final DD 214 upon separation from the U.S. Army. When it's over, it's over, and it was definitely over for me.

the fog is such a problem we could set down and walk up to the crash site."

It was only forty minutes later when I heard the chopper rotate and take off. At first I thought it might be a routine flight and it would be back for us. But, after a while I got real concerned and hustled to Ferguson's office. Charlie was gone. "He left on the chopper," I was told.

"What the hell is going on?" I wondered, and went to II Corps's commo room. The radio man was monitoring conversations between the chopper and the FAC as they flew toward the crash site. They were talking about the dense cloud cover when the first positive news came up. They reported that the radio beacon was moving. Then I heard a lot of excitement on the radio, "Shit, they walked right out of the cloud bank. They're coming out into a clearing right below." I knew for sure it was right where I told Ferguson they'd find them.

When Dick got off the helicopter, he just brushed the whole thing off. I asked the FAC how he was. He just shook his head and grinned. "If I ever have another crash I hope Meadows is with me. He flat took care of my ass."

The plane was at treetop level when it stalled. Trees pushed through the wings, making for a slow descent to the jungle floor. Dick knew the rescue plane couldn't get through the fog bank to the crash site. He did what I thought he would do. He took the pilot to the top of a small ridge, one where we had been on our first time out with the STRATA teams. Then he followed that ridge down to the small plateau below and walked right out of the fog bank into a slash-and-burn area. Ferguson was waiting right at the edge of the fog as they popped out.

Dick had the FAC grab another aircraft for my turn over the AO. The FAC flew the same route and I was barely able to see a little of the downed O-1 beneath the canopy. "We wound up almost upside down," he said. "There was a lot of gasoline pouring out, so Dick got us the hell out of there."

In a few minutes we were circling our practice AO. Dick was right. The area below me presented the same terrain as our mission area in the North. The Da Lat area is like a big plateau with deep ravines, where for years the rivers cut out the land. To go from one plateau to another, you would go way down through the ravines and up the other side. Then you might be faced with a miles-long plateau to cross. If you continued toward Laos it rose up a little bit from the plateau, then dropped off the other side. The drop was several hundred meters into the flat on the other side. The hills were also pretty steep in North Vietnam, and that was the terrain I had set in my mind. The other similarity below was a lack of slash-and-burn zones. Dick's photos didn't show any in our target area. That was because there weren't many Montagnard-type hill people in the North working the steep hillsides.

I called Larry from II Corps and confirmed we were ready for the team. Dick had planned to stay only one day, since he was still busy with teams in the North. But he wanted to go back and take us in to the crash site. He also wanted a souvenir.

Larry brought the team in on a C-47 early the next morning. Our insert aircraft, two Hueys, were not ready yet, so we moved the men to one side of the airstrip for a briefing update. The first business was to strip and secure the wreck of the O-1. The FAC would be along to make sure we took the radio gear and anything of a classified nature. By the time the Hueys arrived we had confirmation that the wreck was still undisturbed. We headed out with Dick and the FAC.

In about ten minutes we were looking down on the crash site. It was still difficult to see under the canopy. We flew large circles around it to spot any enemy movement toward the crash site and dropped down. We went in as if it were a bona fide operation and inserted right at the bottom of the long ridge that held the wreck. On the ground we were about five hundred meters from the ridge where Dick and the FAC had come out of the fog bank. Once we made it to the ridge, we walked right to it.

The aircraft was close to upside down and gasoline was still leaking all over. While my men stood security a safe distance away, Larry, Dick, and the FAC cleaned out the hulk. Dick had his souvenir—the propeller. Once they got it off, two of my Cambodians carried it back to the clearing. Dick, his prop, and the FAC flew back to Da Lat.

We worked our way cross country. We were trying to go the exact distance and cover the exact terrain as the actual mission and trying to establish a time frame for our travel to the target in the North.

We were getting used to each other, and the men were relaxed enough to giggle and mess around. They felt safe, but I didn't know if we were or not. Hell, there were a lot of NVA there, too. Very soon, we started picking up fresh enemy trails. There were the telltale clues: worn and slick trails, displaced underbrush, freshly broken branches, and disturbed jungle floor.

The Cambodians had two moods, jolly and serious. Once we started seeing all the NVA signs, their expressions changed and they turned very quiet and watchful. We had to be prepared for enemy contact at any time.

The only U.S. I knew of were A-camps quite a way from Da Lat in both directions. But it looked as if there was no American unit between Da Lat and the border. The NVA was free to move to and from Da Lat. I didn't know why they had been avoiding us. They had the opportunity to initiate an ambush, but they were choosing not to. I guess their vegetables were too important to them.

Dick had given me strict orders not to engage or pursue them. He had given II Corps our AO and route of travel, and that was the only clearance we had.

He had selected a good area for us. The canopy was very heavy. Occasionally, sunlight pierced through like a knife, making eerie spotlights to walk through. There were huge trees, where the first branch didn't pop out for maybe fifty feet. I never liked to stay down low and moved higher, near the top of the ridge line.

I started looking for a place to RON. I preferred to set the team on the side of a hill where we couldn't be skylined by showing a silhouette on top of the ridge. I would pick out a good terrain feature, move around it to confuse anybody trying to track us, and then, well after dark, go back to it and put down for the night. I found a good place, looking down a ridge on both sides, so nobody could walk up on us.

I didn't send out patrols. We hadn't been detected up to this point, and I didn't want to start leaving signs by wandering around. Our location had thick enough growth and still gave us room to spread out in a good-sized circle. Quon positioned himself facing the rear, where we entered the area. We didn't put out any mines since no one was following us.

We were on the move well before first light. It was midafternoon when we approached the clearing that was to simulate the DZ for the "stay-behind team." It was grass and had never returned to a jungle state. The grass ranged from waist high to over a man's head. Dick and I had anticipated taking three days from insertion to the target in the North. But, with no enemy contact, we were at the practice target in a day and a half. There was no trail like the actual one in the North, so we didn't know exactly how the "stay-behind team" was coming in.

I placed the men behind Larry and me in a thicket on the edge of the grassy area. Their job was to secure our back from NVA ambush while Larry and I scouted the area. With just the two of us moving around we made less noise and were less exposed than the whole team would be.

On one trail, we came across tracks of a weapons carrier. It could have been an antiaircraft piece or a rocket launcher. It had at least two wheels about three feet apart and would be a familiar sight for the photo interpreters. Larry used his PIN-EE camera as I held my CAR-15 down near the track. The S-2 boys would use the gun as a scale and they would know exactly what weapon it was.

The DZ covered a good-sized area, and it took all day long to find the best place to observe the drop. That location meant having to cross an open area on the side of a hill with waist-high grass. We would wait until after dark and then move to the target.

The next day was spent scouting for any signs of trails in and around the DZ. I was looking for something that resembled what we'd find in the North. We didn't find one. We had again positioned the rest of the team behind us. They were sitting just at the edge of the jungle watching everything we did. I didn't think my Cambodians really knew what was going on.

As soon as it was completely dark, I took Larry, Binh, Tranh, and Quon, and we moved on our bellies through the tall grass to the observation position. Tranh and Quon were along to provide security for Larry and me, nothing more. The rest of the team was kept back to secure an area for an escape route if needed.

At about 2300 hours we heard a C-130 drone overhead. Larry and I took the starlight scopes out of their carrying cases and got them ready. I also took out my 7X50 binoculars because it was dark as pitch—no moon. I saw the C-130, just barely, at about a thousand feet. Dick kicked out the bundles and I saw a couple float down above the ridge line, then they disappeared behind it.

Dick had rehearsed some of our Vietnamese mercenaries to be the "inside team" for us. They emerged from the jungle to my right, the southeast corner of the DZ. I could just barely see them with the binoculars, and even at that, only a part of them was visible through the tall grass.

They went to retrieve the drop. They were talking all the time because they wanted us to know they were there. We had live ammo and we were still in a damned war zone and they didn't want us to pop them. The first man after the bundles lit a cigarette—it bloomed out and lit up the scope. It blew the sensors in that sucker. I mean, it flat went out. But the match flame was so quick I couldn't recognize them anyway.

When they got into the drop zone, you couldn't see them at all. We were slightly above them, so they weren't below the vegetation. The background was the hillside. If we had been able to get below them we might have been able to "skyline" them. The best was the 7X50 binoculars. We could get their full outline, but we could not distinguish faces or the uniforms. While they were retrieving the bundles, we changed our position several times to get right on top of them, which on a real mission would be a no-no. The starlight scope was still ineffective. Before we went on the actual mission, we would have photos of the people. But I thought, "If we can't see their faces, what good would that do?" They gathered up the parachutes and disappeared into the jungle.

Dick flew into the DZ by chopper the next morning and came to our location. "Well, how did it go?"

"It didn't go worth a damn. We couldn't identify anything."

"We're running another drop tonight," Dick said. "Can you get closer?"

That night we crawled out to the DZ on our bellies again. We got close enough to hit them with a rock. But I still couldn't make out their faces, even with the starlight. It was just too dark. I tried real hard to see them through the 7X50. But I could still barely see them moving around the DZ. All we knew was that it was people who spoke Vietnamese. Then we snuck around the edge and got down in the lower part. When they lit a cigarette, my eyes weren't quick enough to determine what they looked like.

"We were able to skyline them a little bit, but we still couldn't identify them," I told Dick. "We're going to need a daylight drop or else I won't be able to identify them."

"Maybe you can get down during the daylight hours before the drop," he suggested. "The inside team normally checks out the DZ and sets up their signals before dark."

The signal lights would represent a letter of the alphabet for the month. When the aircraft flew over, he had to confirm the prearranged letter for the drop to proceed. There had to be at least twenty-five meters between the lights to be distinguishable from the air.

"If you can't observe them doing that," Dick went on, "you'll have to go to the village and observe them there."

I still didn't think I would be able to identify any of the inside team even during daylight. But there was one possibility. "Dick, I think we could use a 7X50 with a camera attached and then let MACVSOG pick through the photos for identification." I didn't want to be the one to decide who they were. After two years people change appearance, and the handlers who had put them in were long gone.

About an hour before first light, we started the second half of the mission. I had five days to work our way back through the jungle to Da Lat. This gave me the chance to come down on more serious team training. I talked to the men about things they would do—asked them where they were looking and walking.

On our insertion in the North, after our plane was spotted, the North Vietnamese would send in a team to search. This is when we would maneuver to evade them on the way to the target. So we practiced procedures for movement.

When walking on patrol through the jungle, each man's full attention is directed at a specific field of view—an area of responsibility. But you never want to lose sight of the man in front. Stay four to six yards behind. Stop about every ten to fifteen minutes to just listen for a few seconds. Don't create a track by following in another's footsteps. More than one man will make a trail. Cover any tracks with jungle debris—sticks, leaves, mud.

Breaking branches is a dead giveaway. Don't break off twigs to put in your mouth—a bad habit. Don't push a bush away with your weapon, push by hand. The weapon has a tendency to scar the bushes. Rather than even push against a bush, it's better to go under it. Even with care, a leaf could be turned upside down and it might stay that way. Clothes might catch on thorny vines, leaving torn pieces behind, so try to avoid areas of too thick vegetation, except when being pursued.

Stay off soft or wet areas and away from clearings. Try not to step where the enemy stepped. We each carried a pair of rubber-tire sandals, like the VC wore, in case we got into an area of soft ground we had to cross. I thought this was so much hokum and we never resorted to them.

We moved through the jungle, then doubled back and retraced our path to see if we left any trail. I showed the men how to traverse a ridge without taking a straight-line path, avoiding steep ravines that a man had to climb out of.

In traversing the hillsides, we would come upon little springs seeping out of the mountain. We didn't step in them because they would be loaded with leeches, and they crawled up your trouser legs. Some teams fastened their trouser legs or stuck them inside the boot. That was uncomfortable for me.

I kept mine loose over my boots and just avoided the leeches.

Vietnam presents a lot of different terrain. There was always the slash-and-burn growth of tall grass. The height depended on how long the area had been cleared. If it had been cleared for no more than a couple of years, it would be no more than waist high. This was the work of the hill tribes. They would clear a place and remain four or five years planting and harvesting, then move on. Once they abandoned it, whoosh! up came the jungle with secondary growth thicker than before—some of it taller than a building. The areas they carved out were rarely bigger than a football field—in most cases half. The jungle in South Vietnam was full of them.

The untouched jungle was easier to go through because the underbrush was not as thick as in the slash-and-burn areas. The trees were very tall; the canopy touched and overlapped, shielding the jungle floor from sunlight.

I taught the men to avoid areas in which the enemy can set up. Using a trail was a no-no. If you use a trail, you're going to get shot up. Don't use the very top of a hillside. You're too exposed and there's always going to be somebody on top who's a lookout. So stay about two-thirds up a mountain to conceal your movement. Traverse around, go up on the opposite side of the drop-off. That's the way to follow a mountain range. If you come to the finger of the ridge don't get on the end. Go where the finger joins the mountain and cross there. If you're coming up a ravine, follow it up until the little stream almost peters out and cross. It's the thinnest part of the ridge and you're out of sight more quickly.

When we came to a trail and wanted to cross, we backed up. I would hold up two fingers and point in that direction, signaling two men to peel off in a rehearsed path. I then pointed to two more men and directed them to cross, and so on. As they crossed, the men still covered their assigned fields of view.

When a man crossed he watched and covered as the next man crossed. Everybody watched for the other guy, then we reassembled on the other side of the trail. If it was a narrow path not used much, I held up one finger and pointed the direction each man would take across. I held up my fist if I wanted the men to stop.

Hand signals were very simple so as to avoid misunderstanding. We didn't have to use a lot of hand signals because we had already practiced jungle movement so much. We would point to eyes, ears, or mouth. If we heard the enemy, we held up a hand with the thumb down. Thumb up when it's all clear to move. When we were on a break, I put my thumb up when it was time to move out.

I introduced the men to something they never heard of—a "quail bust" or "covey" maneuver. On my command, a hand signal to "fan out," we would do a fast split. We spread out and zigzagged through the jungle about one hundred yards, coming back around in a circle to see who was tracking us. If the enemy stopped, they were sitting ducks while they were trying to figure out why our trail suddenly split up into a lot of individual trails. While they're thinking about it, BLAM!

If the trail was clear, I would bring the men together with a birdcall. They remained spread out until I called them in. We would come together in about two hundred yards. We practiced about a dozen times.

Each man knew what he was supposed to do in any movement. When the point made contact, the rest would drop to their knees, and the instruction would be to follow my lead—do what I did. In most cases we wanted to get the hell out of there. If the point man did his job, we could split. He had to kill the ones he saw. If he didn't, we would have to finish the job for him. We couldn't turn our backs and run. We'd all be dead men.

I got along well with the team. We just walked all over, traversed and navigated. We hit our extraction point and called the FAC, who had been overhead the whole time.

Once we had a camera rigged to 7X50 binoculars, Dick and I decided to try the mission again. Since we got to the target in only a day and a half, we thought about landing farther back and even asked, "Should we make the insert point farther back in the actual mission?" We mulled it over and asked ourselves, "What if there are villages in between? What about house dogs from the villages? If we have enemy contact, what then?" The upshot was that unless we had more complete intelligence it was better to stick with the original LZ picked for the North.

For the second practice, we decided to take the team to the outskirts of Da Lat in a truck and spend more time en route to the target. But there was one new element added—Captain Ronald R. Glancy, our STRATA S-4. He wanted his Combat Infantryman Badge. He said he heard my team was the best and begged me to take him out to qualify. He swore up and down that he wouldn't influence the mission.

"If it's all right with the S-3," I said, "it's all right with me." His face lit up.

Dick got ahold of me a little bit later and told me he had approved having Glancy on the mission as long as I thought he could stay in the background. "He's really desperate to go," Dick said. "But he still wanted me to assure him that he wouldn't get his rear end shot off."

When the team flew in to Da Lat, we transferred them right to a deuce-and-a-half and headed out of town. We took the road south until it narrowed to where the truck couldn't proceed. We formed our patrol. I told Captain Glancy to walk behind Larry as we started down the trail and to pay attention to all my signals. The trail turned west and soon ran alongside a ravine. We were picking up signs of fresh NVA activity on trails leading away from where we wanted to go. My guess was supply trains.

We had gone about two hundred yards when we encountered a bunch of indigenous carrying big empty baskets. They were old Vietnamese men, and we knew they were up to no good. We gathered them for questioning. We weren't really interrogating them or harassing them, but they were scared because we were armed to the teeth, ready for combat. We asked them questions like "Do you know what's going on up in that area? Do you know if there are NVAs?" We also asked a bunch of questions designed to mislead them—to see if they would slip up and tell us who they were supplying. One said he was a farmer who lived down the trail. But I knew there weren't any houses or anything else, for that matter. Hell, I flew the area—nothing but a trail. I knew they were giving us crap. They were part of a supply train moving in and out of Da Lat.

We took pictures, smiled at them, and told them, "Go ahead." This prompted us to look the area over carefully and cover our tracks. We didn't want them to know we were headed in a particular direction.

Over the next two days we headed almost due west, winding up at the edge of our high plateau about fifteen klicks from Da Lat. The terrain dropped off at this point into a series of deep ravines. By the looks of things, we were getting near the target.

It was late in the afternoon of the third day when we got to the edge of the tall grass that marked the drop area. Larry and I were preparing to start scouting the area for signs of our "inside team" when the FAC called.

"No aircraft tonight. But S-3 wants you to continue the mission. He'll call you in A.M."

About an hour after dark, I had the whole team practice night movement in the jungle around the DZ. Then we crawled through the grass to the top of the ridge overlooking the DZ. Through the 7X50 I could barely make out shapes. It was only because they were playing around making noise that I was able to pick them out at all. I didn't even take the starlight out of its case.

The next morning, Dick was back up on the radio. He asked us to move around to the "village," half a klick from the DZ in the direction of Da Lat. Of course, there was no village, but he had the mercenaries collected there to simulate the village we might have to observe in North Vietnam.

"Take a bunch of pictures," he said.

The "village" was located east of the DZ down a gradual slope that eventually ended at a fast-moving river. Halfway to the river the slope met a plateau. Several ridges ran off the plateau. One ridge came up from a gulch that might have water after a good rain. The men we were looking for were sitting on the side of the ridge in a little campsite. They were talking and really not doing much of anything. We watched them for several hours, right on through the usual two-o'clock native siesta.

I took a whole roll of pictures of the men. The view through the 7X50 was good, but I still didn't think the images would be clear enough for identification. I was satisfied we had done all we could and moved the team out of the area toward Da Lat.

By the time we were a day out of Da Lat I was really tired of the rations. At first light that morning, the FAC was up on the radio.

"Well, boys, what can I do for you today?"

"I wouldn't mind having something decent to eat besides these stinking rations," I told him. "I sure could use a big piece of bread." I was just cutting up with him.

In two hours he returned. "I've got your request for you. Give me some smoke so I can find you."

I moved out into a clearing and popped a white phosphorous grenade. He threw out a bundle. Darned if it wasn't full of French bread. Fresh, too—just out of the bakery. We sat down and ate every bit of it. It was just bread and water, but the bread was so good tasting. Here we were, feasting on fresh French bread in the middle of a war zone. The Cambodians thought it was just great. They looked at me and smiled. I guess they never got treatment like that before. I was their man from that time on.

By the time I got back with Charlie Ferguson at II Corps, I had a lot of notes on locations of the enemy trails we came across. He said he would pass them on to the S-2. But I had this feeling that, if we came back to the area, we'd still be the only U.S. between Da Lat and the Laotian border.

Even though I couldn't identify the men at the DZ with either the starlight scope or my 7X50 binoculars, Dick and I didn't consider the practice a flop. The men got a lot of practice moving in terrain similar to our objective in the North, and we were all getting along very well as a team.

What remained was for Dick and me to figure a way to get the information SOG needed from the night drop. The only way to really identify them would have to be a daylight observation, taking pictures for later identification. And that's what we finally planned to do. We would observe the drop at night and follow them to wherever they took the supplies, where we would wait until daylight to take pictures.

Of course, this wasn't without tremendous risk. First of all, we would be traversing a mountain next to our infilt point to get to the DZ. That would consume three, maybe four days, depending on NVA activity en route. Then we would have to position ourselves to observe the drop without being spotted. If the night drop didn't work for the starlight scope, we would have to locate them again in the daytime in order to photograph them, exposing us even more to enemy detection.

I told Dick, "If you're worried about them, don't supply them. Why risk our necks? And, if they're still ours, why risk compromising them if some of us get caught?" If push came to shove, we both knew the team could be dealt with. "Just bomb their asses," I said. "They're bombing in the North anyway."

WE WERE LESS THAN TEN DAYS AWAY FROM MISSION LAUNCH WHEN MACV-SOG received a startling message from JCS. President Johnson wanted to announce to the world a halt to the bombings of North Vietnam. This was pure political horseshit. It was October and the elections were coming up fast. Vice President Humphrey was in trouble in the polls over Johnson's policy in Vietnam, and the President wanted to salvage his behind.

Colonel Olchovik, Meadows, and Ted Gaweda were upset as hell. Along with a bombing halt, all overflights were also to be stopped, and we had five teams in the North.

Whenever STRATA teams were running, the colonel had an open line to the Air Force's 56th Special Operations Wing at NKP, the 90th Special

Operations Wing in Da Nang, and the 12th Special Operations Squadron in Udorn. He also had F-111s ready on the flight line at NKP for TACAIR support. All were on emergency alert to extract the teams. 0-2 FACs found three of the teams, but two wouldn't answer their radios.

General Westmoreland wanted to know how long it would take to extract the men. He had to give JCS an answer. According to their mission-operation plans, the two teams were probably moving to their assigned exfilt points. To the best of our figuring, they were still four days away.

Request for a delay in halting bombing and overflights was relayed to JCS, who passed it on to the Secretary of Defense and the President. Johnson didn't make his announcement.

Gaweda dispatched fully loaded A-1 Skyraiders from NKP to search the teams' AO and provide support for extraction. Over four days they ran eleven flights into the North, circling at between 1,200 and 1,800 feet, ready to drop down as soon as the teams called. We never knew if we would ever find them by the time the four days ran out. Since we hadn't heard from them, SOG was giving serious thought to leaving them in.

It was very late on the fourth day when the FACs established contact. The word was that the teams saw the planes fly over, but they maintained radio silence, fearing NVA were monitoring their frequency.

But there was one more hurdle. There was a lot of cloud cover. It seemed that everything had conspired against us to get them out in four days. We had a lot of heroes that day. The A-1s, the FACs and the Jolly Green pilots flew into the cloud cover over what was treacherous mountain terrain. Our own SF from NKP were in the helicopters and pulled the men out.

On 31 October, 1968, the President went on the air to announce: "As of November 1st, all air, naval, and artillery bombardment of North Vietnam will be stopped."

At the same time, Gaweda was putting the air crews in for the Distinguished Flying Cross.

"The mission is not off," Dick said. "But the air drop is gone. What do you think?"

I looked at the map and did a quick mental run-through. "We can insert into Laos right on the border and walk the damn twenty-five klicks."

"How long?" Dick wanted to know.

"I'd say ten days in and ten days out."

"Hell, Joe. Can you do it? We can't resupply you or pull you out."

"Yes." I really and truly thought we could do it.

Dick and I put the operation plan together and sent it to MACVSOG. They denied our request and scrapped any further plans to observe the team. Whoever they might have been, the poor men were on their own.

chapter 16

Code Name: Copperhead

Slack time will flat take the edge off a team. And while the President and his Defense Secretary fiddle-farted around with the bombing halt, that's all we had. I didn't like it because I still had one big question unanswered.

"All this training is well and good," I said to Dick Meadows, "But I'd like to see what they can do under fire."

Dick knew damn well I already had something in mind.

"While I was doing recon for the practice mission, I flew over a bridge south of Da Lat that was in a deep gorge. Along with all the enemy signs we came across, I'm convinced that the bridge is part of the NVA supply line in and out of Da Lat. I know about where we can find a group of the little devils and I know I can make contact down there."

Dick brightened at the suggestion. He and I both knew that my men needed a real test.

"Get on a plane," he told me. "Go to Da Lat and check it out. When you get back lay it out and we'll discuss it."

Once in the air out of Da Lat, I asked the FAC to head west toward our old practice AO, a distance of about eight miles. The old landmarks came up fast and my mind flashed with the image of the bridge and its location. I had the FAC circle back well to the south of Da Lat to look for the river I had spotted on the last aerial recon. Sure enough, the plateau below us ended and we zoomed out over a deep, deep gorge. And there was the river. The FAC dropped to a thousand feet above the rim and we followed the river back toward Da Lat.

We were six klicks southwest of the city when that small makeshift bridge appeared way down at the bottom of the gorge. I mean, a long way down in there across a fast-moving mountain stream, which you couldn't ford because it came across the mountain in a torrent like a waterfall. I knew the bridge had to have been put in by the NVA because there were no other indigenous in the area, no farms, no villages, no nothing—and no other military.

The FAC slowed so I could take a long look with my binoculars. I knew contact with the NVA was a good bet down there, but the bridge itself was too juicy a target to leave alone. So I decided we'd have one more mission—blow the sucker.

Just as I took my eyes off the bridge, I saw something else. Coming up through the canopy on the northwest rim were a bunch of little green dots. The FAC and I were talking over head sets. "What's those damn green things coming up from the jungle at us?" I asked.

"Those are tracers. They're shooting at us."

"What are you going to do about it?"

"Shit, I'm going home!"

We flew the hell out of there back to Da Lat. We didn't get hit, but we sure had a good view of them. It made me smile, knowing I had confirmation that the enemy was all in there.

I reported to Dick that I had a "good target." We pored over the maps and detailed the mission. I said I thought it would take three days to hit the bridge.

Dick gave me the nod. "Well, the mission to the North is still on hold, so go on down. If we need you we'll get you back."

"Give it a name," Dick said. "What do you want to call this operation?"

My eyes fell to the snakebite scar on my right forefinger. This was a reminder of my first encounter with something deadly in the woods. "Copperhead," I said. I showed the scar to Dick. "Call it 'Copperhead.' I tangled with the little rascal back in the Smoky Mountains and lived to tell about it."

So the mission took the name. Our AO would be "Copperhead" and every-one on our assigned radio frequency would know me as "Copperhead." I'm not a superstitious person, but I thought the name fit for this first encounter with someone who could bite you back.

Binh, my interpreter, met me the next morning. He was the only one from the camp we let into our OP-34 compound. I gave him a quick brief-ing on the mission. He and the team were already aware I wanted to return to Da Lat and get some NVA. I gave them the word before I went to recon the area. This was probably going to be Binh's first enemy contact and I could see concern cross his face. But I knew he trusted me to carry it off. He was to contact Tranh and tell him to alert the team for isolation the next morning.

Prior to isolation, Tranh would tell me what he and his men wanted in weapons. If I agreed, I passed the list of weapons and ammo to "Stick" Simp-son, our tall, lanky supply sergeant, who would pull from the SOG CONEX grab bag. I always added one more weapon, the M-79 40mm grenade launcher. It could lob a mean round a good distance.

Binh met me at the gate. As we walked to the isolation building, he told me Tranh and Quon were worried about how many men I wanted to take. They were afraid to go into combat with an uneven number. The team would have thirteen, what with me, Larry, Binh, and ten of them. This hadn't come up on the training missions because we weren't looking to contact the en-emy. But, like the Laotians I worked with in 1961, the Cambodians had strong religious beliefs that controlled the way they went into combat. You never wanted to step on their toes when Buddha was involved. I took one man off.

The men of SOG were called "Sneaky Petes." We used it ourselves. In fact we used it first. SF would ask other SF, "Are you a Sneaky Pete?"

"Yes." That's what we did—sneak around.

The whole idea is for the enemy not to know we're in town. To rig ourselves for a mission required team preparation that bordered on the scientific.

During our last practice runs outside Da Lat, Larry and I had begun to refine how we prepared the team for the jungle. On the early exercises, the men weren't really into a lot of sterilization or quietness. But with the pos-sibility of running deep into NVA country, we showed the men how to be as invisible as possible to the enemy. I made certain they understood the noise that a canteen or any other metal object could make and made sure they didn't carry any. We took all their grenades and put them inside a canteen pouch. Exposed grenades could hit something or snag as you moved through thick jungle and detonate. In addition, the canteen pouch had a soft lining that muffled any sound from the cluster inside. We also made a tight load putting extra grenades in the pouch. All ammo likewise went into canteen pouches. You could put seven twenty-round magazines into the one-quart pouch, instead of carrying only the standard-issue four-magazine M-16 ammo pouches. There was another reason. The old ammo pouch was too slow to access—too many snap fasteners. The canteen pouch had one. Also, the ammo pouch was made of the U.S. Army's best rough hard canvas, which made a noise if it brushed up against anything. As a final touch we also taped down rifle sling swivels and all loose buckles.

Inside each of our rucksacks was a lightweight poncho, a camouflaged nylon poncho liner that doubled as a ground cover, two extra pair of socks, a claymore mine and some toe poppers. I was also packing a couple of 2.5-pound sticks of C-4, wires, and detonators for taking out the bridge. There was also extra film for the PIN-EE camera, which I carried in my left shirt pocket.

Since taking a prisoner was always a secondary mission, I had a pair of handcuffs wrapped in one of the extra pair of socks and stuffed into a side pocket of the rucksack. Both easy-access side pockets also held ten days' worth of specially prepared rations. The rucksack also held a collapsible bladder-style two-quart water container, which we would fill up before leaving isolation. I had the only flashlight for the team. It was buried under everything else since I never expected to use it. In the jungle I always knew where I was going.

As I was the only trained medic on the team, I had pressure bandages and capsules of morphine, and carried a blood pack with an IV kit (serum albumin blood-volume expander) in a camouflaged pouch taped to the back cross piece of the rucksack harness.

On the webbed pistol belt hung special-issue plastic water canteens. On this particular mission we would carry three. But we would drink from the two-quart container every chance we could because we needed the canteens reserved as part of our getaway gear.

The belt held all the getaway gear. This was our survival equipment. You might discard your rucksack if you had to get the hell away from a situation, but the belt stayed on.

Since we had more size and girth than our little Cambodians, Larry and I also packed more on our belts. Right in front of me, ready to grab, was my M-34 WP smoke canister, which I had spray-painted black. Next, moving clockwise, were two canteen pouches holding my ammo. Along with the full clip in my CAR-15, I went into a mission with three hundred rounds. Figuring two slugs per NVA, I could create a lot of misery out there.

Then, at my back were a small emergency pouch with bouillon cubes, emergency pressure bandage, signal mirror, orange signal panel (parachute cloth), red, green, and white pen flares, and other items we determined would sustain us for three days if we had to abandon our rucksacks and make a run for it.

Coming around my left side were three canteens full of water and a canteen pouch holding four M-33 baseball grenades, which I preferred to the fragmentation types. My fourteen-foot nylon sling rope hung from the back of my belt—rolled up super tight and attached with the snap link.

Batman never had it better.

The pistol belt was so heavy we had to have carrying harnesses that hooked up like suspenders. Over the harnesses we slung our rucksacks.

The other men didn't have knives, but Larry and I did. I carried my trusty Randall Model 14 while Larry had a Marine K-Bar. I hung mine from the left strap of the harness. I never hung anything on the right side of my body. That's my firing side and I didn't want any junk in the way. Hollywood movies didn't give a shit, but I did. I made sure all the men followed suit. I showed them they couldn't carry anything in a position where the gun could hit it.

My compass hung around my neck and sat in my right shirt pocket. When I took a map, it went into a pants pocket.

We fixed our rations so there would be no hard or bulky containers of any kind—nothing to make noise. Larry and I also created our own diet. We used a combination of dehydrated LRRP rations mixed with CIDG dehydrated rations. The CIDG rations had what looked like fish and some other unidentifiable stuff. It contained more rice than ours, but we considered the rest inedible. After we picked through it we were usually left with only the rice.

In an LRRP ration, one meal held everything the standard C-ration containers had except the LRRP was dehydrated—beef and rice, chicken and rice, and so on. The people who never saw combat wrote instructions that hot water quickened the return to an edible state.

Instead of using an entire canteen cup of water to mix with our full daily LRRP ration, to conserve water we would use only a portion of the ration—mostly the meat. And when you are in that high state of alert you don't eat much, anyway. An LRRP meal would take half a canteen cup of water but our meals took about a quarter of a cup each. That way we consumed less water and food but it was still bulk with the rice.

We mixed the rice from one CIDG ration with our select LRRP ration in its plastic bag. We usually planned two meals a day on the mission, so we prepared twenty meals this way. We rolled up the bags, wrapped a rubber band around them, and stuck them in the side pockets of our rucksack. If the LRRP ration had a candy bar, we'd take the candy bar. After fixing up the rations, we gave what was left to the rest of the team. Hell, they'd eat anything.

During the mission you reached back, plucked one of the bags from the rucksack, added some water to the bag, rolled it back up, returned it to the rucksack or stuck it inside your shirt. After about twenty minutes of movement it would be ready to eat. Once empty, the little plastic LRRP bag was rolled up and put back in the rucksack.

If we got busted by the enemy and had to throw off the rucksack on the run, we knew what to eat in the jungle that would sustain us. For me, it would be Panama all over again.

We had our pick of any jungle uniform we wanted. Supply had a couple of CONEXs full. The camouflage tiger suits I wore in Ban Me Thuot couldn't withstand the hard use in SOG and were especially flimsy when it came to the infamous wait-a-minute vines that filled the jungle. The vines had thorns that were like fishhooks. If they ever got you in the face, ear, arm, or shoulder through the clothes, you'd have to wait a minute, back up and unhook it, or it would rip like a razor blade. The only time I had the tiger suit, the vine almost took it off me. That made a lot of noise, too.

The new Army jungle uniforms were also too noisy. The shirts had big pockets in front and the trousers had big pockets on the sides. Even when well washed and with nothing in the pockets, we still couldn't get them soft enough so they wouldn't make too much noise.

The Vietnamese had their own version of the tiger suit, but it was also made of material too thin for jungle abuse. The fit was lousy for us big Americans, and it wouldn't take long before I had been ripped out of them, too.

I finally decided to use the regular rugged cotton fatigues that we used to starch back in the U.S. Larry followed suit. But our brand-new uniforms had a distinct smell, and I knew the NVA would pick it up. So I had some of the women outside the camp stone-wash them for us to remove the new smell and also give the uniform a slight grayish look away from the olive-drab green—and, of course, they'd also be soft and quieter in the jungle. Besides, the camo design from either the U.S. or the Vietnamese wasn't as good in the jungle as the old fatigues. You could stand back in the jungle and that old U.S. uniform hid you better than the multicolored camouflage uniform.

Our little people followed our lead with their own fatigue uniforms. They were South Vietnamese, made of lighter and cheaper material than ours. We still had tiger suits shipped in for them. In the STRATA camp they liked to wear them starched and pressed. It was a dress-up uniform for them, but on a mission they reverted to olive drab.

Our U.S. jungle boots were leather over the foot with heavy green nylon sides. Inside was a synthetic cushion insert with holes, so that if you walked in water it would mash down and force the water from the boot. They came up to midcalf—about 9 inches—not as high as the black boot. The leather part was black, but I never polished them. This wasn't the B-team back at Ban Me Thuot.

Real team sterilization followed a logical formula to achieve cleanliness of uniform and body. While the team was in isolation prior to each mission, all of the clothes they wore, usually just one outfit apiece, were sent out to be stone-washed in the river to remove all human smell. Meanwhile, we'd make the men run around in their skivvies. The uniforms would be put on the day we left.

You could walk through the camp and smell a man who hadn't washed in a couple of days. Likewise, in the jungle, you could smell the enemy for the same reason. After hunting for so many years and reading books on the human scent, I learned that the hotter it is, the faster and farther human scent will travel. We based our training on this. With the jungle's heavy triple canopy, the heat is fairly well contained and compressed and scent will not dissipate upward and will travel laterally. In a cool climate this is less of a problem.

Anytime you're in the jungle and there's nobody there but you, there's that expected musky jungle smell. Anything that's ripe—bananas or anything else—is very easy to find because there's not an awful lot of wind in the jungle. Any aroma, natural or otherwise, kind of hangs there.

I didn't worry about my Cambodians so much since they had the same smell as the NVA, because they ate essentially the same thing—rice and fish heads, stuff like that. And even though we fed them polished American rice, it still didn't prevent them from smelling the same. Like the Vietnamese, my Cambodians smoked these god-awful cigarettes known as Ruby Queens. Smoking on a mission was forbidden, but even that had already found its way into the body odor.

Since each human group has its own smell, and since body odor from sweat is based on the food you eat, Larry and I were really trying to hide ours. We made sure the whole team washed thoroughly with an unscented soap before a mission, something the agent handlers before me didn't even bother with.

When we chose a place to RON we went in after dark and left before daylight because any length of time in one place leaves a smell, mostly from the food you eat. Even with all the care not to drop any of it, cleaning up afterward, rolling up the pouches and all, the food still leaves a residual scent.

When you take a crap, find a soft area and kick the place up with your boot, then cover your stuff with fresh dirt to kill the smell. Don't urinate into a bush—you'll kill it and that's a definite giveaway.

That's why I would never stay very long in one place.

Dick showed up with maps of our AO around the bridge. The team carefully listened to the briefing as relayed by Binh. The session went slow and easy, allowing for translations in both directions. I wanted the men to speak freely.

By midafternoon the briefing turned to the E&E phase—what to do if the team got busted. As careful as you might be in planning a mission, and as complete and detailed as the intelligence might be, there was no way to determine NVA patrol activity in your AO. You usually found that out when you met in the jungle. So, if the outcome busted up the team, you had to plan points for regrouping and getting yourself back home.

We took our maps and set up locations where the team could regroup, rally points that kicked in if we got split up at various stages of the mission. We selected easily identifiable landmarks from the maps, but when we were into the mission we also picked terrain features we passed, such as an anthill or a scar in a cliff, or a particular tree. There would be an initial E&E rally point. If the enemy made that impossible we had a secondary rally point. We also set up checkpoints that would remain for so many hours and move from checkpoint to checkpoint to safety.

Before we stopped to RON, the point man always had the azimuth to the next rally point set up on his compass. That way you had a better chance at survival when the team was on the run at night.

Once Tranh gave us the high sign that the team was mission-ready, Dick, Larry and I left them in isolation and returned to our OP-34 compound. That's where we laid out our own survival E&E and secret commo frequency.

Our covered truck was standing by at the airfield when the team touched down in Da Lat. We backed it up to the aircraft and Larry and the men hustled in. It was a ten-minute trip to the southern outskirts of the city.

The road narrowed down to the large trail where we had detained the group of old Vietnamese on our practice mission. We didn't see any this time as we got off the truck. But they were there all right—somewhere. The bet was we were under observation. So I wanted to throw them off our trail.

The river that finally ran under the bridge almost began at this point. About twenty meters downhill was a spot to cross and begin our descent off the plateau. The trail continued down a ridge to the west that almost paralleled the river. The trail was well worn and that's the route those old bearers probably traveled. I didn't want to get out on that ridge until we got close to the target because I didn't want the NVA to skyline us with binoculars. We took off across the ridge opposite the NVA trail and moved about a mile, zigzagging all the way through the thick jungle.

About five hours into the mission I called a "covey of quail" maneuver. We split up, left our trail, and doubled back a good hundred yards to see if we were being tracked. Our zigzag path had paid off—we were clear. In another hundred yards we came together and resumed our movement to the target.

I was positive that, the way we were moving, the enemy could not possibly observe us unless they were right there on our tail. And only a freak accident would have them there in the first place.

We worked our way up the side of the mountain toward a little plateau that formed the ridge. We were starting to lose what little light we had through the canopy, and, since we weren't being pursued, I called our RON for right on the edge of the plateau, ready to escape into the gorge if need be.

Quon, our tail gunner, automatically stayed back a ways to see if there was anything along the path we used. There wasn't, so we pulled him closer in. We always set our camps as if we were going to come in contact, each man facing out from a small circle—something you must always do if you intend to stay alive very long.

We could see the lights of Da Lat. We weren't that far—ten klicks to the north. I really wanted to listen to what was going on—to hear any sounds that would reveal NVA positions. We could also see the next mountain across the deep gorge. If there was anybody walking around there, we could easily spot him.

The only noise we heard that even remotely sounded like voices was way downriver from us. The river itself made a little noise rumbling off the hillside.

We stayed off the radio, relaying no SITREP for the time being. I preferred the security of total silence.

We were on the move before first light. In about an hour and a half we had moved five klicks and come upon an NVA bunker complex. We listened for any little noise—any sound of enemy activity—but heard nothing. The bunkers were just holes dug into the slopes and covered with branches and foliage. Their condition told me the bunkers were over a week old. I could see it from the age of the leaves used for building the bunkers—their deterioration as well as the deterioration of the bark on the limbs used for supports of the lean-tos. If the limbs and branches were still "bleeding" they would have just been cut.

The campfire remnants and other signs indicated we had missed the enemy by only a few days. There were two major trails—one from the north and one going east, probably across the mountain and down to the bridge. The trails were worn and slick, and my gut feeling was that both were still hot.

We moved along the trail to the east. On one side was a drop straight down into the gorge. The opposite hill was just as straight a drop. A giant tree loomed in front of us. From my time in the woods, I knew someone had been climbing that tree—shinnying up a lot of times. The bark was slick from rubbing, probably from sandals or bare feet.

My little people could grab the first limb. I turned to Binh and pointed to one of my men, Sok.

"I want him up in the tree. I want to know why somebody's been climbing it."

He went right to the top and found a big limb near the top to sit on. He got excited right away and started jabbering in a loud whisper.

"He's found NVA cigarette butts all over the limb," Binh relayed.

That was their observation point. It was above all the terrain, looking back toward Da Lat. It was sobering news. We knew damn well they could have already spotted us. From that tree Sok could look across the gully to their trail on the opposite ridge.

I had him come down and we walked a few more yards and there was a really big trail almost ten feet wide and as slick as a baby's butt—didn't have a leaf in it. We were awfully close and got our defenses up.

I turned to Larry. "I'm going on down the trail. I'll take Binh, Tranh, and three other men. I want to see where it goes. I'll bet it goes to the bridge. We're real close to the bridge. If the NVA isn't on this side, they're on the other.

"You stay here and secure the trail to the north. I'll have the tail gunner ambush it."

I signaled Quon and pointed where we'd been and he knew what to do— close it off so nobody could cut me off from linkup with the rest of the team. He grabbed his bag and two men and went to shut the door—to plant his booby traps. By now he didn't need any supervision.

Then I sent Sang, the point man, down the trail to the west to secure that side. That left Larry and his long-range radio plus a man for security sitting on top of a bunker.

I instructed Larry, "If anybody sets off the mines, pull the men and circle back around. Go back to where we camped last night. I'll meet you there."

I took the point and waved my men to follow. "Let's check this out real close."

Binh fell in right behind me with Tranh and the others in a string. We were just looking, not trying for contact. We eased down the trail another two hundred yards and wound up in front of a second bunker complex sitting to one side of the trail. They were the same age as the first set, so there was no doubt we were moving through a company-to-company encampment—elements of a larger unit.

In each bunker we found sleeping mats, small bamboo tables, and their little stoves, half submerged like barbecue pits covered with bamboo. We moved on, more cautious yet.

The trail began to circle the hillside and started to climb a bit as we came to yet another bunker complex. These bunkers rose up one side of the trail about forty feet higher than the previous ones and had the same look as all the others—more than a week old. However, the trail we were on was new. It was packed down and was obviously still being used a lot. I signaled the men off the trail right away.

We got halfway to what we expected was another series of bunkers when we heard them loud and clear—NVA. It sounded like a whole bunch of them. About seventy-five yards beyond us was a little draw and on the other side was a little hump similar to the three where we found the other bunkers. We hopped off the trail into the bushes and I signaled the men to stay put.

I crawled and crept and got pretty damned close—less than twenty-five yards. They were just yapping away and carrying on. From the different voices I thought I would see a platoon-sized unit, but the jungle was so thick I just couldn't quite see them. I couldn't tell if they were stationary or on the move, so I had to prepare for an enemy patrol that might come up the trail at any moment.

I diddy-bopped back to the men. "All right, let's booby-trap this damn trail we're on. Three claymores. Put them out."

One man each put out a claymore in the middle of the saddle. I checked the angle of fire so they would kill as many as possible and still leave a space without overlap for catching a prisoner.

All this time we weren't more than forty yards to the first NVA. We moved quickly and silently.

I took Sang and another man and pointed to the big tree that sat against our hillside at the edge of the saddle. They knew just what I meant. They ran the wires from the detonators to a position behind the tree where they could observe whatever came down the trail.

As for going up and down trails, I thought NVA patrols were very poor because they were noisy—you could hear them talking. Some SF thought they did it to let us know they were coming, hoping we would try to avoid them. I thought it was a plain lack of training. Once they gave themselves away, I knew where to set the ambush.

I turned to Tranh. "I want the men to hold their position. We're calling TACAIR down on the suckers."

I moved back with Binh to a position at the edge of the ravine on top of the last bunker we found. I signaled one other man over for our cover.

I whispered to Binh, "Get the FAC."

Binh keyed the PRC-25 and whispered our request. There was no response. Binh tried to rouse them two more times. Still nothing. I kept glancing over toward my men behind the tree. I could see them all right, but from this position I couldn't see the trail worth a damn.

We sat there about thirty minutes. Then I thought I heard a noise. I thought it was a patrol at first, but, as it got louder, I quickly changed my mind. Considering all the bunkers around us, the NVA element I crawled to see was obviously the base camp of a much larger NVA unit.

"Well, shit," I thought. "There's too damn many for five men to tackle. This ain't gonna work."

I went to Tranh, who was between me and the tree. "I'm pulling the claymores," I whispered, motioning for him to follow.

I was now sure of one thing. The noise I heard came awfully soon after we started calling the FAC, so we were being monitored on their radios. When we keyed our radio their HQ picked it up and probably alerted a patrol. The NVA was definitely on the move.

I took the hand igniters from my men behind the tree and stuck them in my pocket. "I don't want anybody to come past you," I whispered.

I quietly disconnected the igniter wires and pulled the claymores from the saddle—no sense wasting them in this situation. I ran back to Binh and the radio feeling we would get busted for sure if the FAC didn't show. Binh saw me and shook his head. No FAC.

I had Binh and our security move back another twenty yards, so if anything happened, we could drop off the mountain and circle back to Larry. We hadn't been in that positiom more than two minutes when my men opened up from behind the tree.

I turned to Binh. "Keep trying the FAC. I'm goin' to see what happened."

One of the men at the tree met me halfway, slamming a fresh clip into his M-16. "NVA . . . NVA. Beaucoup . . . beaucoup," he said in an excited whisper.

The point man was reloading his Swedish K and was standing behind the tree waiting to see if any more would come across. I joined them at the tree and looked around at the saddle. There were five NVA lying there, blown away.

"Did you get them all?"

"I think I did," Sang indicated. He pointed to the bushes on the opposite side. "Some wounded crawl back in there."

"How many? Ten . . . twelve?"

"Beaucoup . . . beaucoup," they said.

And that was for damned sure. Now we had identified ourselves to the whole bunch of them. Everything was quiet and I thought this would be the best time to run out and take what I could find from the dead. That thought was interrupted by Binh.

"Joe . . . Joe . . ." He motioned me back to the radio. "NVA . . . NVA . . ." he reported, reacting to what he was picking up on the radio. The NVA was on the radio two frequencies down. Binh had spun the frequency selector and found them.

They were screaming back and forth.

"What are they saying?" I asked Binh.

Binh was getting excited. He translated, "We've been ambushed . . . killed many, many . . . Americans killed us all . . . need help . . . come help!"

Their HQ responded right away. Binh got wide-eyed. "Unit very near . . . telling them to get in bunkers . . . they're coming."

The HQ unit was coming in so clear I just knew they had to be on the other side of the bridge or on the next ridge down.

"That's way too close," I said. "Get back on FAC. I need his ass!"

The interpreter slipped the frequency back and on the first call FAC was there. He was just getting off the ground in Da Lat.

The FAC broke in, "I read you, Copperhead. Received word from Da Nang that you've been calling."

"We got troubles down here," I relayed. "I think we got a little more than we can handle. We just made contact. We've got five NVA down and we're monitoring more on the radio. We hear that enemy reinforcements are coming to help."

"TACAIR is on the way with some fast death and destruction."

"Do you remember the bridge?"

"Affirmative."

"Head out there and bring them in near the bridge."

"I've got your location and I'll be there in ten."

Binh switched frequencies back to the NVA. They were quiet. I pulled my men from the tree.

In ten minutes FAC was right over us. He was above the deep ravine, looking into the hillside I was on but couldn't spot us through the jungle canopy.

"Where are you at?" he asked. "Mark your position."

I wanted to mark the target first, so I pulled a WP pen flare from my belt and screwed it into its little firing tube. Then I told the men, "Go on back to Larry and secure the trail on the way. Tell Larry what's happening. I'll follow in a minute."

I took the PRC-25 from Binh and wiggled around to a place where I could shoot the flare through the canopy at an angle so it would come down on the hillside where the NVA was.

"I'm marking the target first."

"Okay, Copperhead."

"Okay, I'm firing." I had to practically aim straight up. If I fired at even a forty-five-degree angle, the flare would overshoot them. I pulled back the firing pin and let go. The flare shot almost straight overhead and came down right on top of the next NVA bunker complex.

"Do you see the WP? It went right down on their heads."

"I got it positioned. I'm going to fire rockets."

The FAC let loose and I watched him hit next to my WP.

"How'd that rocket do?"

"Right on it."

"Now, where are you at?"

"I'm right where my flare came out."

"I didn't see where it came out . . . only where it came down. Mark your position and get the hell out of there. I've got TACAIR. We're coming in."

I ran back to the third bunker complex and popped my smoke.

The FAC didn't like it. "You're too damn close to the target. Get the hell away."

I wanted to watch the hill right to the last second, so I ran back up the trail about a hundred yards, just beyond the bunker complex.

"Make sure you save enough bombs to blow out the bridge," I told him. "There's also more NVA on the other side of the bridge and possibly on the next ridge down."

"I'll get all of them. Now, show me some smoke."

I popped another WP. "I'm a good five hundred yards from the target," I said.

The truth was I was standing no more than three hundred yards from the target. If the FAC knew the truth, he'd call off TACAIR. But I knew the jungle canopy would help me by holding the smoke until it found an opening farther away.

It worked.

"Damn, you're a long ways already." The FAC was impressed. "TACAIR is here. We're going to hit it."

A flight of fast movers screamed in and started dumping the world on them. As soon as I confirmed the first impact, I turned to run up the trail, but as the rest of the bombs began falling, the ground shook so hard I could hardly stay on my feet. It was like an earthquake.

I got hold of the FAC. "Can you see the bodies we left in the saddle?"

"I'm not sure."

After some of the canopy had been blown away the FAC radioed back, "I can see bodies." I didn't know if he saw our kill or dead from the air strikes. Anyway, I sure as hell wasn't going to stick around to confirm enemy KIA.

This was the first time I had used TACAIR. When they finished, there wasn't anything left in the way of a target for my men. I thought, "Well, shit . . . now what are we going to do? I guess our training mission is over."

When I got back to Larry, his men were still on ambush on the trail to the north. The jungle was still shaking from the air strikes.

I called the FAC for extraction. "This is Copperhead. Get us out of here."

"Okay, Copperhead, I've got slicks on the way. The infantry is getting ready to come out to mop up for you."

We had one more chore—to prepare an LZ for the choppers. We went back past the first bunker and found a slash-and-burn area. Larry and I handed our knives to the men, who began hacking and clearing an area.

We maintained an ambush to the north and didn't pull it until the chopper radioed it was coming in. We pulled the claymores, leaving the toe poppers in their little deadly holes.

II Corps sent two Army slicks. They hovered just off the cleared area. Larry and his men took the first and I put mine on the second. It was midafternoon, and we had already put in one hell of a day of training since first light.

Charlie Ferguson took me to his S-2 section and I briefed them on NVA locations and where we had left our foot mines and other booby traps. S-2 led me to believe that II Corps was sending infantry in right behind us, but as soon as Charlie and I were alone he told me no one would be in our AO until the following day.

Extensive debriefing awaited Larry and me back in Da Nang. My men remained in their Monkey Mountain camp for questioning by our Vietnamese counterparts.

Dick gave me the final word on the mission. We had come upon major elements of the NVA 240th battalion. F-4s and F-100s tore them up and took out the bridge, but II Corps dropped the ball. They sat on their dead ass and didn't send out an infantry unit until two days later. After all we went through, II Corps had given the NVA forty-eight hours to clear the area. To put it mildly, I was pissed.

Later on, the infantry reported finding signs that the NVA had left the area on elephants. But I didn't believe that. If the infantry had found signs of elephants, they were transporting supplies from Da Lat and that meant the 240th was still in there moving freely.

Now I was really pissed.

chapter 17

Black Death

I rested a day, got a good haircut, and saw to it that the men were cleaned up. They were given Friday, Saturday, and Sunday for R&R, and I went to work on a lesson plan based on the Da Lat experience. That was always the first order of business—correct what we did wrong and emphasize what we did that worked.

Every After Action Report has a "Lessons Learned" component. In it you have to be completely open about your responses to every situation you encountered—all the surprises and all the screwups. This is as valuable as any intelligence you bring back because it may mean life or death on the next mission. It gets incorporated into the next team's briefing and gives you a chance to correct team deficiencies before you go on the ground again.

I thought long and hard about how the men moved and responded to my signals and about how we split for the first time. I never dreamed I would split the team in two. But the trail we found was so hot and was being used so much I couldn't recon it unless the rear was covered.

Another thing was having to set up ambushes on a moment's notice as the tactical situation changed, and then pulling one of them at the last minute because I didn't think it would work. So Larry and I rigged the Monkey Mountain course based on what we had just learned.

Right after Monday morning PT, we hit the ground running. We spent two days at the camp going over the Da Lat mission and putting the men through more weapons training. Then it was on to the backside of Monkey Mountain for three days and nights of real serious instruction. Up to that time we hadn't done any night traveling, but because we might still go into the North, I wanted the men to hone their skills at night movement.

And, from the first day on the mountain, we concentrated on "hasty" ambushes and "quick" defenses. By the time ten days were up, I wanted it all to be automatic. There was another reason for this kind of training—taking enemy prisoners.

For me, taking a POW was always a secondary mission, but STRATA teams had never practiced taking prisoners. If any of the teams we sent north had brought back a POW it meant $300 bonus money to each man. OP-34 offered so much because they knew it would be almost impossible for them. They would have to be an exceptional team to do it.

That was before I came on board with my Cambodians. On every mission we were definitely going to be ready to take a prisoner. I didn't want to get off the ground with a pair of unused handcuffs.

We practiced hasty ambushes, leaving a "hole" in the claymore blast pattern so that we could take a prisoner from the middle of a patrol. Usually, the NVA patrol leader would be from the third man to the sixth man. We wanted our hole there. We'd rather have the NCO or the officer than the others.

Every STRATA man carried a claymore antipersonnel mine. It was about the size of a big book, with a hell of a punch. It had little collapsible stick-like legs to secure it in the ground. The front of this deadly package contained about eight hundred steel pellets that were propelled forward by a C-4-type explosive in a sixty-degree pattern. The mines are rigged for remote detonation by placing electric blasting caps in special holes and running the firing wire to wherever you are hiding. We used a hand detonator that sent a current just by squeezing it.

You could aim the claymore to cover a specific area. The trick was to set up several claymores so that when we ambushed an enemy patrol we'd kill all but one. And that poor chump would be so disoriented and shell-shocked we could pounce on him right away. We'd plan a gap in the blast overlap and watch the patrol move into an exact position before we'd detonate.

It took a lot of practice. The blast and the capture had to be instantaneous. I had my other Cambodian team go out on patrol through the woods and we would simulate hitting them. Then, time and time again, we'd place dummies, set the mines, and see if the men could leave one unharmed.

The bombing halt still had us on stand-down. Dick knew full well that I didn't want my team to get rusty, and he didn't want that either. He was itching as bad as I was to get a team on the ground. That's what we were here for.

On his desk were several missions just decrypted from MACVSOG. "We've got a mission in Laos. It's really not much . . . just a road. You might consider it another practice run." Dick grabbed one of the mission orders.

"Find a tank crossing across a small river that separates Laos and South Vietnam. Intelligence can't find it. From the air they can see the road that leads to the river and can see tanks using the road, but it disappears under the canopy, so they can't find the crossing or the tank park. There's just too much cover."

Dick was right. It wasn't much of a mission, but I thought, "Hell, I might as well go ahead while I've got permission to go on the ground."

Dick spread out the maps. He had the intelligence that accompanied the mission order, but that was already a few days old. We would be given the critical last-minute intelligence just before we launched out of NKP. All we had was the mission site and reports of scattered enemy activity in the area from teams that went in earlier. Until we saw the blowups at NKP and talked to the FAC we had no way to determine our exact infilt and exfilt points or supply DZ. The infilt point was very critical, because we wouldn't know what terrain features stood betweeen us and the target until we picked our LZ. We hedged our bets by picking three possible locations as primary LZ and three more as a secondary LZ for infilt and exfilt and waited to see the recon photos at NKP to fix exact locations.

The team would insert ten klicks into Laos. We would cover a specific sector in which we were to find the foot trail that normally parallels a tank trail, make our way to the tank trail, and locate the exact point it crossed the river into South Vietnam.

Dick said, "Take soil samples in the middle of the road and from each side of the road. Shoot an azimuth at each location, then take pictures looking in both directions. That'll be the drill if you come upon any roads that tanks could use for travel."

This was a procedure we practiced a lot. You dug down at least three inches and put the dirt in a sack. The compass reading was made in the direction the tracks were coming from and heading. Put the azimuth, date, and time on the sack and indicate how far apart in the road each sample came from. With the PIN-EE camera take a shot of the trail and use the length of your weapon as a reference for measurement.

Everything went to MACVSOG in Saigon. That's where the CIA went to work on the samples. Just from the soil samples they claimed they had the ability to determine what went down that road without ever seeing the vehicle. I didn't know how they did it, but their conclusions were certainly accurate.

Even with the cover of the jungle, the tanks traveled mostly at night and holed up during the day. So we were also to find where the tanks were concentrated—where they dug themselves into the side of a hill.

"Secondary mission," added Dick, "take a POW."

Prisoners were now a special commodity because of the ongoing Paris peace talks. This kind of intelligence took on a whole new importance. And we were prepared.

For this mission I didn't want more than ten men on the ground for ease of travel and control. So, remembering Buddha, I passed the word to Binh that I wanted seven of the team on the mission. I told Stick Simpson to outfit the team with M-16s. We could carry more ammo than with the AK-47, plus all that Monkey Mountain training had been with the M-16.

I started memorizing the map of our AO, especially all the landmarks around the target. The AO was approximately ten thousand meters square, with the target in the center. This gave us a pretty large area to roam, if necessary. For plotting and coordinating movements we divided it into a ten-square grid. Each square represented one klick—1,000 meters. We were safe only inside our AO because we didn't know what was going on in any area outside. There might be unknown U.S. or NVA activity.

Our mission ran close to the South Vietnam border, which was just at the east edge of the grid. We had to be careful about U.S. and NVA units operating in that area. The U.S. was running long-range reconnaissance patrols all up and down South Vietnam right along the border with Laos and Cambodia. They set up ambushes and just waited to spring them, so I didn't want to run head to head into one of our own LRRPs, especially with all my Cambodians. They wouldn't know I was there and I wouldn't know they were there. Dick had to make sure they would be kept out of our AO. Dick also had to coordinate with CCN, who launched teams out of Phu Bai deep into Laos.

The isolation building sat a few doors up from the mess hall in the STRATA camp. It had beds and showers since the team usually spent three days totally out of touch with the world. For this mission, the team would be in isolation for two days. We made sure that the men were well rested and well fed. We didn't want anyone on a mission who was tired, sick, or malnourished. A man from the camp was assigned to bring food from the mess. Either Larry or I had to be there when the food was delivered. We would take it inside.

Dick pulled into the camp for the briefing. He laid out the maps and went over the mission. All the team saw was the ten-square grid AO. Only Dick, Larry, and I had seen the full map, and that was for our survival E&E. We let the men study the maps for a short time. Then I gave them my briefing on what we were actually going to do—how we were going to proceed to the target. I didn't go into extensive detail, just the high points. Dick and I elected to save the details for Nakhon Phanom, when we would have better intelligence and the advantage of new FAC photos of the AO.

Since U.S. units were not supposed to be in Laos, the team couldn't count on a safe E&E linkup anywhere except back in South Vietnam. We told the men that if we got broken up to head east and cross into South Vietnam, follow the sound of U.S. artillery, and look for one of our Marine fire bases. We gave them the fire-base locations. Since they would probably look like NVA or VC to the Marines, they were to surrender as *chieu hois* and we'd come for them.

In isolation each man checked his weapon, making sure it was clean and working good, and that he had all the ammo he needed as well as his mines and grenades, and that everything was stored where he wanted it in his belt and backpack. Every man knew what the other man was carrying, down to a single bullet, just in case he needed it. We knew who had the claymores, who had the WP smoke, who had the toe-popper mines.

When you went across the fence, there was one personal item left in the footlocker. Your dog tags. Remember, we were not supposed to be there.

Our sealed black deuce-and-a-half left the camp and traveled inland to the Da Nang air base. The airstrip was one of the most crowded in Vietnam and protected with several batteries of Hawk antiaircraft missiles. We were waved in and moved toward one of SOG's sterile C-123s. The truck backed up to the loading ramp and we walked aboard, unseen by anybody on the outside.

The ramp slammed shut and the "civilian" crew cranked it up. The aircraft was part of a fleet assigned specifically to SOG, in this case the USAF's 90th Special Operations Wing. There were also FACs and TACAIR squadrons detailed to us from bases in Thailand. The crew were really military who had been "sheep-dipped" to make it appear that they were civilians under contract.

We had one thing in common. Our official records had been yanked from military personnel files and transferred to top-secret files in the Pentagon. Their cover went a little further. They went through a phony resignation from the service with a made-up official story. The men became civilians, but their careers in the Air Force secretly went on. The CIA then "hired" them as "contractors."

If any of us were ever caught behind enemy lines, we'd be on our own and in deep, deep trouble.

The sun was low in the sky when we started dropping down as we approached the Mekong River, which separated Laos and Thailand. The Thais were a nation very friendly to us at the time and they supported our operations over there. SOG had cross-border operations deep into Laos since 1965 and into Cambodia since 1967. All the teams used Thailand as an E&E sanctuary.

Nakhon Phanom sits just on the Thai side of the river. Just west of the town was the U.S. NKP facility. It was not only our SOG launch site but an Air Force strike base with all types of jet planes. NKP was a large intelligence operation, and as we made our approach from the southeast we could see radio antennas all over the place. It looked almost as spread out as Tan Son Nhut—a maze of one-story buildings and storage areas.

Another sealed truck backed up to the ramp for us. We were taken to the SOG HQ building, which sat by itself in a secure area behind a tall chain-link fence. The truck stopped, went into reverse, and slowly backed up until it bumped something. The rear flap was undone and peeled back. We were at an open door. The only thing we could see was a hallway. The team was taken to their room and Larry, Dick, and I went to another area for our briefing.

Waiting for us was the rest of our control element: Colonel Olchovik, the

FAC pilot, and the FAC rider—the photographer. The lights went dim and they projected blowups of the recon photographs onto one wall. The image covered the whole wall and showed in detail our ten-square grid AO. We started matching our 1 : 50,000 map grid squares to the photos and began getting a very good idea of the terrain we faced.

Like the areas STRATA teams ran in North Vietnam, Laos was mountainous—up and down, up and down. There was good thick jungle all the way, still with all the virgin timber. As for the height of the canopy above, shit, a hundred feet was nothing. It would be easy to move around in, since the full canopy above held back a lot of undergrowth. You would have to reach a slash-and-burn area to get a good view of the sky. Trees averaged three feet in diameter, with several meters between trees.

The FAC would position himself high enough over the target to include the whole AO and to allow the photographer to get maximum detailed coverage. As each picture came up, I asked the FAC a bunch of questions like "Which way were you flying?" "Did you go down lower?" "Did you move down to take closer pictures of areas that might make good LZs?"

They had everything covered. When they found what they thought were suitable LZs for us, they dropped down to take closer photos. And sometimes they got right down on the deck. It's a miracle we didn't lose more FACs. The FACs had control of TACAIR, and I think the enemy on the ground knew it. Maybe that's why FACs lived so long. Once you fire, you reveal your position and then you've got jet planes on your tail. He was the guy who could put them there.

We went over the latest intelligence about enemy activity in our AO—locations, numbers, movement. According to MACVSOG, we could expect no unusual NVA concentrations around the target. There were also no CCN cross-border teams operating in the area. But Dick would continue to monitor CCN to maintain a clear AO for us.

Dick and I found two infil and two exfil locations good enough for LZs—good enough for the Jolly Greens. We never took the same route out as we took in. I gave them designations as "primary" and "alternate."

Whoever worked the land left the natural slope—there was slash-and-burn but no terracing. For them, that would have been work. That's where I wanted to insert—always on the high portion of the slope so that the enemy couldn't fire down on us. The heavy secondary growth would be tall enough to give us good cover until we scooted into the jungle. I looked for bomb craters near our

LZs. You didn't land in any area where there were bomb craters. The enemy could be lying in them ready to fire on the chopper.

Then we brought in the men. We threw the photos back on the wall and I explained the exact mission objectives. There were no questions. The men were ready to go. We sent them back to the team room while Dick, Larry and I, and the FAC got down to some nitty-gritty.

We'd put an encoding system on the maps in case we needed to use it fast and talk to the FAC. Everybody worked off the same code and grid overlays. It was simple. Each of my basic thousand-meter grid squares was, in turn, broken down into a smaller grid with squares covering one hundred meters of terrain. And the FAC and I further broke those squares down into even smaller ten-meter segments. We used a letter and number sequence for an exact position. "A1A1" might mean ten meters. "A1A2" might represent twenty meters. The full sequence would be a string of these numbers indicating east-west and north-south coordinates. We could call in air strikes or pinpoint our location in a flash for extraction.

For the first time, we would be carrying a "secure voice" scrambler on our assigned FM frequency. This would eliminate delays in transmitting coded messages from a one-time pad. The FAC wouldn't have to take precious minutes to decode it while your butt was in a sling.

Even with the secure voice, we also had an emergency fast encryption system prepared by our commo section in Da Nang to give our STRATA teams in the north sort of a shorthand commo code to talk to the Jolly Green for extraction. The FAC had the decoding information. He always strapped a little notebook just above his knee for these last-minute commo setups. You didn't even have to give your call sign. If he could decipher that message, he knew it was you.

Dick wished me luck and headed back to Da Nang. Larry went to join the team. Now it was time for a private head-to-head session with the FAC. Being Air Force captains and full-blown jet-fighter pilots, FACs really knew their stuff. To a man on the ground, he's next to God.

You had an understanding with the FAC. He did not want to put in TACAIR, and didn't even want to talk to you about it, if you were closer than one thousand yards from the target. Because he wasn't going to be responsible for blowing your ass up.

My mind shot back to the mission near Da Lat. The FAC and I didn't have this kind of conversation. He was worried about me and wanted me out of there. They were usually dropping a lot of ordnance, and with that much falling all around it's easy to get hurt.

I stayed with the maps and blowups to memorize them. My HALO experience came into play. In jumping from high altitudes we had to look straight down on the terrain and analyze it for the jump, so I was used to viewing from high up and knowing in my mind's eye what the terrain was like below me.

When I looked at the blowups, I put myself on the ground and "walked" the route to the target. And it wasn't a straight line, either. Hell, I could "see" it already, and I would for sure be so thoroughly familiar with the terrain and directions that I could navigate through the area without a compass. I didn't have to mark my map at all. Some people made overlays and kept them in one pocket and the map in another. I didn't. If I ever lost a map, whoever picked it up couldn't get anything from it—no intelligence, no nothing. The map I carried didn't even show the grid square we were covering—no boundaries or anything. Once I got on the ground, I would be in my element—the jungle.

The next morning we lifted off at 1030 hours aboard a Jolly Green Giant. The CH-53 was the workhorse for SOG clandestine operations. It was basically a search-and-rescue version of the Marine Sea Stallion, a twin-turbine, five-bladed machine modified with armor plating, jettisonable external fuel tanks, refueling probe, and two 7.62mm mini-guns. The FAC, now called "Covey" on the radio, and a second Jolly Green flew with us as a rescue backup.

At about 1200 we approached the primary LZ. We flew north of the LZ about a good klick. When we got dead north, we made a right-hand turn and went straight in above the tall grass. The rescue chopper maintained a very high altitude to stay out of gun range.

Our pilots didn't want to catch their props in the bushes. So we hovered five to six feet off the ground. All that grass was blown back like a big cushion breaking our fall as we jumped out. You always have to assume the LZ is hot, and, even though you don't see them, the NVA is a quick bullet away. My gut feeling was that they were there, but I felt they would probably wait for the chopper to leave before moving on us. We had to get off the LZ fast.

I faced east and gestured to the point man, who hustled out in front. We moved off the LZ and were quickly in the jungle. The chopper rose above the top of the trees and headed off for a "dummy" insertion. Back at NKP

I had asked for a second insertion as a diversion to confuse the enemy. He was going to land in the LZ the FAC had originally chosen for us, about two and a half klicks northeast of our real LZ.

We moved through the jungle about five hundred yards and I called a halt. We had to find out if there were NVA coming to the LZ to see if anybody got down from the chopper. I put up two fingers and signaled Boua and Sok to patrol to the right. I pointed to Youn and Nim and sent them to the left. The rest of us hunkered down and watched the area between us and the LZ.

Boua and Sok returned and reported hearing something quite a distance away, so we didn't worry about activity to the right. Youn and Nim came back with a different story.

"Yes, there are eight to ten NVA at a little water hole," they said. "The hole is about four hundred yards off. They were just sitting and talking."

We began to hear voices from that direction, but couldn't see them. My guess was that they were moving toward the LZ. About the time I figured those boys at the water hole should have reached our LZ, I heard them fire their AK-47s several times from in front of us, kind of halfheartedly as if they weren't too excited about the chopper coming in.

Within a few minutes we heard more pairs of shots from almost to our rear. I said to Larry, "They've either got us between them and they know it, or they're just marking their locations." I moved the men to the side of our trail and set up a hasty ambush. We sat there for a while.

As always, you could hear the NVA talking as they walked around. At different times they would fire their guns. I knew they were trying to spook us off the ground and make us call for extraction—a common tactic they used against all teams going in. They would circle the area of the LZ and fire constantly—two or three shots at a time—move away and fire again.

To me that was helpful. It told me where they were. Once I knew their position, I could move out. I damn well appreciated them firing.

It still came down to me to decide just how hostile the area was before we passed the point of no return with the Jolly Greens. During our briefing the pilot had indicated that, because of the distance to the target, he could stay with us an hour before he had to return to refuel. Right after that hour, you could still call "prairie fire" for emergency extraction, but you would either have to wait for the planes to refuel, or the FAC would have to get other aircraft from another location. And then you might have to resort to coming out on a wire.

There was only a little time left before we had to commit to the mission. I called the FAC.

"Covey, I've got activity down here. They're behind me and in front of me."

The FAC answered, "I'll hold them as long as I can."

The NVA that were firing in front of me had moved to the right and fired again, real close. I thought, "If that's the same bunch, then they're not coming at me. They're going to my flank and moving toward the LZ."

We pulled the ambush and headed east again. The farther I moved from the LZ, the safer I felt. I told the FAC, "I'm getting pretty close to the drop-off down here. If we can get to the drop-off, you can go."

But our safe time had already elapsed. The enemy hadn't spotted us yet, so I released the choppers. That was it. We were into the mission.

We stopped at the edge of a plateau, where we could dart for cover. The terrain quickly dropped off into the valley, and I could see that same large mountain from the map looming in front of us. It went all across in front, way up to the left, and running down to the right. I thought, "We'll just circle around the edge and see what we can pick up." We moved down to the right a little and heard more firing back to our left. I told Tranh, "Let's move toward that firing."

We followed the sounds, and after a short distance we heard them coming up in the direction we were going, firing a few more shots in the air. Another couple of shots came from very close in front. "Shit, that was close," I thought. "There's got to be a hell of a major trail down there. They're going up and down that trail. Maybe all they're trying to do is scare us off the ground, or else they're marking their patrol locations."

I didn't know which it was, but I was using the sounds to our advantage. The ones below made the mistake by diverting me. If I had continued in that direction they might have seen me. But, by their signals to each other, I was able to track their movement. There was one volley in front, one in back. We zigzagged.

About thirty minutes later they shot again in front, and now they were way out in front. They were running parallel to us and the ones behind us were "chasing" us from the direction of the LZ. I assumed they were tracking us. I said to Larry, "Well, they picked up our trail." It was also a good bet that their trail was really near and running north and south.

I signaled the men to covey out.

We were losing daylight as we eased around to look the place over. We saw some real old bunkers. Still coveyed we eased off the ridge, one at a time. It was pitch dark by the time we reached the edge of the slope and came back together. At this point the slope had a steep incline. I told the men, "Just lie back." We dug in our heels and leaned up against the hillside to wait and listen for a little while.

Our location was well concealed, so I decided to RON right there. We would wait until just before first light to get out. I told the men to use their belts and tie themselves to trees so they wouldn't slip down the side and fall off. They followed my lead and rigged Swiss Seats with their nylon sling ropes and hooked them to their belts through the snap link. They would hang from these as they slept.

We heard firing for another hour after dark, and then it got real quiet. I pulled the binoculars from my rucksack and peered over at the hillside we were going to. I could still make it out. At about 2200 hours, a glow from that direction caught my eye. Here came hundreds of little lights, looking like little candles, moving south in a single line across the top of that hill on our side—the other side being exposed to South Vietnam. Lights at night are deceiving in terms of distance, especially when viewed through binoculars. The hill was still a long ways away, about a thousand meters to the east.

I dozed off. On a mission you never really reach full sleep. You grab it in short spurts because the danger around you always keeps you pumped.

We got up before daylight and eased back around, carefully leaving the hillside because we didn't want to fall or make any noise. A bugle sounded from the hill to the east. We stopped dead. I got its position—the first large knoll where the mountain began, on the Laotian side of it. Then noise began to build from the same location. There was sporadic small-arms fire from a dozen places. We heard a clanging sound, like a gong, coming from where the line of lights originated the night before.

There was a lot of hollering—army commands like "Fall in!" All kinds of stuff was going on. There were people all over the damned place. Then we picked up other sounds back beyond the large group, like a headquarters element.

Larry and I just looked at each other. MACVSOG had put us in the middle of a whole NVA division.

We were sure lucky we hadn't run into any yet. As for all of the single small-arms fire we were hearing, I determined that it was for signaling the location of their patrols. First light was in the sky and now I had to figure the best route past the enemy. Our target area was straight in line with the enemy location. I decided to go south by just five hundred meters.

I said to Larry, "It looks like the little guys are sitting down to eat. It's a good time to get out of here."

We moved down into the valley and by daylight found a major trail ahead. I sent Youn and Nim to recon up one part of the trail and Boua and Sok down the other. They reported no enemy activity. I decided to covey across the trail. I gathered the men and told them, "When you cross that trail, leave no signs. Every man picks a different place to cross." I knew I really didn't have to tell them that. They knew what to do already.

I sent Nim to guard the left and Sok to guard the right. We spread out. On my signal we all crossed at once. We saw no one so we closed back in.

We continued east. In about three hundred yards we came to a very wide grassy thicket between two mountains. There were just a few trees with grass about chest high, so we ducked down to move through. We were just into it when we heard something to our left. Tranh was right ahead of me and wheeled around, signaling us to stop. We ducked down even more. Then he stood up and right in front of him were three men, about three feet apart, in what looked like black pajamas, typical uniform of the VC. Before they even saw him, Tranh stuck the barrel of his M-16 right into the first guy's gut. They just stopped—didn't even put their hands up—just froze.

The men were carrying rations, enough for a platoon for a week or a company for a day. They weren't armed because they were inside their own security perimeter. Of course, so were we. They weren't on the trail—probably taking a shortcut.

I was as surprised as Tranh. There was no odor from the men to announce their presence. They exchanged a few words. I thought, "This is a good chance to cut this mission short. We'll capture the little fellows and take them back." I stood up to get the handcuffs. When they saw me coming out of the grass their eyes got as big as saucers. The first man screamed at the others and Tranh shot him in the brisket. I was close enough to see his shirt fly out in back.

The shot didn't knock him down; he turned and they all ran. They didn't make it. The rest of the team cut them to pieces. Here we were, right in the middle of an NVA division, making all this noise with our M-16s. I figured, "Shit, they can sure tell the difference between M-16s and AK-47s. We'd better do something quick."

I hollered, "Quail!" and we spread out, not losing sight of one another. We went about four hundred yards and came together at a small draw leading up the ridge to the east. We sat down and listened.

We didn't hear anything that might be an NVA response. "What the hell happened back there?" I asked Tranh.

Tranh started talking real excitedly to Binh, who was trying to piece together the translation for me. Tranh's story was: "When the point man of the three walked into me I asked him who he was and where he was going. He replied he was a VC and they were going down to the next unit."

"Why did you shoot that guy?" I asked.

Binh relayed Tranh's answer. "When you stood up, he called, 'Black Death—run!' When he said 'run' I shot him."

"Okay," I told him. It was the sight of me that spooked them. "Black Death" is what they called the teams running our type of missions because we'd go in and call air strikes on them and they didn't know where it was coming from. If they got hit by these teams they would never even see them.

We lay low for about an hour to see if the enemy had picked up our trail. If they had, they were not firing signal shots anymore. I thought about how close we had come to taking a prisoner, and that, if we had taken just three more days before the mission to practice, we might have one in tow.

The men were very nervous and mumbling to themselves. I knew they didn't like the situation we were in. I felt the team was close to bolting. Binh was talking to them and then came to me. He said, "The team leader thinks we need to call for extraction."

Larry had been talking to them and was thinking about it, too. "Maybe, we ought to call 'prairie fire,' Joe," he said.

I knew they wanted to get the hell out of there. They thought they were going to be smeared for sure.

"Shit, no," was my answer. "That's suicide. We're right in the middle of them. Since we're so far down low, we're actually encircled but the NVA doesn't know it yet. If we try to go out here we'll be exposed. And the aircraft would be sitting ducks. If we even attempt it here, we'll be killed when they come in or when we fly out. We've got to move away to higher ground."

After a quick moment to think about it, it made sense to them. They agreed to no extraction.

We moved about two hundred meters up the draw. The point man moved back to us and indicated that there was something up ahead to our left. I held up my fist and the men stopped. I held up two fingers and spread the team out in pairs for a hasty defense, pointing in the direction I wanted the men to go. I said to Binh, "Tell them to wait while Tranh, Larry, and I check it out."

The jungle was as thick as mangrove, so we had to crawl to the edge of this open field. Through the thicket we could barely make out a fresh-cleared area. About a hundred yards away at the opposite northwest corner were several women and old men with baskets under their arms, working—clearing and planting, I guessed.

We were in the low part of the field where the brush was the thickest. Tranh was in front of me. He suddenly had his gun up, aiming at something. I eased up beside him to see what he was aiming at. It was a young girl, eleven or twelve, walking slowly toward us. She didn't know we were there.

The girl kept approaching until she was three feet from the end of Tranh's barrel. I just knew he was going to blow her head off. I grabbed the barrel and pushed it to the ground. As soon as I did, she saw me. I gave her a half grin, hoping to keep her from screaming. Tranh looked at me like "What the hell's the matter with you?" He couldn't figure out why I wouldn't let him shoot her.

The girl didn't show any fear I could detect. She turned around real slow and walked back to the others, and the farther she got from us the faster she moved. She got halfway to them and started mumbling, and all of them headed for the woodline. By the time she got to them she was in a run and talking loudly to them. They all disappeared. She was the only one that saw us.

I always felt that I was so good in a combat situation I didn't have to kill innocent people. I probably won more hearts and souls doing that. I waited until they were well into the jungle before I went back to the men.

We proceeded south a bit and then back to the east a little to continue up the ridge. We continued southeast at least four hundred yards, still going up at an angle, all the while concerned about the locals reporting us to the NVA.

It was very late in the day when we came to a creek just below the top of the ridge. I called a halt and we used the time to fill our canteens. There was something wrong. The creek had mud in it. It was a mountain stream and shouldn't have been muddy at all. Something was going on nearby, at the head of the stream. I wanted to find out what it was, but I didn't want my curiosity to kill me, either.

I quickly moved the men back from the stream and had them covey out again. We went up the hillside, heading northeast away from the stream until we came to a clearing. All the timber had been cut and only the tops of the trees were lying on the ground. They were big trees, so I figured there were bunkers somewhere nearby. Most of the treetops were dead, indicating past activity, but there were a few live ones, meaning the NVA was still cutting there. That meant we were in a hot area. The bunkers had to be on top of the hill somewhere near the stream. That's why the mud was there.

I knew we were on the same hillside as their HQ. It was where I had heard sounds the night before. I knew they were busy trying to get something organized to pinpoint us, and that's why they didn't have patrols out firing shots like before. They knew we were there somewhere.

I figured the best thing to do was circle around to the north until we ran past the clearing, then come back east and go back up toward the HQ. That's the last thing they would expect.

We crossed the fat part of the ridge, where the bunkers were. Everywhere you looked there was a bunker, and I could hear voices out on the end. We crossed where the little ridge hit the main ridge and scooted across and back into the jungle.

Whatever I did was mostly by instinct—survival instinct. I'd say to myself, "Shit, this is no place for us to be. Let's go over there." When danger was close, I could sense it. I guess it started when I was a boy. From the time I was six I'd go out in the woods by myself. I wasn't happy unless I was out in the woods or down on a riverbank.

When we were kids in Chattanooga, my brothers and I would go up on the mountains and play all over, especially in the honeysuckle vines. We might not have known where we were at the time, or what all was around us, but we always managed to get back home—safely.

We stopped halfway up the mountain, as far as we could go. It was dark and we had come to a drop-off. The trees had also been cut down in this area, and we could use the treetops for cover. It looked like a good place to spend the night.

I sent out two-man patrols to secure our area. After downing some rations, I took Quon and went out toward the point where I had seen the trail of lights the night before. We followed the timber cutting about a hundred yards until it got near that trail, and we sat and observed. It was much darker now.

There they were, the same row of lights moving from the top of the hill where the division HQ was. The lights were now about two hundred yards from us, and I could see they were bearers carrying stuff on their heads and backs. It was a resupply train.

Quon and I left our cover and walked within ten feet of the trail of lights. I knew damn well they could have seen us in the moonlight, but they didn't react at all, and we stood there and watched them go. There were women and older men slowly moving under real heavy loads. Their lights were candles. A few had NVA flashlights. There had to be a thousand of them moving close together, and it would probably continue all night.

The NVA could always muster a lot of people for their supply trains. They had them positioned up and down hundreds of trails, living there and waiting to be pressed into service. The bearers would drop off their loads and return for a couple of hours sleep, do their own work in the fields, and regroup for another load. They were amazingly fit. They had been working in the fields ever since they were small children.

The supply trail was a dead giveaway as to the location of the tank trail. The NVA didn't want their foot trails hit by bombs, so they separated the foot trails from the vehicle trails. They sometimes paralleled each other a hundred yards apart, and sometimes the two were separated by a hillside. The bearers we observed were walking a foot trail coming from the top of the hill, so I knew the tank trail was at the bottom of the hill on the other side. Up until now, I hadn't heard any tanks. But I figured we were fifteen hundred to two thousand yards from the target. And the only way to move to the target was to wait for daylight, cross that trail, and go down the mountain to the tanks.

The next morning, the bugle and the gong were loud, clear, and close. I sat and listened to all the noise on the hillside. With daylight I could see the division headquarters on a ridge just below us. After Tet they probably got pushed back to this position, where they had a good view overlooking South Vietnam. We were about five hundred meters away from them and sat with binoculars, looking right down into them.

What I had thought was a drop-off was actually a great big cutout between them and us. It was a sharp draw that dipped down a good bit and right back up. To get to us they would have to come down the trail from their position, come along the ridge in the open, and then up our ridge. All the while we could see everything. We could handily defend ourselves there for a while if we had to, until we got help in.

I had an idea that caused me to smile. "This wouldn't be a bad place to pay them back," I thought as I looked at their position. They were all bunched together out in the open. "Hell, I'm going to bomb the tar out of them."

I told Larry, "If we scatter them, we could probably get across that hill to the other side. After we hit them, they'll be busy trying to build the camp back up and they won't have people for a supply line. We need to get them stirred up or I doubt if we can get across to the other side. Hell, we've seen that same supply train two nights already."

"Shit, let's do it," Larry said.

He keyed the PRC-25 and called for the FAC through the unit's scrambler. There was no answer back. We radioed every fifteen minutes. It was too good a target to miss and I knew we wouldn't get another chance. About midmorning we got him.

"Good morning, Copperhead . . . this is Covey."

Hearing a friendly voice always made me feel a lot better. "Welcome to the war," I said. "I've got a division sitting right here in my lap. The little farts are everywhere. I can't move anywhere without running into them. Get us some TACAIR and put the whammy on them."

"Oh, boy. Let's get 'em." The FAC was definitely excited. He enjoyed using TACAIR as much as we did.

A few minutes later we heard him again. "I've got a stack of fours. Is that going to be enough to take out a division?"

"I'll tell you what," I answered. "It's enough to shake them up so bad it'll take them a while to get back together."

"I've got napalm through CBUs. What do you want first?"

"Put the napalm on them first and set fire to them to create some confusion. Then follow up with 250- and 500-pounders. Then empty the kitchen on them." I gave him the coordinates for the center of the division.

"I'm gonna shoot a WP," he said. "Tell me how close I am."

He let fly with that damned WP.

"Hit that mother!" I yelled.

It looked like it landed right in their frontyard. "You're right in the middle of them," I told him.

"Give me your position," he said.

"I'm about one thousand meters southwest of the target." I had lied to him a little bit. I was a lot closer than he thought I was. It was more like half that. What the hell. I knew I was safe because of where the WP hit.

The FAC gave me a final alert. "They're on the way. Confirm your position."

"We're holding our last position," I assured him. "We're well clear and safe."

Four F-4s screamed in from my right and started with napalm on the backside of the hill, running lengthways to the mountain. The jellied orange fire covered the whole place. Then the second stack came in with the heavy bombs.

As soon as we hit them, Binh and Nim grabbed the radio and started switching frequencies. They acted as if they knew we could pick up the NVA. Sure enough, they had them. You could hear them screaming over the radio. Nim also understood Vietnamese, and he and Binh were just jabbering away at what they heard. It just tickled the devil out of them.

"We're going down the north side!" they were screaming.

I radioed back to the FAC, "They're going down the north side."

The next flight of four hit the north side and gave them hell. Then we picked up another transmission, "We're going down the west side!"

I relayed to the FAC, "Hit them on the west side. They're headed down the west side."

This time, four F-100s came at the west side and unloaded on them. Then the sky lit up and the ground shook from the first drop. We got a huge secondary explosion, as if a big ammo dump went up.

The FAC confirmed, "We've got good secondaries."

Then we lost the NVA on the radio.

The FAC came back. "What do you want me to do with the last stack?"

"Go back over the area you hit the first time," I said. "When they finish with their bombs, tell them to use their guns. Before you leave, put every bit of it on there."

The last four produced two more big secondaries. Along with napalm and big bombs, some of the aircraft had pods with baseball-sized bomblets.

Thousands would go off at the same time. We sat back and watched the fireworks.

"Can you give me an estimate of the kill?" asked the FAC.

You had to give TACAIR a possible kill to report. So I just pulled a number out of the hat for them. "Hell . . . one hundred and five. That sound like a good number to you?"

"Yeah . . . I'll relay it."

After a few seconds the FAC came back, "They're happier than hell with a hundred and five."

After all that bombing, the enemy was moving around a lot, and I knew for certain they were going to be looking for us. But I figured that it would take them the rest of the day to get organized, so they wouldn't be on me until morning. By that time I was going to be on the other side of the hill. So we had to remain concealed. If we were spotted the whole division would concentrate fire on us.

After it had been dark for two hours I moved the men toward the supply trail. As we closed in on it, I looked up and here the little people came again, bigger than life. Another long line of bearers right down the trail.

Even after all that bombing and strafing, they had regrouped and put together another supply train. There weren't quite as many as before, and there was a little bigger space between them. The NVA had most likely pulled every other one to help rebuild the camp and trails.

I signaled a halt and moved real close to the trail. I noticed that every once in a while there would be a pretty good gap between bearers. I was also looking for one other thing—NVA. I knew that within that column there had to be NVA soldiers to keep an eye on what was going on. There had to be some kind of supervision en route. I was just praying we wouldn't encounter one of them when we moved through. But it was so dark you couldn't pick one out if you had to.

It was that same darkness that would protect us, too. We had to take the chance. That's when I decided to walk through them.

I motioned for Tranh. We picked a point in the trail to cross where we thought the jungle would protect us. We returned to the men.

"We'll wait for a space," I told them. "Just wait for them to spread out and go through the gap."

At about 2230 we eased up to within ten feet of the trail. You could hear them breathing. The line was spreading out. I judged their interval at five meters apart. It was now or never.

I took the point.

Sang and Tranh were right behind me. I was worried about the smell—mine and Larry's. I made sure there was a pretty good space between the man I went behind and the people coming up. Going behind the man like that there's less chance of being smelled. I was close enough to touch him, too.

The others came across two at a time, passing through back to back. I knew they saw us for sure, but no one said a word to us. If anything, it was no more than a mumble. They showed no excitement, and we sure as hell didn't. The last thing these poor folks wanted was a firefight. I guess they figured, "What the hell . . ."

We moved forty yards beyond the trail so we could talk. And I'll be damned if we didn't come upon one hell of a bunker complex just over the ridge on the side facing South Vietnam. I thought, "Maybe this was why the bearers didn't make a fuss. They might have thought we were also NVA because we were all operating in the middle of their bunkers." Hell, on a dark night nobody could tell who we were. I planned on that.

The bunkers angled to the northeast away from the trail and ended just where the ridge came to a point and began to drop into the valley. Every ten feet there was a good bunker and still very much in use. We could smell their clothes as we went by. If they were occupied, the people inside were scared to death. They didn't come out and didn't shoot. I guess they didn't know who in the world we were. We checked a few of the bunkers out and found a lot of stuff inside, but no NVA. We followed the bunkers to the point, which was about a hundred yards away from the supply trail.

After crossing through we regrouped at the end of the finger where the last bunker was. Instead of going off the point to the right, we moved to the left and walked northwest off the end of the knoll and doubled back toward the trail a little, just in case someone in the bunkers had observed us moving in one direction. We stopped after one hundred meters on the side of a finger still high on a ridge. We were within a rock throw of the division HQ.

It was about midnight by now and we were tired. I wanted a break to rest, so we'd be fresh for a fast exit in case the enemy discovered us. I said to Tranh, "Let's get a little shut-eye. We'll move before daylight." We were in a very small area, touching each other in a ten-foot circle. One grenade would have got us all, but no one knew we were there.

Barely an hour had passed when we heard heavy artillery coming in about five hundred meters east of us. Larry's eyes popped open.

"Goddamn, Joe, who's doing the firing? They've got to be awful close."

"Shit if I know," I said. "There's no muzzle flash to see." At first, we couldn't tell if the NVA was trying to shell us or if it was the Marines shelling the hillside. The Marines had fire bases almost on the border and could lob an eight-inch shell this far. But they were supposed to have known we were there. So we didn't think the shelling was friendly.

Besides, the impact was only a couple of seconds behind the sound of the gun. We listened carefully and determined the firing was coming from down at the river. They were shooting into the side of the hill facing South Vietnam, but I couldn't locate the position of the guns. I really believed it was the NVA because we had hurt them so bad. The tanks were probably firing rockets at the lower part of the trail we just left.

NVA patrols had probably reported what they thought was our position, because the shells were hitting about where we had crossed the supply trail. They were bracketing as if we had moved in a straight line, but since we zigzagged, we threw them off. Hell, if we had moved like they thought, we'd be under all that iron. Some shells gained on us a hundred yards, landing four hundred meters away.

When the rounds started climbing the hill I told the men, "If they get closer than two hundred meters we're moving back up to the bunkers for cover." I counted thirty rounds, just shaking the hillside. They only got about three hundred meters from us then stopped. Sleeping in the enemy's back-yard definitely helped us.

We slept sitting up.

An hour before daylight, I woke up the men and we snuck off. I took the point. We traveled back to the right making a little circle around the knoll alongside and below the bunker complex, moving single file down the little ridge.

We went about a hundred yards and stopped to listen. Quon came up from his tail-gunner position and said something to Binh. Binh had a worried look. "He says he thinks NVA are tracking us." That was a good bet. I felt somebody had to be in those bunkers where we were last night. And the jungle floor was so thick and wet you couldn't help but make a trail.

Binh had more. "He says he heard a dog."

That added a new danger to our situation. I knew the NVA used dogs against our STRATA teams in the North—little black skinny rascals that were a lot smaller than our hunting dogs back home. They didn't bark hardly at all, and they'd almost be on top of you before you knew it. The dogs weren't really chasing our Cambodians so much as Larry and me, our smell was so different because of the food we ate.

Larry and I were prepared for dogs and carried a mean deterrent—small plastic containers that used to hold insect repellent, but were now filled with CS, a powdered form of tear gas made stronger with a vomiting agent. Just lay some down on the trail, and once the dogs sniff up that stuff it's instant blisters. The mucus membranes in the nose absorb the CS, and the dogs are out of commission for good.

I handed the CS to Quon. He knew what it was and smiled. I told the interpreter, "Tell Quon to block the trail." There was just enough light for him to place the booby traps. We moved on a bit while he went to work placing several mines to alert us in case the enemy was on our track.

Quon's favorites were the toe poppers—plastic foot mines. The device had an inverted spring in it. When you pulled the safety pin it was armed. Pressure on the plunger reversed the spring and detonated the charge— deadly as hell.

Quon was very good at what he did. He concealed them so well that wearing sandals or even barefooted the enemy couldn't tell they had stepped on one. Even if they did, it would be too late.

We left our path and went down the slope at an angle of forty-five degrees. These fingers we were on ran off the larger ridges all the way down the mountainside. The sky was lighting up, and now we could almost see the river. But I didn't want to continue down and make it easy for the enemy to guess our movement.

We crossed over the first finger and we came back a little, actually doubling back on our own trail. We went past it and changed direction, so, if they thought we went off the end, that's where they'd check. The NVA didn't have a clue about what we were doing.

Moving was slow because the vegetation was very thick, and we wanted to listen for any unusual movements. After about an hour we had zigzagged about two hundred meters. We took a water break, which was welcomed by the men and gave me a chance to think the situation over as to what would be the best way to the target. We were inching closer.

Suddenly, our booby traps went off. We got into a quick defensive posture and listened to the havoc we created. The NVA were only seventy-five yards away and we could hear them screaming like demons. When they hit the booby traps, they set one off and instantly another, and then they got into one hellacious "battle" with the woods. When the third went off, they waged another battle, throwing hand grenades and shooting down the finger as if they thought we were there. Two of them were in pain, yelling for help. They had picked up our track and paid for it.

My first reaction was to run back to the ambush point and finish off the ones trying to help the wounded. But further enemy contact was out of the question, especially on this mission. The thought flashed through my mind, "Look at all these devils all through the woods. If we started to fire, they would definitely know where we are, and the chances of getting out would be narrowed to slim."

We used their confusion to move out. This was no time to go down to the target, so we started a sawtooth path traversing the smaller ridges that ran off the main ridge. You go down and come back at an angle, going across, down, and across again, all the while inching south. The movement was just plain instinct.

I thought it would be harder for anybody coming up behind us to shoot straight down at us if we moved at an angle. They might be able to get one or two but not the whole team. We also made less noise that way. They knew we were in there, but as long as they couldn't hear us, we were fairly safe.

There were bunkers all over the smaller ridges we traversed, and we tried to stay between them and the main ridge. The last thing we wanted was to flush any NVA out of their holes.

When our trap went off it alerted the NVA below: we heard the tanks start up and move around down there—short movements as if they were positioning themselves. I figured they were swinging their guns around toward us. I really didn't think they had us pinpointed and was hoping they still figured we were going down toward them. But I didn't know for sure. Things were heating up.

As I came around the next little ridge I could look up to my right into a draw above me. I saw some NVA about seventy-five yards up and signaled the men to stop. I watched the NVA go into a large cave set into the mountain between the ridges of the draw about twenty-five yards from the top. It was big enough for them to walk in, but I didn't see any come out. It was either a big supply point or there was a gun inside. There were a lot of NVA. I thought, "Hell, where are they coming from?"

To traverse to the next ridge we had to cross under the cave as close to the side of the hill as possible. Between us and that ridge was some tall grass. I told the men, "Stay down and follow me. " We stooped down below grass level and scooted across without detection from the front of the cave.

As we approached the top of the next ridge, there were even more bunkers. Every step we took confirmed that we were smack in the middle of one huge NVA unit.

The purpose of the mission was starting to make no sense to me. Why expose a team to the enemy like this when, hell, you should be able to find the tank park and crossing from aerial photos? Just compare the trail to the east and trail from the west. Then concentrate more aerial recon on where the road ran under the canopy.

I tried to figure out what our OP-34 commander was thinking. Why would he risk the men? Why put us in the middle of a division? I felt S-2 knew the NVA division was there. S-2 had to know. But Dick and I were never informed about it. Why did I have to cross all the way through the division just to run a little stupid mission like this? They could have come from South Vietnam in helicopter gunships, landed a ship down there, and done the same thing in five minutes, where it was going to take me ten days.

The answer was simple and hard to accept. They knew I was going to come in contact, and that would verify the division was there. I damn well accomplished *that* mission, all right.

We came up on another small ridge running southeast. We checked it out and found even more bunkers. The men reported hearing people in the bunkers at the end of the ridge. It was a good bet that all the bunkers were full. This was no place for us to be, so we got off that one and crossed to the next ridge, which was mostly thick, tall grass—an old slash-and-burn area giving us good cover.

We could look down on the tank area near the river, about a klick below and to the northeast, but couldn't see them. It was unusual for them to move this much in daylight. Even with the cover of the jungle, the tanks traveled mostly at night and holed up during the day. They would dig themselves into the side of a hill and back up into it. That plus the jungle gave them enough cover from air observation.

I sent two-man patrols both ways along the ridge and they reported no enemy activity—no trails and no bunkers. Quon and the patrols quickly set up security. We set a hasty ambush with two claymores in an area behind us to the north, right where the grass went into the jungle—the direction we thought the NVA might come from if they were following. We were prepared to jump off the ridge in a flash.

The tanks fired up below and started moving around again. Making it down the thousand meters to the river was looking more and more difficult. There were so many of them clanking around we were probably overlooking a tank park. It was at the end of the fingers that came down and made it easy to dig in. They could maneuver the tanks between some of the tall timber.

The men reacted to the noise and turned to look at me. They were flicking at their ears and pointing down the hill where the tanks were. I knew what they heard and I felt their uneasiness. After all our evasive maneuvers we were just a hundred yards from our position the night before. Before our RON we were moving toward the tanks. They had tried to block us by firing into an area we might have reached before we doubled back. They thought we were headed for the border. We were, of course, since the target was right at the border.

The trouble was they were still on the alert for us, and a hundred yards gave us a lousy safety margin. The sounds were getting louder and it appeared that they were making up some of the distance between us. They were now about five hundred meters below us at the bottom of the ridge, just before it broke out into the flat toward the river. It sounded as if they were moving into position—short bursts of engine noise and clanking. I figured they were waiting to find us—waiting for us to make a move. Then they were going to put it on us.

I knew right then this was the best time for extraction, considering our location. The chopper could get in, especially with gunships flying cover.

I called for the FAC. "Prairie fire. Prairie fire. We have to extract."

"This is Covey," he answered. "What's your situation?"

I shot back, "There are some tanks down below our position and we're just about surrounded."

"Okay, I'll get some help."

It was a long and tense thirty minutes before the FAC came back up, "Two Jolly Greens coming in from NKP."

We looked up and couldn't see a thing. It was real cloudy.

"Copperhead, this is Covey. Give me your location."

I gave him the grid coordinates. After a few minutes I heard the choppers. "We're in pretty deep shit here," I told the FAC. "The enemy is holed up in bunkers on all the ridges around me. You're going to have to avoid that."

He was flying almost directly over them real high. I monitored their frequency and heard him tell the Jolly Greens just as plain as day, "Keep your ass above the clouds until I call you down."

He hadn't finished his transmission thirty seconds when here they come through the clouds, "Chump . . . chump . . . chump . . ." a thousand meters north of us and flying right down past the division HQ. The clouds were real low, and the first one wasn't down below the clouds very long when we heard the "tat-tat-tat" of NVA automatic fire, and here he comes down smoking. He crashed in the valley we just came from. The other chopper chased him in. The FAC flew cover over them.

"Are they okay?" I asked.

"Yeah . . . they got them out. No serious injuries. I'll have to get you on another trip."

I didn't think we could hold out that long. The only thing that saved us was the tanks did not want to give away their position. I guess the enemy was concerned over our air power. Consequently, they didn't fire.

It took time to get the choppers in, so we sat tight with our ambush still in place. We had been hunkered down for two hours when we heard from the FAC. "I've got three slicks and two guns coming in from the east. ETA about thirty minutes."

When I heard them coming I popped WP smoke and radioed the FAC, "Tell these guys, 'Don't come up this finger I'm on. Go parallel to the hillside. Come up the little draw. When you get to my ridge, come straight across it.' " I had no more said that when here comes one of the gunships flying right over the tanks and up that damned finger we had been on with all the bunkers. He got four hundred yards from me and I heard "tat-tat-tat" again, and he came screaming by me, smoking. He plowed right into a bunker.

Almost at the same time, the first slick followed my smoke in and sat down right in front of me. I put half the team aboard, and as soon as the chopper cleared the LZ, ran to the claymores. I grabbed them, tossed the caps and wire aside, and hustled back to the other men as the second slick dropped down.

As we jumped in the pilot said, "Got your rappelling gear?

"Yep," I answered.

"Put it on. You've got to get those boys out of the gunship."

We looked at each other. I thought, "Oh, no." Now our butts are on the line because the poor dumb idiot didn't listen. He came over the bunkers right at treetop level and some NVA jumped out long enough to shoot him down. If he had come around from the other side and come across like I wanted him to, the jungle would have protected him.

"Well, let's have at it," I said to the men.

Slicks have a rappelling rig always ready. All you have to do is hook it with a snap link to the Swiss Seat made from your sling rope, and out you go.

We made a big circle a hundred feet above the target, and I looked straight down on it. There was that lousy tank road, and where it entered the river I could see a piled-up rock bed built just below the surface. The tanks probably had only a foot or two of water to plow through to the other side. I still couldn't see the tanks, but they were definitely there somewhere, since the ground had been torn up quite a bit.

All I could think was: "We're damned sitting ducks up here in the air. And we're going to be in even worse when we rappel down to get those men out." We were almost on top of that big bunker entrance. They could just walk out of the cave and shoot us. Hell, we already lost two ships. But it was the tanks below that posed the biggest threat. That's why I called for extraction in the first place.

The slick was going lower and we were positioning the ropes to drop, making sure we didn't kick out any of the sandbags that held the ropes from the chopper. We didn't want any ropes dangling out the door as we came in over the treetops.

I had hold of the rope on one side and three of my men held tight to a rope on the other side. We were at the doors, ready to drop the rope and step out on the skids. Just as we approached the crash site, our pilot told us, "They're out and moving to the LZ. The third slick is going in."

We could see the crew moving up the side of the hill to our extraction point. They had one man under tow. The slick was hovering just above the grass and pulled them in.

"Okay, they've got them," the pilot said. "Only one casualty—the copilot. He's got a big chunk knocked out of his head."

The choppers pulled away and we headed east into South Vietnam. I pulled out my little black notebook and began writing down every detail I could remember. After four days of running through the middle of a major NVA element, with them always hot on our tail, I had a lot to say.

At my debriefing, Dick told me that they had tried to contact me earlier in the mission but had received no recognition signal. "We thought you were dead for sure," he said. That was real news to me.

The Cambodians didn't resent having me on missions. I didn't get the impression they thought I was just another big dummy. They felt safe with me. I know this came out of the training I gave them that no one else would, and from my attitude of treating them as equals.

When we had contact they looked to me for guidance. I could read it on their faces, "Well, what are we going to do now?" I'd give them directions and they followed to the letter with no hesitation.

And even though Larry and I had our E&E and the "shoot them first before they shoot you" plans, they still showed extreme loyalty. I think they would have died for us.

chapter 18

Hot Target

I tried not to stand down more than two weeks at any time. Larry and I had just come off ten days of team retraining on Monkey Mountain, going over all the things we learned from the tank mission. Dick Meadows knew we were ready, but he didn't have anything for us. The mission pipeline from MACVSOG was dry. It was already three weeks since we extracted from Laos and no new missions were coming in to STRATA. The President's bombing halt had closed North Vietnam to us.

But I still had ten teams on the payroll. In the month since the bombing halt, we got off only two missions—mine to Laos and another into Cambodia. The Cambodian mission was a near disaster. The poor men came back sick as dogs. They were too close to the enemy for several days, and couldn't move around to look for water. They ran out and had to drink their own urine.

I was in the OP-34 commo room several times a day looking for missions to grab. It was frustrating. CCN teams were busy, but I wasn't.

Finally, Dick Meadows told me what I wanted to hear. "Joe, why don't you get over to CCN operations and see if they've got anything?"

When I walked in they were already expecting me. I figured Dick had probably called the CCN S-3 captain to tell him I was coming over. I always felt at home there. All the top NCOs at CCN were old buddies of mine. M. Sgt. José Hernandez, who ran the S-3 Operations section, was with me in Panama. "Goddamn, Joe. I've been hearing a lot of stories about you," he said. "What do you need?"

"I just want to check your teletype and pull a mission off it."

"Take any of them you want."

I liked being given the run of the place.

A whole list of missions would come off the teletype at one time. The S-3 took the lists and assigned priorities to them. He selected the ones they *had* to run, the ones they *wanted* to run, and laid out the order in which they would be run. Then he made an operation order for each mission and assigned a CCN team to run it.

I wanted to see the list before S-3 gave these missions to any other teams. Most of the mission orders looked about the same. They were recon missions about checking out trails, stream crossings, enemy base camps, troop movements, and truck parks.

Then I hit one that stood out.

The mission was to "locate and observe a cave inside Laos, and confirm the location as a possible NVA holding area for up to two thousand prisoners, possible U.S." The target was just across the border in Laos.

When you ran into a mission that spoke of American POWs, that got your attention in a big way. Especially one that was reported to involve maybe two thousand men.

And that was it. I took it back and handed it to Dick. "I want to run it," I told him. I didn't have to tell him. He read it in my eyes. Dick and I could always tell what the other was thinking.

The next morning I was on my way to MACVSOG to be briefed on the latest intelligence. But staying overnight in Saigon was the last thing I wanted to do. I hated the cities, and Saigon was one confused city. You didn't know who was who. I felt my chance for survival in the war was better in the jungle than in the city. I made my schedule so that I could get the hell out of Saigon that night.

S-2 had everything ready for me.

The target was about three klicks into Laos. One of our SOG teams had reached the top of a particular mountain and found what appeared to be either an air vent or exhaust vent coming out of it. The point man reported that from the vent he could hear American voices somewhere down inside. He could also hear Vietnamese and a small motor running down below—the vent was probably for the motor, possibly a generator.

There was more. The team's early reports caused FACs to be dispatched for aerial photos. According to the team's After Action Report and debriefings, they didn't find the cave entrance.

The 3-D aerial photos were very good. Through the stereoscope eyepiece you could easily see the mountain, running north and south. You could make out what might be an entrance, but the pictures alone didn't show a cave entrance. It appeared that the trails in and out of the area were going toward what might be an entrance to an underground area—a cave entrance. You couldn't confirm that from the pictures, but there was obviously something there that needed to be checked out.

The CIA was probably on board after the report from the first SOG team and had alerted its clandestine assets to the sightings. Between the team reports and the photos, they thought they had something big. All of the CIA intelligence was there for me to go through. Their sources had captured an indigenous from that area who verified the cave. He wasn't a soldier but a Laotian civilian pulled from that area during a clandestine mission. He had been mistaken for an NVA. He had told his captors, "Yeah, there is a place like that." He said the cave was for prisoners, and *was* holding prisoners.

But the U.S. didn't have any hard evidence—nothing concrete. There had been no U.S. observations of prisoners.

Dick, Larry, and I spent the next day working out the details of the mission. The key information we wanted to get out of the mission was a visual confirmation of whether or not that cave held American POWs. If it did, we had to find where the NVA were camped, locate all their security, determine which side of the hill was best for an assault, find the best avenues of approach, and find a place for putting in a large force of men for the attack.

The images from the 3-D photos were stuck in my mind. When I looked at the map in front of me, I could see myself on the ground walking to the target. There was a stream coming from the north that ran east along the northern edge of the mountain. It curved west, following the natural contours at the base of the mountain, came back around the edge of the mountain and headed south. At the point where the river turned south there was a little draw in the terrain. You could look straight west and see an indentation that might be the entrance to a mountain cave.

The map showed that when you were at the top of the hill you were two klicks from the border, but you could observe the mouth of the cave about another klick away—a day's walk from the border.

I told Dick I thought we could launch directly from our site at Phong Dien, land just inside the South Vietnamese side, and walk across the border to the target. No need to launch out of NKP. We would also be in west of A Shau, so our vital E&E plan would be simplified, too. We could make our way back across the border to the U.S. fire bases—a day or two walk— rather than go to an LZ somewhere in the jungle.

Of course, not going to NKP for mission launch meant I wouldn't have the advantage of the FAC's photo blowups, but the 3-D photos gave me enough of a mental picture of the area around the target. I had the terrain down.

I hit Dick with one more thing. "I'll tell you what we're going to do. We're going to do all the requested intelligence, and after we've completed the area recon . . . we're also going to take an NVA prisoner."

Dick just smiled. The mission was perfect for it.

The idea was to take an NVA guard and bring him back to Da Nang for interrogation. And I wanted to take the guard myself. Larry and I took the team to our Monkey Mountain reaction course and began practicing for it. Like other times, we used some of our other STRATA Cambodians as stand-ins for the NVA "guards." They loved doing it. It was a big step up from pulling targets.

My team really got excited. Up to now, in all our training, taking a POW was secondary to the mission. Once the team heard we were planning to take a prisoner they got more interested in this mission than the ones before. A POW guaranteed a bonus for them—the equivalent in Vietnamese money of $300 U.S. The other thing they liked was that we would be close to the Vietnamese border, making it easy to escape back.

We trained for a week to take a prisoner my way—not walking up on him. Make him walk to me—into *my* trap. When the enemy walked up on you, everything he did was a reaction to the surprise. So we set up a situation whereby we would take him our way. That meant using our old trick of getting him between two claymores. The NVA sent out a lot of patrols with four, five, and six men. That was the size patrol we wanted. We needed a POW who was young and a bona fide NVA. We practiced placing the trap to daze him good, then we had to make sure our side security took out the others not killed by the blast.

Taking a prisoner was not everybody's long suit. We had a lieutenant from CCN who wanted to take a POW something fierce—a feather in his hat. So his team set an ambush on a trail. Along came an old man with a cane. The lieutenant jumped out and confronted him. By the time the old man got through beating him upside the head, that was the end of the lieutenant's attempt to take a prisoner. The old man continued his way down the trail.

I elected not to give any potential prisoner that kind of opportunity to get the best of me. If we came upon a lone NVA, I would spring at him face to face. To our figuring, the best approach was to disable him with a blow from the steel butt plate of my CAR-15. If I could get close enough to him to pop him a good lick, we had him for sure. Then we would cuff him. As always, we had handcuffs, tape, and extra rope for this exact purpose.

We practiced quite a bit, and in the training I was always able to subdue our "catch" every time we sprang a trap.

We were ready.

I took the men back to our STRATA camp and put them in isolation. Then I got with Dick to finalize the last details of the mission and prepare the team briefing.

There had been a change.

MACVSOG had nixed our request to insert into Vietnam and walk across the border into Laos. They wouldn't let us out on this side because of my Cambodians. We would be landing in the midst of Marine and other U.S. patrol activity, and my little people could easily be mistaken for the enemy. SOG still wanted to maintain launch control from NKP, but Dick did convince them to change the launch orders allowing us to fly from Phong Dien to insert into Laos.

In picking a new LZ we drew our customary circle three klicks out from the target. Within this three-thousand-meter radius we selected our primary infilt and secondary infilt, and primary and secondary exfilt. We elected to land in Laos about one klick northeast of the target. The river turned there. The LZ would be dead west from where we would fly over the border.

As always, the three days of isolation were spent checking and rechecking equipment and making sure we had all the ammo we needed. All belts were full. Our mines were where we wanted them and ready to grab, canteen pouches were tight with grenades. Rations were packed. Everything hanging or carried was again rigged for silent movement, including several pair of bracelets for our prisoner. Team sterilization was complete. We ran over the mission again and again, maps and all, including the E&E plan and routes.

By the end of the third night of isolation, the men were well rested and fed. In my room at STRATA HQ I closed my eyes and walked through the mission.

At first light the closed black truck pulled up. Dick had been in communication with MACVSOG and passed to me and Larry the secret radio frequency we were to use for our own E&E if events caused us to get away alone. He also had some encouraging words. "Joe . . . the men I talked to in SOG and CCN are glad you took the mission."

Larry and I crawled into the back of the truck, and we drove to the small airstrip where our King Bee waited. We followed the drill, backing up to the aircraft and exiting the sealed vehicle directly into the aircraft. As always, no one outside was to see the team from isolation on. We were by ourselves— no S-2 or S-3 to escort us. Dick had said either he or the S-2 would meet us at the mission launch site.

Phong Dien sat on highway 1, fifteen miles north of Hue. It was a busy place. The 1st Air Cavalry was there along with a unit of the 101st Airborne. That meant a lot of choppers and fixed-wing. Dick had laid on slicks to carry us into Laos. This would be our first time taking the UH-1D on a cross-border insertion.

The King Bee put down on a remote but familiar part of the airstrip. We had been brought there from the tank-crossing mission. Looking around I couldn't see our slick. When we arrived, all our support was supposed to be already standing by, then it was only a matter of transferring from King Bee to the Air Cav or SOG helicopter unit that would carry us to our mission location and support us. That particular helicopter unit was not there.

The King Bee pilot said he couldn't just sit there, so we climbed out onto the tarmac. I didn't know the exact time we were to be inserted, just that it would be a short time after we got to the launch site. So I had all these Cambodians with no markings and two U.S. with no markings sitting out on this damned open airstrip. We presented a very suspicious picture, and it was a good way to blow your cover. We were all ready, with the adrenalin flowing, each man quietly going over in his mind his part of the mission—not talking at all through the tension.

I knew by instinct that something was screwed up. It was the kind of an error that just didn't happen accidentally. I was really getting anxious about our aircraft when a Jeep came running up to us. It was the S-2.

"Your mission is on stand-down for a while," he said. "There's something going on, and I don't know what it is. They're jumping around at SOG . . . looks like we got a rescue going." I looked over toward the flight operations building, and there was a Jeep with Dick Meadows heading my way. There were so many planes in and out I never saw his aircraft come in. Dick wasn't alone. More SOG teams were landing. That settled me down real quick. It wasn't my operation that had a flaw; something bad was happening.

Dick pulled up and jumped out. "Come here," he said. "I want to talk to you."

He started to take me aside, but I never liked keeping things from my men. "Can't the men hear?" I asked.

"No . . . c'mon over here. I have to talk to you."

We walked to a spot off the tarmac, trying to get away from the noise. There were choppers everywhere bringing men in.

"This is what's happening," Dick began. "CCN has got a recon team that's getting their ass kicked and they're surrounded."

I said, "Well, send in one of their STRIKE forces. That'll take the pressure off."

Dick shook his head. "We already did, and they're under siege along with the recon team. They're all trapped. We're forming a rescue element to go in and break the siege."

That was one hell of a situation. A STRIKE force was a beefed-up team around thirty strong. So, between the two SOG units, Dick was talking about breaking through the NVA to rescue over forty of our men.

"I'm putting together a reaction force," he went on. "I've got approximately forty men from CCS as a Hatchet Force, which will be my headquarters element. CCS is also sending up Mad Dog's team." Dick looked me in the eye. "Joe . . . you've got a special sense of where the enemy is at any time in the jungle. I want you to lead us in—be my point team."

I knew damn well he had me plugged into the operation from the start.

"I'll let you go back to your mission when we get back," Dick said. "It shouldn't take more than a couple of days to do this."

That was good news. I wanted to be the one to find that cave full of Americans. "Hell, you're the one that wrote it," I said, "and you're the one who can scratch it off."

Dick checked his watch. "Mad Dog and the rest of the men from CCS should be here soon. We'll leave when the slicks arrive. Go brief your men."

Just as I was turning, Dick caught me with a grin. "You couldn't have gone on your mission anyway. I was taking your aircraft for this rescue."

I knew it would be difficult for my team to go from being on a high, ready and concentrating on one mission, only to change in the middle of the stream. But I explained to them there was really no choice. Our men were in a bad fix in Laos. My Cambodians were disappointed at first then perked up with the knowledge that there would be a lot of men on the mission. And they really lit up when they heard Dick Meadows was commanding the mission and they would be running alongside a legend—"Mad Dog" Shriver.

Sfc. Jerry Michael "Mad Dog" Shriver. When we first met I thought he looked more like a "Snake" Shriver. He was a slim six feet two and his little people followed him like Lilliputians with Gulliver. His team was akin to mine, but they were mostly Vietnamese mercenaries. He had trained them and they stayed together on missions.

Unlike some of the other U.S., he dressed in the thinner Vietnamese fatigues. He wore the big olive-drab scarf around his head—the one we used as an arm sling. He would blacken his face. Shriver was one rough-looking character. He didn't like our rifles at all. All he often carried was a big knife on one side and a pistol on the other. Most times he went out with a .9mm pistol and a big .357 hog leg.

The story was that he got the name "Mad Dog" after charging a machine gun with just a pistol in his hand. The sight scared the pants off of the NVA, and they ran like hell. There were rumors he had a necklace made up of the ears of NVA officers. I never saw it.

His intention was not to come back alive. He was going to stay. He was a bit deranged—every war has men like him—but I didn't mind being around him. He would have done anything for the U.S. troops. Laying down his life didn't mean a thing to him if it would accomplish something.

The force from CCS, along with Mad Dog's mercenary team, were on the ground. With my STRATA team, Mad Dog's men and Dick's own CCS HQ element, we had a reaction force of 110 men.

Dick liked what he saw. "Hell, with this many men behind me, I can go in anywhere I want to."

Meadows was very much in his element running our kind of mission— it was in his blood. MACVSOG had told Dick he couldn't go on any missions. They felt he was too valuable as the STRATA S-3. But there he was, pumped up and in command. He had been itching for some combat and had put the whole rescue mission together before MACVSOG could yank him.

THREE SLICKS AND THREE GUNSHIPS CAME IN FOR US, DEFINITELY NOT ENOUGH to take us all in one trip. Dick took Larry and the rear half of my team, with my tail gunner, Quon, for the first insertion. It was a strange feeling. It was the first time Larry and I had been separated going into a mission.

It took an hour for the Hueys to make the round trip. I loaded up the rest of my team and we lifted off, flying almost due west. I was anxious about Larry and the other men.

Our LZ was about six klicks inside Laos. It was very close to the teams in trouble. The gunships had worked the area over before the first wave arrived. Dick and the first elements went in on an old slash-and-burn area on the side of a mountain, just below the top—too small for anything but one chopper at a time.

We circled around waiting to go in. The gunships hovered overhead, waiting to respond to any enemy threat. I took the lead helicopter in. The chopper slowed just above the tall grass and we were out quicker than lightning. It peeled off as another slick hit the same mark. And then that one was off as the third slick dropped in. Our men were off fast. The third slick sped away, leaving the three gunships circling and watching.

The first men had security out around the LZ. I caught up to Dick to find out where my men were. He gestured toward one side of the LZ. "The rest of your men are right down on the point. They've already had enemy contact."

"Shit," I thought, "this is a hell of a way to start a mission."

When I got to them they were gathering together and preparing to get farther off the LZ. One of my little people had taken a bullet clean through the leg. It was a slight wound—going through the flesh and missing the bone.

"What the hell happened?" I asked Larry.

He was a little embarrassed. "We were down just a few minutes. We were feeling our way around trying to secure the LZ when this NVA stood up in the grass. I guess he couldn't get away as we came in so he just hid there. He hit Sok in the leg and then made a break for it. We fired at him, but he got away."

My man's wound wasn't serious. I wanted to medevac him but he refused. I went back to Dick and "complained."

"Damn, Dick, what are you doin' getting one of my men shot up. I can't leave them with you for five minutes."

Dick just laughed. "Get on down there," he ordered.

That was the kind of attitude that held down the anxiety and sweaty palms. In less than five minutes he came to me with the route. Dick had all the maps and intelligence. He already had it planned.

With my team at the point, we moved out to the north. Dick pulled his CCS and HQ element in behind him and had Mad Dog bring up the rear. Although Larry thought they were fired at by only one NVA, I knew that if there was one, there were more. I told Binh to warn the point man to watch out.

Every time we moved in the jungle, I knew that I had to be ready to take the point myself. If it got real spooky, Sang, the point man, sometimes became very nervous. It had happened a few times before.

I was also a bit uneasy moving with such a large force. We were making a lot of noise. There were no usable trails. I hated trails, anyway. So we followed the ridge line, staying to the side of the ridge. I didn't want to give the enemy a chance to skyline us.

We moved from the LZ quite a way over to another ridge. Then Dick had us stop in a spot that was in defilade just below the crest of the ridge, so he could make contact with the teams in trouble. His transmission was short.

"We'll stay here awhile," he told us. "Joe, you shut the door."

Since it was almost dusk, Dick organized four recon patrols to check out the areas around us before it got too dark. The patrols included two lieutenants and men from his HQ element, and some men from Mad Dog's team. They moved off the ridge in different directions.

I took my team and retraced our path a bit. It was a tried-and-true maneuver to shut the door. I set up a small ambush, scattering my men in case the enemy didn't follow our exact trail. I set up the watch in pairs, so our trail was always under observation. Larry and I paired up with Tranh and Binh.

We weren't at the location thirty minutes when we heard shooting from the direction of one of the patrols. One of the lieutenants hustled back to Dick and reported they had found a heavily traveled trail going off the hillside. They also heard sounds from what was probably a village ahead. As they moved toward the village, they walked up on an NVA guard just standing there with his weapon slung over his back. He didn't even know they were there. They shot at him to wound him, and he was knocked to the ground. When they went to take him he tried going for his gun. The lieutenant shot him again, this time killing him.

Dick and I just shook our heads. It was an example of inexperience, plain and simple. The young lieutenant probably got excited when the man started wiggling around for his gun. Hell, he was shot in the leg. The lieutenant could have used a good butt stroke to the head to calm him down.

Another patrol that went off the mountain on the other side also heard the people down in the village. They found a trail to it that also went back toward where the American teams were surrounded. Dick sent two teams to different areas near the village. One got close enough for eyeball contact. They reported seeing women and children and that the place was full of NVA.

Meanwhile, the other recon patrols reported more NVA roaming the area. If any NVA followed us, they stayed well clear and safe. We knew they were there from the earlier contact where we landed. Dick pulled in the patrols.

He felt we would probably get probed that night and got on the radio looking for some U.S. artillery capable of hitting the village. The FAC found a Marine artillery battery within range just inside South Vietnam. We were surprised to find the Marines so close to the Laotian border. Dick requested a fire mission for outside the border—way outside the border—and got approval.

Dick was in hog heaven. He had come up through the ranks in Korea as an artilleryman. He ordered a few rounds for range and the ground started to shake. Dick "walked" the second round until he got it right where the trails led—right where they shot the NVA guard, five hundred meters down the valley from our location. The second 155mm round was close enough so that Dick needed to relay only one adjustment to the fire. The next round greased dead center of the enemy position and we shelled the hell out of it—you could hear the people screaming.

Dick turned to the patrol leader. "Are you sure there were NVA in that village?"

The patrol leader confirmed what they saw. Dick called in another fire mission, and another group of 155s rained down. In case any NVA tried to get away, Mad Dog set up an ambush on one of the trails and a lieutenant took ten men along another trail. There was no enemy contact.

We began preparing for the next day—the linkup and rescue of the teams in trouble. We decided to RON where we were, and go in to break the siege at first light.

That plan wouldn't last another hour.

Just before dark, Dick got the news that the siege was broken and that our slicks were on the way to extract the SF. The NVA had pulled back, probably frightened by the gunships covering our arrival and the picture of us coming in with a force of 110 men. Dick's artillery barrage was obviously the last straw for them.

We started to relax, thinking we would be out the next morning. My mind went back to the POW cave, and I started to get excited again. But in the very same transmission, Dick was handed another mission.

There was a Marine infantry company bottled up on a mountain right at the Laos–South Vietnam border. They were fogged in and had almost been wiped out. Half of their men were dead and most of the rest were wounded. They were sitting ducks on the hill, being torn apart by enemy ambushes and infiltrations. We were to link up with them, reinforce their position, and lead them off the hill.

"What the hell are those boys doing on the border?" Dick wondered aloud.

Right away, Dick, Mad Dog, and I started going over the maps to lay out our route. We were still about six klicks into Laos and figured it would take two to two and a half days to link up. From the moment we got the mission, Dick was in radio contact with the Marine company. Through the FAC we received the Marine frequencies and call signs from Ted Gaweda in Da Nang. The Marine call sign was "Delmar" and they were calling us "Charger." All our communications were being relayed by SOG channels through the 1st Marine Battalion HQ, then on to A Company, sitting atop Hill 1044, which split the border.

The night was quiet. That gave me a chance to go over in my mind how we were going to get to the Marines. I shut my eyes and started to "walk" the terrain—every ridge, finger, and draw. I wouldn't need Dick's maps or a compass. The area was full of NVA, and if the absolute worst happened and the enemy hit us full force, I didn't want to be standing there with my finger up my nose trying to read a damned map. I wanted to be alert every step of the way. I wasn't like Mad Dog. I wanted to get out alive.

Just before dawn we started our movement down the ridge headed northeast, back toward South Vietnam. My team was still on point. Right behind me was Dick's headquarters element within a rock throw of me. It was up to me to coordinate the movements of all the men. We had so many, getting separated was a problem. For our internal communication Dick used his favorite call sign, "Sugarfoot." I was "Copperhead" and Mad Dog was . . ."Mad Dog."

We zigzagged our way over the fingers that ran from the ridges toward the border, staying out of the bottom of the fingers until the last minute. We proceeded down the mountain a few hundred meters, using the terrain to our best advantage, looking for trails and making certain there was no enemy in front of us or to our flanks.

At 0700, about two hours into the move, my point man and team leader hit the dirt. I heard Sang's Swedish K cut loose. Everybody froze. I was out of position, hanging back with Larry, and couldn't see anything because of the thickness of the jungle. Then Tranh opened up. I ducked down and ran up to him with Binh close behind. Tranh pointed to a tree about three feet in diameter, fifty feet from us.

"NVA . . . NVA!" he said in a loud whisper.

Just then the NVA stuck his head out, and *bing*! My point man splintered the bark above his head, popping him back behind the tree.

I ask Binh, "How many are there? Does he have a gun?"

Binh quickly interpreted for Tranh. Tranh was very excited.

Binh gave me his reply. "One man. We don't think he has a weapon."

"Tell the men to keep his ass pinned down there," I said. "I'm going to take him. When I get near the tree, tell them not to shoot anymore 'cause I'm going to jump in there and capture him."

Binh relayed it to Tranh, who passed it to the other men.

Then I grabbed Binh. "You're coming with me."

We started sneaking toward the tree, which was at the edge of the ridge. Out of the corner of my eye I could see that Binh had taken a hand grenade from one of his pouches and had pulled the pin. I had my CAR-15 ready as we eased down the ridge. My men were sniping at both sides of the tree as we approached it from one side. Every time the guy peeked out they peeled the bark by his head.

I stopped about ten feet from the tree. I could see the NVA every time he moved, crouched at the base of the tree. I could grab him anytime, except that I was too close to the line of fire set down by my men. I started to straighten and got ready to pounce. I was just about to tell Binh to order the men to stop shooting when machine-gun fire exploded the dirt at my feet!

The bullets were flying from down in the creek bottom behind the tree. The barrage ripped off the whole dirt bank under me. My men reacted and suddenly I had two lines of fire coming my way. I dove behind a little tree not nearly big enough for cover.

As my men opened up, an explosion and flash stunned me. My only thought was that I had been hit by the NVA below. I got off half a clip down the hill in the direction of the machine gun.

I had this hot pain in the middle of my forehead. I really didn't know what hit me. I reached for the wound and pulled out a thin metal fragment. It was a fragment of grenade—Binh's grenade. He must have pitched it between me and the big tree when the enemy opened up. It stung for a few seconds.

"Damn it Binh, you almost put it in my lap." I had to control my anger. Cursing at any of the men was a no-no.

Binh just shrugged.

We were at the center of the hill and couldn't see to the creek bottom behind the tree. Whoever it was must have seen my boots at the edge of the ridge.

After about three minutes of return fire the NVA machine gun stopped. I signaled my men to stop firing. I waved the team down toward me to get a better angle on the enemy position. They dropped down the hill well off the enemy's flank.

I turned back to the interpreter. "Let's get us a prisoner."

We lunged at the tree. But the man was gone, probably darting down the hill while we were concentrating on the machine gun.

We were joined by men from Dick's HQ element, and we started down the hill for a careful search. There was no fresh blood trail leading away from the tree, but I knew Binh's grenade got him, too. He was a lookout for the men below.

We found a water hole fed by an underground spring. There was some blood on the other side of the ditch, where the machine gun was. We searched a hundred-yard area, finding nothing more than spent ammo casings around the water hole. I felt we were close to something. Those men had to be part of a larger enemy force.

I reported to Dick that we missed taking a prisoner. In two days we had lost two chances to take a POW. I just shrugged. Dick was understanding. "Joe, you couldn't help it," he said.

My team completed a sweep of the area, and they began jabbering among themselves. I asked Binh what was going on.

"Oh, they're talking about knocking the bark off the tree onto his head."

They were laughing about it and going through the motions mimicking the NVA's actions. I knew they wanted to see me catch him. They didn't know I was afraid my own men were going to shoot me. Then I laughed with them. For them it was a sign of approval.

We remained at the water hole an hour, using the spring to fill up everything of ours that needed filling. It didn't take long to run through water on a mission. One ration used half a canteen cup, and none of us knew how long it would be before we found water again.

As on every mission Larry and I carried the heaviest loads. We carried all the smoke and other stuff on our belts, which were full from the buckle all the way around to the back. We had also filled the two-quart collapsible plastic containers in our rucksacks. Larry also had the ten-pound PRC-25 radio, so the rest of us divided up his mines and claymores. Larry and I wound up moving through the jungle with a minimum of sixty pounds, sometimes seventy, hanging from us. That sure kept the legs built up.

Dick moved us out.

My usual techniques of quiet movement through the jungle were difficult to follow with a force as big as ours. We were just making too much noise. The others didn't take the precautions we took. I could hear Dick's HQ element clanking behind me. I began thanking my lucky stars that only me and my team would carry out the other mission to the cave.

I was alert to the possibility that we were being followed and observed by NVA, but I also had the feeling they didn't want to make contact, given their losses whenever they sent out a patrol.

Farther up from the water hole we found a major NVA trail leading off in the general direction we were headed. Coming from up the trail we could smell the unmistakable pungent odor of cooking fish. The trail was coming from my left and running to the right toward another ridge to the east.

We backed up a bit and took positions alongside the trail. I moved back to Dick. "There's one hell of a big trail down there," I said. "What should we do about it?"

"I'll send a patrol up on it," Dick answered. He moved back to Mad Dog and had him pick some men to investigate the trail. Mad Dog was gone no more than twenty minutes, when he came back with sightings.

"We could see the beginnings of a village up there," he reported. "It's sitting just below the crest of the ridge. I couldn't hear anything or spot any activity at all."

Dick mulled the situation over for a few seconds. "We'll move on the village slowly and carefully," he ordered. "Mad Dog will take the left flank and Joe will take the right. Move out when you're ready."

My team and Mad Dog's team stayed off the trail as the rest of our element walked along the trail. It was well beaten-down and led toward the village—about five feet wide and packed solid. There had been a lot of traffic. It confirmed my earlier feelings that the area was crawling with NVA.

Up ahead, my point man stopped. I could sense something was wrong. I moved to Sang and saw his knees shaking. Sang also sensed the NVA all around us. Hell, there might have been thousands out there. Sang was scared he was walking into a bullet. I understood that. You had to be patient and understanding with these men. They knew I would never have put us along a trail like that. It was suicide. But Dick had placed us there and that's where we had to be. Sang asked if we could get off the trail. I had no choice but to relieve him and take the point myself. Hell, he was shaking so bad he was no good to us, anyway.

The village ahead was hidden under a heavy canopy of tall trees. The vegetation and jungle was so thick that it was impossible to see the village from the air. There were trails leading in many directions out of the village, dropping down the sides of the hill into the jungle below.

Dick sent Mad Dog around the backside of the village, and had me move to the front, which faced north toward the South Vietnam border. With weapons ready for anything, we approached the front of the village, where all the little entrances came out to meet the main trail, which at that point was wide enough to be a road. The trail came up and circled around the village. Part of the trail split off and headed farther into Laos.

All of the huts faced the front. There were no huts on the right side of the trail. Mad Dog had no contact on the backside, and came around to link up. Our senses were as alert as could be. Bullets could come from any direction—from the huts, from the trees, or they could pop out from underground tunnels and blow your head off.

We moved in. There were still no people, but you could tell that they had been there the night before. There were about a dozen hooches, all in a row. That was different from anything we encountered before and indicated it might have been a place where ammo bearers spent the night. There were no signs of animals, a good indication that no families occupied the village. The hooches were hastily put-up bamboo huts with makeshift beds and floors swept clean. The fireplaces were cold, but there were other signs of life.

The paths and trails in and out indicated that the village was in use. It had obviously been there a long time—the ground had been well beaten down all around. A lot of people had probably lived there, including a lot of NVAs. The villagers had diddy-bopped out already, frightened off by our presence in the area.

I slowly made my way from hooch to hooch. In the third hooch I found a brand-new 9mm Tokarev pistol lying on a makeshift cot with a whole bagful of 9mm rounds. The Tokarev was the kind of weapon used by an NVA psychological officer. If a village was big enough—twenty or thirty families—one of those bad boys was always assigned. The goons would take over a village, keeping the poor farmers in line with threats, intimidation, and murder. He might have been living in that hooch, staying off by himself.

The Tokarev made a great souvenir.

The find automatically put us on a higher state of alert. We searched a little more thoroughly, but didn't find food or additional weapons and ammo. If the stuff was buried, they had done a good job. There were some bunkers, but they were empty, too.

We put security on the trails. The main trail went off to the right toward Laos's eastern border with South Vietnam, so we had to shut that off. Mad Dog found another big trail going north in the general direction we were headed. We quickly shut that door, too.

By the looks of things, we had missed the inhabitants by minutes. But I felt they were near. I was sure they had a hole in the ground full of people somewhere close. We couldn't take the time to look for tunnels or caches. We had already been there an hour, and we had to get to the Marines.

Dick ordered us out of the village, and I moved my team back on point. Because Sang got so rattled as we entered the village, I decide to lead all the way to the Marines.

We moved through the jungle, still making a lot of noise. We came upon a large trail heading straight down the mountain in the direction of the

Marines. It was an automatic death trap, and I didn't want to cross it. My men were happy. They read my mind. We doubled back up the side of the mountain toward the village a little ways. The trail reappeared at the saddle that connected the ridge we just left and the next one to the east of us.

I ordered a halt and walked back to Dick. "Look, I hate these damn trails," I said. "We can get to the border going straight across country."

"Well, we'll just try it," he replied.

We proceeded off the trail, but the jungle was so thick and the terrain so steep that the men behind us began slipping and sliding all over the place. It was too hard for them to go down and come back up in our zigzag pattern of maneuver. It just wasn't working.

Dick caught up with me and shook his head. "Joe, we can't take the time. We got to get over to relieve the Marines. The trail goes in the right direction. Let's take it." Dick was confident we had enough men to handle anything, plus he knew he could call in artillery with devastating results.

We climbed back up near the next ridge and put half the men on the trail and placed the others in elements at the flanks. This way we could move down the trail and hopefully not get trapped.

Trails scared the dog shit out of me. It was like going in and coming out by helicopter—you were so damned exposed. Once I was on the ground and in the jungle I really didn't mind being in. The area might be full of NVA, but it was "my territory."

On our first few days in Laos we hadn't followed any trails. The terrain was open enough to allow us to travel without any restrictions. But, as we got closer to the border, the hills became steeper and the jungle got thicker. The paths along our avenue of travel were along the ridges of the hills. So, with as big a group as we were, there was no way to vanish into the jungle. We were marching right down the trail, keeping "four" eyes open for the worst.

We followed the main trail as it wound its way east and then north. We could see another large ridge ahead, between us and the border. The trail led through another saddle, connecting the mountain we were traversing to the one close to the border. We figured that when we got to that ridge we could see right into South Vietnam, maybe even see the mountain the Marines were on.

We reached a small connecting ridge and I stopped dead in my tracks. There was a long wire lying across the trail. My first thought was claymore wires, and that we were walking right into an ambush. I signaled the men to get off the trail and we all hit the dirt. There was no immediate enemy contact and I dashed for cover. My men were quickly into a defensive posture as I ran back to Dick, who had stopped at the saddle.

"What the hell's going on, Joe?"

"I think we got claymore wires up there. There might be more."

Dick alerted all the men. Sure enough, there was another wire stuffed down into the bushes. Dick took a good look at it. "It's a commo wire," he said. He pulled on it and it appeared to continue back to the village behind us and up to the ridge in front of us. Dick's radio man hooked a telephone to it, something we always did in these cases. The line wasn't hot. It was dead.

The wire I came upon was also dead. They probably were commo lines for an NVA unit headquarters or an NVA forward observer directing fire across to South Vietnam. We decided not to follow the wires any farther than the ridge.

The trail rose off the connecting ridge onto a higher ridge atop a big, long mountain running northwest to southeast. Even with the thick jungle, we could see South Vietnam to the northeast. Below and in front of us were the river and valley that were at the base of the next mountain, which climbed toward the border between Laos and South Vietnam. The Marines were on that mountain, at a position about two o'clock from us.

The top of our ridge was egg-shaped and flattened out pretty good, with a lot of cover. Dick put his headquarters element near the middle of the ridge, and sent Mad Dog to secure the opposite end to the southeast.

Suddenly, there was some commotion from Mad Dog's element. They had found fresh graves on their end of the ridge, just before it dropped off. The graves were right below the trail, which continued through to the border.

"We'll RON here," Dick said to me. "You go back to the ridge and shut the door. I'm going to dig up at least one."

I alerted my men to prepare an ambush back along the trail. I headed back toward the ridge to pick positions for them. I eased through the bushes and stepped out onto the trail.

I was face to face with an NVA!

There he stood not ten feet away, his weapon slung over his shoulder. He couldn't have been more than eighteen if he was a day. He had that look of "What the hell are you doing here?"

As always I had my CAR-15 around my neck in the firing position. I got the drop on him and could have blown him away on the spot. That very thought raced through my mind, but I also thought I should take him prisoner.

I didn't want his hands at his sides, so I motioned with my weapon for him to raise his hands. He was so agitated he couldn't keep still, so I signaled again a couple of times. All I saw was anxiety on his face. Suddenly, he turned around and bolted down the steep sides of the mountain, disappearing into the thick jungle below.

I just stood there shaking my head, thinking, "Shit . . . what the hell am I going to do now?" I had the little guy cold, too. I took a couple of shots, but he got away clean. The jungle was just too thick. There I was, trying to get him to raise his hands, and he thought I told him to run. I started to laugh.

The shooting sent my men down into their defensive posture. I walked back and told them, "Just stay here until I get back." I walked over to Dick at the grave site.

"What was that shooting all about?" he asked.

"Dick, you ain't going to believe what happened. Damn it, I had one right in front of me but the scared rabbit got away. I went onto the trail and ran right into him."

"Why didn't you just kill him?"

"I thought I could take him prisoner. I could have killed him easy but I just couldn't see shooting him point-blank. He took off as hard as he could through the jungle."

"Well, go back and shut that door good this time."

I positioned my men farther back down the trail, where they would have a better and longer view of anyone coming up. I found two places where the men could look right down the trail in the direction of the village. I put my Cambodian team leader, Tranh, and another man down near the end. I put Larry and Binh a little ways back from them behind an old downed tree. I put several more of the team out in pairs in a half-moon configuration covering the trail. I let them know I wanted a POW and to fire at their legs.

I placed the last two men in a position about fifty feet from the first two. As I took a few steps back to check the coverage, all hell broke loose.

Tranh and his buddy had suddenly opened fire.

I hit the dirt next to Binh. He motioned toward the trail. I crawled over to Tranh's position. They were shouting, "Two NVA. Two NVA! One here . . . one gone!"

Larry and I ran onto the trail, and there he was, not ten feet away, lying at the edge of the bushes. He was shot in the leg and trying to tie a tourniquet with a dirty brown rag. I didn't see a weapon or grenades. I stuck my CAR-15 in his face. He looked at me, and his eyes got real big. Then he fainted dead away.

I looked around to see if there were any more. The trail was empty. I said to Larry, "Cover me!"

I grabbed the NVA by the collar and dragged him as fast as I could back through the jungle to our position, out of sight from the trail. I was upset that the men missed like that. They were watching the trail and taking aim. It was another case of trying not to show your displeasure with them. Hell, I let one get away, too.

There weren't any more signs of enemy activity, so I dragged our first bona fide POW back to Dick. He was an older man, in his twenties. He was a muscular NVA who had obviously been in combat before because, in the short time it took me to get to him, he had almost put the bandage around his leg.

"Well, we got one this time," I said to Dick, pointing to my trophy. The NVA began to revive and started mumbling. The medic was on him right away, but the man didn't seem in too bad a shape.

Dick's men had dug up one of the graves. It was an NVA officer. "We can assume the rest are NVA as well," Dick said. "We've got an epaulet off him and some documents."

From the smell, he had been there a long time. We doubted there would be any U.S. buried there. They would never be buried alongside NVA or other Vietnamese. Dick covered the grave back up.

I returned to my men and placed them back in their positions around the trail. "I don't want any more prisoners," I told them. "Any more come down this trail, I don't want any more damned misses. I want those men killed. The hell with this business of letting them get away."

Larry and I walked back on the trail where we had found the NVA and carefully checked the place where the other one escaped. There wasn't any blood where he disappeared. I said to Larry, "Damned if he didn't escape down the same route as the one I came face to face with. I'll bet it was the same NVA, too. He's a slick one, ain't he?"

About sunset we were getting some early fog. Dick walked up to my position at the backdoor. "The medic's done a pretty good job on the prisoner," he said, "but we can't carry him with us across the border. We'd have to carry him in a stretcher and that'll slow us down. We've got to medevac him out if we're going to keep him alive. So I need you to clear an LZ for the chopper."

There was the crack of small-arms fire from up around Mad Dog's position. Dick ordered some of his headquarters men up the ridge and we followed. As we approached Mad Dog, a couple of single shots slapped through the trees.

"What's going on, now?" Dick asked Shriver.

Mad Dog pointed toward a depression just across from our position. "They got snipers across that opening."

The NVA had come into the area and started sniping at some of Mad Dog's men. They were well hidden in the trees at the edge of a slash-and-burn area about seventy-five yards away. A few more shots rang out and we had a man down. It was one of Dick's headquarters men getting hit while moving toward Mad Dog's position. He had taken a round in the chest.

My men were also taking sniper fire from the next ridge over. They were right at the near edge of the clearing. When they stuck their head around a tree looking for the enemy there was a "zing," and another bullet ricocheted off. The fire appeared to come from a couple of locations. My men started shooting just to draw the enemy fire to pinpoint his exact location.

The problem was that the slash-and-burn area under sniper fire was the best place for a chopper to land. It sat in a draw down the right side of the trail to the west, between us and the mountain with the village. It was partially overgrown with bushes and grass, and big enough for one chopper to set down.

I showed the spot to Dick. "The only place we can take the prisoner out is right there," I told him. Every few seconds a bullet came through the trees. They could see us, but we couldn't see them.

Dick looked the spot over and said, "Joe, you've got to take your team down there and clear the LZ for the chopper. You've got to get to the other side and shut the NVA off."

I shook my head a bit. "Well, I don't know if I can or not. The darkness will help us. We'll try to get down in that draw, wait until they open fire, then maybe we'll get close enough to shut them down."

Mad Dog had his own plans to take out the snipers. He brought up a couple of M-72 LAWs. "They might be in bunkers," he said, "so we'll clear it with the LAWs, and we'll throw some fire into the area to run them off."

He didn't waste any time launching the antitank rockets into the area. Fifteen minutes later the enemy started firing again. He was well positioned and hidden in the deep part of the jungle.

I grabbed Larry and we moved into the tall grass, keeping our heads down. We found a small section in defilade that would give us enough cover from sniper fire. We could mark the LZ, then crawl into the tiny draw, lie down, and cover the LZ. Dick could bring the chopper in on top of us.

We headed back to Dick with our assessment. He had the FAC on the radio. "We can't secure the LZ before dark," he told him, "so we can't have the chopper in before dark." Dick wrapped up his call, and we could see he wasn't too happy. "I've got confirmation on the medevac chopper," he said. "But not until midnight." It was now almost dark and the snipers still had to be dealt with. Every once in a while another round came our way.

Dick's solution was predictable. "Enough of this crap," he said. "Hell, I'll just bring the artillery back in. I'll walk the artillery right up on them. Let's do it before it gets dark."

Dick called up the same Marine artillery base that supported us the first day. Once he registered them for that first target, we were already under their fan. The pounding began. Dick started the 155s landing back in the lower part of the village behind us and walked the artillery right through the village. He walked it up to within two hundred yards of our location, and that was awful close. They sounded like they were going right into our pockets.

"Hold that registration," he told them. "You're firing right where we want you to fire. Hold that registration."

Dick had zeroed the guns well. The NVA firing stopped—at least for the time being. But we didn't have the chopper there yet, either. Dick wanted to hit them again just before the chopper arrived, giving me time to get in position to clear the LZ.

"If they mess with us tonight when the chopper comes in," Dick said, "you take care of anything close, and I'll hit them with the artillery again."

Dick turned his attention to our POW. He was a master at interrogating prisoners. He had a lot of experience from his NCO days running teams. Dick held the SOG record for capturing thirteen enemy prisoners. Along with his interpreter, Dick slowly and methodically got the man to spill his guts. The man also handed over documents indicating what unit he was from.

The medic had finished working on our own man who took a sniper's round. It was one of CCS's Vietnamese mercenaries. He was one very lucky soldier. The bullet had entered his chest, gone around his rib cage, and on out by the shoulder blade, missing all vital organs. He was all bandaged, walking around telling everybody he wanted to stay. So Dick planned to extract just the POW.

But there was always one element you couldn't control—nature.

It was almost midnight, and the fog was rolling in thick, covering our position. We could hear the chopper approach, but couldn't see him. We could hear him stop overhead, but we still couldn't see anything through the fog. My men and I were on our feet moving toward the open LZ.

Dick called us back.

"Joe, this fog's so thick the pilot can't get through, you might as well stay here. He's got his landing lights on and we can't even see it. And he sure as hell can't see the landing area. He's afraid to come down blind, so he's coming back in the morning at first light."

First light was bad news. We wouldn't have a chance to go down and clear the area under the cover of night.

An hour before first light we got the message that the chopper was again airborne. But we weren't finished with bad news. Dick came over to me and said, "I've called off the medevac. Your man died."

"What about the guards?" I rushed back, looking for the medic. He was highly trained and one of our best. The man shouldn't have died. I found the medic standing over the prisoner.

He rolled the man over. There was a lot of blood. "We had him covered up to keep him from going into shock. When we turned him over we found this pool of blood under him. The bullet had come out the back of the leg and he was lying on the exit hole. I guess during the night he squirmed around and worked loose the pressure bandage."

The medic and I could figure what really happened. The Vietnamese medic who guarded him overnight let him bleed to death. We couldn't make any accusations since we had forty of them with us. "The hell with it," we said.

I removed the personal documents he still had. There were some postage stamps and letters. He had written a letter to his sweetheart that was six months old, telling her about killing all the "imperialist Americans" and that he would be home soon.

I was familiar with the feeling.

The medic and I wrapped him in one of our nylon camouflage blankets and laid him out next to the trail where it went into the woods. We made sure he would be found, so that his people could give him a burial.

After "feasting" on LRRPs, Dick, Mad Dog, and I met to discuss our move on the Marine position.

Dick spread out his map. "We need to coordinate our linkup with the Marines." He pointed northeast to the border. "That's them . . . on top of that other mountain right on the border . . . Hill 1044. Before we depart our position we need to make contact and determine the best way to approach. The last thing we need is for them to think we're the enemy. I figure they're all shell-shocked, and here *we* are, coming at them from Laos."

Dick looked right at me. "Joe, I want you and your team to continue the point. I want you personally to make first contact with the Marines. What do you think?"

Right away I wished I had been born blond. "Damn, Dick . . . look at me. I'm dark, too. I'll look like a real NVA to them." That's when I remembered my red bandana—one of those old country-type red and black ones. "Tell the Marines the point man will be wearing a red bandana around his forehead."

Dick relayed my message to the Marine unit, and indicated our approximate path of travel and angle of approach up the ridge to their position. Their condition was deteriorating, and we knew they would be more trigger-happy than ever.

Our big concern was that we wouldn't know exactly what part of the ridge we were coming up on until we were almost on it. Hell, anything could happen to divert you. So Dick was going to alert the Marines again just before we got to the top of the ridge and tell them exactly how many yards we were from them. We would tell them to have a man meet us at that position, and again go over our recognition signal. Any accidental contact could be dangerous for us both, and I didn't want to get blown away by a U.S. Marine.

We proceeded down the side of the ridge. The mountainside was full of enemy signs as we moved down toward the stream below. We spotted a number of little trails and some disturbed sections of jungle. We wanted to wind up down at the stream at a point we had selected on the map.

We entered a small draw—a deep indentation near the stream. As we closed in on it, I could hear some activity ahead. I passed the word back to the other men. The streambed below finally came into view. It was deep but the water was down to a trickle that time of year.

We held the column back inside the jungle until we could check out the area. Dick sent out a couple of patrols. They reported trails along the stream running northwest to southeast and a lot of signs of the enemy. There were no sightings and no contact.

Areas around the stream were hard packed where the enemy had camped. In the streambed, I came across a buried piece of commo wire. I pulled on it. It ran back to the bank behind me and up ahead to the other bank. My men dug up several more wires, too. There were trails going every which way. There were definitely NVA all around us. We thought we could make enemy contact at any time. They knew we were there, but they were definitely avoiding us. They had been avoiding us all along.

I guessed at several reasons. They might have identified Mad Dog and got spooked. It could have been a fear of Dick's artillery fire. It could even have been their caution about who was leading the Americans through the jungle so well.

After a few hours it was obvious they had left the area and were probably far enough away so that they posed no immediate threat. We passed the word back to Dick, but it was still no time to let our guard down.

The men broke out of the jungle and quickly moved across the stream into the thicket on the opposite side. A little before 1200 hours, we arrived at the southwest base of the mountain that rose to Hill 1044 and immediately started to traverse up the hillside toward the northeast. You could tell you were almost in South Vietnam because the timber had been blown all to hell. The finger coming down off the mountain was all secondary growth. We had to grab for the bushes and pull ourselves up and along.

My team was no more than a hundred feet up the hillside when we suddenly came upon an unexploded 500-pound bomb. The dud was lying in the bushes on the ground fully exposed—about the size of a man's torso. We looked around for more and, sure enough, found a couple of 250-pounders. We got the word back to the men to watch for the bombs and not to touch them. We told them to move single file and in each other's footsteps.

We were less than a klick from the Marines and worked our way around half a dozen more bombs, including a couple of thousand-pound monsters. As we zigzagged up the finger, it was like climbing uphill through a mine field.

We were almost on top of the Marine position and way ahead of Dick's men. I took off my soft hat and wrapped the bandana around my head. I turned around to Larry. "Get Dick on the radio." Larry made contact and handed me the receiver.

"Sugarfoot . . . this is Copperhead. I'm about ready to break out up here. You better call them and let them know." The Marines were probably scared to death and I knew we were going to look just like the enemy to them.

After a few minutes, Dick called back. "Copperhead . . . this is Sugarfoot. Delmar is expecting you. I told them you're in eyeball range. They will meet you. Recognition signal is your red headband."

The thick growth ended suddenly. I signaled my men to stay back. Larry stayed right behind me. It was a tense situation.

I broke out in the open. I was near the top of the ridge, at the edge of the Marine perimeter. The bombs had completely destroyed everything, not just a little bit—everything. It was like being on another planet. There were no more trees. It looked as if someone went through the area with a giant lawn mower and leveled them. What was left was nothing but stumps and splinters—all chopped to pieces. And the whole area was gray with fog.

I could see up the ridge. I focused on one lone Marine standing about forty yards up from me. He was all bug-eyed, weapon in the ready position. I kept saying to myself, "Don't move, mister . . . don't move."

"Hi!" I said. I tried to smile.

The Marine just stood there. With that wild look in his eyes, I could tell he didn't know where the hell he was, or what he was doing. More Marines waited thirty yards farther up the ridge behind him. It was a good bet they were ready to shoot. Even though it was a distance to their position, we could see each other clearly.

I pointed at my bandana. "I sure hope this poor Marine ain't blind," I thought.

I signaled my team to follow as I slowly walked across the little clearing toward him. I lowered my gun to my side, barrel down. I kept constant eyeball contact with the Marine. With all my little people following behind, I didn't want the guy to get nervous and fire.

The Marine watched me just as closely. I could sense he was still not sure about us, and I just knew his finger was tightening on the trigger. With my gun down, I was wide open. I was looking for any sign that would send me to the dirt.

I was within twenty yards of him when Larry grabbed me from behind. "Stop," he whispered. Larry pointed down to the ground. My legs were already pushing against a tripwire. The wire was at midthigh—at my crotch. I had walked into a "goodnight ambush." All along I had thought the path was clear.

I looked to the left and saw a hand grenade hanging there with the tripwire attached to the pin. "Get it," I told Larry. Larry followed the wire to the grenade and grabbed its handle. He snipped the wire.

When you booby-trap with a grenade you straighten the pin, making it loose in its hole and easy to dislodge. Just a little bit of pressure will slide it out. We were real close to getting our ass blown up. Another half step, and blam! No more family jewels.

Larry passed the word back to Dick to have the men check the ridge very carefully for more booby-trap surprises.

I closed the gap between me and the Marine. He was a young, dirty, and tired lance corporal. I was a little pissed. "What the shit you tryin' to do— kill us? You were supposed to clear the area for us."

He was shaking. "We didn't know it was down there . . . maybe one of the guys who got killed put it out there . . . that's all I know."

Hell, those scared soldiers hadn't even been down that far.

We held at that location as Dick and the rest of our men came through. Mad Dog automatically shut the door with his men, and Mad Dog could shut one tight.

The Marine position atop Hill 1044 was a scene of total devastation, the likes of which I had never seen before. The stench of the place was terrible. Bodies and body parts were all over. You couldn't keep from stepping on them. Many of those who were still alive had been wounded. Their bandages hadn't been changed in days. All the men were absolutely filthy. Some of the wounded were pretty bad off, walking around like zombies totally unaware of what was going on around them.

One Marine casualty with half his head blown off sat on a log beside us. He was still wearing his backpack. Two captured weapons were sticking out of either side. A third was slung over his shoulder. He refused to part with them and even lay down to sleep on top of them. He didn't know where he was.

Our CCS medic was the busiest one of us. The Marine medics had already used every medication they had and were in such a desperate situation that they wrapped the wounded in layers and layers of bandage. Fortunately, we had taken a large amount of medical supplies for our original rescue mission and were prepared to treat a large number of casualties.

The Marine company commander was a very gutsy Lt. Wesley Fox. He and his gunnery sergeant had bravely held the company together. A Company, 1st Battalion, 9th Marine Regiment, had been ordered to finish cleaning out the remnants of the largest NVA weapons and matériel cache of the whole war. The battalion's Company D had fought its way up the hill earlier and found over nine hundred weapons of all kinds, eighty tons of food, and two hundred tons of ammo buried in B-52 bomb craters. According to Fox there were enough weapons, ammo, food, and other supplies to outfit an entire Marine regiment. Helicopters had been carrying the booty out ever since and by the time A Company was given the hill almost everything had been hauled, leaving them the mission to deny the enemy what was left.

Fox told us that when they came to the hill his company was 150 strong. Over half had been killed and most of the remaining were wounded. Every patrol had been ambushed, resulting in either one wounded or two killed every time out, every day. There on the hill they were getting probed and hit every night. They took cover in the B-52 craters, but it was still not much protection from the repeated satchel charge attacks.

Resupply had been impossible because of the enemy and the fog. Whenever choppers tried to fly through the fog, the noise attracted an NVA tube popper and also a lot of small-arms fire. The chopper would abort the mission. So there had been no medevac and no food. They were stranded up there.

Fox said that the men had been through a lot of battles even before coming onto Hill 1044. He lost all his officers on his last enemy engagement and his platoon sergeants took over as platoon leaders. The ranks were also pretty well torn apart. Battalion reinforced him just before he was ordered to his present position. And now he was facing an even worse situation.

One by one the Marines came around to see if we had any food to spare. They were very hungry. What a pitiful sight. Hell, we went into our original mission with ten days worth of food, and since we were used to eating only two meals a day, we had consumed only a few days' worth. We gladly shared what we had. I usually took only one meal a day, so I offered them the rest. I showed them how to prepare our special LRRPs with water. They loved it.

They were so grateful they brought us weapons from the NVA cache. I took two brand-new Chicom SKS rifles still in cosmoline, even though it meant loading myself up more. But the blond stock was so pretty.

Mad Dog scared them to death, and they stayed away from him. He had that frightening look in his eyes. Hell, I liked it. The jungle was the best place for it.

Our big task was securing the area from probes and infiltration. Lieutenant Fox handed us the western half of the ridge, the portion most exposed to Laos. Fox had told us most of the attacks came from that direction. The Marines could then concentrate all their resources on infiltration from the South Vietnam side.

Our security formed an arc. My team sat at the northwest tip of the ridge, with the Marines at our east flank. A Hatchet Force from Dick's HQ took positions behind me on the other side of the ridge. Mad Dog's men closed the back door along the southwest finger we came up, and then took positions between us and the Hatchet Force, overlooking a draw to the west that faced Laos.

It was a good bet the NVA had followed us until they got to the end of the finger near the base of the hill about a hundred yards below. We expected that they would come up that draw between fingers. Shriver placed a Marine M-60 machine gun so that it pointed down the draw. Then he placed his men along both sides of the draw to catch the enemy in a crossfire.

For cover, Larry and I placed two large tree logs over a bomb crater, with a small space for us to squat between. Dick found a hole near us. Except for their foxholes, the Marines didn't have any cover at all.

We kept making grisly discoveries all around us. Lieutenant Fox had told us, "If you want to find out how many NVA were killed in the B-52 raids, just go around the hill and kick up the dirt." Just underfoot were a lot of fingers and hands and a tremendous number of bodies that were blown to bits. The craters were full of them, stinking worse than shit and crawling with flies and bugs. It reminded me of the mass graves from the Nazi concentration camps, except that the NVA bodies were blown all to hell. The torsos looked like grenades had gone off inside them.

The food situation for the Marines was really desperate. Dick and Lieutenant Fox were on the radio to the 1st Marine Battalion HQ trying to figure how to make a blind drop on radio command. It was something SF Pathfinders did, but the fog was so damned thick the control on the ground might not be able to tell if the aircraft was right overhead.

Dick was disappointed. "We can't work it out for now," he said. "We'll try for morning."

It was getting dark. Before I settled down for the night, I visited every team member. I gave each a case of grenades, another present from the Marines. "If you hear anything down below," I said, "just pull the pins and roll them down the hill." They were all smiles. All afternoon their morale had been low. They had been expecting a mass raid from all sides. It wasn't hard to figure out why they thought that. They had never before seen anything like Hill 1044.

I went over to Mad Dog. He had just put the final touches to his ambush. He always had that look on his face like he was ready to kill, and he was. His men were in good spirits, too. I checked on the Hatchet Force, then moved back to my little bunker and decided to crap out. Larry and I tried to remain alert, but it was real hard to keep from dozing off.

All of a sudden, a blue flare went up and all hell broke loose at Mad Dog's position. His M-60 was just barking away. Being only thirty yards from him, we were getting a lot of ricochets. Larry and I ducked down behind our logs. My men started rolling their grenades down the hill. In a flash there was a real battle going on. Green tracers lit up the night.

As bullets from the ambush flew overhead, Larry and I jumped over the logs and darted to the first ridge. If any NVA had made it through Mad Dog's ambush we were ready to finish them off.

The grenade explosions, the machine-gun fire, and the automatic-weapons fire were all mixing together. Suddenly, two more different-colored flares went up. Mad Dog yelled for his men to cease fire.

It was over.

I motioned to Larry, "C'mon, let's find out what the hell went on." We hunkered down and made our way to Mad Dog's position. We could hear him laughing. It was the first time I ever saw him grin.

"Those sons-of-bitches tried to come up that draw and my men started talking to them," he said. "They thought it was more of their own NVA buddies. My men talked them up the draw right into the face of the goddamned machine gun, and we just let go. We shot the living shit out of them!" Shriver acted like he had won a championship.

Mad Dog's men began shooting when the NVA lit their first flare. It was a blue flare meaning "Open fire!" The instant his M-60 fired on them, there were two other flares in rapid succession—one was yellow ordering them to "Attack!" immediately followed by a green one telling them to "Withdraw!" By the time the NVA realized they had been sucked into an ambush, it was too late. Everything went down fast—a Mad Dog trademark.

At first light the word of the encounter was spreading through the Marines. They were all laughing. Mad Dog's ambush was one hell of a morale boost. The Marines said it was the first night since they had been on the hill that they didn't suffer a man either wounded or killed. What's more, they couldn't get over the actions of our own little people pulling the NVA up the draw.

Dick and the lieutenant had just returned from the draw. Fox was elated. "Damnedest thing I ever saw," he said. "The whole draw is soaked with blood." There were no bodies to be found. Right after the ambush, Mad Dog heard the NVA taking out their dead and left them alone to do it. I was surprised he didn't chase them all the way to North Vietnam.

The fog didn't give us a break. We heard an aircraft overhead. They were trying the blind drop. The chopper sounded just above tree-top level and you could hear the stuff coming down. The Marines whooped it up as Lieutenant Fox sent out a recovery team. But it didn't succeed. Dick relayed the word that they didn't find the drop. Lieutenant Fox determined that the parachutes had come down somewhere between our hill and Battalion HQ to the east.

Dick, Mad Dog, and I were real concerned about the tactical situation. In our defensive position we were sitting ducks for NVA probes. And the condition of the Marines was getting worse.

"We need to get them and us off this hill," Dick said. "Weather or no damn weather, we've got to get out of here. The Battalion HQ is four klicks west. Get the men ready."

That was good news. I wanted to get the hell away from that graveyard.

Dick went to coordinate with Lieutenant Fox, and Mad Dog and I rigged for a fast departure. It was something we did a lot. Dick returned shaking his head and looking a bit unhappy.

"I offered to assist Fox in carrying his dead and wounded. He said his men would want to take care of their own. Then I volunteered us to take the point. I wanted you to be the point man, Joe. But they don't want us to take the point. Fox said it was their battle and they wanted the point. I didn't agree with any of this but I did get us the flanks. Mad Dog, you take the right. Joe, you take the left."

The Marines left a small contingent on the hill to destroy the rest of the NVA cache. A lot of the stuff had been sitting around in slings waiting for choppers to take away, but the fog shut everything down. There was a thousand-pound bomb crater full of ammo and hundreds of brand-new weapons.

The Marines wanted to give Mad Dog the M-60 he used on the ambush, but that sucker was just too heavy for the kind of mobility we were used to.

We moved off the hill with most of the Marines carrying their dead and wounded. It was very steep on the backside of the hill, and the going was slow. We were moving northeast, paralleling the border. Shriver was on the flank below the Marine point element and I was just above it. Dick and Lieutenant Fox had us on a connecting ridge, where the clouds and fog had reduced the visibility to about fifty yards.

Suddenly, there was a terrific explosion as the Marines blew the NVA weapons cache. The ground shook under my feet as the whole side of the hill went up. I thought, "Well, at least all those bodies got buried and put to rest."

We traveled about four hundred yards and crossed over a saddle toward the first finger of the next ridge. The Marines on point stepped right into an ambush. The first mine tore apart one Marine and a B-40 rocket dropped another.

"Damn that Fox, anyway," I said to myself as we hit the ground.

The whole lead platoon was under enemy machine gun and RPG fire. Lieutenant Fox rushed another platoon into the area and they laid down heavy return fire. The enemy was quickly reduced to occasional small-arms sniping.

Three Marines were down. One was sitting there very agitated. I ran to help him. He was a big black man and he had his pants down around his knees, feeling all around his crotch.

"Goddamn . . . goddamn," he said, smiling. "This is my third one and I still got my tools. And I'm goin' home. Thank you, Jesus!"

He was laughing out loud. His legs were full of small fragments from the B-40, but he was one lucky Marine. Another Marine ran up to help and I took off back toward Dick. He and Lieutenant Fox were in a heated discussion about something. I could almost swear Dick was getting ready to belt him. After a few minutes, Fox nodded his head and Dick came my way.

"Fox has two dead and four wounded," Dick said. "They think they got a wounded NVA. They want to kill his ass. I got Fox to let us have him. Let's go check it out."

We ran to the Marine point element. We could see their weapons pointing at a tree to one side of the saddle a hundred yards ahead. I was hoping the platoon leader could hold his fire. Dick and I carefully moved along the edge of the saddle. Sure enough, there he sat, on the ground behind a big root wad, with a shoulder wound. Of course, seeing us scared the devil right out of him. It should have. If he moved one finger, he was dead. We searched him thoroughly for weapons. His body was still in shock from the wound, so he wasn't in a lot of pain yet. Near him was an empty rocket launcher. He was probably the RPG man.

I had my men pick him up, and we took him back to the main body of the Marine unit. Our medic took quick care of the wound and Dick's men put him under guard. There were a lot of angry Marine eyes watching as Dick's men made a hasty litter with logs and a poncho. To guarantee we wouldn't lose another one, he was tied to the logs.

There was no more enemy contact, so Lieutenant Fox ordered us back on the trail. Dick stayed with the prisoner to interrogate him.

We hit a pretty heavily traveled trail, really a road wide enough for a vehicle. B-52s had chewed it up, but it was likely the enemy used it to get to Hill 1044. We moved onto the trail behind the Marine point. The litter was right behind me and Dick was still talking to the prisoner. The Marines still wanted to kill him.

We spent three hours traversing from ridge to ridge. Then we began to pick up the sound of helicopters way ahead. At about 1200 we came up on the tail end of the 1st Marine Battalion HQ security perimeter. Up ahead was Tam Boi, the mountaintop battalion CP, right in the middle of VC territory. The sky was filled with choppers, constantly going in and out carrying wounded. Lieutenant Fox took his company right on into the battalion area. Dick went with Fox to report to the HQ.

Dick joined us with word that the Marine battalion commander wanted us to shut the door for the whole battalion. News about our past success had obviously reached the CO. We were happy to oblige. We positioned three M-60s on a ridge with overlapping fire. Then, to complete the security, the men laid out mines and other favorite booby traps. Mad Dog and I worked out a roster for manning the M-60s through the night.

The fog rolled in again and nobody could get in or out of Tam Boi. We were at the battalion backdoor for three days.

Early on day four the weather was finally clear. And it was noisy as the dickens. Choppers were coming in and out. Dick had our POW at the LZ for evacuation. Men from A Company showed up to thank us for our help. They brought boxes of C-rations to return the favor for us sharing our food with them. The men looked a lot better than when we found them. Their extraction was imminent and that got our hopes up, too.

But when Dick returned from the LZ, he had news I didn't want to hear. We weren't going to be extracted but lifted to a hill overlooking Tam Boi to provide security for the battalion's extraction.

They flew us by chopper, C-rations and all, to a long ridge east of Tam Boi. We landed to find mostly grass and a few bushes. To the southwest we were looking into Laos. Our job was to secure the extraction area until all Marines and equipment were safely out. Five klicks to the north we could see a lot of helicopters lifting Marine 155s from Fire Support Base Turnage, probably the one that supported us on the whole mission.

Dick told me to set my team as headquarters for our operations. Our hill was really bareass bald. There was no cover, so the Marines brought us shovels. I had never used an entrenching tool in combat. In the jungle, you didn't need to dig for cover. But there was a first time for everything.

The digging was often interrupted by ground contact from below. Enemy activity was everywhere below us. We were in a great spot to sit and watch it all. Especially the Marine aircraft diving in and out, barrel-rolling back and forth, hitting the enemy. I was having a blast. They were shooting the shit out of those suckers.

But Mad Dog couldn't stand being in a grandstand. "Shit, I'm goin' up on that ridge, and I'm goin' to kill me something," he said. "I can't let the Marines have all the action."

Dick just humored him. "If you feel that way about it, go on. But keep me informed."

The ridge ran east about five hundred yards, then turned south and climbed a long way before making a bend to the southwest. Mad Dog took his men about three-quarters of a mile down the eastern side of the ridge and dropped out of sight into the jungle. He could flat smell the enemy.

He wasn't gone two hours when we heard his men cut loose. Suddenly joining in were a couple of twin-engine OV-10s. They dived down, let go with their rockets, climbed, and made barrel-roll loops, and dropped back across the enemy quick as lightning. Back and forth, back and forth, one behind the other, kicking asses every which way.

Mad Dog came storming back mad as hell. He had a squad of NVA walking right toward a killing zone full of claymores, when one of his men jumped the gun. They only killed two. The rest scampered back from the ridge.

It wasn't until just before 1200 the next morning that the weather finally cleared. Tam Boi came alive. The sky over the battalion LZ was filled with Marine CH-46s and Army CH-47s. The helicopters also alerted the enemy. Mortars and B-40 rockets rained down on the LZ.

The Marine helicopters were having a hell of a time trying to land through the enemy fire. They pulled away and flew way out of the line of fire. But the pilots from the 101st Airborne had the guts. They flew right through the curtain of mortars and small-arms fire. There were a lot of heroes flying those choppers. They were really taking care of business. It must have embarrassed the Marine pilots, because they started landing, too.

The Marines had a good fire-suppression plan and threw everything they had at the enemy positions. There was so much ordnance in the air it gave us the greatest Fourth of July show ever. Artillery and 81mm mortars hit the west flank, more artillery came down on the southern flank, and OV-10 gunships cut up the enemy to the north; 4.2s mopped up everything else.

The extraction of Tam Boi went like clockwork. The last Marines were also off FSB Turnage. "Chute up!" Meadows ordered. That meant put your gear on and get ready to move.

Six of our slicks took us off the ridge—eleven days after we landed in Laos.

The coffee at STRATA HQ never tasted better. Ted Gaweda stuck his head in the door to tell us Dick and I were due at I Corps HQ in forty-eight hours for a private debriefing with Lt. Gen. Richard Stilwell, Corps commander, and that we were going to be decorated by the general for our actions on the Marine rescue mission.

"I initiated the paperwork myself," he said proudly. "I think Dick is going to get the DSC as an impact medal, and by the time we get all the paperwork in on it, it'll probably be downgraded to a Silver Star. Joe, you're supposed to get a Silver Star impact medal and it'll be downgraded to a Bronze Star. That's the way they normally do it."

Dick and I thought we might get some kind of decorations, but those were major ones.

When we arrived in his office, Stilwell stood between his desk and a large situation map covering the back wall. We stood at attention. His greeting was polite. Dick presented all our findings. From the intelligence we got off our prisoners, we reported a regiment-sized NVA element operating in I Corps area.

He seemed very dissatisfied with what we were presenting. In fact, he maintained that our information was wrong. "No, they couldn't be there," he said. "I got them on my map right . . . here . . . in IV Corps area."

The man was telling us that what we gave him wasn't true.

"There's no way those men could have come from the same unit," he went on. "They might have been assigned to it at one time, but that unit is way down in Cambodia." He poked at the map, where he had posted that very regiment on the Cambodian border next to IV Corps' AO.

Dick stood his ground. "Well, we can't help that, sir. This is what we got off both POWs." Dick and I glanced at each other with a look of "What the hell's going on here?" We kind of shrugged our shoulders. All our information had come from POWs picked up at two different locations. Their documents pointed to the same large NVA unit being located in our mission AO—I Corps area.

What gave our information credence were the multiple enemy contacts, starting with our initial position six klicks into Laos, on across the border to Hill 1044. We had pointed to the action at the water hole, action at the mountain where we called in artillery, all the signs of NVA as we crossed back into South Vietnam, and the enemy attacks on the Marine position. And what about the siege of our CCN teams? All those NVA had to come from somewhere.

So essentially Stilwell was calling the bare facts we had a bald-faced lie. He could sense that we were not happy at all with the way the interview was going. On that, he was absolutely correct. It always showed in my face when I got peeved. Dick couldn't hide his feelings, either.

Stilwell brought the conversation to an end and went through the motions of telling us we did a good job and all. But Dick and I could tell we were swimming in bullshit. The general took a medal from his desk, and called a photographer who was waiting outside. He pinned the Silver Star on Dick, shook both our hands, and, after the photograph, dismissed us. Dick and I just looked at each other, saluted the general and left.

We had obviously made the man very nervous—so nervous that he gave

Dick the wrong medal. When he realized his screwup, he just left the DSC sitting there and pushed our butts out the door.

I came away embarrassed. I could accept not being put in for the award in the first place. But to be put in for it and to be told the I Corps commander himself was going to give it to me, and then to show up only to be dismissed empty-handed—that was embarrassing as hell.

Gaweda was dumbfounded. "I'm sorry, Joe," he said. "I don't know what went wrong. That's not the way it was supposed to be. You might have only received a Bronze Star later on, but Stilwell was going to pin the Silver Star on you because we sent the paperwork up."

Dick did get the Silver Star officially, and, thanks to Gaweda, I received a Bronze Star after all.

But there were a lot of questions that needed to be answered about what was going on at I Corps headquarters. Good intelligence was being brought in, but it just wasn't being used, and good men were dying as a result.

Stilwell probably had his staff dispose of our information to cover his ass and the asses of a lot of other commanders.

chapter 19

Vietnam Ghosts

"**J**oe, it looks like you're not going out anymore." Dick knew I'd be disappointed at the news. He sure as hell was right. I had a month left in country and was still looking forward to finding that POW cave in Laos, but it was no longer our mission. We were back from our encounter with General Stilwell only a few days when the word came down from MACVSOG that no more Americans would run across the fence with the STRATA teams.

"We've got another job," he said. "Saigon wants us to train teams from CCN to stay on the ground long enough to complete their missions."

Even after all their time and preparation, the CCN missions were being terminated within twenty-four hours—some within two hours. This had to stop.

MACVSOG had recognized my ability to take a team deep into enemy territory, get to the target, and come out untouched. It was a record most other SOG teams running with mercenaries couldn't claim. It all came down to training and experience. There were a lot of young E-5s coming into SOG and arbitrarily being assigned teams to lead. Up to this point their only jungle-fighting experience had been the SOG school in Long Thanh. The men had most likely never been to leadership school, either.

They took command of eight to ten Vietnamese mercenaries who had been exposed to all kinds of contact. They were thrown together with maybe two other U.S. who were just as green. Nobody knew enough about each other. They got their mission and went out across the wire into a foreign country, no American troops anywhere around. It would be the first time this American team leader had been out there, and it would get the mercenaries thinking, "Maybe we should or maybe we shouldn't trust him. At the first sign of anything happening, let's get him to call 'prairie fire.' "

There was usually no hard reason to call off their mission. So either the mercenaries put the fear of God in them or else the NVA pulled their old tricks, firing in the air to make them think they were surrounded. Our E-5s spooked easily. That had a lot to do with most of the SOG team failures. Not only were missions quickly aborted, but SOG teams were taking casualties at a rate of about 40 percent.

CCN sent us three ten-man teams, each with seven Vietnamese mercenaries and three Americans. The Americans were new in country and had just acquired their teams. I had to make sure they were trained to stay on the ground the full ten days, or long enough to complete the missions. They were to learn the terrain, their men, and enemy tactics well enough so they wouldn't call "prairie fire" prematurely.

The areas outside of Da Lat were a natural choice. I flew over the jungle to pinpoint the AOs for the teams, then Dick and I worked out the missions. In Da Lat, I briefed the teams and immediately inserted them into the jungle. Their three AOs formed an arc that swung from north of the city to southeast of the city. Each was to treat this as a bona fide mission that might invite enemy contact. NVA were all in there, and contact was always a possibility. I was like a mother hen, flying over them every day with the FAC or in a chopper, talking to them. I moved them all over and had them make intelligence reports and SITREPS. They all spotted enemy movement of some kind.

The young team leaders were energetic, very attentive, and gung-ho. Some of those boys could read a map and compass real well, but they couldn't read the land and sometimes wound up down in gorges and places they didn't expect. They also didn't know enough to avoid a straight path to their objective. The training forced them to learn the terrain, learn jungle movement, and work as a team. We kept them on the ground for ten days. It was a hell of a good reaction course, and they did well.

I was particularly impressed with one team leader, a tall, lanky fellow who talked slow like a country boy—as if he just came out of the woods somewhere in Tennessee. He had the best team of the three and knew how to operate in the jungle. After the mission, I told Dick that SOG had a damn good soldier there. My opinion of him was right. He went on to win the Distinguished Service Cross for gallantry.

That young soldier reminded me a lot of Mad Dog Shriver, but Jerry Shriver was one of the many heroes who never made it back.

There's more to war than guns and bullets. You also try to demoralize your enemy by waging a war of nerves. There were extensive psychological operations mounted in North and South Vietnam. Our side dropped leaflets all over the countryside, urging the NVA and VC to give up a "losing cause" and guaranteeing them safe passage through our lines and plenty of food and care when they came over.

MACVSOG's OP-33 also had airplanes flying along the border transmitting "messages" from phony insurgent bases in the North, calling for all true patriots to rally against the Communist regime.

Of course, two can play at that game. Ho Chi Minh had his "Hanoi Hannah." Like her sisters before her—Axis Sally and Tokyo Rose—Hanoi Hannah broadcast a constant stream of propaganda to our troops, designed to weaken their resolve to stay and fight.

I don't know what effect it had on other U.S. soldiers, but for SF the broadcasts took on a personal tone. The teams from CCN, CCC, and CCS were singled out as particular targets by Hanoi Hannah. "Black Death," as we were called by the enemy, had caused them such sheer hell the NVA placed a bounty on our heads. Dead or alive, we were worth a lot of money to the men who could bring us down.

Our last whereabouts would be broadcast, largely from reports by NVA patrols who found their dead comrades or from the lucky survivors of air strikes that seemed to come out of nowhere.

Mad Dog Shriver was the most feared and hated of the lot. His ambushes were legendary—on both sides. Hanoi Hannah used his code name "Mad Dog" in her messages, warning him that he was marked for death. Shriver wasn't the least bit intimidated. He was elusive as hell, and as his deadly successes increased, so did the bounty.

Sfc. Jerry Michael Shriver had a reputation among other SF as a loner and a bad-ass, and the way he looked when he came out of the jungle would scare you. After the Marine rescue mission, he stayed with us, waiting for a ride back to CCS. That night he went to our little bar in the rear of the OP-34 building. Some of the other men commented that the evening would end with him shooting up the place. "He does it all the time," they said.

My reaction was disbelief, unless, of course, someone pissed him off. So I went to the bar out of curiosity and sat down with him. There weren't but three in there along with one of our signal men behind the bar. I was alerted to leave him alone. "Just let him drink," I was warned. "He'll get drunk and probably pass out at the table." I talked to him for about an hour, and, for the life of me, didn't find a hostile bone in his body.

The stories of Shriver shooting up bars were true, however. Jerry thought highly of the men who were brave enough to run with a team, and wouldn't associate with anyone who was not running. Jerry hated "barroom cowboys"—the kind who hung around mouthing off about missions that were total bullshit. These would be the ones he'd shoot at. I knew the feeling. We had a couple of cowboys at SOG who would shoot up a bar, and that was the closest they ever got to combat. That kind of thing went on all over South Vietnam.

I never did pay much attention to Hanoi Hannah, although a lot of the other SF did. After a couple of successful missions, it didn't take long for you to be put on her list. Team radio transmissions were always monitored by the NVA, and, even though we were careful to either code or scramble our calls, some team-leader code names and call signs got broadcast in the clear. The enemy was able to piece the fragments together and eventually identify some of us by code name and deed.

When Dick Meadows and Gerard Wareing were running teams out of CCC in Kontum, they were early members of this exclusive club. They wore it like a badge.

I was told there definitely was a bounty on the men running STRATA. Initially, Hanoi Hannah was probably talking about the mercenaries we were putting in the North. But after my ambush and air strikes near Da Lat, and the havoc I called down on the NVA division headquarters, I was most likely one of Hanoi Hannah's new targets. I never heard her broadcast my "Copperhead" call sign, but that didn't mean I wasn't on her hit list.

I never found out if these bounties were legitimate, but MACVSOG took the threat seriously. Larry and I couldn't leave anything to chance. We had to assume that was her way of trying to get my men to compromise the team—to maybe shoot us and try to collect the bounty. That's why we had our own E&E.

Shriver kept extending his tour and, unfortunately, was living on borrowed time. His very next mission out of CCS would be his last. We were told he had a gut feeling that the mission into Laos had little chance of success, that he balked at going out—something very uncharacteristic of him. The mission planners knew the area was too heavily fortified, but, like many other missions of theirs, an SOG team was forced to go in against the odds.

They set Jerry down right in the middle of an NVA unit, and the team got shot up bad. There was so much NVA fire that the choppers couldn't get back down to pick them up, the area was just too damned hot. Jerry managed to see to the extraction of some of the team, but he remained on the ground. Near the end, he was reported to have built a bonfire to draw the bad guys into the LZ. He was seen around the fire as the enemy was converging. The last thing they saw of Shriver, he was running across a clearing, headed for a tree line, firing his pistol as he ran.

Then the rumors started. There was a story that, about three days after his disappearance, Hanoi Hannah broadcast they "had" Mad Dog Shriver. There was no word on whether he was dead or alive. There were also some wild-ass reports that the NVA had got Shriver to work for them. We chalked that up as just more of Hanoi Hannah's horseshit.

I was haunted by Jerry's very last words to me in the bar in Da Nang. He had just been to the States between tours, but found he couldn't adjust. "I've come back to stay, Joe," he said. "They'll bury me here." He meant it. I could see death in his eyes.

The only possessions he left the world were a German shepherd and $35 cash. Jerry Shriver was later posthumously promoted to master sergeant. I don't think his body was ever recovered.

The real shame of it was that SOG never took into consideration a team leader's instincts regarding a mission. Most of the men were senior NCOs, who knew the jungle and the enemy situation better than anybody. They had gut feelings about the danger and chances of success on missions. Some of my buddies who were killed or wounded sensed something was wrong way before they were inserted. Sfc. Ron Brown was attached to CCN and given a mission fifteen miles into Laos. He was one of the original members of the Army's Golden Knights—a veteran of over a thousand free-fall jumps. He had a gut feeling about the mission—it didn't feel right. But he wasn't afraid. He went into a hot area, called "prairie fire," and was shot off a string during exfilt. He fell back into the jungle and was never seen again.

Sfc. Paul Adair was luckier. His chopper came in on a bomb crater for their LZ. There were no bushes for cover and he sensed danger. As he slipped down onto the runners he dangled in the air just long enough to spot a lot of boot prints on the ground. He hollered to the pilot to abort, and as he turned back in to the chopper, an NVA green tracer tore through his knee.

I never had a negative feeling about a mission. Dick and I put together good operation plans and I followed up with extensive team preparation. What got us through were my instincts about taking a particular route or a bold course of action. All of SF's senior NCOs relied on their instincts. Their feelings should have counted with their commanding officers.

Jerry Shriver didn't want to go on that last mission, and he's still there.

THERE'S NO WAY TO PUT VIETNAM BEHIND YOU. SOMETIME, SOMEWHERE, YOU will meet another SF who will bring word of a lost buddy, or tell you who picked up where you left off. The network that exists among SF runs twenty-four hours.

It was April 1970 and it had been almost ten months since I lifted off from Tan Son Nhut for the last time. News from SOG came from the man who replaced me as STRATA agent handler. He sought me out at Fort Bragg and found me in the middle of a field exercise. It was our first meeting, since he had not yet arrived in Da Nang when I left.

We talked about the teams. The news wasn't good. My Cambodians hadn't survived their very next mission after I left.

Right after they were inserted into Laos, they got into it with the NVA. They were in a large grassy area, trying for an extraction and calling for air support. TACAIR was slow in responding, and the FAC and photographer were overhead trying to protect them.

The NVA were coming from all sides, and the FAC was firing his WP rockets at the enemy along the edge of the woods to keep them away. The dry grass was set ablaze. The team stayed in the grass too long and was engulfed. The point man managed to run through the fire, but the others burned and blew up from all the explosives they carried.

Seeing that the men were burning, the pilot flew closer to the ground in an attempt to help, but he lost control of his aircraft and crashed. He and the photographer were killed. These were the same men I worked with at NKP.

The luckiest one was Tranh, my Cambodian team leader. He wasn't on the mission. He had developed a bad case of bursitis in his shoulders from lugging his heavy rucksack so many times and had been made the STRATA camp gate guard. Sang, the point man, was so badly burned he didn't survive the hospital.

CCN was under pressure to get more insertions on the board, but almost every attempted LZ was being compromised. My reading of the problem placed the failure on the inexperience of the U.S. team leaders. But, for some reason, CCN believed that they had double agents among the Vietnamese mercenaries and began sending all-indigenous teams on what looked to me like suicide missions.

"Rumor Control" was working overtime to quash reports that this was part of an organized program to send these good men to die to keep SOG clandestine operations secret. Hell, some resupply drops were reportedly booby-trapped to explode in the face of teams our intelligence thought were compromised.

What I learned next really set me back on my heels. We talked about the two-thousand-man POW camp in Laos. What was curious was that my replacement knew all about the mission—about the earlier team reporting American voices. SOG obviously still had that mission on the table after I left.

I asked him if any other team picked up the mission and ran it. "No," he said. "They B-52d it."

He could have been bullshitting, but I doubt it. The fact was that President Nixon had approved secret bombings of Cambodia and Laos the year before. They were called "menu" bombings—with target code names like "Breakfast," "Lunch," "Snack," and "Dinner." Only the President's closest advisors knew of the operations—not the Congress or the public. To cover these missions, the B-52s would take off assigned to recognized South Vietnam targets. As they closed on Vietnam, some would be sent new coded coordinates in Cambodia or Laos, and then peel off toward their real targets.

Between 17 and 18 February 1970, B-52 raids over South Vietnam were stopped for about thirty-six hours while bombers were diverted to Laos to destroy Pathet Lao and North Vietnamese targets around the Plain of Jars. That's when they also must have hit the bunker.

I thought, "Damn, if they B-52d a whole mountainside that had a cave that could house two thousand men, you know where those POWs are right now. They're buried. Regardless of the number, they're buried."

We both realized that would stir up a hornets' nest like nobody had ever seen. We dropped the subject.

I OFTEN THOUGHT ABOUT THE COURAGE OF THE MEN I KNEW. THERE WAS ALSO the other end of the scale. The deserter. The defector.

There were reports of sightings, but you had to sift through the surprise and anger on the part of the patrols when they ran across one of their own who had gone over. It's a good thing I didn't see any. If there was anything that would have gotten me killed, it would have been that. I would have gone to extremes to get one of them.

When I was in Ban Me Thuot an A-team reported a Caucasian running with the NVA. The sighting was brief and unconfirmed by any other team. There was a Marine patrol who said they saw an NVA antiaircraft unit with a five-foot-ten white "advisor." A Russian? Maybe. Maybe not.

When you spotted something like that, you had to be awfully careful to ascertain whether that man was under duress or not. In other words, was he there voluntarily or was he there against his will as a prisoner?

In SOG, a team had reported seeing a Caucasian with the NVA, not being guarded, by a river on the Laotian side near the seventeenth parallel. The Caucasian stripped down and washed in the river. The SF were on a ridge and could look down with binoculars but couldn't determine if he was U.S. or Russian, or from some other Eastern Bloc nation. The team was directed to stay and observe. I never heard if he had been identified.

Mad Dog also reported seeing a six-foot white guy and hearing his southern accent.

We always got reports of deserters, but they were hushed up. If it was reported in the debriefing, I'm sure the team was told to shut up about it. "This is a classified deal" was the order. I don't know what happened to the after action reports, but the men on those teams will carry the secrets forever.

Bull Simons was called on to stage a daring rescue of some seventy POWs held in a North Vietnamese prison in Son Tay, twenty-three miles west of Hanoi. A successful rescue so deep into enemy territory would be a propaganda bonanza and give all our troops an incredible boost in morale. It would also put the enemy on notice that we weren't going to sit by and take their crap.

Dick Meadows was one of the first men the Bull put on his planning team. Dick was called to Washington from Fort Benning, Georgia. It was late in July and I was in the Nantahala National Forest climbing a five-hundred-foot bluff. I didn't know it at the time, but I was at the top of Dick's list for the assault phase of the raid.

The first inkling of something in the wind came when some of the other men on our field exercise were released to go back to Fort Bragg. Some returned, some didn't.

When I got back to Fort Bragg I started asking questions. The men were surprised to see me. "Joe, what're you doin' here?" they asked. "How come you didn't volunteer for that mission?" Now I was really agitated. I breezed into the office of Col. Elmer Monger, the group CO. He acknowledged that my name was on a list submitted by Simons for a mission.

"I could only let just so many people go," he said. "I need the rest of you men to run the unit."

In a way I could see the colonel's point. My team was in a state of readiness damned few other teams maintained. But I still wanted a chance to go with Bull Simons. The man was a legend.

I went to see the Bull, whose office was always open to us, and asked if I could volunteer for the mission. Simons shook his head. "I'm sorry, Joe. I've already interviewed every man and the names have been approved by Washington. There's nothing I can do about it now. We're committed to the men on the list, and we can't change that. That includes the alternates. Everyone is already down in the training area. They're just waiting on me."

I wished him luck and left. Somewhere between Simons and Monger I was pulled off the list. That was the end of it.

The raid was one of the most extensive missions of its kind, ever. But it came up dry. Months before the mission, the prisoners had been moved. Simons and his men were never informed. A handful of intelligence types knew that there was always a fifty-fifty chance that no POWs would be found.

From the time the mission was planned, there was never any hard evidence that prisoners were still in Son Tay. At least, none that was passed on.

About sixty days before the raid, SOG began running Son Tay target data with recon teams of indigenous on the ground, observing movements in and around the prison area. Placing the "spooks" was largely the work of CCN in Da Nang. A six-man OP-35 recon team of Montagnards from CCS was pressed into service, too. These were men trained by SOG for Bright Light pilot-recovery operations, and they were very much at home in the mountainous terrain of the North. With overflights still a no-no, the recon teams were taken to a forward launch site and inserted virtually on the so-called DMZ. They were to walk from the border to positions near Son Tay prison. It was one hell of an extended operation.

C-130 Blackbirds, full of whiz-bang electronics, listened from positions up and down the Tonkin Gulf. None of the men on the ground were able to confirm, one way or another, POWs inside the prison. Spy photos from high-altitude SR-71 aircraft had clouds in the way.

Thirty days before the mission, the recon teams were pulled off the target. That meant that ground intelligence would have to come from whatever "controlled American source" was bought and paid for among the native population. That kind of intelligence was usually unreliable as hell.

The upshot was that the Son Tay raiders didn't have up-to-date target information from the ground. On all my missions, I went in with intelligence that was no more than twenty-four hours old.

The raid was carried off beautifully. "Negative prisoners" was the word from the assault force. It was a letdown for everybody, but Simons brought all his men back without a scratch.

The raid was a wake-up call for the NVA. American POWs were moved from wherever they were to new locations. About ten days after the raid, an OP-35 Cambodian recon team, operating in the CCS AO just across the fence in Cambodia, had a sighting of twenty-one U.S. POWs being moved to a high-hilltop location. CCS was able to confirm the sightings through locals trained as agents by the OP-35 teams.

The report was relayed to OP-35 headquarters in Saigon, and Donnie Vickers, the CCS sergeant major and S-3 operations sergeant, began planning a rescue. Since the POW location was almost inaccessible from the ground, CCS was considering an airborne assault. But JCS in Washington wanted to keep the lid on, and MACVSOG was told to get CCS to back off.

They were ordered to let Saigon handle everything and not to breathe a word of the sightings to anybody. "Just forget it," they were told.

As far as I know, no further attempt was made to rescue them. Another goddamned political decision.

There were a lot of stories about why the Son Tay prisoners were moved way in advance of the raid. The most popular was that flooding of the nearby Song Con River threatened the compound, and the POWs were moved as a safety precaution. That explanation was strengthened with revelations that secret U.S. cloud seeding in Laos had created the monsoonlike rains in the first place.

Another reason was that the NVA was going to renovate the prison prior to inviting an International Red Cross team to inspect the place.

My feeling is that these were cover stories made up to hide the fact that there was a leak at the highest levels of the U.S. government—a leak that both sides wanted to conceal. President Nixon was furious at the leaks to the press about his secret bombings, so it was also possible that word of the Son Tay raid was passed to North Vietnam sympathizers.

Anytime a mission of that nature failed to achieve its objective I would say to myself, "Some skunk in Washington who was against our involvement leaked the information." And whoever it was had probably been doing it all along.

The Army had its own ideas about leaks—the Vietnamese wives of our soldiers. This resulted in a directive prohibiting any U.S. military from marrying foreign nationals from any theater of operations.

In war, anything is possible.

chapter 20

Playing with Penelope

The Army was always testing new concepts to "modernize" the battlefield. Some of the schemes were downright harebrained. Some showed a little intelligence. And a few worked to perfection. There had to be combat simulations to test the stuff and SF were often selected because of their training and Vietnam experience.

The Hunter-Liggett Military Reservation in California sat on land originally owned by Howard Hughes. The U.S. Government acquired the property and turned it into a laboratory to create the Army of the future.

The civilian contractors and their military project officers probably had the legend of Mr. Hughes dancing in their minds when they set out to build a computer-controlled combat course. What they wanted to do was run patrol-sized infantry units through simulated battlefield conditions.

The brains behind the operation sat in Fort Ord at the Combat Developments Command Experimentation Command (CDCEC). They were proud of their creation.

Then *we* showed up.

Capt. Michael Lewis, a veteran of CCC out of Kontum, commanded our six-man team. I was team sergeant and had excellent men behind me: Sfc.

Richard Altman, Sfc. Jose Guerra, Sfc. John Irwin, and SP4 Arnold Mc-
Dowell. Mac was the only one that hadn't been to Nam, but he had excelled
in our strategic recon exercises.

The orders said we were being assigned along with a B-team to thirty days
with the Experimentation Battalion at Hunter-Liggett. Major Claude Matchette, the B-team commander, hadn't given us a clue as to what kind of "experimentation" we were in for. All we knew was that we were going through
a new course called SIAF—Small Independent Action Force. Captain Lewis
and I figured that was a fancy name for "recon."

We had arrived two weeks ahead of the course to get accustomed to the
topography and to learn to navigate the new area. There's a difference in
your pace based on the slope of the terrain, roughness under foot, and thickness of the undergrowth. We knew we would probably be training real hard
and real fast, so we learned what to expect when we were told to "go one
hundred yards" or "move ten klicks."

We soon realized that the B-team wasn't going to give us any support to
prepare for the course. They were supposed to support all the A-teams by
setting up patrol training and putting us through exercises to perfect our
navigational skills. But the B-team sat on their butts and drank beer while
we worked. All they had to do was follow the SOP Lewis and I presented to
Matchette back at Fort Bragg.

Lewis and I had done something that hadn't been done before in the 7th
Group. We dug into our SOG background walking the jungles of Southeast
Asia, and came up with a team SOP. It had everything: where you put your
rations, your compass, your maps; descriptions of the jobs of every man in
every situation; how you moved, how the point man moved, how the tail
gunner moved; areas of security depending on your position in the team;
how to set up and run a hasty ambush; how you cross a danger area; what
happens if you lose one of your helicopters en route; how to make dummy
inserts; setting up an LZ and a DZ and actions in them; how to react if ambushed; what your responsibility is if something happens to the team leader;
what actions to take if you can't make contact with the FAC; actions at a
rally point and what determines a rally point; setting up the E&E; how to
handle tension and nervousness from all the action; when to let off steam,
and a lot more. A hell of a lot more.

It was a first.

But Matchette got all the credit for it because it went through 7th Group only under his signature, and lo and behold it reappeared at Hunter-Liggett as part of his B-team SOP. Unfortunately, it just sat on Matchette's desk like a decoration.

So we did the B-team's dirty work. We set up the PT course, the obstacle course, and navigation exercise. We opened up *our* SOP and passed the information around to the other A-teams.

Lewis was boiling and told Matchette, "Don't *help* us anymore. Don't come over to our area. We will be training, and we will make you look good. Just don't talk to us at all."

The B-team couldn't have taught us anything, because they didn't know anything. They kept their distance and we made them look good.

There was one hitch—a little wild pig called a "peccary." Howard Hughes had introduced them into the area as a game animal, but they survived and got real mean. Our briefings at Fort Bragg had told us about them—warning us not to try to trap them—that they would charge with their sharp little tusks. It was the time of year when they were protecting their young, so we were on alert.

The first incident of man vs. pig came early. We heard someone shouting and found that an A-team soldier had gone into a thicket with a bunch of the little rascals. His buddy was three hundred yards above on a hill standing a peccary "watch" and yelling out their positions until the man came flying out of one end like a cannon shot.

The peccary wasn't the only hazard we were warned about. We always had a medical briefing about any area of operations. They would tell us about poisonous snakes and insects, contaminated water and food, and infectious diseases. The briefing officer had reported that the biggest danger to us around Hunter-Liggett would be VD. That was because of all the hippie communes scattered throughout the nearby hills. A lot of military were getting VD. That was a real surprise. I didn't think any soldier in his right mind would mix with those people.

Along with the peccary sightings, one team did report seeing a "hippie hole," where the long-haired freaks were swimming naked. We made a note on our maps, because if any of my team ran into them, there would be hell to pay.

Our SIAF course was different from what infantry units had been exposed to. It had been reworked to test LRRP-type units—units whose mission was recon and intelligence gathering, not contact. We were going through with nine other teams of SF, Navy SEALs, Marine Force Recon, and Air Commandos in order to validate the course—prove that it would do what it was designed to do.

Or prove that it wouldn't.

We were the first team out and started tearing their ideas apart from day one. We were taken out to a great big clearing. The grader had all six of us stand facing each other in a little circle like points on a clock. They had sixty stakes placed in the ground, from twenty-five to a thousand meters away, each at a particular compass azimuth. The grader would say, "On azimuth so-and-so, tell me the distance to the stake." You turned around, shot your azimuth, looked through your field glasses, identified the stake, and figured the distance. The whole team was given a chance to confirm it and report to the grader.

We had to pick the twenty correct stakes. The course designers had already calculated the odds—the expected score for an "average" unit. That was their first mistake.

The second mistake was made by our grader. "If you guess it right on the mark," he said, "I'll give you a case of beer."

We got them all, and with no long discussions, either. They were flabbergasted at how good SF was. The computer said we weren't supposed to get that many right. Hell, nobody ever told *us* that! We had twenty cases of beer, too.

That ended the betting.

The main part of the course was set up for infilt operations. The civilian contractors were given SITREPs and AARs from patrol action in Vietnam. They fed all that into their computers and came up with all kinds of combat situations. When a unit ran into a target that the computer put there, the "proper reaction" was already in the computer, and the team's reaction to the situation was automatically compared to it.

It looked great on paper.

The big problem was that the civilian contractors didn't know diddly about what recon was all about. They hadn't been there. Even the military who watched over the program hadn't been there. It was all theory, and theories could get men killed.

There was a twenty-five-kilometer course through the mountains. We were to walk it several times, observing assigned targets, reporting enemy signs and activity, and evading detection. Seismic and acoustic sensors were placed throughout. They were similar to the air-dropped seismic intrusion devices—ADSID—and acoustic SPIKEBUOY listening devices that were placed all up and down the Ho Chi Minh Trail. The course controllers were supposed to be able to tell where we were at any given time.

But they really weren't prepared for our type of recon team. They assigned us this young captain—a damned non-SF "leg" at that—to umpire a five-day, long-range, cross-country navigation exercise. When he briefed us we knew right away he didn't know squat about SF operations.

From the time we were inserted into one end of the test area, he was in constant radio contact with the HUMRO—the human resources officer at the operations center—relaying questions as to why we were doing this or that, and making entries on his score sheet.

The main point of the five days was to find out how good we were at spotting targets at night. To us, that part was a piece of cake. Our main concern was the leg captain blowing our cover. Lewis assigned Irwin and McDowell to keep an eye on him.

"Make sure he keeps his head down," Lewis said. "Watch his movements, and don't let him hurt himself or hurt us."

I wanted to make damned sure the young man knew how serious we were about our missions. I took him aside and said, "If you make us look bad I'm gonna damn sure kill you."

I could tell from his face he believed that I would.

We started screwing with the computer right away. We dropped right into the same things that were so routine to us in SOG. We'd "communicate" with the FAC and set up radio codes keying the squelch in a pattern for "yes" or "no." We'd zigzag all over the place, sometimes retracing our paths. Our umpire and the controllers at the other end didn't know what in hell we were doing. Every time we tried to explain our movements and actions it blew their minds, and they always came back with "That's not part of the exercise. It does not compute. It does not compute."

They didn't have a clue.

But we spotted almost every target and reported a lot of "enemy" movement. They had live bodies roaming in and out of our AO, both to observe and be observed. Hunter-Liggett had a lot of underbrush, so we'd move out at night and stay hidden in the daytime. On several occasions we observed the bad guys in the valleys below us while we were resting, wrapped in our ponchos. They were so easy to predict. They never saw us.

Sometimes, when we suspected we were being observed, we went into areas we weren't supposed to be in, and gave them a false location. We'd get a message real quick, "No . . . you're not there. Report your location. Report your location."

It became such a game with us we gave the computer a name—Penelope. By this time, the young captain had gotten such a kick out of running with us he became a real member of the team and fell right in with us. Penelope didn't stand a chance.

February in those mountains was biting cold. We were observing a target at night and trying to keep warm. We couldn't break cover with a fire, so we all huddled tight around a cigarette lighter. It didn't warm us worth a damn, but we made like it did. We'd rub our hands and say, "Boy . . . that's good. I feel a lot better."

The weather at 0300 was the coldest yet. With only ponchos and liners, it was extremely uncomfortable. Like any other mission, John Irwin, the radio operator, slept with his rig. Penelope called.

"What is the temperature at your location?" As if we carried thermometers.

Irwin came up on the radio, "Well, Penelope . . . we are using a rectal thermometer, and it registers down at the bottom."

After a pause, they said, "We don't understand your last transmission."

John spelled it out. "We're freezing our goddamned asses off!"

I couldn't hear their response, but John started giggling out loud.

"What are you laughing at?" I asked.

"It will not compute . . . it will not compute." John was doubled up.

They didn't bother us anymore about the weather.

The whole next day, we kept saying, "It will not compute . . . will not compute," laughing our heads off.

As we were finishing up that phase, we had to move through this one highly sensitized area, where there was a sensor covering every square foot of ground. This was a lot different than walking through areas with regular combat-style sensors. The place was all wired in. They could tell within twelve inches where we were on that part of the course. It allowed the "live enemy" to get awfully close to us and not make contact. Even though it was very dark we could see them, but we never did panic—something the HUMRO expected us to do.

All the while, Penelope was throwing questions at us. "If you saw an enemy patrol, would you drop down and take them under fire?" "If you saw them, and had enough time, would you hide and let them go by?"

Captain Lewis reminded the HUMRO that any answer we gave would have no effect on a real combat mission—there were so many variables. That irritated them.

We kept them irritated. And scratching their heads. On the next series of exercises, we proved the computer wrong on almost every count. The civilian contractors thought they had figured within thirty minutes when a recon team should get back off a particular type operation. We'd always come back early, sometimes by two hours.

We always gave them more than they asked for, too. We even took soil samples, but they didn't have any idea how to process them. We had to tell them why it was so important to intelligence gathering.

Halfway into our final week we were taken into a classroom. Two civilians were waiting. The older one was holding a gun that looked like something out of a science-fiction magazine.

"What kind of Buck Rogers contraption is that?" we asked.

"Boys . . . this is a laser target illuminator."

"Oh, damn," I thought. I suddenly understood why we were given such a thorough eye exam back at Womack hospital.

We sat down and the class began. The laser gun looked like an M-79 with a 4X scope on top. It had been developed at Redstone Arsenal, Alabama, and test-fired at China Lake, California. The older civilian was one of the men who developed it. He was our instructor, and we were going to be the first to fire it in a military exercise.

It wasn't the "death ray" we read about in the comic books. Its batteries didn't generate enough power to kill a man, although it could injure his eyes. The beam was meant to "splash" a target thousands of meters away. The bounce from that splash would be picked up by sensors in an attack aircraft miles from enemy detection, and that plane would let fly a laser-guided missile.

BOOM!

SF would infiltrate enemy territory, find the target, and "splash" it. No aircraft would appear on enemy radar or be reported by any observers. They wouldn't have any idea where on earth the bomb came from.

At the end of two days of training, we put on special goggles and fired it. It shot out a pencil-thin red beam in a series of pulses. It was a neat gizmo. The instructor said the device had the power to send a beam three thousand meters with hardly any spread or drop in altitude. The hit, or splash, was called that because that's just what it looked like—like dropping a stone in water.

The only caution was that the target should be a clear shot, with nothing in between to deflect the beam. The smallest object, even a leaf or a blade of grass, could screw it up, and the possibility existed that the beam might eventually ricochet back toward the gun. The last splash was what the bomb homed in on.

You kept the trigger pulled until the pilot reported he was "locked on." The computers and the bomb did the rest. In addition to our riflelike version, they were testing more powerful helicopter-mounted target designators.

The evening of the firing we went back into the mountains and made our way to the top of a hill with a deep valley below. Across the valley was our target, three thousand meters away. Through our binoculars we could see it was a big sign, the size of a building. We were excited that we were chosen as the first soldiers to fire the laser.

We picked a bald hill to lie on. I got behind some big rocks, and drew the stock tight into my shoulder. I trained the scope on the big X in the middle of the sign. It was a perfectly clear shot—obviously planned that way.

Our aircraft was an A-4 attack jet out of Miramar Naval Air Station near San Diego. He was circling way out, waiting for our contact. Captain Lewis gave him the azimuth heading.

"Roger that. I'm thirty miles out on azimuth. Fire your gun."

I fired the gun.

"Firing," Lewis relayed.

He no sooner got the last syllable out of his mouth than the pilot came back, "Locked on."

In a few seconds the sign blew all to hell.

My first thoughts were, "Damn. Send me back to Vietnam with this thing. I could tear up the NVA real good and they won't ever figure out what hit them."

That was our only time with the laser. The next day we were back with one last crack at Penelope—a recon patrol exercise with a mock artillery position as our target. We got to the top of a mountain and saw it through our binoculars a thousand meters away, clean over on the next mountain. We saw people moving about and called in the coordinates.

The HUMRO radioed, "What is your action toward this target?"

Captain Lewis just shook his head. He grabbed the radio. "Penelope . . . we'd like an air strike."

"Denied. Not available."

John Irwin had a big grin on his face. He got on the radio. "Request permission to fix bayonets and charge!"

The HUMRO took a few seconds. "Will not compute . . . will not compute."

Our young umpire was trying to control himself. "You were supposed to 'report and evade.' That's Penelope's solution." Finally, he just had to let go. The whole idea of us charging down the hill, across the ravine, and up the next hill had us all laughing like crazy. We didn't even have bayonets.

The leg captain became our only casualty. And that was from those devilish dehydrated rations. We didn't want C-rations weighing us down, so we voluntarily took the stuff out on the course. The scientists had come a long way since we were test guinea pigs, and we were also wiser about eating the rations with a proper amount of water.

The leg was real curious about the "candy bars" we had. "What are you eating?" he asked.

"Lurps . . . L-R-R-Ps," I answered. "Special dehydrated food for long-range patrols. The astronauts eat it."

"Let me have one."

I gave him one and he loved it.

"Damn . . . that's good. Give me another."

Captain Lewis gave him another, but warned him, "Be careful with that stuff. You've got to eat them very slowly. If you don't, you're not going to like the next thirty seconds."

The poor guy didn't know to give each ration enough time to absorb the liquid in his stomach before downing another one. He asked for a third. And a fourth.

It was just a matter of time.

When it hit him, he was hurting bad. We gave him all the water we were carrying, but that wasn't enough. We were at least five hundred yards from the nearest water—a stream.

Irwin got on the radio to the HUMRO, and reported the problem and our location. The HUMRO didn't believe where we were. They had four observers out trying to find us and we had eluded all four.

"You can find us now," Irwin told him. "We're breaking cover." Irwin gave the coordinates of the stream and asked for a medic to meet us there.

We half carried the captain down to the stream, and he drank and drank. The B-team medic was worried about him going into shock, and gave him an albumin injection to pump him up until we could get him out of there.

Even after all that, we still had to convince the course controllers we had been where we said we were. It was the same after every exercise, and every time our young captain confirmed what we said. We were kind of aggravated because they would believe him, but not us.

When all the points were added up, the best any of the other teams could do was 70 percent. We had a combined score of 99 percent and blew all their theories to hell.

After a long debriefing and a mountain of paperwork, Major Matchette pulled Captain Lewis and me into his office. He said, "All right, guys, who leaked the scenario to you?"

They actually thought we knew what was in the computer.

"Nobody, you asshole," Lewis barked. "We used our head." After all those days in the bushes, the captain wasn't about to be diplomatic. "Nobody fed us a fucking thing. We got nothing."

We left Matchette and the course controllers still wondering how we did it. The answer was in our SOP and in all those days in the jungle.

As far as Penelope was concerned, "It will not compute . . . it will not compute."

chapter 21

One for the History Books

When I got back from Vietnam, I didn't expect a parade, but I damn well didn't expect to be spit at either. Every GI, wounded or not, had to fight another war.

Stories of dissension in the United States were getting back to us troops, and I often thought what my reaction would be if, and when, I encountered any antiwar types. My first taste of this came less than a year after I returned from SOG.

It was March of 1970, and I was in the middle of Operations and Intelligence School at Fort Holabird, Maryland. This was a continuation of earlier O&I training that had been interrupted by my second Vietnam tour. It was an intensive course dealing with techniques of interrogation designed to loosen the tongues of POWs. The men teaching were real pros, and they showed us that more good intelligence could be gathered by working on a man's mind than by any physical punishment. It was an eye opener.

We were living in a civilian area of Baltimore, and drove back and forth to the school. There was a lot of antiwar activity, and we had to be very careful not to wear uniforms until we got to the fort. The Army even got us quarters in the small communities on the edge of town—the quiet sections where we didn't have all that hostility—and rented rooms from families. A couple of the men who were staying in a hotel very close to the fort had their vehicles vandalized—knife scratches and cut-up tires from the low-lifes who came out from under their rocks at night. The men eventually moved out.

O&I was a tough school and was strictly for SF. There was a lot of studying at night, and by the time you went to bed you were real tired. We had no time for going to the bars or restaurants. Considering the mood around us, that would have been a mistake, anyway.

It was a bad scene. One time, as I was leaving the fort, the little punks had the road blocked. There was one standing in the damned road right in front of me. I put the pedal to my 1968 Chevy short-bed and ran over the bum. I didn't kill him, just knocked him out of the way. The MP was standing right there. He just grinned, so I went on my way. "If they want to do their peace march, go to Washington," I thought, "but don't harass me. I was only doing what I was told to do." I was mad.

It didn't end there. In April that year, my team was on exercises in Pisgah National Forest. Near Lake James, we had set up an HQ at a Boy Scout camp. One evening, as I was sitting on the porch of my cabin, a small bunch of antiwar hippies came walking up the dirt road. They probably spotted our military fatigues. One of the real ugly ones came close to the porch and shouted right at me, "You all are baby killers!" The rest picked up the chant.

It took all the control I could muster to stay on the porch. Finally, I couldn't take it anymore, and came down to him face to face. I got into a real mean voice and said, "I work for the President of the United States, and if he orders me to kill your baby, I damn well will kill your ugly-ass baby!"

All the color drained from that long-hair's face, and he ran back to his buddies. They beat a hasty retreat.

So the military had a real problem with its image—the Army in particular. The JFK Special Warfare Center was even redesignated as the JFK Center for *Military Assistance*. But it took a Special Forces sergeant to come up with an idea that would not only shine up our image but be a good field-training exercise as well.

It was a dandy.

The idea was to retrace the path of Meriwether Lewis and William Clark—cover some 2,800 river miles and over 400 mountain miles from St. Louis to the Pacific! It was a bold operation put together by S. Sgt. Sigfredo Llorens of the JFKSWCEN.

Michael Lewis and I heard about it first. "I've already started writing it up," he said. "What do you think?"

We got excited right away. It would involve twenty-nine men—two twelve-man A-teams in the boats and five support personnel following in vehicles loaded with supplies and extra gear.

Llorens was following a tradition among Special Forces NCOs—making sure the A-teams stayed ready for anything. That meant constant training, both physical and mental. A team sergeant would often create operations to keep his men tough. As long as the JFK Center's training objectives were met, these plans were usually approved. Llorens was so convinced that the reenactment was a good proposal that he dug into his own pockets to the tune of $150 and called authorities all along the Lewis and Clark route, finding out about road conditions and property rights along the way.

The operation plan started through channels, and Captain Lewis and I kept our fingers crossed that it would be approved. By the time it hit the desk of Brig. Gen. Henry Emerson, the center's commander, it had been endorsed by practically everybody. Old "Gunslinger Six," as he liked to call himself on the radio, jumped on the bandwagon and sent it down with his approval.

There would be two A-teams on the expedition, one from the 5th SF Group and one from the 7th—since both were headquartered at Fort Bragg. The groups were free to choose their men.

Colonel Elmer Monger, the 7th Group CO, called Captain Lewis into his office. It was such a natural thing. Here, the 7th Group not only had a team leader named Lewis, but his team was regarded as the hottest in the Group. Hell, I thought we were the best in the whole damned Army.

"Take the best people from Group," he told Lewis. "You have total control of who goes."

Coming off SIAF at Hunter-Liggett, we didn't have a full team of twelve to offer. Half the men were either in a school or assigned elsewhere, so I had to fill out the team. The new men would have to possess the physical stamina and level of training my team was noted for. We could handpick from the fourteen hundred men in the group by any method of our choosing.

The Army provided copies of the Lewis and Clark diaries and plenty of maps. Michael Lewis, Lt. Earl Howell, our new XO, and I spent hours and hours in skull sessions and preparation. Conditions along the rivers had changed a hell of a lot since 1804. Much of the Missouri had been dredged and straightened to handle river traffic, and the rest of the river system was full of dams. So we had to add some dead reckoning to Lewis and Clark's notes about currents and geography.

After all was said and done, the team leader from the 5th Group agreed that ours would be the lead boat, and that I would be the navigator for the whole exercise. I would have insisted on that, anyway.

Our support element would stay ahead of us and meet us at predetermined camp sites. We would be in constant radio contact with them and with Fort Bragg through long-range commo.

It was midday on May 13 when we flew over East Alton, Illinois, which sat a little north of St. Louis at a bend in the Mississippi River just above where the Missouri began. I was jumpmaster. It was a beautiful day with very little wind. We parachuted into an airfield and got a terrific reception from the crowd. As we landed, trucks came from all directions to pick us up. It was quite exciting.

They took us to our waiting advance team, and we turned in our parachutes. We strapped on our rucksacks and combat gear and marched into town. We didn't get far, because the town had a big feast ready for us in a restaurant. After that great welcome, we marched over to Wood River to a spot across from the mouth of the Missouri, where Lewis and Clark built and launched their big keelboat for the first river portion of their journey. There was a small park dedicated to them.

The advance team had already put four sixteen-foot plastic assault boats into the water. They were powered by 40hp Evinrude motors that the 1st SF Group had shipped from Okinawa to the scuba committee at Fort Bragg.

The next morning, we piled in and floated down the Mississippi for a big ceremony at the Gateway Arch. The mayor of St. Louis gave us a replica of a coin that Lewis and Clark had traded the Indians, as well as other trinkets to present to the museum at Fort Clatsop, Oregon, where Lewis and Clark ended their trek west. We had mapped out a timetable that would put us there 4 September.

It was one heck of a send-off.

As we headed up the Missouri an amazing thing began to happen. People from all the small towns came out and cheered us. Some even escorted us to their docks. They would take us in, feed us, and send us on our way.

Our reception in Jefferson City was also terrific. People poured out to see us. While we were there, one of our support trucks diddy-bopped to Fort

Leonard Wood to get two more plastic boats, to spread out our load and give us a better shot at the current.

In Kansas City the people swarmed all around us. There were a lot of Vietnam vets in the crowd. Our showing up meant a lot to them.

The Army Corps of Engineers gave us more up-to-date maps of the river above St. Joseph. From now on, the Missouri would be close to what Lewis and Clark found—wild to the first dam in South Dakota—not controlled like it was between St. Louis and St. Joseph, where the dredging made the river stay in its banks. It was also getting blazing hot on the river. We stripped down to short sleeves and changed into the olive drab cutoffs all of us wore for scuba training. It made for a good tan.

All the river towns, big and small, opened up to us. As we moved through Missouri, Kansas, Nebraska, and Iowa, boats from all over came up to bring us to shore. There were always picnic tables full of food just waiting for us. And there were good, solid people who crowded around and gave us a pat on the back. We had found the *real* America.

In Omaha, they gave us the key to the city and made us honorary citizens. The local race track dedicated the sixth race to us, calling it "The Green Beret Purse." After that we were guests of honor at an Omaha Royals baseball game. We participated in the flag-raising ceremony, and the stadium gave us a big round of applause.

In South Dakota we put into the big, beautiful Lewis and Clark Lake behind the Gavins Point Dam. It was the first time we were on still water. We made good time. This was a beautiful part of the world. We were often tempted to pull to the banks and explore, but had been briefed and warned to stop only at dams or under bridges. That was state land. The rest belonged to the reservations, and the politicians didn't want to upset the Indians.

The big news was that the Indians were more upset that we *didn't* stop to see them. They'd come up to those locations where we landed and sit around chitchatting with us. They were very friendly. A lot of them were working some good-looking farm land. When we explained why we bypassed them, they all shook their heads and laughed.

The lakes behind each dam eventually turned into their natural river form—moving and changing—and very difficult during rainstorms. In some places the water would slam over the boat. We were afraid we would take on too much water and often pulled into some cove to wait it out and bail out the boats. These places were usually in the middle of no-man's-land.

We encountered three more dams and a huge system of reservoirs and lakes, and passed by the Cheyenne River and Standing Rock Indian reservations on our way into North Dakota. At every dam we had to land and carry those six heavy iron motors to the other side. Each took three men to carry, and there was no comfortable way to do it. Then we had to climb back to get the boats, the gas cans, and all the gear. It took awhile to get over one dam that was a quarter-mile portage.

Outside of Bismarck, we pulled into a camping area near the spot where Lewis and Clark spent their first winter with the Mandans and met the Indian woman Sacajawea. The descendants of those Mandans held a little powwow with us. Sfc. José Guerra looked almost as Indian as the natives and they took to him right away. They held a ceremony making him a "brave." He was given an eagle feather and welcomed into the tribe. The bald eagle was an endangered species, and the U.S. had forbid the hunting of the bird, even by the Indians who coveted its feathers as a symbol of manhood and strength. Hell, they were dressing up in feathers way before there was a U.S.

Even though José got the feather, we felt the honor was meant for all of us. The Mandans were good people. All the tribes we met were good people.

The river was taking us through fabulous country—deep gorges and vast plateaus. There were also long stretches where we didn't see a soul. We sometimes went days between towns. We were eating C-rations and getting very tired of them.

In the middle of one really remote stretch in Montana we had spotted one large solitary tree on the riverbank and pulled over to camp for the night. The news from the 5th Group team wasn't good. They were far behind and one of their boats had broken down. "Damn . . . we're going to have to be here a couple of days in no-man's-land," I thought, "and all we got is C-rations."

Captain Lewis was the only one to carry a weapon, an over-and-under .22/.410 fold-up survival gun. It was time to put it to use. I dug out some shells I always carried, and asked Lewis for the gun. "I'll be back in a little while," I said to the men.

There was a long flat open area from the river to a mountain range. I walked up to the base of the mountains and into a game preserve. I stopped short at a gang of coyotes, who were resting quietly. As I doubled back across the hillside there she was, a pretty little doe asleep in the buck brush right below me. That's what I was up there for, and I got her with one shot to the head.

When Michael saw her all he could say was "Joe . . . you killed Bambi's mother."

Well, Bambi's mom cooked up real good. We tied her to a spit with wire from our C-ration boxes and roasted her all night long over a slow fire. Michael Lewis didn't have any problem eating his fill. By the time the other boys had closed in to us, we had eaten the whole damned thing.

It was our fifty-ninth day on the river when we reached the headwaters of the Missouri just outside of Three Forks, Montana. Three streams came together there to form the Missouri—the Madison, Jefferson, and Gallatin.

It had taken two months to get this far, and we were really happy to make it over 2,000 miles. The men had a christening: Captain Lewis and I got thrown halfway across the Madison. We swam for about an hour, then loaded boats and motors onto one of the support trucks. The gear would be put on a C-130 back to Fort Bragg. When we finished the overland phase, we would be paddling RB-15 rubber boats from Orofino, Idaho, to Astoria, Oregon.

That evening, we started final preparation for our walk across the rest of Montana and Idaho. Since it was going to be over four hundred miles on foot, we made sure we had plenty of dry socks.

That night we slept very soundly.

In the morning we walked into Three Forks, with every intention to walk on through. But the townspeople wouldn't hear of it. One of the businesses offered us breakfast. The word had been spreading that we were in town, and the streets were full of people by the time we got back on the road. They clapped loudly as we marched by.

At this time of the year in Montana, it was very hot in the middle of the day—sometimes reaching 110 degrees. It was at least that by midafternoon. We knew from the start our biggest problem would be our Vietnam jungle boots with their steel plates. We knew that we were going to walk a long way in a short time, and that the feet were bound to bake. But, in our early preparation, the Army wouldn't give us special shoes. We had written a couple of shoe companies to get some hiking boots. We didn't get a single reply. Since nobody knew about our expedition in advance, I figured when they received our request they probably asked themselves, "Who the hell is this?"

We had already figured that the walk would take thirty days. We were trying for eighteen to twenty miles a day as long as we could stand it. That would not be easy to do, considering all the gear we were carrying.

As soon as we got a few miles west of Three Forks, we found from a map that the route went way down to the southwest around the corner of a mountain and came back. We could see where we wanted to go, about five miles away. We thought that the best way to travel was to cut straight across the mountain; then we could drop back down to a paved road on the other side. The road led halfway down the mountain back to the original highway that ran from Three Forks to Butte.

It was a slow climb to the top, and we began to realize that was one big mistake. It may have been a shortcut, but it was in the heat of the day and the ground was hard and hot from lack of vegetation. By the time we got to our first camp, there were blisters all around.

The feet were so bad on a couple of men you could see tears come out of their eyes. I tried to instill in their minds that, if they got in the truck, they wouldn't get credit for making the full trip. Captain Lewis didn't like that idea. He wanted to give them credit, anyway. But I wanted them to use the last bit of gumption they had to complete the walk. We finally did put a couple on the truck.

By the morning of the second day most of us had mended enough to continue. But the team from the 5th Group still had one man that had to be put in a truck for a day. For the rest of the walk, we determined that it would be better to walk three hours in the morning and three hours in the evening, even if it meant after dark. We followed the primary route of Meriwether Lewis. According to their diary, Clark would go off the trail to investigate something, then link up with the party on down the trail.

We made it to Pipestone Pass and the Continental Divide. At about 6,400 feet we could look to the northwest and see Butte, on the other side of the Divide about ten miles away. We made our descent and stopped at the outskirts in a pretty camping area. As we were setting up for the night, a bus rolled up loaded with Boy Scouts. They were there to meet us. They camped right along with us, and it was great. We showed them some survival tricks and they didn't want us to quit. I don't think we ever went to sleep.

They walked with us into Butte. By the time we reached the Naval Reserve Center armory, the boys had hiked almost ten miles. Most of them had awful sore feet, but they didn't care. The parents wanted our medics to treat them before going home. It was quite a sight. While we treated their feet, a doctor from the Reserves was treating ours.

When we got to Missoula, the antiwar types came out. It was a college town and a tiny group heckled us as they carried signs and shouted their slogans. None of them had the guts to face us. The National Guard must have had problems before, because their compound had a tall wire fence around it. That evening we were greeted by a nice crowd. But the welcome was marred by demonstrators, who harassed the good people coming to see us. As a consequence, we didn't think it would be advisable to stay more than a couple of days.

On the twenty-eighth day of our walk we stood on a small ridge of mountains in Idaho's Clearwater National Forest and could see Orofino, Idaho, to the west. We were all feeling a lot better, since we could almost see the end of the walk. With two days to spare, we had it licked. We could also make out the drop-off into the Clearwater River on the other side. That would begin our final water route to the Pacific. We continued to walk after dark, so that the next day all we would have to do was go downhill into Orofino.

In the morning we double-timed the last three miles with full field gear. We had made it to Orofino. Well, most of us made it. Each team had lost men along the way. We lost Larry Hunt and José Guerra and the 5th lost its XO. The men were sent back to Fort Bragg on emergency leave, disappointed as hell.

There was a big reception for us at the VFW hall, but we didn't want to spend all of our extra time partying. We used that time to rest and double-check everything for the final push to Fort Clatsop in Astoria, Oregon.

After two days, we were more than anxious to get on with it. We put two RB-15 rubber assault boats into the Clearwater and headed for the Snake River. It was rapids all the way and we enjoyed every minute of it. We were flying.

The Clearwater ran through the northern rim of the Nez Percé Reservation, and they showed up in large numbers to follow our progress. They gave us one hell of a send-off as we paddled toward the Snake. They jammed almost every bridge, cheering and whistling. The river cut through some high, sheer banks, and the bridges were at least fifty feet above us. As we approached one, the Nez Percé were dangling six-packs of beer. When we got close, they dropped them!

I thought, "Oh, no . . . drop in the water. Drop in the water." From that height the six-packs were like bombs; if one hit it would tear up the boat. But the current was so swift we dodged them all. Every time a six-pack hit the water, it busted open and every can went in a different direction. The next thing I knew I was in the boat by myself.

It was quite a sight. The men were floating on their backs, feet in the air, picking up the beer and stacking the cans on their stomachs. Men, boats, and beer were moving together with the current. When we went out of sight of the Indians we were still chasing the beer, and they were just hooting and hollering at us.

By midafternoon we came to the first slack water, making for hard rowing. We were getting near Lewiston, where the Clearwater and Snake joined. Lewiston was at the border with Washington. Across the Snake was its sister city, Clarkston. The people of Lewiston had several events organized for us, but first we had to meet with the new commander of the 7th Group. Colonel Monger had retired and the new CO was Col. Joseph Love.

Love met us at our quarters at the local junior high school right after we came off the river. He showed up as we were unloading the support trucks. He wearing a green beret and low-quarter shoes. He was out of uniform! Every real SF wore his Class A dress uniform with trousers bloused over boots.

Then the colonel opened his mouth, and the first thing out was a stupid scolding. "You look like a bunch of ragtags," he said. "Every one of you needs a shave and a haircut . . . and that's what I want you to do." He didn't ask how we were, or thank us for a job well done. The second thing that came out of his mouth was "Get rid of those short pants. They're not regulation."

Hell, cleaning up was on the agenda anyway whether he knew it or not. After the colonel left, I had to walk around to cool off. That smart mouth had me steaming.

We had made good time from Orofino and put ourselves on stand-down in Lewiston for two days. The townspeople held a great big ceremony for us in a big park in the middle of town, and we showed our appreciation with certificates making them "Honorary SF."

But it took the good ol' U.S. Army to bring us back to earth. Captain Lance Guilford, the CO of our support team, had received a radio message that the governor of Oregon and a ton of bigwigs were going to personally honor us at a real big banquet in Portland the *next* night. They were going to truck us to and from. This was news to us. We had never figured to spend any time in Portland. We really didn't have any extra time to give them. Without checking with any of us, an Army public-relations man had dropped the ball.

Captain Lewis told Guilford to telephone the governor's office. "Tell them we just don't have the time . . . but thanks anyway," Lewis said.

If you want to upset a politician, that's the way to do it.

When we pushed off into the Snake River we were back on our original schedule to Astoria. Real soon, we started getting the fallout for standing up the governor. We were catching flak on all the radio stations. "Can you believe that?" they were blaring. "The Green Berets turned down the governor's invitation!" It was just a big, fat misunderstanding. Only the politicians got bent out of shape.

It took a long five days to reach the Columbia River at Pasco. We put in for the night above McNary Dam, the first we came to on the Columbia. The northern banks of Wallula Lake backed up to within fifty yards of the railroad tracks that had run alongside the river for miles and miles. There was a wind blowing, and we decided not to fight it. We pulled our rubber boats onto the banks, and set up camp between the tracks and the water. There wasn't much room, so we were rolled up in our ponchos close to the tracks. It turned out to be too damned close.

About 0200 the ground started to shake, and before we knew it one of those damned trains was speeding toward us. If you were ever to be afraid, that was the time. That sucker sounded like it was going to run on top of every one of us. He was long and loud, and when he finally passed we moved to the other side of the tracks and a lot farther away.

As we got closer to populated areas, navigation became very simple. All we had to do to determine where we were was tune in the local radio. All the stations were continuously broadcasting our location. We decided to play games with them. We would double back and hide. Then we would hear the radio say, "Where are they at?" Then we'd wait and travel at night. "We think they're down by the dam," the radio would report. They sometimes sent a plane looking for us.

Because we had canceled out on Portland's big welcome, we decided to spend the night on the Washington side of the river, across from Portland. As we paddled up to the docks just above Vancouver, folks started lining the riverbanks, waving and cheering. Those were the people who mattered. They loved us.

The final leg of the Columbia was very tough. We were fighting the tides, the wind, and an occasional sandbar. It was often dark when we caught the tide. Captain Lewis had our Fort Clatsop arrival ceremonies pushed back another day. Fortunately, the good people of Astoria were sympathetic. They understood their river very well. Less than twenty-five miles from Astoria we pulled off on the Washington side near the small town of Cathlamet. We climbed a mountain and through our binoculars could almost see the mouth of the Columbia and the coast.. Cathlamet gave us a big welcome. A gentleman who owned a fleet of tugboats treated us to a swim in his pool, and his wife even washed our clothes. The city fathers then gave us a huge steak dinner.

When we finally got to Astoria, it was very late, and we were very hungry and tired from fighting Mother Nature. We stopped at Tongue Point Coast Guard station at the eastern edge of town. They opened their big kitchen to us.

Astoria stuck out into the Columbia, so the next morning we began a four-hour row around it to the Pacific side. We passed giant ship docks absolutely packed with people. They were throwing beer at us and all. We headed for the Astoria Yacht Club, and the closer we got the harder we rowed. When we pulled up, the other team was a mile behind. We were so glad to be at the end we could have fought a hundred-mile-an-hour current and still made it.

The next afternoon, 5 September, we paddled across Youngs Bay to the inlet of a small river named for Lewis and Clark that ran south paralleling the coast. The original expedition went up that river to build a winter home, Fort Clatsop.

It was a very nice ceremony. We presented the expedition museum with the Stars and Stripes we had brought from Fort Bragg, and raised it above Fort Clatsop. Then we gave the museum the Lewis and Clark coin and other artifacts from St. Louis. They had a presentation for us, too, and unveiled a plaque with our names on it.

What made the whole exercise so great was the response from people in the towns and villages spread out along the route. They took us in like we were their sons. What we saw was the real America.

In a way, for us Vietnam vets, it was the parade we never had.

chapter 22

The Rest of the Story

We had just come off ten days of grueling desert survival training in Arizona when Michael Lewis and I got the word through the 7th Group chain of command that the Army wanted us in Washington for a presentation ceremony. We were to meet with the Secretary of the Army and General William Westmoreland, the Army Chief of Staff, to receive congratulations on the success of our Lewis and Clark expedition and to present them with commemorative paddles from the trip. Michael and I were flattered, to say the least.

There was one hitch, however. We didn't have the paddles anymore. All our Lewis and Clark paddles had been snatched up by the men and given to everyone and their brother, including the governor of Oregon, the Special Warfare Center itself, and a general from Fort Monroe. The Center Public Information Office had gone to great lengths to make fancy framed mounts with plaques and a map of our route. They handed us their handiwork, and we were to provide the paddles.

We drew some from supply but they looked too new. The day before we left for D.C., our men assembled in the barracks parking lot to see us off. Lewis stood on the blade of one paddle and I stood on the other. The rest of the men grabbed the handles and dragged us along the lot. When the paddles looked appropriately worn down, we wiped them off and mounted them for the presentation. The only giveaway was the handles with the finish still unblemished. The real paddles had all the paint rubbed off. Where we were going, who the hell was to know? When PIO picked them up for shipment, nobody said a word.

Kathy and I dropped the kids with a neighbor in Fayetteville and drove to D.C. Captain Lewis was in his own car, happily on his way to stay with one of his D.C. honeys. Michael had a lot of girlfriends in different places, and this particular one—a woman named Ruth—lived in Vienna, Virginia.

We stayed at the Holiday Inn in Alexandria, which was close to the Pentagon, and took the next morning to see the sights, since Michael and I weren't due at the Pentagon until midafternoon. It was a crisp February morning, which gave the place a scrubbed-down look.

Michael met us back at the motel right after lunch. He was carrying his uniform on his arm. It was wrinkled as hell. "I don't know how it got so wrinkled," he said. "It was in good shape the last time I wore it."

"Did you have to run around to some girl's house to find it?" asked Kathy, wanting to say a whole lot more. Kathy had come prepared with a steam iron to make sure the creases in my class As were crisp. She laid out Michael's uniform on the bed and gave it a good going-over.

After the ceremony with Westmoreland, we were going to be guests of the Sierra Club at a banquet in our honor. I reluctantly left Kathy at the motel, telling her I didn't know if I would be back that day at all or how long the dinner would be. As always, she understood.

The halls in Department of Army were beautifully paneled, with a thick olive-drab carpet underfoot. I lagged a little behind Michael and tried to look into all the offices along the way. I always wanted to know what really went on in that place. There were a hell of a lot of colonels not doing very much as far as I could see.

We walked into an outer office—kind of a reception area. There were more generals than I had ever seen in one spot. It looked like the damned Milky Way. They were waiting for us and formed a reception line as we came in. As Michael and I started shaking hands, I recognized one of them and my blood started to boil.

There in the reception line stood Lt. Gen. Richard Stilwell himself—the jerk that gave Dick Meadows and me such a hard time back in Vietnam.

As I got closer I knew he recognized me, but I could tell he didn't relate it to that time in his office at I Corps.

"I think I know you, don't I?" he asked.

"Yes, sir." That's all I said, and I didn't say it with a smile, either.

I was trying to control myself. I really wanted to tell him, "You ought to remember us. You're the one who called us a liar." But that wasn't the time to do it. It had been over a year and a half since Dick and I met in his office in Hue, but I'll never forget the face of that sorry soldier, no matter how long I live. I wondered if the true story of his intelligence screwup would ever be told.

Without saying any more, I immediately stepped to the next general. At the end of the line was Robert Froehlke, the Secretary of the Army. "Just call me Bob," he said.

Just before entering Westmoreland's office, one of the generals' aides handed us the ceremonial paddles. They looked real good.

The generals followed us in, along with Army photographers. The Lewis and Clark route map was already there sitting on an easel. We presented one paddle to Froehlke and one to Westmoreland. Michael went to the map and did a quick briefing on the conduct of the mission. After a short question-and-answer period Westmoreland excused the generals. Froehlke took the cue and excused himself. The general wanted to be alone with us.

He stood in front of us as Michael and I came to attention. Westmoreland told us to be at ease. He said, "Gentlemen, this will be a private talk in strict confidence, so you can speak openly and freely."

Westmoreland turned to me first and asked for my comments on Lewis and Clark and on the state of things at Fort Bragg. I was concerned about saying anything, so I just said, "It's going all right from my standpoint, sir." At the time it was—from my standpoint. I had a good team and we were treated well. But there was a lot I could have said.

Then it was Captain Lewis's turn. Westmoreland had a lot of questions about Lewis and Clark, and Michael was very positive about the expedition.

"Well, captain, how are things going at Fort Bragg?"

Lewis cut loose.

"Sir, we have E-6s and E-7s out there swinging blades on the lawn at JFK—picking up pine cones. We've got highly trained troops—good folks—pulling SD, like men going up on post and moving furniture from one warehouse to another. The XVIII Airborne Corps commander doesn't know what to do with SF and has assigned us as post support—something he's shoving down the throat of the folks at JFK because he's a two-star and all we have is a one-star. We're unpopular with the post commander and his whole staff because they've got this idea that we're prima donnas and somewhat rank-headed. But they have no conception of the responsibilities these SF have in the field. And now they've got these men pulling these stupid-ass details. Sir, the morale is going into the toilet. The next time they have a mission, how can they be expected to perform top-notch?"

Westmoreland just took it all in without saying a word. Boy, did I want to join in. But, hell, I was just an E-8 in a no-man's-land filled with brass.

Like Lewis, I was unhappy with all the stupid details assigned to SF men that pulled us away from training, but I didn't say anything about it. I was always unhappy about the details and the fact that they were transferring out a lot of SF, trying to cut back on SF because of Vietnam winding down. SF at Fort Bragg were in limbo—between the heaven of serving our country in a time of crisis and the hell of head-shed idiocy.

Captain Lewis had come up for air, and I thought he was finished. The general thought so, too, and was about to dismiss us when Michael dropped his bomb.

"Sir, the underlying reason for the mess at Fort Bragg is all the unqualified officers assigned to JFK Center. I think the Army is trying to dilute the leadership of SF by giving us non-SF-qualified, and worse, non-SF-oriented officers.

"You go through the Center and all you find are staff officers with no SF background—especially the senior officers. The Group commanders aren't being screened for SF background. It's almost as if any officer with an SF background was automatically excluded."

Westmoreland just nodded his head. I felt that Michael was getting in real deep, but he wasn't trying to be derogatory, just concerned. In any event, Captain Lewis was on a roll.

"One of the things that's hurting the morale of the NCOs was here they are trying hard to keep a tradition going and knowledge going, and every time they get a new commander at company and field-grade level they have to teach the man about SF."

Lewis had finished. Westmoreland thanked us for being so candid and we were dismissed. My impression was that Westmoreland didn't seem to be too concerned about what Lewis said. I thought, "Boy, I should have said something about this, or about that." But Michael had pretty well said it all, and if that wasn't enough to impress Westy, I didn't know what would.

Captain Lewis and I were escorted back to the garage and we pulled out for D.C.

The Sierra Club held its meetings in one of those old Washington brownstones behind the Capitol building. They gave us a very warm welcome, and we were ushered into a beautiful dining room with a large banquet table. There were thirty-four chairs, and as I looked around the room I just knew there was an important person in every one of them. The club president sat to my right at one end of the table and Senator Barry Goldwater sat at the other end.

Before the meeting came to order the man sitting on my left leaned over to me and introduced himself. "I'm with the project that developed the starlight scope, and I'd like you to be my guest at the development center. What do you think about the starlight scope?"

The guy didn't know I had firsthand experience with it in SOG. "I really don't think much of it," I said, and let the poor man have it. I gave him some details on why I didn't like it and how I thought it could be improved. The man just looked at me and didn't say a word. After I finished he said there were new models coming out with improvements but didn't say anything further about me coming to the plant. Then he kind of clammed up and wouldn't have anything more to do with me.

The meeting was called to order. There was a small prayer and then dinner. After a short business meeting they called on us. Michael gave them the lowdown on Lewis and Clark. Then they made a small presentation to me and Michael. The author Freeman Felden gave me an autographed copy of his new work, *The National Parks*. It was a beautiful book and I was honored to receive it.

Back at the motel I told Michael that Kathy and I would meet him in the bar at 2200 before he headed back to Vienna. When I got to the room, Kathy was frantic. She was all shook up because General Emerson's office at Fort Bragg had been trying to find Michael and me all night. Brig. Gen. Henry Emerson himself, and Bunny Knowles, his secretary, had already called four times about us. Emerson's office demanded to know where we were and kept asking, "Just what the hell did Captain Lewis say to Westmoreland?" Kathy didn't know what was going on.

They called the motel because they didn't have Lewis's number. It looked like they started calling right after we left Westmoreland's office, wanting to know where we were and what was going on between us and Westmoreland. The calls were angry and threatening to the point of frightening Kathy.

I phoned Fort Bragg and found out JFK Center knew everything Lewis had said to Westmoreland in private. But what they had attributed to Lewis in Westmoreland's office had been blown way out of proportion—it didn't even sound like what had actually been said. It was so off base it was easy for me to deny.

I really didn't have to lie when I told them, "No, Captain Lewis never said anything like that. He didn't say anything detrimental to the Center. . . . He never said anything like that. We just had a few words to say. Westmoreland wanted us to say more. He wanted us to open up and talk to him. In fact, Lewis was a foot from me and I didn't hear him say a damn thing like that."

Anyone that has played the children's game Rumor can appreciate what happened. By the time the word got from the Pentagon to Fort Bragg and then bounced around inside the Center, it was different—totally different from what Captain Lewis had said in what we thought was confidence.

"As soon as you get ahold of him, have him call us immediately!" they demanded.

When I told Michael, he just shrugged it off. "Hell, I'll call them when I get back to Vienna and straighten their ass out." Most people would have been scared to death, but Michael wasn't worried a bit.

It was way past midnight when they called back again to check.

"Boy, Michael must have said something really bad," Kathy said.

"No Kathy . . . he didn't. He just spoke the truth."

"Then maybe you ought to give them his telephone number."

So I did.

When I got back to Fort Bragg, I was expecting the worst, but I never heard a peep out of anybody. Except Michael Lewis. He told me General Emerson called him that night at about 0300.

"The whole Center was pissing in their pants," Michael said. "Emerson's chief of staff was first on the phone. 'I have the general on the line. I want you to compose yourself and think about what you're going to say.' In reference to what? I asked him. Then the guy gets a little icy. 'Reference your conversation with General Westmoreland.'

"Joe, he tells me that they got a call from the Pentagon. Then he proceeds to ask me, point by point, if I said this or that about the center to Westmoreland. He tells me that the whole center staff had been up most of the night because of it. So I told him, 'Sir, I don't have any idea what you're talking about.' Hell, Joe, I lied like a rug because I thought it was such an innocent conversation. And besides, Westmoreland promised us everything we said was in confidence. Was that ever a lying bunch of bullshit.

" 'Captain, what I want to know is what you're going to tell the general.' So I told him I was going to tell the general we don't have any idea what Westmoreland is upset about. 'Sergeant Garner and I didn't say anything controversial. We didn't slip or spit. As far as I know, everything went well.'

"Then Emerson himself came on and said roughly the same things. He wanted to know what was going on—why the twenty-one generals were in the room for this tiny presentation. Hell, I don't know why."

The shit had really hit the fan with a big SPLAT! The good ol' boy network was being threatened. There were some very concerned folks. If there was anyone you went to school with and you're an officer in a relatively high position, and you sponsor this guy for whatever reason, and you find out you've made a mistake, you aren't about to take the heat for that. What you do is make this buddy of yours look good one way or the other, or pull his butt out of the fire. Because, otherwise, it's guilt by association.

When the word reached Fort Bragg about our conversation with Westmoreland, there were people slapping their asses to cover their bottoms. The Center called people in that night to go through the officer-assignment records for the past six months.

Two things that remained unanswered was how Fort Bragg found out about our conversation with Westmoreland and how it happened so fast. Was the office of the Army Chief of Staff hot? And, if so, who was listening?

Or did Westmoreland pick up the telephone and alert Emerson to clean up the records at the Center?

chapter 23

Greenlight— Return of the Bag

I didn't volunteer for the SADM firing team. The word came down directly from 7th Group headquarters, which controlled Greenlight, the top-secret project built around SADM, the special atomic demolition munition, the man-carried nuclear bomb.

Volunteering for something like that was really not a smart move. During training and testing you could get into a lot of trouble. If you made the slightest mistake, it meant a black mark on your record, and you might eventually find yourself reassigned somewhere else. SADM teams were tested by Forces Command (FORSCOM) inspectors—men who took no prisoners. On a test there was no other score allowed than one hundred percent. If you made 99.9 percent in assembling and arming the device, you were dead! If you actually failed their test, the Group commander could be relieved of duty, that's how touch and go it was.

So, when the 7th Group commander and his S-3 picked a team to be SADM trained, I'm certain they discussed choosing the team with the best men: "We need a team sergeant and team leader we can trust."

Beforehand, all I knew of the SADM device was from team talk with other SF that were in the program, and the knowledge that I had been the very first man to jump with the bomb back in 1960. It was early in 1970 when my team was chosen to represent the 7th Group as the SADM Firing Team.

Some other SF questioned why I took it on.

I looked them straight in the eye and said, "Hell, if it comes down to a nuclear exchange, your chances are no better than mine, right? So what difference does it make if I'm carrying one?"

Now, barely four years later, we were about to place the device on a real live target. The makeup of the team had changed a bit, what with the nature of SF assignments and all, but the Army always tried to maintain the integrity and readiness of the SADM firing team—a policy that probably cost me a spot next to Dick Meadows on the Son Tay prison raid.

It was a crisp February morning. The sun was breaking above the tree line as I hung a right off Chicken Road and slowed to a stop at a high chain-link fence topped with razor wire. I was at the "Bird Cage," a tightly secured area located at the southwestern edge of Fort Bragg's Macridge training area. Armed guards carefully checked each man's ID against a name list that included our pictures and waved us through the gate into the Greenlight training compound.

There were ten of us—a full A-team minus one officer and one NCO. Out of the ten, only four men played key roles in jumping with the bomb and placing it on a target. These men were charged with knowing the device inside and out—and with knowing what it was capable of. They were also expected to have the skill to infiltrate the most heavily guarded target.

The team leader was Lt. Dan Schilling, "Dirty Dan" to us, about six feet three, a slender and wiry Missouri boy. He was a West Point grad, but you'd never know it. Schilling was the shirtsleeve type. He'd dig in with the rest of the men when there was a job to be done. He liked to read and refused to have a TV in his house, saying it turned the mind to mush. But, boy, could he work a bottle of Jack Daniels. Schilling kept a scrapbook full of Jack Daniels labels, each label with a story behind it—stories of where he was and what he was doing at the time. He didn't have a West Point ring; he recalled the motorcycle accident at Fort Benning when he was knocked out then came to with no wallet and no ring.

Our demolitions man was S. Sgt. Gerard Infanger, dark haired and tanned, with a stocky build. I had known Infanger from our days at JOTC in Panama.

Gerry was from Deer Park, New York, and spoke very good English. He was proud to come from a familly with military in its blood. Infanger's uncle was one of the first paratroopers in World War II—in the 501st Parachute Infantry Regiment. He became an officer and was later killed on an island in the Pacific. Gerry's father was a Pathfinder with the 508th in Europe and said that there were only two outfits worth joining: the Airborne and the Rangers. Gerry discovered college wasn't for him, and he got hold of a recruiting pamphlet about SF that said, "We take the best of the Rangers and the best of the Airborne." He worked at getting SF-qualified, went to OCS, and had been a captain before Westmoreland's Reduction in Force (RIF) shakeout gave him no choice but to accept an NCO grade to stay active. His Army training included nuclear-chemical target analysis.

Sfc. Gary Gilmer was our radio operator. He was the smallest on the team, with not much hair at all. But he was one tough little man. He came out of Vietnam with a bunch of Purple Hearts and the holes to prove it. He always pointed out that his marksmanship kept him alive. "Getting shot at is not the problem," he'd say. "Getting hit is the problem. It would have been worse except that I made it a point to double-tap every target—hit him in the head and chest."

Almost everyone in SF knew him as "Goofy Grape," a call sign he earned in Vietnam. He was on the Cambodian border calling for artillery. The G.I. at the other end asked for Gilmer's initials but had trouble hearing his "Golf-Golf" over the air. He asked to have it repeated again and again. Gilmer got really steamed and spit out, "Goofy Grape, you deaf son of a bitch!" The name stuck from that time on.

Everything about the nuclear device was critical. There was no room anywhere for error. Our training was constant. From our first sight of the bomb in early 1970, we had thorough training every six months. We would begin with two weeks of intensive classroom instruction at the Bird Cage and then move on to Camp Mackall for another two weeks of hands-on testing. Then, once a year, a team from FORSCOM put us through a technical-proficiency inspection (TPI), with all the marbles riding on the outcome.

This was one of those times.

As always, our training was being handled by civilians from the Field Command of the Armed Forces Special Weapons Center. The SADM came from Fort Bragg's Nuclear Weapons Support Branch. An armed guard would bring it to us. It was a simulated device, accurate in every detail including explosive parts, but with no nuclear material.

The SADM traced its roots back to a slightly bulkier device of the mid-

1950s called the T-4. The original application was as a "cratering" charge for a proposed canal from the Gulf of Mexico to Lake Nicaragua, then to the Pacific. Five devices were planned for the excavations at one kiloton each, but Nicaragua backed out.

The JCS then asked the nuclear experts at the Los Alamos labs to design a small "suitcase" bomb that could be emplaced behind enemy lines by Special Forces and other unconventional warfare teams against such targets as tunnels, bridges, dams, airfields, ports, terminals, and communications centers.

The solution was to modify an existing artillery round, adding special arming and timing capabilities. And there it sat—the SADM man-pack nuclear bomb.

The device was a little less than two feet long and had the same shape as the end of a regular bomb. The timing and arming mechanism was about the size and shape of an upside-down World War II hand grenade. As nuclear bombs go, the SADM was called a low-yield weapon, but when it went off it still delivered in the .01 Kt to .10 Kt range, and, considering its small size, could kick ass.

The bomb was pretty much self-contained and was one hundred percent sealed. The timer, the most classified part of it, was in seconds, minutes, and hours. There was also an "instant" setoff, if you had the nerve. Almost 90 percent of our training was on the timer with its tamper-proof backups. The first step was setting the timer, the next was arming it—there were several sets of "rings" to manipulate. Once it was set you couldn't deactivate it.

When you reached your target, you needed to be damn well sure of your orders to set the timer and arm it. The final word was not a team decision. We were to wait on target for an encoded radio transmission giving us a mission "go" or "no-go." The whole thing was designed not to alert the enemy that anything suspicious was going on under their noses and to give us enough time to withdraw.

One of the more popular ways to hide a clandestine radio transmission was from the flyover of a regularly scheduled "commercial" aircraft. The "pilot" might transmit in the clear on an assigned frequency—obviously monitored by the enemy—a key phrase or sentence. The message might come several hours before the prearranged time of detonation, allowing us to vacate the target.

The routine of the aircraft doing the flyover could not be altered. If there was a transmission time arranged, it was because that aircraft always crossed over or near our area at that time. If we were going to do it in Cuba with its twenty-mile airspace, any one of the many commercial flights that fly just outside that twenty-mile limit could easily transmit to a team on the ground. We'd be waiting for the transmission at the prearranged time, never knowing what aircraft it came from. In advance of the mission our briefing would simply say, "They'll be transmitting on 'this' frequency at 'this' time with 'this' message." It might even be a "weather report."

In a "no-go" scenario we might have to pull it off the target and get rid of it—destroy it. You could destroy the device without setting off the bomb. Before timing and arming, you could blow the bomb in place with an explosive and not have a nuclear detonation.

We took training at the Bird Cage for two weeks. At the end of the two weeks we knew to expect an exercise at Camp Mackall, which would add another two weeks. It was there that all of the classroom work would come together under the critical eyes of FORSCOM inspectors.

We began loading our gear early Monday. It was a familiar drill. We were mission-ready with all our full-alert equipment—weapons, communications, medical kits, rations, full rucksacks, and parachutes. Inside the C Company area our activity raised little curiosity among the other SF. Men were always in transit—going to and from training or preparing for missions. It was business as usual for SF. If we said anything at all to other SF about the training, it was always referred to as Greenlight. We never called it SADM or mentioned "nuclear" outside of the team.

We accepted the SADM assignment as an honor—another feather in our hat. We always knew we were the best team in 7th Group and could do the job better than anyone. Group headquarters knew it too. We brought a lot of skydiving trophies back to the 7th. No one could top our teamwork.

Camp Mackall Military Reservation was a totally self-contained training site. We would be locked up for two weeks with armed guards standing over us at all times. For a SADM team, what went on inside was our moment of truth.

Over the years every SF out of Fort Bragg had come to know almost every inch of Camp Mackall. My team alone had run dozens of missions there. In fact, we left our mark.

During early demolition training at Camp Mackall we were running live simulations. We did a lot of experimenting: we had a feeling we were writing the book on SF demolition exercises. Seaboard Airline Railroad tracks looped around the northern perimeter of Camp Mackall and dropped southwest toward Rockingham. We were simulating blowing the tracks to derail the train. We would set up a dummy charge, just a pop, to complete the mission. The exercise was boring as hell.

So we decided to make things more interesting by placing a more substantial charge a lot closer to the tracks. When the next train came by, we blew out windows. How we all kept out of jail I'll never know.

Our reputation was well known within the ranks of the XVIII Airborne Corps. They hated us. During field-training exercises when my team played the aggressors, we would harass the hell out of them. They would complain to the umpires that we weren't playing fair, with the ambushes and all. Our response was, "Hey, when you're in combat, who's going to be fair?"

In war, nobody celebrates second place.

We weren't the only SF at Mackall for SADM tests. Firing teams from several other SF Groups were busy in their team areas already. The U.S. had a stockpile of almost two hundred SADMs, with units in the United States, Italy, West Germany, and, according to some reports, South Korea.

We didn't know the order of the team tests, so we made the most of our time, going over all our classroom training and notes from the very first day we were assigned the SADM. The FORSCOM TPI was set up in three phases—written test, hands-on test, and the application test—placing the device on a target.

On day three we were notified that our call would be the following morning. From prior tests we knew this was our cue to set up security around our camp with barbed wire.

We were called as a team into the heavily guarded training building, and our IDs were again checked against their name list and pictures. Waiting inside were FORSCOM SADM personnel. Phase I was always a bear. We were even tested on stuff we might never use.

Among other things, we were expected to know how to place the device for demolition under water. All SF were SCUBA trained, so as a SADM team we might well find ourselves on an amphibious operation. We were taught how to submerge the device out of sight and float it below the surface without sinking to the bottom. Charts and tables told us how to prepare the device in its container to stay submerged by putting a specific amount of air in the container around the device. We could emplace it against a dam or in a harbor where the heat and radiation benefited the kill ratio.

The next day was taken up by hands-on tests. You couldn't be nervous at that point. Each man was put through the paces of setting the internal timing mechanism and arming the M-96 firing device. Gerry Infanger was the clock expert on the timer. On a mission we would rely on Infanger and Lieutenant Schilling to manipulate the clock system, although we all learned it.

This was the first time in the testing that we physically handled the bomb. We all had a good feel for it and really learned to respect its potential. The particular device we were given was the MK-54 Mod 1, weighing in at about forty-five pounds. That was the weight I first jumped in 1960. But we now had more to carry. The device had a form-fitting jump container, shaped much like the bomb itself. It was a thick, Styrofoam-type shockproof case, which added fifteen pounds. When you left the aircraft you were jumping sixty pounds above and beyond the full field load already strapped to you.

It was a leg-breaking weight.

As a team we had already jumped the device several times. On those jumps we carried the bomb in its case only if we didn't have to lug it to a target. When we were given a mission to take it to a target, I jumped with it rolled up in a sleeping bag inside my rucksack.

The final test phase was the application phase. Even after two weeks of classroom instruction and two testing sessions, FORSCOM still didn't show us how to get it on a target. That part was left to the unconventional-warfare skill of SF. That was the fun part. That was the excitement. That was my specialty.

FORSCOM had us run mission simulations that were as lifelike as possible, since the whole idea was to prepare us to place the SADM somewhere in the world. We would run small missions on the ground at Camp Mackall under close watch of an armed guard, who was usually the umpire of the exercise.

We had targets for placement—like a small dam near Mackall's north cantonment area. We had to set the timer and arm for detonation. In moving toward a target, our team was especially mindful of the safety of the bomb. Because of the excess weight we would switch off between the men as we moved, so care had to be taken not to damage the timer or arming mechanism. There was no smoking around the device, and any safety infraction by any member of the full team, even something that anyone else might think insignificant, was cause for a bad mark on the team's record.

The Army figured that SADM missions would most likely begin with infiltration from the air and that the higher the altitude the greater the chance for surprise. That's why HALO jumps were such an important component of the SADM program, and that's where we excelled.

At Fort Bragg we often HALO-jumped as a windup to our Greenlight training. On a designated SADM-team training day, we could even devise our own missions and run them, including dropping with the device from as high as twenty thousand feet. There was the usual armed SADM guard, who was also SF and part of the Greenlight program. The only time the device left his sight was when we went out of the aircraft with it.

Waiting for you on the ground would be another armed SADM guard, and he'd stick to you like glue. Eluding him would have been easy for us. But you didn't play games with SADM. The bomb was serious business.

To maintain team integrity, everyone assembled on the first man out. A moving aircraft automatically dispersed everyone as they jumped, so the team had to make up for that dispersion by changing body position and tracking through the air back to the first man out. With the first man also carrying the weight of the bomb, and maybe even its case, that was extremely difficult. The rest of the team, loaded down themselves with full-alert gear, still had to stabilize and help the bomb carrier maneuver. But we were expert HALO jumpers, and it was all in a day's work for us. Once we popped at eighteen hundred feet we had the advantage of the newly modified MC-1-1 parachutes which were much more controllable than the Army's old T-10 rag.

In the northern portion of Camp Mackall there was a small airstrip that could handle a C-130. We loaded up, accompanied by an armed guard. Our FORSCOM jump was very basic—a static line drop from the usual 1,250 feet. The device was in its case inside my rucksack.

We landed back at the airstrip dead on target. Another armed guard was waiting for us at the DZ and took control of the bomb. There was no makeshift mission this time—no target for us. And this surprised us a bit. The jump marked the termination of the FORSCOM testing.

Back at our team camp we got the word. Lieutenant Schilling relayed the news that we were going into isolation the next morning for a mission with the device. No more was said, but we knew we'd be out of touch with the rest of the world for the duration.

Kathy always knew to expect the unexpected. My team was one of seven "severe-alert" A-teams on immediate call to hot spots around the world—part of the antiterrorism Joint Contingency Task Force. We practiced a lot. We'd get a "mission" in the middle of the afternoon, HALO in to a friendly foreign country, go to a particular target, rescue a "political prisoner" and return him to a secure area, then be extracted. Our wives would never know where we went, but they accepted the fact that their SF men led this kind of life.

Isolation. We were locked in the training building. At one end was our team room—an open space similar to a barracks day room, outfitted with cots and a small table. We found the remains of a "sand table," confirming that other SF teams had already been through their isolation period and were probably well into their missions.

We were ushered back into the same room used for our testing a couple of days earlier. The mission operation order had come down from the 7th Group S-3 and signed off by the 7th Group commander. The target was a hydroelectric plant—a dam. We were to place the SADM nuclear device on a civilian target secretly. The dam was on the Pee Dee River and formed Lake Tillery, a popular fishing and boating spot located six miles to the west of Mount Gilead, North Carolina.

We were briefed with all the current target "intelligence": aerial and other "spy" photographs, location of enemy movements and concentrations—in this case a platoon of Marines from Camp Lejeune—civilian areas, friendly contacts, and transportation and communications information. The briefing included operation time schedules and target damage requirements.

When you prepared for this type of exercise, the controllers told you how much of the target they wanted out of commission, and for how long. You had at your disposal target damage information broken down into how many months or years the dam would be out of commission, depending on what part of the structure was blown. There was also a chart that showed the amount of damage downstream from the disabling or destruction of any specific part or section of the dam. You could even blow parts of the dam without any devastation downstream. It was already calculated in the charts.

Speaking of charts, our intelligence had on file schematics of every major dam in the world, with each dam divided into targeted parts that could be disabled or destroyed by the SADM along with calculations as to how long the dam would be out of commission after a specific detonation. So when a SADM firing team was given a mission, the results of a successful emplacement had already been calculated.

Our mission was to knock out the dam at Lake Tillery for forty-five days, and we were shown a little square marking the area at the dam to be disabled—in our case the hydroelectric generators. The tactical situation called for harassing the "unlawful government in power" by cutting the flow of electricity, while not exposing innocent civilians to wholesale flooding of their homes. The yield of our device and the pattern of destruction had already been calculated to destroy only portions of the dam. It was also calculated the fallout might affect the locals.

They sent us back to the team room. It was up to us to figure out the best location for the device in order to take out the generators for the forty-five days. That might have been the easy part. Then we had to figure avenues of approach to the dam and avenues of access to the prime location, where to emplace the device to avoid discovery for the several hours it might take before detonation, how we could leave a man with the device waiting for the signal to set the timer and arm, and how to get him out the next morning. Our plan had to match their expectations. If the mission controllers didn't approve our briefback we would be told to refigure. We'd be sent back to the team room to recompute the placement of the device and rework our maneuvers to get it on target.

Gerry Infanger was the best demolitions man I had run across in my entire SF career, and his was the task of selecting the best spot for the bomb. He buried himself in the target data and photographs. When he finally smiled, we knew he had it. Infanger chose to place it on this one rock on the spillway side of the dam. He was very precise in that.

"How come you're setting it here?" asked one of the men.

Gerry gave us the setup. "We're supposed to knock out these three turbines without cracking the dam, right?"

We chimed in, "Right."

"Well, I saw all these films of the OSS blowing dams and bridges during World War II. The key part of a generator is the shaft. It has to remain perfectly balanced. Once a blast knocks it off center it'll twist itself to death."

With his finger, Gerry traced a circle around the generators in the photograph. "So we've got a bomb that can deliver .10 kiloton." Gerry moved his finger back to the rock. "We're going to take out all three generators at the same time . . . from here."

We trusted Gerry's assessment, so now it was up to us as a team to figure how to get by the Marines at the dam and put the bomb on target. We studied different ways to get in, such as using a strong swimmer—like me—with a snorkel to swim upstream at night, holding on to the rocks and pulling a rope behind me. Then, after climbing onto the rocks below the dam, I'd pull the others along.

Another plan was to approach the dam at night from the lake side, snorkel down to the dam and sling a grappling hook over the concrete wall, scale it using the nylon rope, then rappel down the opposite side to the target area.

Each idea had its pluses and minuses. Approach from the spillway side meant fighting the pressure of a mean current near the turbines. Scaling and rappelling also had a major drawback—the Marines could "skyline" us as we came over the top, especially if it was a clear night.

In either case an E&E plan would involve a water escape at night while the Marines were on guard. However, given the intelligence we had at the time, these were the plans we took into the briefback.

Day 2 of isolation was briefback time. We were ready with our own sand-table map of the dam and surrounding AO. The thing was a work of art, with the various land and water features done in powdered cake coloring and crushed-up crayon. While we worked in the team room we could send out for any materials we needed.

Dan Schilling proposed HALOing in the device since we had a lot of success on other occasions. But, to our disappointment, the controllers nixed it in favor of a more conventional static line drop. The altitude would be low enough so that we could make eyeball contact with the DZ. That made them feel better.

After the team briefback, every member of the team briefed the operations officer on his part—first the team leader, then the team sergeant, then right on down to the medic. Every part each of us played on the mission had to be accepted or it was a no-go.

Infanger put on a real show. He was talking "overpressures" and "underpressures." Because he'd gone through the Prefix 5 school for nuclear weapons at Fort Belvoir, Gerry was armed with an arsenal of technical terms to sling around.

The controllers were impressed with our detail, but when they applied Infanger's computations to their own we were told that the device had to be placed at another point: inside the plant's control building, a structure sitting to one side of the three generators.

It was back to the team room. We frankly didn't give a damn about their bullshit philosophy of going into a foreign country and finding the "ideal" place for a nuclear bomb. Hell, once we were in that foreign country, we would put it on the easiest location to get to. We would be the only ones there, and who the hell would ever question us? And as for setting off a nuclear bomb to do a certain degree of precalculated damage, our idea would be to blow the whole damned target all to hell. Shit, it was war.

But we played the game. Refiguring our maneuvers based on a new placement of the device was no problem at all.

Day 3 of isolation. We gave our final briefback. This time we also had to brief the Marine "aggressor" commander. We laid out our infiltration plans. He was smug with confidence. "Oh, my boys ain't gonna let you do that. No . . . uh-uh . . . I'm sorry."

Well, we had heard that before. The silly ass didn't realize that, in a real war, we would probably kill all his men to get to the target.

That night we moved out to the airstrip where our C-130 was waiting. Inside was an armed SF, who watched over the device. Since I was team sergeant and was going out with the device, I was responsible for its security once we left the aircraft. So, according to the orders, I was the only one on the team that was supposed to carry live ammo. I would have a loaded .45 sidearm. Well, Dirty Dan, Gerry, Goofy Grape, and I thought that was a bunch of baloney. We secretly brought along some .223 ammo that fit our M-16s. Nobody was going to take our bomb or even get near it.

I didn't want to screw with the SADM container's extra fifteen pounds, so I took the bomb out and rolled it up inside my mountain sleeping bag. For extra measure, I lined the bottom of the rucksack with some socks.

When we were over the DZ, the pilot turned on the green light, but the jumpmaster had the final call to go or no-go. Twelve hundred feet below us the DZ ran north and south. It had been prepared by the 7th Group S-3. It was lit by small flares and marked by the usual method, an inverted L. The winds were blowing below twelve knots—a good safety margin. I signaled the O.K. and out we went.

It was an easy descent. Two hundred feet above the ground, I released the rucksack to the full extent of my drop line. The device dangled fifteen feet below me as I swung toward the DZ. It made a soft landing and I came down on my feet right next to it.

We landed in a tight circle, left our parachutes with the men at the DZ, and headed west toward the dam. An experienced A-team was in its element moving in the dark of night. To keep up a decent pace through the woods, Schilling, Infanger, and I would switch off carrying the bomb. Gilmer already carried a heavy load with his radio gear. All of us had Vietnam under our belt and, given our cargo, we treated this mission with the same respect as moving through an area infested with NVA.

With the dam in sight, we set up camp for the night at the edge of a swampy area. It was a dairy farm and we bedded down alongside a barn. Like the DZ, we were on private land. The Army always had to get permission from the landowners, and we treated them with courtesy. SF trained a lot in these hills and we wanted the locals to be happy to have us around.

Lieutenant Schilling had climbed a small hill ahead of us to do a first recon. He returned to report what appeared to be a platoon of Marines guarding a railroad bridge that spanned the Pee Dee River on the spillway side.

So far, so good.

Gilmer slept with the device in the bottom of his sleeping bag.

At first light Schilling went out to recon the area again. The tactical situation had changed overnight. He observed at least a company of Marines dug in along the whole front entrance to the dam and all around the tall chain-link fence. They were obviously on 100 percent alert. This new development would complicate our plans.

He also observed something else—something very interesting. An old pickup truck with garbage cans showed at the front gate at 0600. The Marines didn't bother to check the cans in the back thoroughly before sending it on. Inside the gate, the truck stopped at the control building—the same place where we were to place the bomb. The garbage man got out, grabbed a can, and went in. He made several trips in and out carrying garbage cans. Then he drove back to the gate—a total time span of about twenty minutes.

Bingo!

Schilling figured that he and Infanger could put on civilian clothes and go in and out with the garbage-man. It was so simple and so outrageous— just the kind of mission that does work. The garbage man idea really caught our fancy. We quickly dismissed the other ideas. Hell, as a team we hadn't failed yet!

The evaluator for the exercise was Sgt. Maj. Charlie West. He was a tall, skinny SF who had a favorite saying that identified him. Everyone called him "That's Not My Job West." He was a damn good SF who expected you to do *your* job. As the evaluator, Charlie knew what was going on at all times. It was his responsibility to be on top of both sides of the exercise.

West had set up a meeting point for coordination. It was a little café on Route 3. That night Lieutenant Schilling put on civilian clothes—we always carried civvies with us—and made his way to the café to meet with West, the local deputy sheriff, and an engineer from the dam.

West explained the change in Marine tactics. The platoon had fallen asleep at their guard positions on the bridge. Another SF team had snuck up on them and made off with their weapons. The Marine commander— the same officer who told us our plans wouldn't work—chewed out the Marine platoon leader, a young lieutenant who was aging fast. According to West his words were, "If the Army makes you look bad one more time, you're all walking back to Camp Lejeune!"

Schilling outlined his plan. West thought the idea was terrific. The sheriff's deputy was all in favor of it, too. The dam engineer confirmed the garbage man's schedule. He was just a resident of that rural area who had the contract. The deputy offered to drive Schilling and the dam engineer to the garbage man's home.

On any field training like this the key is the SF who first contacts the local civilians. If they liked that person, they were immediate recruits into the exercise. Lieutenant Schilling was first rate and quickly won over the garbage man—got him "signed up" to help us without ever revealing what we were carrying. He was told what he could expect in an actual military situation— that guerrillas would have come to his house, murdered him and his family, and taken his clothes and truck. He agreed to go along with us all the way.

Schilling returned to our camp with the complete layout of the garbage man's route. If he and Infanger could get through the gate, we knew we had it made, and if we needed to "sacrifice" a man it was all part of the lifelike nature of the training. If it had been an actual military operation, sacrificing a man would be nothing at all. What the hell, we knew that once we took a nuclear bomb on target—if it came to the point of actually employing nuclear weapons—that would be the end of it anyway, and if any of us survived it would be a miracle. We accepted that.

The four of us stayed with the bomb. Infanger slept with it that final night. Sfc. Richard Altman, the team's O&I NCO, had followed us on the jump and had the job of security for the operation. Altman and his five men were deployed in pairs and in position nearby to keep people out. They had loaded weapons as well.

The local law enforcement had no idea we had men with live ammo.

In the morning the garbage man met us at the barn. He was ready to play. Schilling and Infanger put the bomb, wrapped in my sleeping bag, in a garbage can and covered it with garbage. Off they went. I took the rest of the men to the hilltop for close observation. If it had been the real thing, we would have been snipers ready to provide escape cover if anything went wrong.

The garbage truck drove up to the Marine checkpoint with the garbage man, Dirty Dan, and Gerry in civvies, all acting like it was routine. Schilling waved, Infanger waved, and the garbage man waved. The Marines lifted the lids for a quick check, then the Marines waved, and in they went.

Once at the control building, Dan and Gerry took the garbage can inside and removed the device. The real garbage man went about his business loading cans into his truck. Gerry climbed up onto a platform and Schilling handed up the device.

With the SADM there was a two-man rule—the device could never be left with one man. However, in a real war, the only rules are the ones that let you win. Schilling violated the rules right away.

After putting Infanger on target, Dan just decided to nose around. Schilling showed his spunk by walking into what was obviously an employee break area, and got a Coke and some candy from the machines. Several Marines showed up and asked him for change. Dan didn't miss a beat. He carried on a conversation with all of them gathered around the machines, including the Marine lieutenant and another officer. Schilling always tested limits and just wanted to see how far he could go. That was one of the reasons I liked him so much. He was just like me.

The rest of us remained on the hilltop watching it all, observing the comings and goings, always on alert just in case they had to be rescued. We were always within striking distance.

Right according to plan, the truck made its way back to the gate. The gate was opened and Lieutenant Schilling and the garbage man waved goodbye as they drove away from the dam.

Marine math: three minus one equals three.

Back in the control building, Infanger sat with the bomb, waiting for the signal to set the timer and arm.

That night the rest of us were back in the woods prepared for the flyover and the transmitted code to "go" or "no-go." We knew that when the plane flew over and said, "Do it," that would be our point of no return. There would be no other communication whatsoever. The SADM timer would be set and the device would be armed.

At 0300 the next morning it came. From somewhere overhead we received a coded CW. Gilmer checked his one-time pad and decoded it.

"It's a go," he whispered. "Blow it!"

Schilling and I eased as close to the dam as we could and relayed a prearranged "go" signal on the small radio. Following his instructions to the letter, at 0600 Infanger would set the timer and arm the bomb to detonate at 0700. Once he set the clock, he had to be out of the dam, and we had to be clear of the area. We would wait for Infanger to leave the dam on the next garbage run.

At 0600 the garbage truck was late. It arrived at 0615 and Infanger again became a garbage man. At 0645 the truck returned to the Marine checkpoint with Gerry and the garbage man. The guards just waved. They drove past Charlie West, who was hanging with the Marines near the gate. West had been watching the comings and goings. He didn't bat an eyelash, but if any of us had been intercepted, Charlie would have taken over the device immediately.

When West got back to the barn, Gilmer was the first one he collared.

"Where's the device?" he demanded.

Gilmer was surprised by the question. "It's on target and it's detonated."

"No, no. They gave you a 'no-go' message."

Gilmer planted his feet. "No, they didn't." He showed West his log and what code was "go" and what was "no-go," then pointed to his one-time pad and what he had written out. "That's the 'fire' message."

"Well, they were supposed to send you the 'no-fire,' " West said. "On account of all the Marines being there we didn't want all you guys getting captured."

"Hell, we didn't get captured. Like I said, the damned thing's on target and it's detonated."

The message from the aircraft had been transmitted in reverse. Somebody up there had confused the codes for "fire" and "no-fire"!

A highly classified nuclear bomb was sitting on a dam in a civilian area, unattended. Charlie went screaming back toward the dam, picking up the Marine lieutenant and his company commander on the way. West pointed toward the Marine contingent. "Gentlemen, I hate to tell you this, but it's 0700 and these people right here are all dead. Those other people out there are severely burned, and those three fishermen out on the lake are dead."

The Marine captain was bewildered. "What do you mean?"

"Come with me. I want to show you something," said West.

Charlie took them to the control building. "What's that up there?" He pointed to an olive-drab canvas bag.

"It looks like an OD canvas bag," the lieutenant answered.

"Right. And those of you who survived the blast are radiation exposed and are all gonna die." Charlie looked right at the lieutenant. "Do you remember yesterday morning when the garbage truck came through?"

The lieutenant pulled out a note pad and pointed to an entry. "Yes, sir. We got it right here."

"How many went in there?"

"It's right here. Three men."

"How many came out?"

"Two."

"How many went in this morning?"

"One."

"And how many came out?"

The lieutenant again checked his notes. "Two."

"And that didn't ring any bell?"

There was still no light bulb.

Charlie just shook his head. "Son, a nuclear bomb just went off and ninety-nine percent of your men were killed . . . and you ain't the one percent!"

Within an hour a helicopter flew in with the Marine battalion commander. He relieved the lieutenant of command and sent him back out on the same chopper.

The poor idiot wasn't one hundred percent serious about his job. The reason my men and I succeeded was that we were.

In Vietnam, that got a lot of men killed.

chapter 24

Every Trick in the Book

There was always a possibility that SF would have to fight where it was cold, so we had winter training north of Flagstaff and learned to ski and survive in the snow and ice of the San Francisco Peaks.

But we had no idea what *real* cold was like until we hit Alaska.

It was the middle of January and our whole C-team boarded C-130s to Anchorage. We were headed into five weeks of arctic exercises, and our instincts told us we were being readied to operate in the kind of conditions the Russians were used to.

Sixty miles from the Alaska mainland was the Soviet mainland. But we were even closer than that. The little U.S. island of Inalik—Little Diomede to anyone who's not Eskimo—was right on the territorial line across from its larger brother Ratmanova—Big Diomede to anyone who's not Russian. There were only two and a half miles between them across the Bering Strait. Hell, you could almost skip a stone from beach to beach.

We had a lot of sensitive installations in Alaska, mostly early-warning radar stations pointed at the Soviet Union. But the most inviting targets were our huge naval petroleum reserves above the Arctic Circle in an area called the North Slope, and an even bigger one—the oil fields at Prudhoe Bay.

Then there was the Trans-Alaska Pipeline—almost eight hundred miles of it, twisting over some of the most inhospitable terrain found anywhere. It was a commercial project, but its security was everybody's business, especially ours. Once it was finished, it would be a nightmare to patrol.

That's where the Eskimos came in. It was called the Alaska National Guard, but it was really the Eskimos. We were going to spend two weeks training them in the fine points of intelligence gathering and observation.

That would be later. Our first job was some cold weather training of our own.

We had flown nonstop from Pope AFB and had left behind sixty-degree weather—sixty degrees *above* zero. When the command "Chute up!" was given, we were handed heavy felt-lined ski masks. The Air Commando crew chief warned us to remove the masks right after we hit the ground. If we didn't, perspiration would build up, and we'd get frostbite. We elected to forget about the masks altogether.

The jumpmaster was a major from the C-team. From the way he stood at the door to spot, I knew it was a political selection.

The green light went on, and the crew chief cleared us to jump. It was one hell of a shock to the system. Damn, it was cold, even through the long johns and layers of uniform and baggage. We were over Elmendorf AFB, outside of Anchorage. As soon as I looked at the ground, I knew the major and the pilot had screwed up. Blackbird pilots were supposed to be the best pilots in the Air Force, being able to put you out within ten meters of the target. But our position didn't look good. We were in one hell of a wind, and we were let out way too low. To add to the problem we had to contend with a herd of bison below.

Gerry Infanger had his own troubles. He had caught the prop blast, got turned around, and almost lost his goggles. They got fogged up and he was having trouble seeing the ground. He went in on instinct. When he hit the ground, he still had twists in his canopy, but he was unhurt.

The next task was getting off the DZ. It was covered with three feet of frozen snow, and there was no way to walk on top without it breaking underfoot all the way to the ground. We had packed snowshoes, but we weren't given the time to get them. Loaded down as we were, it was one hell of a chore to walk. We were getting real hot and sweaty, and by the time we made the one klick to Fort Richardson, several from the other teams had frostbite. That's when they sent vehicles to pick up the rest.

After the jump we were in a bar with the Air Force hotshots that dropped us. They admitted that they had sent us out on a sea-level reading. That meant we were a lot less than twelve hundred feet above the DZ. They also told us they had a forty-knot tail wind, so we were flying about eighty knots too fast when we went out. Most airborne soldiers would have been really messed up. But, being SF, we had the MC-1 steerable parachutes and the experience to hit the bull's-eye.

At post supply, they issued us cold-weather tents, little Yukon stoves, equipment sleds, and second sleeping bags. "What do we need two for?" I asked.

"You'll find out," the supply sergeant said. "You put one inside the other. And make sure you've got a lining underneath."

We spent the next three days learning to erect the tents and to pack and haul a sled called an Ahkio. It looked like a seven-foot-long banana-split bowl, and was a Finnish design. When fully loaded, it weighed over two hundred pounds. It was meant to be pulled by three or four men, rigged in waist harnesses and shoulder straps. But SF, who were tougher than anybody, needed just two. Your best skier held it from behind to control the movement. So two SF were really pulling more than three hundred pounds in the snow.

The tents were team-sized—lightweight and quick to put up. Each had a squad burner, a little square tent stove more commonly called a Yukon stove. It sat on folding legs and had a set of pipes that stuck together for a smokestack. It was for cooking and heating and would burn anything.

After we practiced erecting our tents and rigging the Ahkios we had a competition. Every team lined up with its sled fully loaded. The instructors blew a whistle, and everybody hauled ass through the woods on a cross-country course. At the end you set up your tent. The team that set up camp the quickest won a case of beer. As far as we were concerned, it was a time to have fun.

We'd hold back and wait for some of the tents to be put up, then run over them with the sled. We'd go out of our way to knock them down. Before it was all over the other teams started knocking us into the snow. The men who finally won had to pick themselves out of the snow a bunch of times.

Even under those conditions, we maintained a regular fitness schedule, taking PT every morning. We did it like we did back at Fort Bragg—in T-shirts. Talk about some people doing some jumping around—you didn't have to count. The men automatically started jumping to keep warm.

One morning we loaded everything, sleds and all, in a deuce-and-a-half. "You're goin' out in the country," they said. "You're going to be taught cold-weather survival."

Our instructors were senior officers and NCOs who were experts in cold-weather operations. We headed east out the backside of the post into the Chugach recreational area. It was a beautiful place, but it sure was cold. I thought the Army would have been better off taking the men that were so highly skilled in jungle warfare and keeping them razor sharp in their specialty. Then, do the same with SF cold-weather experts. My jungle experience wasn't worth a damn in the snow.

Gary Gilmer, on the other hand, was from Montana, and he was eating it up.

After a couple of hours, we rolled into an area with a lot of trees. Between some of them the wind had piled the snow into twenty-five-foot drifts. We were in the foothills of a small mountain range and were surrounded by some pretty desolate stretches.

We were beginning to lose the sun when we finally pulled to a stop. For most of us it was really lunchtime, but up there the daylight lasted only a few hours. We climbed out of the trucks, and our lead instructor started barking orders about where he wanted us to set up. "Put your tents here . . . here . . . and here." We were spread out in a large, rough semicircle with the B-team headquarters in the center. He checked every one of us to make sure the tents were proper and that we were safe from frostbite.

There wasn't much doing that first afternoon. We thought we might turn to pinochle when one of the boys showed us a map. He had a big smile. "Look at this. We're right . . . here. And here's that highway that goes from Anchorage to Greely and Fairbanks. The map shows a built-up area right . . . there. I'll bet they sell beer."

We didn't bother checking with Captain Charles Aycock, our team leader. The guy never cared what we did as long as it didn't impact the mission. Fifteen of us put on our World War II Army-issue cross-country skis—"suicide slats" we called them, since they didn't have safety bindings. I pulled out my compass and away we went, heading into the night across a country we had never been to before.

And, lo and behold, ten miles later we came out on the highway, and there was a great big beer joint and dance hall at the edge of this little town. We went inside and found the strangest thing. The place was owned by an old SF from my days in Panama, Charlie Harris!

He recognized me right away, and almost did back flips. He couldn't believe it. "Where the hell did you come from? I didn't hear a plane fly over. Put all your shit in the corner. The drinks are on me."

We hadn't seen each other since he was in front of me in a chow line in the jungles of Panama. He had gone on to become a helicopter pilot in Vietnam, saved his money, and bought the bar.

Charlie worked hard to try to get us drunk, but we only drank a little bit. We did eat his hamburgers, though. We traded stories until about two in the morning. On the way out the door he gave us bottles of whiskey, and we'd stop every once in a while to take a little of the medication.

We got back to camp about 0400. It was hard to sneak in since we were giggling and laughing and making all kinds of noise.

The instructor didn't give many classes the next day, so as soon as it got dark even more of us got together, and WHOOSH! There we went, back across the snowfield ten miles. We stayed until he closed.

The next morning, the lead instructor struck his tent. Captain Aycock wanted to know what was going on. "I thought we were supposed to stay out here ten days."

"Ten days, hell," the man said. "Anybody that can get up in the middle of the night, ski ten miles to a beer joint, and ski ten miles back—and do it two goddamned nights in a row—sure don't need no instruction from me."

The guy wasn't SF.

"They're yours, captain. Take them back to Anchorage."

We never did let a free minute go by without some kind of physical activity. Alaska, as cold as it was, was no exception. Just a short ski run from Fort Richardson was Arctic Valley. The military had their own slopes there that were lit at night. When the temperature was anywhere between twenty above and twenty below, they were open. We got lucky and skied right up to the 2300 closing time every night.

At the beginning of our third week the other A-teams were given exercises spreading them out over the southeastern part of the state. Our team was assigned to Fort Greely to train the National Guard Eskimos.

It called for another drop, and I was counting on the C-130 pilots to do a better job of getting us over the DZ this time. Fort Greely was about 175 miles from the Arctic Circle, and was the Army's cold-weather test center. It was bound to be a lot colder than Fort Richardson.

It was.

When we hit the ground it was like landing on concrete. It was forty below. With a good wind, it could reach eighty below.

We had a good wind.

There were moose all around. We kind of spooked them when we dropped in. We didn't know if they were going to charge us or what. The ground party quickly escorted us off the DZ to a remote part of the post. Our quarters were a plain old Quonset hut with a Yukon stove and fold-up portable bunks. Two other Quonsets would house the Eskimos who would be flown in from outlying villages.

We had a few days to familiarize ourselves with the post, and to lay on food, equipment, and supplies. The cold-weather test center was north of the heart of the post. Occasionally, we'd hear a siren, and suddenly see a lot of folks moving around.

"What's the siren for?" we asked.

"Oh, that's the work whistle," we were told. "When it gets to forty below or more the temperature is right to start our operations and everybody goes to work."

Outside of the testing and sometimes field exercises, there was not a whole lot for people to do at Fort Greely, the place was so isolated. The only entertainment was the NCO club. It had a poolroom and showed movies every night.

But the team didn't fool around at the bar. There was a ski slope on the post, so we skied over to it the first chance we got, and turned on the lights ourselves. The motorized tow was shut down, so we just pulled ourselves up the rope.

We did all our skiing wearing two layers. Even at forty below we still built up moisture underneath going up and down those hills. If you couldn't dry somehow, you were damned sure going to freeze. Once we finished on the slopes, we skied right back to the little Quonset hut and got by the stove to dry and change clothes.

We skied and jumped every night until the MPs ran us off.

On the fourth day, the Air Force started flying out to all the villages, bringing back the Eskimo Guardsmen. Each village was like an outpost for the Army, and the men liked drawing a Guard paycheck.

They were part of the 2nd Eskimo Scout Battalion. When we saw them it was like looking at pictures from the geography magazines. What a rugged bunch! Their squad leaders introduced themselves. They were the elders of their villages. There might be ten from one village, but the young were never in charge. Some were fairly well educated, and interpreted for us.

We had this one, the only one from his village. That sucker looked just like he stepped out of the Stone Age. He spoke an ancient dialect that even the other Eskimos could not fully understand. After some real strained conversation, we found out he was from a tribe that had come from Siberia not too long ago. The Eskimos worked out a "language" between them, so the man could follow our instruction.

We took him to the NCO club and introduced him to beer. "Bee-ull . . . bee-ull," he called it. We let all the Eskimos come to the club. They had plenty of money and loved spending it. This was like their two weeks of "summer training." Some said that was the only break they had in their life from hunting, and when they couldn't hunt, they spent the rest of the time fishing. That was their "work."

Tourists were a source of income for some of the villages. Ivory carvings made them a lot of money. They brought some with them—those boys didn't miss a trick. The price was outrageously high. We thought we could persuade them to sell it to us cheaper, but they wouldn't have any of it. They thought of us as tourists, too.

We gave them ten days of classes. It was more to school them in intelligence gathering than anything else: how to sight things out of the ordinary—things that didn't belong. We told them it didn't make any difference how slight it was. If it was the tiniest bit out of place, note it and report it.

Of all people we ever trained, these men definitely knew the landscape. Although most of them were more like coastline watchers, the oil pipeline was a major concern. Several of the villages sat in the vicinity of the pipeline, and although the oil companies had their own people to watch it, we trained the Eskimos to spot anything suspicious. Each village was linked to a commo net by radio, and we schooled them in procedure.

We made one miscalculation at the start of training. We put two weeks of C-rations in their Quonset. At the end of the first week they had eaten every bit. We forgot that they were used to eating a lot of food, especially a lot of fat, to handle the temperatures. So, midway through the training, we had to call for a resupply.

It was going to be a night drop into the same DZ where we had parachuted in. We already had several nights of eighty below, and even in the heated Quonset it was cold. Captain Aycock had placed his last can of Schlitz under the Yukon stove before retiring. When he went for his brew the next morning, it was frozen. Now remember, beer contains alcohol. We kept our radio and beacon batteries inside our clothes next to the skin, so they would be warm enough to work.

The DZ was clear of packed snow. It was forty below, and the snow was more like little rocks of ice that the wind would blow into the trees. We'd throw a cigarette butt on the ground, and the whole team would huddle around it like a big fire, going, "O-o-o-o . . . ah-h-h-h."

One of the Eskimos held the beacon for the plane. We were given only a four-minute period when we could transmit, so the pilot had to be in and out in those four minutes. You held the beacon with two hands to keep it oriented to a certain degree heading. For our drop that meant pointing directly into the wind. The only way the man could hold it was for someone to brace him from behind.

Captain Aycock came up to help. Even though he was wearing one of those big parkas with the fur hood, Captain Aycock's chin protruded as he held the man. In those four minutes he received frostbite. It wasn't long before the skin turned dark, just like a burn. Later, it began to peel.

One of the last exercises for the Eskimo scouts was extraction by Skyhook. It was an extreme measure, and you had to be in one hell of a fix to use it. You're harnessed to a rope that is lifted hundreds of feet by a balloon filled with helium. A C-130, equipped with special "hooks" in the nose, snags the rope just under the balloon and yanks you off the ground. After a short time under the belly of the plane, your rope is hooked to a winch that reels you up the tailgate.

We used to do it a lot at Fort Bragg, until the first failure. That was when the rope broke on General Joe Stilwell, Jr. He fell a few feet and broke some bones. Ever since then, we practiced with a two-hundred-pound dummy.

The C-130 circled overhead and came in low, dropping a bundle containing the harness and rigging, the balloon and two cylinders of helium. Unfortunately, it was so cold that the fill nozzle of one cylinder snapped off on impact. Now we had only one useful cylinder. Because of the wind we could only get the balloon and the dummy up about two hundred feet. The C-130 made a few passes but it was a no-go. The pilots really needed five hundred feet for a successful grab. But, even if we had the balloon fully inflated, a live man would surely have gotten frostbite.

We scrubbed the mission and turned the gear in to an Air Force man who was overseeing the operation. He never knew it, but I kept the five-hundred-foot rope.

We were in the final phase of training when I got a radio message from Fort Richardson that there was a telegram from Kathy. My father had died. "We've got an aircraft ready to pick you up," they said.

"What day did he die?" I asked. The telegram indicated five days earlier. "Well, hell . . . there ain't no need for me to go." If I had been notified earlier, I would have been at the funeral. We never were close, but I would have been there. He had been put away, and that was that.

Once the Eskimos were on their way back to their villages, the real work began. Pipeline sabotage and terrorism were uppermost in the minds of Department of Defense. And who better to test security than SF? After all, we blew the Panama Canal and went through a company of Marines to put a nuclear device on a dam. SF was also successfully running missions against nuclear installations all over the U.S.

Ours was to be the first mission against the pipeline.

The first thing we did was "borrow" four snowmobiles from the Fort Greely MPs. We grabbed them from under their noses and ran all over, hitting pumping stations and pipeline sections along a fifty-mile stretch. The post had helicopters searching for us, but every time they got close, we threw a white sheet over us and made like a snow drift.

Another favorite trick was driving headlong into the mounds of snow caught by the trees and piled up at the edge of the road. Sometimes that snow froze solid as a rock, but in most places you could dive into it and cover up.

When we turned in the snowmobiles, the MPs were ready to hang us for larceny. "Hell, no, that ain't larceny," we pointed out. "That's all part of the damned exercise. How can you 'steal' from the enemy?" They calmed down when they realized that if we had been terrorists hellbent on sabotage, everything would be fair game.

We wound up "blowing" the pipeline in 127 different places.

But that wasn't the end of our guerrilla operations. Fort Greely was holding arctic maneuvers involving Rangers from Fort Richardson and infantry from Fort Lewis, Washington. They were in the rugged hills of the Yukon Command Training Site, east of Fairbanks.

Our mission was to disrupt the exercise "by any means possible." My team always took that literally. We were given ten days to do it, so there was no time to fool around. Gathering intelligence about the operation was the first order of business.

We took off any insignia that might say "SF" and walked into Fort Greely's field mess. We stood in the chow line along with all the other hungry soldiers and airmen. There were so many men thrown together we slid right in—nobody the wiser. It was great. We could pick up all the talk and just eat like hell.

Since I had my master sergeant stripes, I went back in the NCO section and ate with all their top noncoms. There was the usual pissing and moaning bullshit, but there was stuff that caused my ears to perk up.

The nerve center for the war games was the ground-level operations center below the airfield control tower. That's all I needed to hear.

Captain Aycock was all smiles. "Well, shit. If we can infilt that easy, why not try for the command center?"

We had a young specialist 4th class leg assigned to us temporarily from Fort Richardson. He was part of our DZ ground crew, but really didn't know what SF operations were like. So we figured if we sent him to hang around the tower, he wouldn't stick out. We also wanted him out of our hair as we developed our plans. We cleaned up his uniform and gave him a patch we had scrounged from post supply. Sending him to the tower proved to be our best move.

When he got there he made like he belonged. He must have looked so innocent they thought he was really assigned there. The very next day he ran into our Quonset all excited, jumping up and down, "You ain't goin' to believe this, you ain't goin' to fuckin' believe this. There is one captain over there that's got all the call signs, frequencies . . . everything on the whole operation in one big notebook. I was standing beside him. He was running all the air missions—food, medevac . . . everything."

We all knew it had to be the air S-3 for the war games. That would be our target. The young SP-4 had done his job as good as any guerrilla. We told him as much and sent him back.

"Oh, hell," we all said. "How are we going to get this guy?"

That's when Captain Aycock went to work. He checked around the post and found that the S-3 was up from Fort Richardson. He went to a pay phone and called Anchorage. Starting with the switchboard at Fort Richardson, he began making inquiries, and in a short time came up with some good intelligence on the S-3. We had his name, his wife's name, and the name of his brand-new baby daughter, born just before he came up to Fort Greely.

The plan was simple. The best usually are. I would dress as an MP, walk into the tower, and give the S-3 a cock-and-bull story to make him think there was an emergency concerning his new baby. I'd have him follow me outside to a vehicle and capture his ass.

Aycock went to the town of Delta Junction, which was just outside Fort Greely's north gate. There was a small motel there owned by an old trapper and his wife. One of our men had hunted this area before and knew the couple. Aycock rented three rooms as our guerrilla headquarters.

"I got one hell of a deal," he told us. "The old man is happy as shit to rent anything this time of year."

We went to the MPs and laid out our plans for the provost marshal. We wanted them to know exactly what we intended to do, so we wouldn't have a running gun battle as we took our prisoner through the gate. They agreed to respect our operation and not interfere. Hell, we could have been anybody giving *them* a cock-and-bull story, too.

We had to procure MP identification, mainly arm bands. The MP first sergeant was a master sergeant like me and gave me everything I needed. I used my own rank insignia on a standard pile cap that everybody on post ran around with.

When we came away from the provost marshal, I was an MP master sergeant.

We had been running around in a four-door International Scout supplied by the exercise umpire—an E-7 from the C-team. There was enough snow on the hood to hide the fact that it wasn't an MP vehicle. That night, with Clifton McClain, our big, muscular heavy-weapons man, as driver, we took off for the operations center. The umpire was sitting next to McClain. We had briefed him on our plans, and he loved the whole idea. I felt he really wanted us to pull it off.

We pulled right up in front of the building. I got out of the back of the Scout and, with no hesitation at all, walked into the operations room. It was busy as hell and very noisy.

"Is Captain Martin here?" I shouted. Everything stopped when they saw I was an E-8 from the provost marshal.

"Yes, I'm Martin."

It was the S-3. He was holding the operations book. I kept my cool. "Sir, is your wife named Sarah?"

"Yes, she is."

I had his interest. "Do you have a child named Jennifer?"

"Yes, I do."

I really had his interest. "Well . . . something's happened and we need you to come to the provost marshal's office so we can talk. Would you please come with me?"

I could tell he was worried. He threw on his parka, tucked the operations book under his arm, and I held the door for him. McClain stood at the Scout and opened the door for him to get in the backseat. We were so damned proper.

He slid in and I slid right next to him. As McClain slammed the door, I stuck my pistol in the captain's ribs and announced, "You're captured."

"Goddamn" was all he said. "Goddamn."

The umpire in the front seat turned around and said, "Good!" McClain hauled ass out of there. We went out the front gate right by the MPs, and took off toward the motel.

Once inside we tied the man up. "Joe, he doesn't have the book," Aycock said. "I searched him and it's not there."

"Shit, he had it when he got in the car," I said, and walked outside to the Scout. He had stuffed it behind the seat. Without the book, all those men were stuck out in the snow with no supply and no communication worth a damn.

Gilmer had kept our C-team headquarters in Fort Richardson updated on our progress. When he reported that the "package" had been delivered, our colonel was jumping for joy. He and the Infantry colonel had been bumping heads all along, and he was so tickled we had screwed up the other man's war games. They had to call off the whole operation.

But that wasn't the end of it. The Infantry colonel found out where we were and sent four goons to take care of us. We heard a hard knock on the door, and when the umpire went to open it, there were four of the biggest boys I had ever seen in uniform. They grabbed the umpire and started dragging him to their Jeep. He kept kicking and screaming who he was, but they paid no attention.

McClain ran out the door to help. McClain was a martial-arts expert, with knuckles that were hard as rocks. The fight was about to get interesting. As two of the goons fought with the umpire, the other two jumped on McClain. Well, you don't grab McClain. He sent one guy flying, locked his arm around the other one's neck and just knocked the shit out of him. KA-CHUNK!

The umpire had planted his feet against the side of the Jeep so he couldn't be pushed in. McClain waded in and tossed the other two aside like sticks. He wrestled one to the ground and began pummeling him like a windmill. The other goon yanked the fire extinguisher from the Jeep and ran toward McClain to hit him in the head.

He never got the chance. I pulled out my .45 and whopped him on the back of his head. When he dropped, the fight was over.

The motel owner wanted to throw us out because there was blood on the sidewalk. We had six inches of snow on the sidewalk, but the old man still said, "That damn blood will be there till next year.. I'll never get all of it up. The guests will see that and won't stay here."

Captain Aycock managed to calm him down. We weren't about to leave until the colonel ordered us back.

Our CO radioed that he was getting congratulations from all over. But the best was a call from the Infantry colonel. "That's the first time I ever had a post commander beg. He was pleading, 'Please . . . give me back my man and my book.'"

When we got back to Anchorage for the debriefing, all they talked about was how we "ended the war."

The Fort Richardson commander still threw a big going-away party at the Officers Club for all the SF, and after five weeks of operations it was a good time to let off steam. The post surgeon brought in three women wearing ponchos and introduced them as go-go dancers. The ponchos came off and they were practically naked. They started shaking to the music and stripped all the way.

Back in the crowd three well-built SF also took off their clothes and jumped onto the dance floor, flapping in the breeze. We always thought officers were strait-laced and rigid. We were wrong. When they let it go, they really let it go!

When it came to dirty tricks, SF had it down pat. But every unconventional-warfare team had that trademark. The SEALs were no exception. A team was billeted at Fort Richardson while they practiced along the coast and in the harbors. They had wrapped up their exercises and were also whooping it up at the club.

As you entered the club, you walked under the hides of a huge polar bear and an even bigger Kodiak. Spread out as they were on the wall, from toe to top of the head, there had to be twelve feet of pelt each. They were the biggest animals I ever saw.

The next morning, as we were preparing to leave, we had a shakedown. I mean, a *shakedown*. The MPs ordered all of our bags opened, and everything was searched. They were looking for the animal hides. During the night, both had been stolen right off the wall!

The SEALs had flown out before dawn, and that's about when the skins were discovered missing. I didn't know how they did it, because they had a whole lot less gear than we did. Their bags had to be smaller than ours. We weren't the only ones searched. Every unit leaving Fort Richardson was searched. But, because of what we had done to the war games, we were automatically prime suspects, and the MPs made a special effort to search us. The hides never showed up. Those SEALs were definitely my kind of men.

But to this day, I believe those MPs still think *we* took the hides. Our reputation was preserved.

chapter 25

One More Call

Getting out of Vietnam didn't mean the U.S. was leaving that area of the Pacific. The British had temporarily contained the Communists in many parts of Malaysia, but the Red Chinese and Russians were drooling over a long chain of islands that sat between Malaysia and Australia, perfect stepping stones for their terrorists and insurgents.

The area was Indonesia, a string of thousands of islands that stretched along the equator for about 3,200 miles. Most of their national territory was made up of Sumatra, Java, Kalimantan (the southern part of Borneo), Sulawesi, the Maluku Islands, and the western portion of New Guinea.

There were tremendous natural resources at stake, like oil, wood, tin, coal, coconut, and tobacco. The Portuguese and the Dutch were the first major powers to fight over the area way back in the early 1600s.

The Dutch became the big power in Indonesia and kept a tight rein until the Japanese overran the place during World War II. The Dutch had sold the native populations on being their protector, but that claim turned to crap.

The Japanese gave it up in late 1944 when things began getting desperate for them. The Dutch tried to step back in, but a young nationalist named

Sukarno wasn't taking any more of their crap. He led a resistance movement against both the Dutch and the British, and after some fierce battles and a lot of negotiating, an Indonesian republic was established. The only trouble was that the Dutch still pulled the strings. More fighting started and it took the United Nations to get the Dutch to back off.

The U.S., which had left the area right after the war, was up to its neck in Korean Communists and knew it better get back in. So, in 1950, we made like Mr. Nice Guy to the new government and started pumping millions into Indonesia to support their "internal security." Military hardware started flowing and we built up our influence.

The scene was set for the Communist PKI, a small but growing bunch. They started agitating for "real" independence. The government kept them down most of the time, but this was going to be the way the Russians and Red Chinese would make their power grab.

Our relationship turned sour as Sukarno and his followers saw the U.S. as just another evil colonial power wanting to dominate them. The Russians and the Red Chinese pounced. In 1965 and 1966 the U.S. wasn't given the time of day as the Chinese Communists poured into the country with tons of military aid and "advisors."

Then, the Communists shot themselves in the foot. The PKI became real aggressive, and that caused a lot of friction with Islamic groups. Sukarno's romance with the Russians and Chinese was over. Things came to a head when the PKI wanted to create a separate army of armed peasants. The Indonesian Army, which Sukarno held in an uneasy alignment with the PKI, balked. Rebel forces, made up of pro-Communist military, PKI, and other followers, quickly staged a coup, but it backfired.

The Communists murdered six Indonesian generals and fatally wounded the five-year-old daughter of one of them. The citizens were enraged. Angry mobs began a "holy war" against PKI members in the villages and against the Red Chinese and Russians. Several hundred thousand were killed. The Russians were wiped out. Many Dutch were cut down, too. Ol' Sukarno, who had played footsie with the Communists, was in deep trouble, and the government turned to General Soeharto to restore order. Soeharto was commander of the army's strategic reserve and powerful as hell. The U.S. knew this was a man it could deal with, and we started playing footsie with Soeharto.

U.S. aid to the tune of $13 million a year gushed in. On top of that, starting in 1974, we gave them foreign military sales credits so they could buy more U.S. military equipment.

And that also meant the arrival of U.S. advisors, like me.

I was in the middle of preparations for the Alaska exercise when, out of the blue, Dick Meadows found me. I was very happy to see him again. He hadn't changed in the six years since our SOG days in Da Nang—he was still jumping at clandestine assignments. He was on his way to Indonesia to set up Mobile Training Team (MTT) operations and alerted me to look for a request for volunteers coming down from 7th Group. He didn't provide any details and was on his way as quick as he came in.

Not a full week went by after I got back from Alaska before the call came for men to fill MTTs. The location wasn't mentioned, but I knew this was Dick's doing. I had just gotten a company and was on the promotion list for sergeant major, but pushing papers wasn't my style. If Dick was on a mission, something was definitely going on and I wanted to get in the middle of it. I was the first to volunteer.

When the orders were handed out I had been placed on a seven-man MTT to Indonesia. We would be in country for more than three months, teaching jumpmaster and pathfinder techniques to Indonesian Airborne officers and senior NCOs—the elite of their paratroopers. I was excited.

Everything necessary was already at the training site in Indonesia. We took our own parachutes along with the usual travel bags and rucksacks full of survival gear. I was the only one on the team who had medical training, and although I wasn't officially assigned as team medic, they handed me a large kit of medications and aids, more stuff than I had ever seen a medic carry. We were supposed to keep a low profile on the mission, and if any man was injured, we did not intend to take him to one of their hospitals.

Civilian clothes would be our uniform all the way—cheap wash-and-wear that was perfect for the steamy islands. We had sterile jungle fatigues for the mission itself.

The trip was long and tiring. We flew Piedmont Airlines from Fayetteville to Washington, D.C., and hopped a TWA flight to San Francisco. We slept overnight at Travis AFB, and the next afternoon we took off in a USAF Military Airlift Command jet headed to Thailand, with a stopover in the Philippines. We had already crossed the international dateline and made it to Bangkok the "third" day. A Thai International plane got us to Jakarta, the capital of Indonesia.

Jakarta was packed like Hong Kong, with about 4.5 million people. We were met by an embassy driver in an International carry-all who took us through some pretty ugly streets, filled with beggars and homeless children—lots of homeless children.

The embassy compound was an oasis. The main building was large and beautiful, looking like something the Dutch might have built. We processed in at the office of the U.S. Defense Liaison Group. It was a fancy cover name for all our military operations in country. They put us up for the night at the embassy house in the rear, but there wasn't much time to rest. We had to coordinate all our transportation and arrange for food. We hit the commissary and loaded up. Liquor at the embassy was dirt cheap.

The next morning we were on our way to Bandung, a long eighty miles to the southeast. That's where we would be staying while we trained the Indonesian Army. We made our way under thick tropical rain forest and through large fields of rice to an area of rolling hills that rose to a small range of mountains. Bandung was a city of over a million. Like Jakarta, there were homeless kids and beggars all over. On the side of a hill was a pretty residential area filled with flowers. All the houses were well-kept and looked very European. Our embassy-provided house was right in the middle of them.

The exterior was deceiving. Inside were a concrete floor and walls and hardly any furniture. The bedrooms had two army cots each and that was it. There was no bathroom like we were used to—just a slow, trickling shower. It was very primitive. We would be living out of our suitcases the whole three months.

We were very hungry, so our driver took us to another embassy house for a hot meal. A communications MTT was staying there, and when I walked in I was met by a bunch of old buddies from the 7th Group. They were just putting dinner on the table.

The embassy employees had their own contacts and saw to the hiring of older women for cooking and washing. Before we finished eating, our driver had people hired. They would bring their whole families and move into rooms at the back of the house.

Then Meadows walked through the door. "What took you so long?" he asked with a great big smile. "I've got a whole battalion just waiting for you."

Dick told us we were the last MTT in country. The original plans to send eight had been dropped—shelved because of one soldier's letter to CINC-PAC. Part of the contingent that went in ahead of us was a three-man weapons and small-arms repair team. As they were about to leave, one of the men wrote a letter to the admiral in Hawaii and told him everything was screwed up. He said he went there for a small-arms repair course but the Indonesian general who was in charge of all the equipment for the training was on vacation. The second in command, a colonel, wouldn't order the cases uncrated without the general's authorization. The team wound up trying to conduct the course out of a little bitsy tool box. The guy said it was a waste of his time and that he had spent ninety days away from his wife for nothing.

That one letter rattled the stars at Department of Army, and JCS canceled out on some sixty SF due to come to Indonesia. But our MTT was too far into the planning stages to be scuttled.

"You're here to help these poor warriors jump without killing themselves," Dick said. "They lost a whole battalion in the sea because they couldn't jumpmaster worth a damn." Dick wasn't more specific. "Keep your eyes and ears open and maybe they'll tell you all about it."

Early the next morning we drove out into the countryside toward Batujajar, the Indonesian special forces and airborne center about ten miles from our house. A small village butted up to the camp and was mostly soldiers' family quarters. There was a small airstrip to one side, with helicopters, several new C-130s and one C-47. The camp held the airborne division of the Indonesian Army. Once into the compound we could see that most of our training gear was in place ready to go.

We presented ourselves to the Indonesian commandant and his staff. It was the same old bullshit all over again. The higher-ranking officers were "royals" who came from powerful families that were close to the government. We gave the staff our lesson plans for approval—more politics—and were taken around the camp by the commander of the paratroop battalion we were there to train. Major Soegiyarto was a down-to-earth guy, who was well respected by all the officers of the division. The man quickly earned our respect as well.

The process of approving our lesson plans took three days. That gave Sfc. George Fails and me a chance to check out the gear and get to know the officers and top NCOs. These were the men Fails and I had to train to jumpmaster. They had all been in quite a few battles already. Some were well decorated—survivors of the battalion that drowned. They were already qualified jumpers, but they were using vintage Russian techniques. That had already cost them a lot of men, and it was up to our MTT to school them in our techniques—the best in the world.

The embassy was going to hire interpreters, but the government didn't want any civilians around military operations, so the Army gave us some young officers who spoke English well enough for our training. To our amazement, almost all the officers spoke two foreign languages. In their version of OCS, it was required. They were taught English and Chinese. They considered one the language of the "friendly country" and the other was of the "enemy country."

"Which one are you?" they would ask.

They were afraid of the Red Chinese and had not decided about us. They really didn't feel that they could trust us because we had just finished pulling out of Vietnam. They had learned English to keep a close eye on us.

The Indonesians had a good reason to be on edge. A lot of their islands had been under occupation for years, and it wouldn't have taken much to overrun them again. The Dutch and the Portuguese were still enemies to them, and they were waging a campaign to reclaim all the islands. In fact, it was a year earlier, during an attempted night drop onto the Portuguese-dominated island of East Timor, that the paratroop battalion fell into the ocean and was lost.

A new government in Portugal had determined that East Timor was too damned expensive to keep as a colony, and set it loose. Since then three factions had been scrambling for control. There was the Timor Democratic Union—UDT—that wanted to maintain ties with Portugal; the Apodeti, who wanted to be a full part of Indonesia; and Fretilin, who advocated immediate full independence. Fretilin was Communist-controlled and the strongest of the three.

Time was running out for the Indonesian government and the situation on the island was getting desperate. If they were going to mount another surprise attack, it would take our training to do it. This was their only airborne unit. You could always tell when you were messing with the elite. There were always generals around—like the armies we trained in South America.

Every morning began with Fails giving PT. We emphasized that the men had to maintain their physical condition. Each group we put through had one week in the classroom and two weeks in the field. We taught them the function of their parachutes and reserves, and how to inspect their equipment. The second week was spent on the outside rigs. We showed them how easy it was to screw up by hooking a man to the airplane mockup all wrong to produce a complete malfunction. We taught them to spot all the things that could go wrong. We put men in parachutes incorrectly and made them correct it. We timed them, from putting on the parachute on through inspection and loading into the plane.

Their last week was in the air "jumping a buddy." Each man made six jumps—three as jumper and three as jumpmaster. Jumpmaster techniques included a lot of map work, sessions with the pilot, and final calculations in the air—spotting landmarks and the DZ and taking into account wind drift. Once the plane was airborne, a jumpmaster rarely sat down. With the Indonesians, the first thing we had to work on was getting them relaxed to the point where they would unfasten their safety belts and stand in the open door watching the ground and talking to the pilot for course corrections. In the past, as soon as they got the green light they jumped, not knowing where they were. Hanging out the door was new to them.

The weekend after I jumped my first group, Major Soegiyarto asked me to help train the army's competition parachute team. They weren't exactly the Golden Knights, but that's what they were striving for. The major said they needed my kind of skill to whip the team into shape for an upcoming national meet. Thanks to Meadows, Soegiyarto knew all about me before I arrived.

I couldn't refuse.

I liked to play around with them to show what could be done. I would dive down and stop just over a man's back, do a flip to come right even with him, and watch his eyes widen.

Java was beautiful from the air—green and lush. We could see they had good rice farming. They even worked the fields at night. You could see them carrying lights. I asked the officers about that. "They're catching frogs," they said. There were a lot of edible frogs that found their way into the downtown restaurants. Frog legs were always on the menu. They were very small frogs, but didn't taste bad at all.

You would think from the many shops and farms that the people were prosperous, but there was a lot of poverty in Bandung. You had to walk around all of the poor lying in the streets. There was a lot of prostitution. The girls sat around in the nightclubs. If you wanted one, you ordered from the bartender and paid him just like a drink.

We drove by a beautiful park with benches and waterfalls. The place was full of girls. Our driver said they walked the park day and night. When we asked about them he laughed. "No . . . No . . . not girls." Apparently, the city had a lot of homosexuals.

There were other Americans in Bandung besides the MTTs. Our team officers, Capt. Norman Bruneau and Capt. John Baker, had been invited to a party thrown by two U.S. civilians. The rest of the team went along. The civilians lived on the outskirts of town in a pretty villa closed in behind a wall. Captain Bruneau introduced us to the two men, in their early thirties. Each had a beautiful Indonesian girl hanging on to him. Two other girls just walked around the room. They spoke English and seemed to have more education than the street girls. They lived there.

The two men tried to feel us out about what we were doing. It turned out they knew almost as much about our mission as we did, but we didn't know anything about them. Their story was that they were doing a "geological survey." They made a big point of telling us all about their "work." It felt like they were expecting us to go back and report it to the Indonesians. There was definitely something about them that told us it was a cover. I nosed around the place and didn't see anything—instruments, equipment, or charts—that would suggest they were what they said they were. It was all a lie. We stayed away from them after that.

We got along real well with the battalion officers, and one by one they eventually got around to visiting us at the embassy house. For some reason they felt more relaxed around us after we broke off from the two "civilians."

Some of the higher-ranking officers even invited us to play tennis. That was a mistake. They were damn good and whipped our butts.

The training went extremely well. The paratroopers turned out to be some of the best students I had anywhere. But we had one who just could not pass, regardless of the amount of training. Over a bottle of orange drink we discussed the old sergeant with the colonel. "You can't flunk this man," he said. "He's been our first sergeant for a long time and it would be a terrible thing for him."

The colonel had a proposition. "You give me a list of the men in the order you think they would perform on an actual mission. We will know that man isn't qualified but you will graduate him, anyway." I knew what they were after. I also knew I didn't want to go through the same bad situation I had in South America when I was training jumpers for the Colombian Army.

It happened when one man froze on the jump tower and flat refused to budge. Even after an officer gave him a good tongue lashing he still wouldn't go. He was taken away from the tower, and later that night I saw him running back and forth in front of the other men. He was wearing a yellow helmet. The next morning he never showed for class. The poor fellow had committed suicide.

"The sergeant *will* get his jumpmaster wings," our Indonesian colonel said. The deal was that the Indonesian Army would never have him jumpmaster a jump. I agreed. It would have been a terrible thing to have another man kill himself because he couldn't bear the shame and disgrace. I guess it was in their culture.

When they graduated, that old sergeant was the last on the list. The whole battalion gave him an ovation. Hell, he wouldn't have graduated grammar school in the U.S.

Each man on our MTT was also presented with Indonesian jump wings. We had earned them since we jumped with each group out of the plane. Then the division commandant threw a big goodbye party for us, and we were on our way back to the States.

It was always gratifying when our training resulted in a successful mission. A month after we returned to Fort Bragg, a letter of thanks arrived from Major Soegiyarto. The skydiving team had taken first place.

But it wouldn't be until late in the year that the whole parachute battalion would be tested.

By August, conditions on East Timor had deteriorated into civil war. By September the Communist Fretilin occupied most of the territory, and in late November they tried to set up the Democratic Republic of East Timor.

On 7 December 1975, Indonesian "volunteer" forces, led by our trained airborne unit, landed at Dili, the capital of the former Portuguese eastern half of the island. Fretilin had put together a force of twenty thousand, which the departing Portuguese had armed. A massacre followed at the hands of the Indonesian military and, unfortunately, many civilians considered to be Fretilin supporters were also cut down.

The very day before the invasion, President Ford and Secretary of State Kissinger had wrapped up a state visit to Jakarta. They had left no doubt with the Indonesian government that an "independent" East Timor was unacceptable. In other words, the President had given the nod for the invasion.

Because of the international turmoil that the U.S. expected, the State

Department was hoping the Indonesians wouldn't do it with our equipment. Well, what else were they going to use? All their training was on our stuff!

East Timor became Indonesia's 27th province in July 1976.

The government had a great retirement plan for a senior officer. When he retired he was given an island to protect as a province chief. Whenever I looked at a map of the area, I would wonder which of all those tiny islands was given to my friend Major Soegiyarto.

chapter 26

Shutting the Door

The position of company sergeant major had its downside. I was stuck in the B-team HQ doing administrative stuff—pushing papers.

I missed being a team sergeant—especially of the best HALO and SADM team in SF. But the team was in capable hands. I had turned over the reins to Richard Altman.

The upside of being sergeant major was that I was in a position to make sure the team stayed together. I arranged for them to work for the Airborne and Electronics Test Board, jumping and evaluating new HALO parachutes.

I also did my best to jump with them on their test jumps. It tickled me when they said, "Boy, we could tell when Joe was jumping. He'd be the last one out and the first one down." I would dive through them.

But there was just so much a body could take. Twenty-one years of maintaining physical toughness; twenty-one years of staying ready to run missions anywhere in the world. Then there were over thirteen hundred career jumps, to boot.

My right knee had never fully recovered from surgery to remove a lot of torn cartilage—cartilage ripped while on winter skiing maneuvers in northern Arizona. I rehabilitated myself with swimming and bicycle riding until I was back running five miles a day with the men. But I could see the end of the road.

I put in for retirement. It was brought about by plain old wear and tear. I also felt that, after twenty-one straight years in SF, I had done everything that had to be done.

When the President had called, I was ready.

The Army dangled one more carrot in front of this old mule. I was offered the job of command sergeant major of the U.S. garrison in Puerto Rico. It would have been a plush job. Too plush. My place was with the troops. My mind was made up.

I wanted to retire to hunt and fish.

The Army might have stopped recruiting, but other people in the government wanted me to "work" for them. A man I didn't recognize pulled me aside in the NCO club. It was a straightforward question. "Would you consider going overseas to train men in clandestine operations?" He never indicated where or identified himself.

I didn't know if he was CIA, or some foreign agent, or what. I did know that I had run into CIA in Laos and Vietnam who I once knew as SF. Because of our training, we were their best candidates. The other possibility was that this was a trick—a test to see if I would be a security risk in the future.

I looked him in the eye and said, "No. Hell, no. When I leave here I don't want nothin' else to do with it."

"Thank you, sergeant," he said. He left without another word. I didn't tell anybody, because that had happened to almost every top SF who was about to retire. If I had not been approached, I would have been surprised.

I retired very quietly—at home on leave. I didn't want a ceremony. There were so many retirement parades those last few years in SF I didn't want to put the men through another one. Hell, they were having enough formations as it was. I wanted to forget it. It was over.

I took Kathy and the kids back to Missouri. She had cared for me and the children all those years, and I wanted to pay her back a little bit. I had her away from home over twenty years, and she wanted to go back. If I had had a home to go to, I would have wanted the same, but I didn't. In the years I was married, I spent more time with Kathy's folks in Missouri than I ever did with any of my family. I built her a big house way out in the country.

From time to time the county sheriff would pass the word to me that I was being watched. "Before they left," he said, "I assured them that all you were doing was hunting and fishing."

Then Joey called from Oklahoma City with this wild tale of being stopped at the Canadian border.

I never had a fear of anything. Not even retirement.

Glossary

1-0: One-Zero, cross-border team leader's designation for tactical and communication purposes.

1-1: One-One, cross-border team's second in command— at times also used to denote the radio operator.

A-1: World War II–model, single-engine aircraft, highly maneuverable, known as the *Skyraider*.

A-4: Single-engine turbojet attack aircraft, known as the *Skyhawk*.

A-6: Twin engine turbojet attack aircraft, known as the *Intruder*.

AAR: After action report, formal written account of a mission.

ABN: Airborne.

AC-47: Armed version of C-47 aircraft, with three side-firing 7.62mm MXU-470 mini-guns, known as *Puff, Dragon Ship*, or *Spooky*.

AC-119K: Armed version of C-119 aircraft, with four mini-guns and two 20mm cannons, known as *Shadow*.

AC-130: Armed version of C-130 aircraft, with Vulcan 7.62mm XM-134 cannons, six barrels per cannon firing 6,000 rounds a minute, and night-vision devices, known as *Spectre*.

ACH-47A: Armed version of *Chinook* helicopter, with M-5 grenade subsystem, 2.75-inch rocket pods, two M-60 7.62mm machine guns, M24A1 20mm machine guns.

ACOUSID: Clandestine seismic and acoustic sensor – transmits audio on command.

ADSID: Clandestine seismic sensor, free-fall dropped from aircraft, buries itself, has a small antenna that resembles a tropical plant.

AFB: Air Force Base.

AK-47: Soviet-designed automatic assault rifle using 7.62 x 39mm ammunition, muzzle velocity of 2,330 feet per second.

Alpha-Bravos: military mnemonic alphabet. A=alpha, B=bravo, C=charlie, D=delta, etc.

AN/GRC-9: (*Angry-9*), Bulky long-range generator-powered radio.

AN/GRC-109: (*Angry-109*), battery-capable modern replacement of above.

AN/PRC-10: Early FM field radio, later replaced by PRC-25.

AN/PRC-25: FM field radio, line-of-sight transmission usually limited to 25–30 miles.

AO: Area of operations.

Ao dai: Vietnamese pajamalike garb. Vietnamese women wore ankle-length dresses split at the hips over baggy pants. Men's smock reached to the knees.

Apache team: six-man reconnaissance and intelligence-gathering team.

APC: Armored personnel carrier.

ARVN: Army of the Republic of (South) Vietnam.

ASA: Army Security Agency.

AWACS: U.S. Air Force transport aircraft equipped with sophisticated radar and communication equipment.

Azimuth: A horizontal compass angle measured clockwise from a fixed reference point.

B-40: Enemy rocket round fired from an RPG-7 launcher.

BAR: Browning automatic rifle, World War II vintage.

Barroom cowboys: EM who stayed away from field operations but claimed mission exploits in the bars.

BDA: Bomb damage assessment.

Black operations: Top secret, clandestine activities.

Blackbird: Lockheed C-130 aircraft with highly sophisticated secret communication gear, radar-deflection equipment, and terrain-avoidance radar (TAR). Painted charcoal on top and light color on bottom.

Blood pack: Serum albumin blood volume expander medical kit with intravenous capability.

C-3: Puttylike explosive.

C-4: Plastic explosive, M5A1, configured in a 2.5-pound, two-inch-by-two-inch block called a *stick*.

C-46: World War II version of DC-3.

C-47: Twin-engine, propeller-driven World War II–era transport, known as *Gooney Bird*.

C-119: World War II–vintage twin-boom cargo aircraft, known by paratroopers as the *Boxcar*.

C-123: Twin-engine, propeller-driven, cargo/troop-carrying aircraft.

C-130: Lockheed four-engine turboprop, known as *Hercules*.

CAR-15: Colt automatic rifle, XM177E2 automatic carbine, 5.56mm submachine gun, shorter version of M-16, telescoping stock, advanced flash hider, better hand guard.

Cammies, camo: Camouflage-patterned combat uniform.

CAS: Controlled American source (CIA intelligence source).

CBU-25: Cluster bomb unit, antipersonnel.

CBU-46: Cluster bomb unit, antipersonnel.

CCC: Command and Control Central (SOG).

CCN: Command and Control North (SOG).

CCS: Command and Control South (SOG).

CDCEC: Combat Development Command Experimentation Command.

CDEC: Combat Development Experimentation Center, Jolon, California.

CH-21C: Modified version of helicopter known as the *Banana Boat*.

CH-34: Helicopter carrying cargo or eighteen troops, known as *Choctaw*.

CH-47: Helicopter carrying thirty-three troops or cargo or artillery pieces, known as *Chinook*.

CH-53: Marine *Sea Stallion* used for SOG operations, called *Jolly Green Giant*. Search-and-rescue version of the CH-3 *Sea King*. Twin-turbine, five blade-rotor, armor-plating, jettisonable external fuel tanks, air refueling probe, two 7.62mm guns. Normal cruising speed of 172mph.

CHICOM: Chinese Communist forces.

Chieu Hoi: Open Arms policy. Program set up to encourage VC and NVA to defect without fear of retribution.

CHINAT: Chinese Nationalists (Taiwan).

CIA: Central Intelligence Agency.

CIB: Combat infantryman badge.

CIDG: Civilian Indigenous Defense Group. Locals sympathetic to the U.S. cause, recruited into A-camp companies.

CINPAC: Commander-in-Chief-Pacific.

CN: Nerve gas, can come in powdered form.

CO: Commanding officer.

Cobra gunship: AH-1G, with rockets, 40mm grenades, 7.62 mini-guns.

COMUSMACV: Commander, U.S. Military Assistance Command Vietnam.

CONEX: Container-Express, steel shipping cases, six by six feet or eight by eight.

Cosmoline: Jellylike lubricant antirust coating for weapons.

CP: Command post.

CS: Tear gas, can come in powdered form.

CTZ: Corps Tactical Zone. Corps area of combat responsibility.

CV-2: Twin-engine turboprop aircraft, medium capacity, short takeoff, known as *Caribou*.

CW: Continuous-wave, Morse Code radio transmission.

CZ: Canal Zone, Panama.

Daisy cutter: 15,000-pound bomb for leveling and clearing aircraft landing sites.

DASC: Direct Air Support Center, receives TACAIR request from FAC pilot, staffed by both Army and AF.

DCI: Director, Central Intelligence.

DEFCON: Defense Condition, a graduated level of alert.

Defilade: Protection from hostile observation or fire using a natural obstacle, such as a hill or land depression.

DET: Short for *detachment*.

Deuce-and-a-half: 2.5-ton truck.

Doublet antenna: Two long antenna wires used for long-range transmission, length determined by the radio frequency.

DRCP: Dummy rip cord pull. An initial free-fall practice exercise with the jumper attached to a special 15-foot static line.

DT: Defensive targets.

DZ: Drop zone.

E-4, 5, 6, 7, 8, 9: Enlisted grades—corporal, sergeant, staff sergeant, sergeant first class, master sergeant, sergeant major.

EM: Enlisted man/men.

E&E: Escape and evasion—an emergency route for survival in hostile territory.

F-4: Twin-engine turbojet supersonic tactical fighter, known as *Phantom II*.

F-100: Korean War–era single-engine turbojet, used in Vietnam as a FAC observation plane.

F-105: Single-engine supersonic fighter-bomber, modified versions known as *Wild Weasel.*

FAC: Forward air controller—pilot who flies over the battlefield, relaying calls for air strikes and/or team extraction. Flew O-1E *Bird Dog* or O-2 *Oscar-Deuce.*

Fan: The perimeter (circle) created by the maximum range of a camp's mortars or supporting artillery.

Fast mover: Jet aircraft.

FO: Forward observer—ground-based director of artillery fire.

FOB: Forward operations base with command and logistic elements.

FORSCOM: Forces Command headquartered at Fort McPherson, Georgia.

FSB: Fire support base—semifixed artillery emplacement.

FTX: Field training exercise.

FULRO: *Front Unifié pour la Libération des Races Opprimées* (United Front for the Struggle of Oppressed Races)—1964–65 Montagnard anti-government uprising in the Vietnam highlands.

Gunship: Huey (UH-1B) equipped with rocket pods, vulcan cannon, machine guns.

H-21: Helicopter known as the *Banana Boat.*

H-34: Single-engine helicopter, known as *King Bee* by Special Forces and *Choctaw* by the Air Force.

HALO: High altitude, low opening—describes classic military free-fall.

H&I: Harrassment and interdiction fire.

Hatchet Force: Reconnaissance team of U.S. and CIDG with mission to relieve pressure on an A-team in hard contact with enemy.

Head shed: Slang for *headquarters.*

HEAT: 85mm High-explosive antitank warhead—NVA used it against human targets.

Hmong: Dominant Laotian hill tribe.

Ho Chi Minh Trail: system of NVA supply roads and trails running south from North Vietnam, through Laos and Cambodia.

Hoi Chanhs: VC ralliers (VC responding to U.S. PSYOPS and/or those POWs who joined U.S. cause and were reinserted behind VC lines to rally).

HQ: Headquarters.

HUMINT: Human intelligence (sources).
HUMRO: Human resources officer.

IAR: Immediate after-action report.
IL-28: Soviet medium-range bomber.
Indian country: Slang for enemy territory.
IRBM: Intermediate-range ballistic missile (Soviet SS-5).

JCS: Joint Chiefs of Staff (Pentagon).
JFKCENMA: John F. Kennedy Center for Military Assistance, Fort Bragg, North Carolina. Later "less militant" designation of JFKSWCEN.
JFKSWCEN: John F. Kennedy Special Warfare Center, Fort Bragg, North Carolina.
JOTC: Jungle Operations Training Center, Panama.
JSOC: Joint Special Operations Center—old interservice coordinating umbrella for the Delta Force.

K-Bar: Marine- and SF-issue knife.
KIA: Killed in action.
Klick: Slang, meaning kilometer (1,000 meters).

L-19: Fixed-wing, single-engine observation aircraft *(Piper Cub)*.
LAW: Light antitank weapon, shoulder-fired M-72 66mm rocket with one-time disposable fiberglass launcher.
LDNN: South Vietnamese commandos, trained by U.S. Navy SEALs.
Leg: SF slang for non-jump-qualified infantryman.
LLDB: Lac Luong Dac Biet—South Vietnamese Special Forces (in name only).
LRRP: Long-range reconnaissance patrol.
LRRP rations: special dehydrated food designed for extended exposure to harsh field conditions.
LZ: Landing zone for aircraft.

M-5: Medium-sized medical kit.
M-14: First-generation modern U.S. automatic assault rifle, firing a 7.62mm x 51mm shell.

M-16: Next generation of above, firing a 5.56mm shell with a muzzle velocity of 3,200 feet per second.

M-26: Fragmentation hand grenade.

M-30: 4.2-inch mortar.

M-33: "Baseball" grenade.

M-34: White phosphorous grenade (WP).

M-60: 7.62mm machine gun.

M-79: Shotgun-style 40mm grenade launcher.

MAAG-L: Military Assistance Advisory Group—Laos.

MACV: Military Assistance Command Vietnam.

MACVSOG: Military Assistance Command Vietnam, Studies and Observation Group.

MC1-1: First-generation (official) steerable parachute.

McGuire Rig: Extraction device invented in the early days of SF in Vietnam by Sgt. Charles McGuire.

MFF: Military free fall, later became HALO.

MI: Military Intelligence.

MIA: Missing in action.

MIKE: *MIKE Force*—a well-armed quick-response force used to help an A-team in distress and/or help recapture an area.

Montagnards: Warrior hill people of Vietnam.

MOPSUM: Monthly operational summary.

MOS: Military occupational specialty.

MPC: Military pay certificate (redeemable scrip/voucher).

MRBM: Medium-range ballistic missile (Soviet SS-4).

MSF: Mobile strike force—a reaction or reinforcing unit made up of U.S. A-team personnel and many CIDG personnel.

MTT: Mobile training team—SF advisors to foreign military units.

NAD: Naval advisory detachment, Da Nang.

NCO: Noncommissioned officer, usually a sergeant.

NCOIC: Noncommissioned officer in charge.

NKP: Nakhon Phanom, Thailand. STRATA mission launch site.

NVA: North Vietnamese Army.

NWSB: Nuclear Weapons Support Branch, Fort Bragg, North Carolina.

O-1: FAC observation aircraft, single-engine, known as *Bird Dog*.

O-2: FAC observation aircraft, twin-boom, known as *Oscar-Deuce*.

O&I: Operations and Intelligence.

OCS: Officer Candidate School.

OIC: Officer in charge.

One-time pad: Encryption pad with several five-character letter groups on each page. Radio operator used each page only once and used pages in order until pad was exhausted.

OP-30: Umbrella designation for highly clandestine SOG operations.

OP-31: SOG Naval unit specializing in secret riverine operations.

OP-32: SOG Air Force unit.

OP-33: SOG unit specializing in secret PSYOPS and radio operations.

OP-34: SOG unit specializing in secret cross-border operations.

OP-35: SOG unit specializing in secret enemy ground studies.

OPLAN: Operation plan.

OSS: Office of Strategic Services, World War II predecessor of the CIA.

OV-1A: Reconnaissance rocket-firing aircraft, known as *Mohawk*.

OV-1B: Reconnaissance aircraft armed with electronic surveillance such as side-looking airborne radar (SLAR).

OV-10: Twin-engine, twin-boom, lightweight armed reconnaissance aircraft, known as *Bronco*.

PAB: Plastic assault boat—16-foot fiberglass hull.

Pathet Lao: Laotian Communist forces.

PBR: U.S. Navy river patrol boat.

PC-1: *Paracommander* parachute, based on the MC1-1.

PCF: U.S. Navy "black boats" known as fast patrol craft.

PIN-EE: Camera, 35mm, used for intelligence gathering.

PLF: Parachute landing fall—a small platform used in jump training.

PRC-25: AN/PRC-25, FM field radio, line-of-sight transmission usually limited to 25–30 miles.

PRU: Medical kit with heavy drugs, larger than the M-5 kit.

PSID: Patrol Seismic Intrusion Device.

PSYOPS: Psychological operations.

PSYWAR: Psychological warfare.

PTF: Navy fast patrol boat, two 50mm guns amidship, 900-mile range at 35 knots, very quiet engine, known as *Nasty Boat*.

Puff: AC-47. Armed version of C-47 aircraft, with three side-firing 7.62mm MXU-470 mini-guns, also known as *Dragon Ship, Spooky.*

Quad-50: brace of four .50-caliber machine guns.

Randall knife: Randall Model 14 attack knife, favorite of some SF.

R&R: Rest and relaxation.

RB-15: Fifteen-man rubber assault boat.

RECONDO: Recon Commando, designation of LRRP school in Nha Trang.

RF/PF: Regional Forces/Popular Forces—All-Vietnamese unit, recruited from villages, separate from SF, sometimes with a MACV advisor, known as *Ruff-Puff.*

RIF: Reduction in force. Program to pare the swollen ranks of officers. Men given an opportunity to remain active at an NCO grade until they have enough time accumulated for retirement.

RON: Remain overnight.

RPG: Rocket-propelled grenade. Also refers to Soviet RPG-7 launcher for shoulder-fired 85mm HEAT B-40 antitank rocket, used against human targets by NVA.

RTO: Radio-telephone operator.

S-1: Command staff personnel section.

S-2: Command staff intelligence section.

S-3: Command staff operations section.

S-4: Command staff logistics section.

S-5: Command staff civil affairs section.

SA-2: Soviet SAM (surface-to-air missile), effective to 59,000 feet.

SAC: Strategic Air Command.

SACSA: Office of the Special Assistant for Counterinsurgency and Special Activities, Pentagon.

SADM: Special atomic demolition munition – man-carryable nuclear device.

SAM: Surface-to-air missile.

Sand table: A topographic model of an AO, used in planning a mission.

Sapper: NVA/VC commando armed with a lot of explosives.

SAS: Elite British Special Air Service, counterpart to U.S. Special Forces.

Satchel charge: Explosives with a time fuse in a suitcase or carry-bag. Deadly enemy infiltration weapon.

SCUBA: self-contained underwater breathing apparatus.

SEAL: Sea-air-land, Navy/Marine clandestine forces.

SECDEF: Secretary of Defense.

SECSTATE: Secretary of State.

SF: Special Forces, Special Forces soldier.

SFG: Special Forces Group.

SFOB: Special Forces forward operations base.

Shadow: Armed version of C-119 aircraft, with four mini-guns and two 20mm cannons.

SIAF: Small independent action force.

SITREP: Situation report.

SKS: Russian/CHICOM semiautomatic rifle.

Slick: Slang for UH-1D helicopter with M-60 machine gun.

Snap link: Steel mountaineer connector ring.

SOG: Studies and Observation Group.

SOP: Standard operating procedure.

SOUTHCOMM: Southern Command, Fort Amador, Panama.

Spectre: AC-130. Armed version of C-130 aircraft, with Vulcan 7.62mm XM-134 cannons, six barrels per cannon firing 6,000 rounds a minute, and night-vision devices.

SPIKE Team: OP-35 cross-border team of ARVN Rangers, Nungs, and Montagnard mercenaries sent to harass, interdict, gather intelligence, and direct air strikes.

Spikebuoy: Air-dropped free-fall acoustic sensor that buries itself.

Spooky: AC-47. Armed version of C-47 aircraft, with three side-firing MXU-470 7.62mm mini-guns, also known as *Puff, Dragon Ship*.

STABO: Extraction harness developed in the Vietnam RECONDO school by Major Robert L. Stevens, Capt. John D. H. Knabb, Sfc. Clifford L. Roberts.

Starlight scope: Image-intensifier night-vision device.

Static line: 25-foot paratrooper lanyard that automatically deploys parachute.

Stay-behind team: usually a mercenary team dropped deep into North Vietnam for an extended period.

STRAC: Strategic Army Command (vintage 1960s), also acronym for: *Skilled, Tough, Ready Around the Clock.*

STRATA: Short-term reconnaissance and target acquisition.

Strike Force: Thirty- to forty-man man highly mobile search-and-destroy force.

SWCEN: John F. Kennedy Special Warfare Center, Fort Bragg, North Carolina

Swedish K: 9mm submachine gun

T-7/9: Air Force bailout parachute, 28-foot canopy, used by early Army jumpers and heavily modified for skydiving.

T-7A: Reserve parachute, 24-foot canopy.

T-10: Army-issue 35-foot paratrooper canopy.

TACAIR: Tactical air – all aircraft in support of ground troops.

TASS: Tactical Air Support Squadron.

Tet: NVA and VC lunar new year offensive, 30 January 1968.

Tiger suit: striped, camouflaged jungle fatigues

TOC: Tactical Operations Center.

Toe-popper: Antipersonnel mine—round, about the size of a small tuna can. Dig a hole, push it in, and twist the lid.

TPI: Technical proficiency inspection.

TTY: Teletype.

TUC: Time of useful consciousness prior to debilitation due to lack of oxygen in the blood—HALO free-fall term.

UH-1B: Small troop-carrying helicopter, known as a *Huey*.

UH-1D: Workhorse model, known as a *slick*.

URC-10: Small emergency AM radio, voice and beacon signals, known as *Whisper Radio*. (URC-4 was earlier model.)

USAF: United States Air Force.

USDLGI: United States Defense Liaison Group, Indonesia.

USNAD: U.S. Navy Advisory Detachment at Da Nang

USSOUTHCOMM: United States Southern Command, Fort Amador, Panama.

VC: Viet Cong.

Viet Cong: *Việt Nam công-sam*, indigenous Communist guerrillas.

Viet Minh: *Vietnam Doc Lap Dong Minh Hoi*, Vietnam Independence Allied Committee, first organized to fight the French.

VNAF: South Vietnamese Air Force.

WIA: Wounded in action.

WP: White phosphorus (grenade), known as *Willie Peter*.

Index